# Business Data Communications

# Business Data Communications

**Manish Agrawal**
College of Business
University of South Florida

**WILEY**

**JOHN WILEY & SONS, INC.**

| **VP & Executive Publisher** | Donald Fowley |
| **Executive Editor** | Beth Lang Golub |
| **Editorial Assistant:** | Mike Berlin |
| **Marketing Manager:** | Chris Ruel |
| **Designer** | Seng Ping Ngieng |
| **Production Manager:** | Janis Soo |
| **Senior Production Editor:** | Joyce Poh |

Cover image © Barrett Lyon, The Opte Project

This book was set in 10/12 Times Roman by MPS Limited and printed and bound by Malloy Lithographers. The cover was printed by Malloy Lithographers.

This book is printed on acid free paper.

Founded in 1807, John Wiley & Sons, Inc. has been a valued source of knowledge and understanding for more than 200 years, helping people around the world meet their needs and fulfill their aspirations. Our company is built on a foundation of principles that include responsibility to the communities we serve and where we live and work. In 2008, we launched a Corporate Citizenship Initiative, a global effort to address the environmental, social, economic, and ethical challenges we face in our business. Among the issues we are addressing are carbon impact, paper specifications and procurement, ethical conduct within our business and among our vendors, and community and charitable support. For more information, please visit our website: www.wiley.com/go/citizenship.

**Library of Congress Cataloging-in-Publication Data:**

Agrawal, Manish, 1969-
    Business data communications / Manish Agrawal.
      p.   cm.
    Includes index.
    ISBN 978-0-470-48336-7 (pbk.)
      1. Business enterprises—Computer networks.  2. Computer networks.  3. Data transmission systems.
    4. Information technology—Management.  I. Title.
    HF5548.2.A47   2010
    004.6—dc22

                                                  2010045253

Printed in the United States of America
10 9 8 7 6 5 4 3 2 1

# Brief Contents

Companion website: http://www.wiley.com/college/agrawal

# Table of Contents

**Companian website: http://www.wiley.com/college/agrawal**

# Preface

*The mind is not a vessel that needs filling,*
*but wood that needs igniting.*
—PLUTARCH

This text is designed for a one-semester undergraduate course in Business Data Communications. Data Communications is one of the growth areas of the economy because information exchange is becoming an increasingly important part of people's lives. This book focuses on providing working knowledge of data communication concepts and technologies that most students are likely to encounter within the first five years after graduation.

This book tries to most effectively utilize the time frame of a semester-long undergraduate class with about 40 hours of instruction time. Unlike many other information systems classes, which typically have a unifying theme—for example, SQL in database development, or the Waterfall model in Systems Analysis and Design—the data communications class easily transforms into developing familiarity with an alphabet soup of technologies—QAM, ASK, 802.3, IP, TCP, UDP, HTTP, SMTP, IMAP, DHCP, DNS, NAT, ARP, RFC 1918, subnetting, BGP, and 802.11, to name a few. The challenge in this class is to develop a unifying theme to help a student who is new to these technologies, so that the student is able to see how all these technologies are components of a unified system that enables data communications. All the design choices made while developing this text are based on this single goal.

The goal of the text is to help students, the future innovators of business and technology in our society, to understand the common principles underlying computer networks. In pursuit of this goal, at every possible occasion, the book addresses *why* networking technologies are designed to work in their current form. Hopefully, this focus on *why* will help students recognize opportunities for profitable innovation in their careers, even in contexts that are unrelated to data communications.

## Key features

The book incorporates a number of features to improve student comprehension. These include:

- *Reinforcement of a unifying theme throughout the book—"efficiency of network resource utilization."* Research suggests that the brain assimilates new ideas better when these new ideas are linked to existing ideas in the brain. The unifying theme helps build these connections. All modern data communication technologies are motivated by the need to most efficiently utilize the extremely expensive network infrastructure—cables, bandwidth, routers, exchange points, even IP addresses. If at first a technology makes no sense to a student, they should be encouraged to please step back for a minute and try to assess how this technology improves network resource utilization. Network operators would not invest in using a technology unless the technology was absolutely necessary to improve the utilization of network resources in some way. This idea of improving resource utilization is reinforced in almost every chapter. Examples include multiplexing in Chapter 2, broadcast in Chapter 3, IP addressing in Chapter 4, flow control in Chapter 5, address reuse in Chapter 7, point-to-point communication in Chapter 10, bandwidth utilization in Chapter 11, and frequency reuse in Chapter 12.

- *A focus on describing why technologies have been designed to work the way they do.* When students understand why a technology works, it helps improve comprehension, long-term recall, and, potentially, helps the idea in other contexts. Resource utilization efficiency (as described above) is the most common explanation for data communication technology design. But other factors are important too. Examples in the book include layered architectures in Chapter 1, signaling in Chapter 2, multi-part addressing in Chapter 4, three-way handshake in Chapter 5, hierarchical naming in Chapter 7, and modulus operation in Chapter 13.

- *A focus on covering a core set of data communication technologies.* Trying to cover every possible networking concept within one class, particularly at the undergraduate level, hinders student comprehension. Accordingly, the book takes the minimal set of technologies that are absolutely necessary to enable computer networking in organizations—Ethernet, TCP/IP, ARP, NAT, DNS, DHCP, routing, subnetting, and security—and focuses on showing what each of these technologies does, why each of these technologies is necessary, and how each technology works. Focusing on the most essential topics enables more detailed coverage of essential topics such as packetization, IP addresses, subnetting, route aggregation, and DNS. Every topic that has been covered is discussed in reasonable detail so students feel confident in their abilities to apply them at work and to discuss them with professional experts in the industry and in job interviews.

- *Hands-on exercises with every chapter.* Students repeatedly state that they understand more from hands-on exercises than from lectures. Every chapter in this book has hands-on exercises that help students use and understand the networking concepts covered in the chapter. All personal computers come with easy-to-use networking utilities that students can use to learn more about the capabilities of their computers. Many exercises are based on these utilities. Examples include tracert in Chapter 1; ipconfig in Chapter 3, 4, and 8; ping in Chapter 4; netstat in Chapter 5; and nslookup in Chapter 7. There are also spreadsheet exercises that help students understand amplitude modulation (Chapter 2) and CDMA (Chapter 12). Finally, some end-of-chapter hands-on exercises use other interesting software. These include Wireshark (Chapters 6, 11, and 13), OPNET (Chapters 10 and Chapter 14), and BGPlay (Chapter 9).

Some of these hands-on exercises are unique to the book. For example, the Wireshark exercise in Chapter 11 uses wireless packets captured using AirPCap, so that students can see the fields in the radio header to see the transmission frequency channel selected. The spreadsheet exercises demonstrate technical concepts such as modulation and multiplexing using simple spreadsheet exercises.

- *Business case in each chapter.* To show students the business use for the technologies covered in the book, each chapter ends with a case study that shows the business or social impact of the technology covered in the chapter.

- *Network design case integrated throughout the text.* To help students see how all the technologies covered in the book integrate with each other in an enterprise network, there is a network design case that runs throughout the book. In each chapter, students make design choices to meet user requirements for the technology covered in the chapter. The finished exercise can also be included in students' portfolios for job interviews.

## Book outline

The book may be seen to have four parts: (1) introduction, (2) technology layers, (3) supporting technologies and systems, and (4) managerial issues.

    The introduction (Chapter 1) provides a high-level overview of the book, the need for computer networks, and their evolution to their current form. It describes why layering and packetization are done to deliver information. Part 2 (Chapters 2–6) covers each of the five layers in the TCP/IP technology stack in detail. Since upper layers in all layered systems depend upon services from the lower layers, it is easier to understand the operations of lower layers than that of upper layers. Hence the book uses a bottom-up approach, starting from the lowest layer (Chapter 2) and ending in the topmost layer (Chapter 6). Part 3 (Chapters 7–13) covers the supporting data communication technologies such as WANs, routing, and subnetting. Finally, Part 4 (Chapter 14) covers managerial issues in networking, such as standardization, legal issues, and network design.

## Supplements

The following supplements are available to help instructors and students:

- PowerPoint slides are available for all the chapters. These slides include all the figures used in the book and can be used to highlight the key points in the chapters.

- There is a companion website for the book, which is referenced at various places in the text. The companion website includes technology standards, particularly the easy-to-read RFCs such as IP, TCP, HTTP, SMTP, and NAT. There are also articles from the mainstream media that are relevant to the class. The goal of the companion website is to get students to devote a meaningful amount of time outside class hours going over the assigned readings and to get a broader understanding of data communications. I assign 3–4 readings from the website for every meeting and devote about 20 minutes at the beginning of each class to discuss the assigned readings for the day. A side benefit of this approach is that by the end of the class, students become comfortable reading these kinds of technical articles and reports.

- There is an Instructors' Manual with answers to the end-of-chapter questions and about 20 multiple choice or true-false questions per chapter for use in tests.

This text is the result of my own adaptations over the years of material covered in existing data communications texts. The result seems to work well for my students, and hopefully will work for everyone who uses the book.

## Acknowledgment

I would like to acknowledge three people who are especially important in planting the seeds for this book and for giving me the confidence to write it. My PhD advisor, Prof. H. R. Rao, at the University at Buffalo, encouraged me to teach Business Data Communications when it was time for me to teach a class while doing my PhD. Without that start, I probably would have never taught this topic. Over the years at USF, Joe Rogers, the university's network expert, has been very patient in sharing his expertise with me and responding to my questions about computer networking. Joe also went over the book to help remove technical errors. Finally, a friend from college and former McKinsey consultant, Bhasker Natarajan, gave me the idea to write a book when I asked him for productive ideas to keep busy in my spare time. He assured me that it was easier than it appears and would not take longer than two weeks to complete the first draft. That encouragement was enough to get me started, though it certainly took longer than two weeks to complete the first draft of the book.

I am grateful to Beth Lang Golub, the Information Systems editor at Wiley, for having faith in me, a first-time textbook author, when I approached her with the idea of a new text in Business Data Communications.

Special thanks are due to my department chairs, Stan Birkin and Kaushal Chari for their constant encouragement. Finally, I would like to thank the reviewers of this book, who gave very constructive feedback and pointed out errors in earlier drafts. The book is better because of their efforts.

## List of reviewers

Kemal Altinkemer, Purdue University
Robert J. Bonometti, Shenandoah University
Thomas Bruckman, LaGuardia Community College
Susan J. Chinburg, Rogers State University
John Day, Boston University
Ana Maria De Alvare, St. Thomas University
Kurt DeMaagd, Michigan State University
Jahyun Goo, Florida Atlantic University
Bill Hammerschlag, Brookhaven College
Xiaorui Hu, St. Louis University
Annette L. Kerwin, College of DuPage
Subodha Kumar, University of Washington
Lei Li, Columbus State University
Thomas Martin, Shasta College
Masoud Naghedolfeizi, Fort Valley State University
Harry Reif, James Madison University

Kala Chand Seal, Loyola Marymount University
Sushil Sharma, Ball State University
Sumit Sircar, Miami University
Changsoo Sohn, St. Cloud State University
S. Srinivasan, University of Louisville
Ashok Subramanian, University of Missouri St. Louis
Steven Zeltmann, University of Central Arkansas

## About the colophon[1]

It is unlikely that a single book can teach everything worth learning in any subject. An approach that tries to fill a "bucket of knowledge" is therefore necessarily futile. A more productive approach is to recognize the boundless potential and spirit of inquiry of the human brain. Recognizing this, at every opportunity, this book tries to show why Internet technologies work the way they do—what the challenges were and how the adopted solutions solve these challenges. It is hoped that this approach will ignite students' curiosity, motivate them to look for common principles underlying computer networking, and maybe even improve the ways we currently operate and use computer networks. Maybe some ideas from the technologies discusses in the book could even be usable in entrepreneurial ventures.

## Notations

*Definitions are in italics.*

Remarks are in shaded boxes

---

[1] A colophon is a brief comment, usually located at the end of the text, providing finishing touches to the text.

# Photo Credits

## Chapter 1

Page 10: Morse Telegraph: DEA/A. DAGLI ORTI/DeAgostini/Getty Images, Inc.; Page 10: Thomas Edison: Hulton Archive/Getty Images, Inc.; Page 10: Alexander Graham Bell: Time & Life Pictures/Getty Images, Inc.; Page 10: First Internet: Computer History Museum; Page 10: Almon Strowger: SSPL/Getty Images, Inc.; Page 10: Apollo 11 astronauts: Courtesy of NASA; Page 13: Furniture: juuce/iStockphoto; Page 13: Gym: Dr. Heinz Linke/iStockphoto; Page 13: Box: Carlos Alvarez/iStockphoto; Page 13: Truck: Grafissimo/iStockphoto; Page 13: Minivan: Frances Twitty/iStockphoto; Page 28: Web page: Courtesy of St. Cloud State University.

## Chapter 2

Page 37: Internet's undersea world: Courtesy of Telegeography; Page 44: Sunbeam: Sebastian Meckelmann/iStockphoto; Page 57: NYC, 1900: American Stock/Getty Images, Inc.; Page 61: NIST smart grid conceptual model: Courtesy of National Institute of Standards and Technology.

## Chapter 3

Page 67: Ethernet connector on PC: Author; Page 68: Early Ethernet diagram: PARC (Palo Alto Research Center, Inc., A Xerox Company); Page 69: Early Ethernet diagram: Robert Metcalfe, David Boggs; Page 70: Hub-based Ethernet: Author; Page 71: Flyer: Author.

## Chapter 4

Page 106: US maps: Intelligent Direct Inc.; Page 120: ARIN web page: Used with permission from ARIN.

## Chapter 6

Page 154: Search advertising: Courtesy of Google; Page 155: Map of world wide web: Opte project; Page 167: Wireshark interface: Courtesy of Cacetech.

## Chapter 7

Page 207: Home router web interface: Author; Page 208: Websites: Courtesy of Yahoo!; Page 211: UCF home page: Courtesy of the University of Central Florida.

## Chapter 9

Page 253: ARIN webpages: Courtesy of ARIN; Page 254: bgplay interface: Courtesy of Route-views project.

## Chapter 10

Page 258: Neighborhood intersection: traffic merging into interstate: Courtesy of Google; Page 259: Early Internet: Courtesy of the Computer History Museum; Page 268: Reaper UAV (Drone): Ethan Miller/Getty Images, Inc.; Page 271: OPNET application interface: Courtesy of OPNET.

## Chapter 11

Page 287: Wireshark interface: Courtesy of Cacetech; Page 295: WiMAX data rates: adapted by author.

## Chapter 12

Page 303: Morse Telegraph: DEA/A. DAGLI ORTI/DeAgostini/Getty Images, Inc.; Page 303: Thomas Edison: Hulton Archive/Getty Images, Inc.; Page 303: Alexander Graham Bell: Time & Life Pictures/Getty Images, Inc.; Page 303: First Internet: Computer History Museum; Page 303: Almon Strowger: SSPL/Getty Images, Inc.; Page 303: Apollo 11 astronauts: Courtesy of NASA; Page 304: Landline adoption: Used with permission from ITU; Page 310: cellphone adoption: used with permission from ITU; Page 311: cellphone technology evolution: Courtesy of the Association for Information Systems; Page 313: cell phone towers: Courtesy of Antennasearch; Page 318: maps of Bangladesh: Courtesy of CIA; Page 318: woman with cellphone: Courtesy of Grameenbank; Page 320: Alexander Graham Bell's diary: Courtesy of the Library of Congress.

## Chapter 13

Page 343: bgplay interface: Courtesy of the Route-views project; Page 345: Albert Gonzalez: Courtesy of U.S. Secret Service; Page 347: Wireshark interface: Courtesy of Cacetech.

## Chapter 14

Page 358: nessus interface: Courtesy of Tenable security; Page 369: OPNET interface: Courtesy of OPNET.

# Introduction

## CHAPTER 1

*Any sufficiently advanced technology is*
*indistinguishable from magic.*
—ARTHUR C. CLARKE

## Overview

This chapter describes why computer networking is important and why you should care to know about computer networking. It introduces the TCP/IP technology stack that underlies most computer networks. At the end of the chapter you should know:

- why computer networks are important
- why data is sent on computer networks as packets of information
- the important tasks that must be performed to deliver each packet of information to its destination without error
- the standard technologies that accomplish these tasks (the TCP/IP stack)

After the TCP/IP stack is introduced in this chapter, the rest of the book will describe how each of the technologies in the TCP/IP stack works.

## Definition

*Business Data Communications is the movement of information from one computer application on one computer to another application on another computer by means of electrical or optical transmission systems.* In everyday language, business data communications is also called computer networking. The two terms will be used interchangeably in the text. *A transmission system that enables computer networking is a data network.* For example, the computers in your home, together with the wireless router, are a data network. All the cables, routers, and other data-carrying equipment of your ISP constitute another data network. The computer in your university are also organized as a network. Figure 1 shows the three networks.

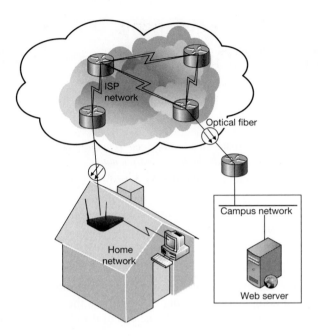

**FIGURE 1**  Data networks

Practically speaking, a focus on data networks is very useful because it helps us understand how the popular computer networking applications such as web browsing and e-mail, work. But an even bigger benefit of focusing on computer networks comes from a learning perspective. It turns out that a common set of technologies supports all computer networking applications, not only web and e-mail, but also all distributed applications such as client-server database applications. The basic principles behind data network technologies have not changed in almost three decades, and are not likely to change in the immediate future. Therefore, understanding these technologies will not only help us understand how modern data networks work, but will also be useful to understand any developments that may occur in computer networks in the near future.

As you will hopefully see throughout the book, computer networking involves some very interesting challenges and equally interesting solutions. The result is that one device, a humble desktop computer, can perform many conceivable communication tasks—web, e-mail, video and music downloads, chat, instant messaging, VoIP telephony, and queries on remote databases. In all likelihood, the desktop will also be capable of running new communication applications that entrepreneurs like you will come up with in the future. This makes computer networking an exciting technology to become familiar with.

Most homes and organizations have another network—the phone network. Phone networks are extremely important because a lot of business information is exchanged in phone conversations. An overview of phone networks is provided in Chapter 12.

# Utility of computer networking

Let's start with the basics. Why should you care about computer networking? After all, when people talk about IT, the picture that usually comes to mind is of large databases and rich user interfaces, not computer networks. So, where do data networks fit in from a professional point of view? Are they important enough for you to spend an entire college course studying about them?

It turns out that computer networking is one of the most essential components of the modern economy. Most corporate computer applications use computer networks for storing and retrieving data from databases. Almost every organization depends on computer networks for communication using e-mail or chat. Almost every home and office depends upon computer networks to share resources such as printers and files. Almost every large retail chain depends upon computer networks to get real-time data on the inventory in its stores for just-in-time fulfillment. Almost everybody with a computer depends upon the Internet to search for information.

In fact, computer networks are so pervasive that they play a vital role even in places where their role is not very obvious. For example, the case in Chapter 9 shows how gas stations use computer networks to send real-time data on fuel levels to central information systems which use this data to calculate optimal fuel delivery schedules.[1] The case in Chapter 2 shows how the plans for improving energy efficiency in the United States depend upon the use of sensors and computer networks to exchange real-time information between power consumers and generators. Communication networks have become such an integral element of our daily lives that even experts in risk management find it difficult to imagine life without functioning communication networks. For example, in Chapter 11, we see that in the immediate aftermath of Hurricane Katrina, the city leaders of New Orleans were virtually cut off from the outside world for some time because their emergency plans had assumed that basic phone service would remain intact after a hurricane. Computer networks came in handy in this case because, even though land lines and cell phones were down, city leaders could obtain an Internet connection and make phone calls to the outside world over this Internet connection.[2]

Another measure of the importance of networking in general (including voice and video) is the fact that the information-exchange industry is one of the world's largest industries by revenue. Firms in this category include all the large carriers such as AT&T, Verizon, and Bell South. It is easy to see why this industry may command such large revenues. If you look at your own monthly expenses and add up all the bills you pay to stay connected (broadband Internet connection, phone, cable, and cell phone), you are likely to find that your information-exchange expenses are one of your largest monthly expenses. Add up the expenses by most families and businesses in the country to stay connected and you get a sense of the size of the revenues collected by

---

[1] Worthen, B. (2002). Drilling for every drop of value. *CIO Magazine*: 7.
[2] Rhoads, C. (2005). Cut Off: At Center of Crisis, City Officials Faced Struggle to Keep In Touch; Mayor's Inner-Circle Spent Two Days in the Dark; Web Phone Became Lifeline; Police Chief Rips a Server Free. *Wall Street Journal*. New York, NY: A1.

the information-exchange industry. This course introduces you to the technologies that support one of the largest industries in the world.

The importance of networking has also been measured from another angle. Evidence suggests that telecommunications infrastructure is a driver of economic activity. Economic progress requires telecommunication infrastructure to support it. This has been observed in both developing and developed countries, even though only the developed countries have well-developed sectors of the economy that depend heavily on telecommunications. Though this evidence is based on data from 1970–1993, and the telecommunications infrastructure studied was telephone networks and not computer networks, it points to the role of information exchange in economic development.[3]

Another estimate released in 2009 shows the economic importance of computer networks. The advertising-supported Internet represents about $300 billion of economic activity in the U.S., representing slightly over 2% of the total U.S. gross domestic product (GDP). The advertising-supported Internet directly or indirectly employs more than 3.1 million Americans, or about 1% of the U.S. population.[4] The Internet is not a toy anymore; rather it has become an extremely significant component of the U.S. economy.

Not all effects of computer networks are so benign. Computer networks expose organizations to security attacks from around the globe. More than 40 million credit-card records were stolen from the databases of retailer T. J. Maxx by attackers because its computer networks were insecure. Computers at national security targets such as the Pentagon and NASA are routinely attacked in attempts to steal information or simply to demonstrate technical competence. In recent years, this has led to significant hiring of information security experts.

With so many users online, the total volume of traffic on the Internet is huge and continues to grow rapidly. An estimate made by CISCO, one of the largest companies in this sector, suggests that the total volume of Internet traffic in 2008 was 7,394 petabytes per month.[5] Written numerically, this number is 7,394,000,000,000,000,000 bytes of data on the Internet per month. And this number is growing at the rate of 42% per year. There are few other business statistics that are already so large and yet are experiencing such high growth rates. Internet traffic growth is being driven by both consumers and businesses, with consumers driving a larger share of the growth recently. This is because of the emergence of video as a major Internet application. Video files are huge, and a single video file downloaded by a home user can be equivalent to over a month of e-mail traffic volume generated by a business user. Traffic volume is still largest in North America, but continents outside North America are experiencing higher growth rates. The highest growth rates are in Latin America, driven by the entry of new Internet users in these countries. Table 1 shows the growth rates in internet traffic by geography and user category.

---

[3] Dutta, A. (2001). "Telecommunications and Economic Activity: An Analysis of Granger Causality." *Journal of Management Information Systems* **17**(4): 71–95.
[4] Interactive Advertising Board, "Economic Value of the Advertising-Supported Internet Ecosystem," 2009. Accessed at http://www.iab.net/insights_research/947883/economicvalue (accessed 11/09).
[5] CISCO Systems (2008). Cisco Visual Networking Index—Forecast and Methodology, 2007–2012.

**Table 1** Global IP traffic forecast by CISCO

|  | 2006 | 2007 | 2008 | CAGR 2007–2012 |
|---|---|---|---|---|
| **By type (PB/month)** | | | | |
| Internet | 3,339 | 4,884 | 7,394 | 42% |
| Non-Internet | 895 | 1,693 | 3,353 | 55% |
| **By segment (PB/month)** | | | | |
| Consumer | 2,641 | 4,359 | 7,674 | 49% |
| Business | 1,586 | 2,193 | 3,008 | 35% |
| Mobility | 7 | 26 | 65 | 125% |
| **By geography (PB/month)** | | | | |
| North America | 1,471 | 2,419 | 3,997 | 43% |
| Western Europe | 886 | 1,354 | 2,267 | 52% |
| Asia-Pacific | 1,307 | 1,963 | 3,151 | 44% |
| Latin America | 118 | 189 | 332 | 61% |

## Careers

As impressive as these statistics are, as a student, your primary concern should be—what is in it for me? Why should I study computer networking? Will it help me in my job search? Is computer networking a rewarding career path? The numbers are again very encouraging. All indicators suggest that computer networking is indeed a very rewarding career path. According to estimates prepared by the Bureau of Labor Statistics of the U.S. government, whereas overall employment is expected to grow by about 10% from 2006 to 2016, the category of "network systems and data communications analysts" is expected to grow by 53%.[6] Most impressively, this is the highest growth rate among all jobs categories classified by the BLS. Total U.S. jobs in this category were estimated to be 262,000 in 2006 and this number is expected to grow to 402,000 by 2016. This is an addition of 140,000 jobs, which ranks 23 among all occupations in terms of jobs added. Therefore, if you choose to build a career in computer networking, the prospects are very favorable. Not only is computer networking vital to the economy, it can also be great for your career.

# Technology milestones

Hopefully your curiosity to learn more about computer networks has been stirred. We now begin a discussion of the technology behind computer networks. Modern computer networks are extremely capable. To attain these capabilities, networks have also become quite complex. To better understand modern, complex networks, it helps to start with the simplest early networks. We will look at the important developments to see how

---

[6] http://www.bls.gov/emp/emptabapp.htm.

each development improved the capabilities of computer networks. While innumerable developments have contributed to the present state of networking, four developments stand out—the telegraph, multiplexing, switching, and packetizing. Each development has improved the efficiency of computer networks in terms of increasing the data-carrying capacity of computer networks, using the same network resources.

## The Telegraph

One of the earliest instances of using networks to send data was the telegraph. Samuel Morse patented the telegraph in the U.S. in 1840. This was almost 40 years before the invention of the light bulb, which was patented by Thomas Edison in 1880. The telegraph is important because, for the first time, we were able to use wires to send information to far-off places. The system was simple and looked as shown in Figure 2.

To send a message, the sender would connect and release the switch as required. When the switch was connected, the electromagnet would be energized and pull the marker to one side. This scratched a line on the paper at the receiver. To send meaningful messages using this system, Morse also developed a code, called Morse code, which coded letters and numbers as dots and dashes. For example, the letter *a* is coded as a dot and a dash. To send *a*, the sender would connect the switch for a short time, release it, and then connect it again for a slightly longer time. This would create a short line and a long line on the paper at the receiving end. An operator skilled in Morse code could interpret this set of short and long lines as the letter *a*.

The simple telegraph system has two major ideas that are relevant for modern networks. The first is that information is carried as energy on the wire. The sender powers the line on or off depending upon the message to be transmitted. The receiver interprets the varying patterns of electrical power on the line as the message. As we will see in Chapter 2, information transmission requires some detectable change at the receiver in response to changes created by the sender.

Just like the telegraph, modern networks also transmit information as varying patterns of energy on a wire. This is the only known way of causing some detectable change by the receiver in response to some action by the sender. This is called signaling. Signaling is covered in Chapter 2.

The second idea demonstrated by the telegraph is the need for coding. If information can only be sent as energy transmission being turned on or off, we obviously need to express all letters and numbers in terms of energy transmission going on or off. This expression is called coding. The telegraph used the Morse code, which expressed characters

**FIGURE 2** Telegraph

as dots and dashes. Converting back from dots and dashes into human-readable messages is called decoding. Though Morse code is no longer used, modern networks do express letters, numbers, characters, pictures, sounds, etc., as codes. Instead of dots and dashes, we now use 0s and 1s to build coding schemes such as ASCII and UNICODE.

The telegraph also shows that systems reflect technological capabilities of the time. Later generations of the telegraph replaced the electromagnet and paper strip with speakers, which vastly improved the speed of the telegraph. However, speakers did not exist at the time of the Morse patent. When you see a technology solution in this text or elsewhere, it often helps to ask why things are done the way they are. Often, they are work-arounds just to make things work. NAPT (Chapter 7) is one such work-around. Or, they reflect the limitations of technology at the time of its creation. For example, the relatively small packet size (1,500 bytes) in Ethernet (Chapter 3) is one such example. Removing these work-arounds and technological limitations is an excellent opportunity for students to apply their knowledge in innovation and entrepreneurship.

## Multiplexing

The second major telecommunication innovation was multiplexing. While it is useful to be able to send a message over a wire, it is even more useful to be able to send more than one message over a wire at the same time. *The ability to combine multiple channels of information on a common transmission medium is called multiplexing.* Thomas Edison invented a multiplexing telegraph in 1874. This device carried four messages at the same time (two in each direction), allowing one cable to send and receive two messages simultaneously.

Why is multiplexing so important? The answer lies in the economics of communication networks. The biggest costs in networking are often the costs of laying cables. Multiplexing allows the fixed costs of installing and maintaining one long-distance cable to be amortized over multiple messages. This is quite similar to the idea of dividing a single interstate expressway into multiple lanes. It is very expensive to build highways. Highways become affordable because lanes enable multiplexing by allowing more than one vehicle to use the interstate at the same time.

In fact, though technologically feasible, data communication would be prohibitively expensive without multiplexing. Consider an example of what would happen without multiplexing. If multiplexing were not possible, your cable company would need to bring 200 cables into your neighborhood if they offered a 200-channel package and wanted to let users choose any of these 200 channels at any time of the day. Without multiplexing, the cable company would also need to bring one cable into your home from the neighborhood access point for each additional TV you installed at home. Without multiplexing, there could only be one radio station in one location. Multiplexing allows multiple radio stations to beam their signals over the same area where listeners can tune into the station of their choice. Multiplexing is used in modern networks to transfer the data being sent by all the users in one location over a single link to the next destination. For example, a single fiber-optic cable carries all the traffic leaving your university to the ISP.

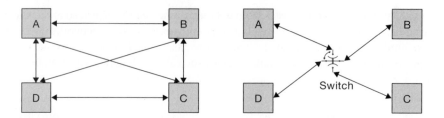

**FIGURE 3** Switching

## Switching

The third major development in communication was switching. Multiplexed networks can become even more efficient if the same wire can be used to connect different locations on an as-needed basis. *Transmitting data between selected points in a circuit is called switching.* Consider the example in Figure 3, where we have four locations to be networked together. Without switching we would need six cables to connect these four locations. In the example, all data from A to B would go over the cable A-B and data from A to C would go over cable A-C. By adding a switch to the network, we only need four cables. Clearly, adding a switch can reduce the cost of networking in this case if the cost of laying two cables exceeds the cost of adding a switch. As the number of networked locations increases, the advantages of switching increase further. Adding a new location to a non-switched network requires connections from the new location to all the other locations. For example, adding a 5th location to the non-switched network would require four new cable links (one each to A, B, C, and D). In the switched network, the 5th location would only need one more link—from this new location to the switch. The earliest switches were human-operated; you may have seen operators working on switches in war-time movies.[7] Later switches automated the switching process.

You can see that the network is beginning to get complex. The switched network adds a device to the network—a switch whose sole function is to facilitate communication. The network is also becoming more difficult for lay users to understand because they don't see the switch, even though all communication passes through it.

## Packet switching

The previous three developments in networking (telegraph, multiplexing, and switching) were completed by the end of the 19th century and led to the rapid expansion of phone networks. Compared to the next development, packet switching, these three developments are also quite intuitive to understand. The next major development in networking was packet switching. *Packet switching is the process of routing data using addressed packets so that a channel is occupied only during the transmission of the packet.* Upon completion of the transmission the channel is made available for the transfer of other traffic. The first packet transmission occurred on Oct. 29, 1969, in California.[8]

---

[7] A good example is the 1937 audio-visual clip "Spot News," available at http://www.archive.org/details/spotnews1937. The use of switching begins around the 2:15 mark.

[8] http://web.archive.org/web/20080308120314/http://www.engineer.ucla.edu/stories/2004/Internet35.htm.

Packetization squeezes out further efficiencies in the switched network. A traditional switch establishes connections between end nodes based on network needs. For example, when user A dials user C, the switch connects user A to user C. Now A and C can send data to each other, but if A wants to send data to B or D, he must wait for the switch to close the connection between A and C and to create a new connection from A to B or D. By contrast, in packet switching, all users are always connected to each other. When A sends packets of information to the packet switch for delivery to C, the switch receives these packets and forwards them on to C. If A simultaneously has some data to send to B, it can pass the data for B to the packet switch, and the switch will instantaneously forward the data to B.

Why is packet switching more efficient than traditional switching? If A and C are conventional phone users, the advantages of packetization are not very significant. After all, if you are A, and are talking to C, there is generally no reason for you to also be connected to D at the same time. However, if A, B, C, and D are Internet users, the advantages of packet switching are immediately obvious. User A may be working on a document stored on file server B, sending a page for printing to printer D, while listening to music stored on media server C. Packet switching can allow all these communications to occur simultaneously. In large networks with multiple users, the advantages of packet switching are even more compelling. If A, B, C, and D represent large networks, John in network A could be chatting with Joe in network C, while Jane, also in network A, could be chatting with Alice in network D. A traditional switched network would have to alternate between connecting the pairs John (network A)/Joe (network C) and Jane (network A)/Alice (network D). Quite likely, users will experience slow performance as the switch tears down the previous connection and establishes the new one. In a packet-switched network, John, Joe, Jane, and Alice would simply send packets of information to the switch, and the switch would forward the packets to networks A, C, and D depending upon the destination of the packet. Users are likely to see instantaneous response with such a setup.

Figure 4 shows the four developments described in this section on a timeline. For reference, two landmark developments—the first phone call and man's landing on the moon—are shown below the timeline. It can be seen from Figure 4 that circuit switching technologies served global communication needs for almost a century. Packet switching has only become widespread in the last decade or two.

Packet switching is quite complex. At the sending end, the data needs to be broken down into small segments, and each of these segments has to be labeled and addressed correctly to create packets of data. Each individual packet has to then reach the destination across the network. At the receiving end, the data in the packets has to be rearranged back into the correct order with the data in other packets. This is a very complex operation. Complexity is almost always undesirable and is tolerated only when it is absolutely necessary. Modern networks introduce the complexity of packet switching only because it offers considerable efficiency over circuit switching. Experiments suggest that packet switching[9] can be up to 100 times more efficient than circuit switching.[10]

---

[9] The term "packet switching" is attributed to Donald W. Davies of the British National Physical Laboratory who used the term in 1965 to describe a network that chopped data into packets of 1024 bits each.
[10] Roberts, L.G., "The evolution of packet switching." *Proceedings of the IEEE*, 1978, **66**(11): pp. 1307–1313.

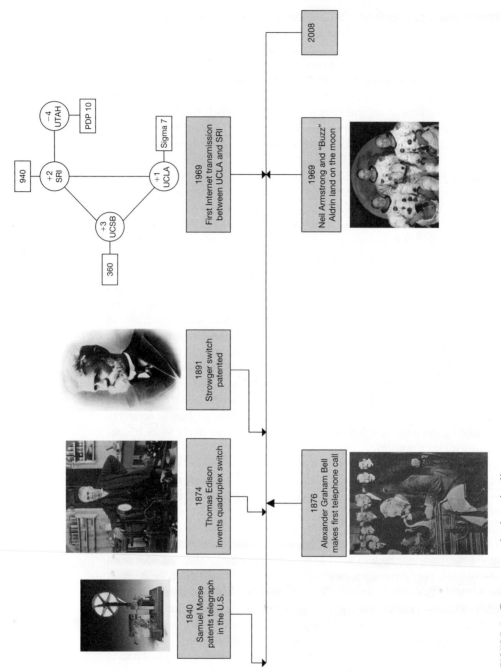

**FIGURE 4** Data communications timeline

## Circuit switching vs. packet switching

Traditional switching (used in phone networks) is called circuit switching because it establishes circuits between senders and receivers. *A circuit is an electronic closed-loop path among two or more points for signal transfer.* Figure 2 is an example of a circuit. Packet switches between networks are called routers. *Routers are devices used to interconnect two or more networks.* Routers are very sophisticated devices and can route packets between senders and receivers even if they (the routers) are not directly connected to either the sender or the receiver. They do this by locating other routers on the network that are closer to the destination and by transferring packets to these routers for further routing.

An easy way to identify whether your network is circuit-switched or packet-switched is to see its billing practices. A network that bills you on a per-KB or per-MB basis is likely to be packet-switched. This is because the resources consumed in a packet-switched network depend upon the volume of data transferred. A network that bills you on a per-minute basis is likely to be circuit-switched. This is because the resources consumed in a circuit-switched network are proportional to the time duration for which a connection is maintained, whether or not any data is transmitted over the connection. Another way to tell the difference between circuit switching and packet switching is based on whether the network is "always on." If the network needs to dial in to its destination, it is a circuit-switched network. If the network is "always on", it is a packet-switched network.

The difference between circuit switching and packet switching is analogous to the difference between the landline phone and Skype. On the phone, you dial a number and wait for the call to be connected. On Skype, you simply click on a friend and send a message. There is no connection set-up or tear-down in packet switching.

Because routers can locate other routers closer to the destination and can do so in real time, packet switching also improves the robustness of networks. A router will stay connected to the network as long as it can find at least one other router to connect to. This robustness of packet switching was the primary motivation for the U.S. Department of Defense to fund the development of packet switching. By contrast, if a link fails in a circuit-switched network while a call is on, the result is a dropped call.

With the exception of Chapter 12, this entire text focuses on how packet transmission works in modern networks.

# Packetization

*Packetization is the process of breaking down user data into small segments and packaging these segments appropriately so that they can be delivered and reassembled across the network.* Data segments produced by packetization are generally called packets, although as you will see in Chapters 3 and 5, the terms *frames* and *datagrams* are also used to denote some specific kinds of packets. Packetization is therefore the idea of sending information as small blocks of information. By contrast, circuit switching sends data as a continuous stream of information.

Each packet has two parts. The body of the packet is the segment from the original data carried by the packet. The header is the information added during packetization to aid the delivery of the packet to the correct destination and for the body of the packet to be correctly reassembled with the bodies delivered by other packets.

Packets are analogous to letters sent in the mail inside envelopes. The useful information in the mail is the body of the letter. However, to ensure that the letter reaches the correct mailbox and is read by the intended recipient at the destination, we add additional information such as an addressee name and mailing address to the letter. When the recipient reads the letter, he generally does not care for most of this additional information. He is only interested in the body of the letter. Overhead such as a mailing address is added only to ensure that the letter body reaches the intended recipient. Similarly, once packets are processed by the receiver, the additional information such as addressee, destination address, etc., is discarded by the receiver. The header information added during packetization is also called packet overhead because it is the unavoidable information cost for packet delivery. The receiver does not care for most of the information in the header, but the body cannot be delivered to the receiver without the header. Figure 5 shows a comparison between data packets and letters.

There is a very good analogy for packetization from business—knock-down kits. Traditional furniture stores have to deliver every item of furniture in specialized trucks, often by specially trained personnel, raising costs. In knock-down kits, large and unwieldy items such as furniture and home gyms are broken down into kits for reassembly at the place of use. Each box in the kit can be lifted by an average-bodied person. Knock-down kits demonstrate another advantage of packetization—ease of transport. Once knocked down into small-sized packets, even large furniture items can be transported by end users in domestic vehicles (Figure 6). The trade-off in using knock-down kits is the effort involved in reassembling the furniture at home using instructions that come with the kit. Just as knock-down kits can carry objects of any size using a common transport infrastructure, modern packet networks serve as a common infrastructure for all forms of information, including phone, video, and data. By contrast, traditional circuit-switched networks are generally tasks pecific with separate networks for voice and video.

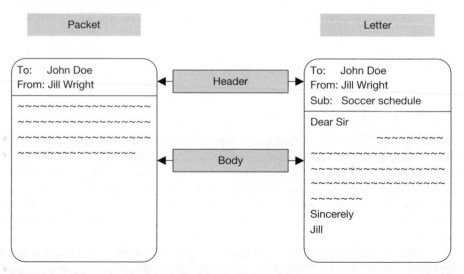

**FIGURE 5**    Comparing the structure of data packets and letters

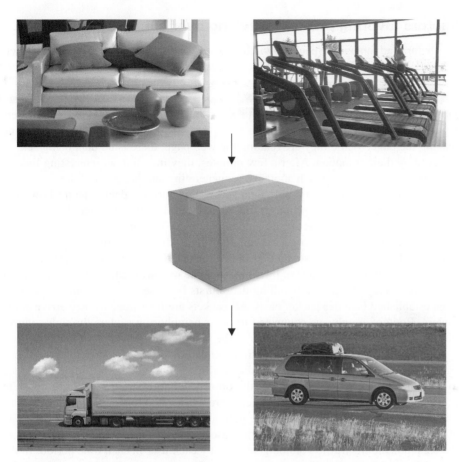

**FIGURE 6**  Knock-down kits as the business version of packetization

Reportedly, IKEA introduced the idea of knock-down kits in furniture retailing. In 1952, Gillis Lundgren, an employee at the fledgling retailer took the legs off a table to fit the table into a customer's car. Beginning the following year, the company began to mass-produce furniture using flat-pack design with a focus on making it easy for customers to transport the furniture in personal vehicles from the store. The reassembly effort at home was worth it because lower transport costs sharply reduced furniture prices and increased sales.[11]

The rest is history. IKEA's flat-pack methodology rocketed them past the competition. Company founder Ingvar Kamprad has written, "After that [table] followed a whole series of other self-assembled furniture, and by 1956 the concept was more or less systematized. The more 'knockdown' we could produce, the less damage occurred during transport and the lower freight costs were."[12]

---

[11] http://www.ikea.com/ms/en_US/about_ikea/the_ikea_way/history/1940_1950.html.
[12] Jason Jennings, "Less Is More: How Great Companies Use Productivity": Portfolio, 2002.

## Factors favoring packet switching over circuit switching

The natural advantage of packet switching over circuit switching in improving network utilization is further enhanced by two factors. The first factor is that the typical user of Internet applications demonstrates very "bursty" behavior. *Burstiness refers to short periods in which large volumes of data are uploaded or downloaded by the user followed by long periods of minimal activity.* Consider a typical web browser. Users typically click on a link to download a web page, and then spend considerable time reading the page. While they are reading the web page, there is no data being sent or received by their computer. After a few minutes, they may find an interesting link on the page and follow it to reach another site, generating another burst of data.

Circuit switching is very inefficient at handling bursts of data. Imagine how inefficient it would be if each time a user followed a web link, the computer had to set up a connection to the target server, download data, wait for some time in case the user wanted to revisit the same target server, and finally disconnect from the target. Not only would the wait time to set up the connection test the patience of the end user, the connection would be idle most of the time when the user was reading the page. Packet switching is very efficient at handling data bursts because no new connections need to be established on a per-packet basis. All packets are forwarded as they arrive at the routers. Routers are always connected to other neighboring routers through connections that can be shared by all the users of the router.

By handling packets from multiple senders addressed to different receivers, packet switching aggregates network data traffic. Aggregation is a simple technique to "smooth" traffic because it is generally observed that different users have different traffic patterns and when all these patterns are aggregated together, the average traffic volume is much less bursty than the individual traffic volumes. Figure 7 shows an example of traffic being generated by three users browsing the Internet. The heights of the bars indicate the traffic volume generated by each user in each time period. In the figure, each individual traffic pattern is bursty. However, the sum of the three traffic patterns, shown with the title "Total" is less bursty. Network designers can then design data-links such that the relatively steady, aggregate traffic volume represents, say, 70% of the overall traffic capacity of the link, ensuring suitable link utilization.

The second factor that has led to the popularity of packet switching is Moore's law. As computers become more capable while getting increasingly cheaper, communication link costs have become the highest-cost components of networks. Therefore, ensuring high utilization of communication links is the top priority for modern network carriers. Since computers are now inexpensive, we can afford to dedicate routers, which are essentially specialized computers, solely to the task of routing packets. Routers aggregate packets from multiple users and improve link utilization in bursty networks. This can make packet switching 3–100 times more efficient than circuit switching.

**FIGURE 7**
Aggregating traffic
from multiple users

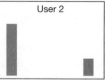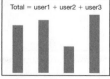

As a bonus feature, packet switching also improves the reliability of the network over circuit switching. This is described in more detail in Chapter 12. Routers can automatically discover alternate routes, skirting dead or damaged routers. End users obtain network connectivity as long as at least one path between the sender and the receiver can be found. Though carriers are now interested in packet switching primarily for its efficiency of link utilization, reliability was the primary reason the federal government was interested in packet switching during Cold-War times and funded its early development. Packet switching promised information networks that would survive even if some intermediate communication nodes were destroyed by the enemy in war.

## Layering

Now that we know we are going to packetize data, we can begin looking at how packetization is actually done. The hardware and software that performs packetization is designed using a layered architecture. *Layering is the practice of arranging functionality of components in a system in a hierarchical manner such that lower layers provide functions and services that support the functions and services of higher layers.* The end user interacts with the topmost layer. The lowest layer interacts with the wires carrying the signals.

Layering is common when extensive coordination and monitoring is needed to accomplish goals. For example, most organizations are layered, with each layer given well-defined goals. At the top level, CEOs meet stakeholder goals. CEOs are helped by VPs, who may be helped by area managers, who may in turn be helped by fresh college graduates acting as foot soldiers in the organization (Figure 8).

Layering is also common in computer software. At the topmost layer are the computer applications and at the lowest layer is the computer hardware. End users interface with computer applications such as web browsers. Applications depend upon the operating system for tasks such as accessing hardware resources for printing, saving files, etc. The operating system, in turn, depends upon device drivers to interact with hardware.

For example, when you click on the *Print* button on your browser, your browser requests the operating system to print the document. Your operating system sends the document to the driver of your default printer, which sends the correct sequence of commands and information to the printer to print the page (Figure 9).

There is a strong tradition of using layering to add functionality to computer software. Hence, networking software is also organized in layers. For example, you may have upgraded a version of your web browser or switched to a different web browser. You could do this without changing any other network capabilities on your computer because the browser application is a layer of software that is independent of other layers that enable networking. It is also easy to move between wired and wireless computer networks without changing browsers or e-mail clients. Again, this is possible because the network access functionality is defined in a layer independent of the applications layer.

Arranging software functionality in layers offers many advantages. An obvious advantage during development is specialization. Experts can focus on delivering the functionality of each layer, interoperating with neighboring layers through well-defined

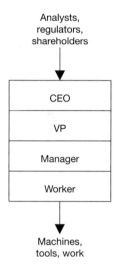

**FIGURE 8** Layering in organizations

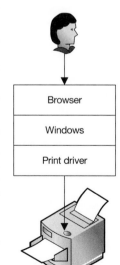

**FIGURE 9** Layering in software

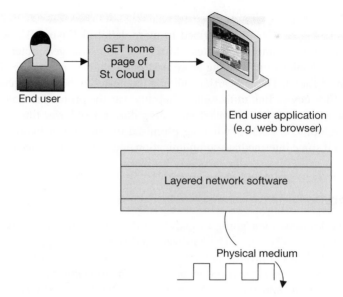

**FIGURE 10**   Network layers

specifications. Interface designers working on the topmost layer can focus on human/ computer interaction issues. Programmers developing device drivers can focus on transaction speed and printing features. However, the greatest advantages of software layering are during operation. Individual layers of software can be upgraded without changing other layers. In the software world, we all know how most applications even offer to upgrade themselves automatically. This is possible because the applications are an independent software layer and application upgrades do not require operating system changes. Similarly, upgrading graphics capabilities or adding sound capabilities to computers does not require modifications to existing applications. It is comparably easy to introduce new technology at any layer if it does not affect other layers.

Figure 10 shows the overall context of the layered network system. The end user uses applications such as web browsers to access network resources. The application interacts with the topmost layer of the layered network system. The layers process the request layer by layer until the lowest layer transmits the user request as signals over the physical medium. The browser and the physical medium are considered to be outside the layered network software.

## Typical packet structure

At this point we know that computer networks send information as packets. If you visit a web page, your browser gets that page as packets from the web server. These packets are reassembled before the page is displayed on your browser. Each packet contains a part of the web page, and some additional information, called header.

We also know that networking software is organized in layers. So, how does layering affect packetization?

Layering affects packetization by organizing the information in the packet header in a layered manner. The remaining chapters will look at each layer in detail. The big picture is provided here.

For packetization to work reliably, five essential tasks need to be performed. Together, these five tasks ensure that packets will reach the correct destination, have no data errors, and will serve user needs. The five tasks are:

**(1)** specifying user commands

**(2)** segmentation and reassembly of packets

**(3)** identifying and locating the destination on the network

**(4)** error control to remove errors during signaling

**(5)** signaling

Networks perform these five tasks in a well-defined five-layered sequence as follows. When a user needs network service, he invokes the appropriate user command and passes the appropriate data to the command (for example, the URL of a web page). This happens at the topmost layer and completes Task 1—specifying user commands. The header at this layer carries the user command.

If the data is large, it needs to be broken up. This is done in the next layer, completing Task 2—segmentation and reassembly of packets. The header at this layer keeps track of the different segments. Each of these packets has to be delivered to the correct destination. To do this, the next layer takes each segment and adds the appropriate destination address to the segment. This completes Task 3—locating the destination. Routers along the way look at these destination addresses and send the packet to the next router. *Each link from one router to the next router is called a hop.* We have to ensure that no errors are introduced while the packet is being transferred over a hop. Therefore, the next layer transfers packets carefully toward the destination, network by network, router by router, hop by hop, from your home network to your ISP's network, and to the target web server's network, ensuring that the packets are not damaged as they cross a network. This completes Task 4—error control. To perform errorchecks, this layer adds error-checking information at each hop. Finally, within each hop, the last layer sends data as signals necessary for information transfer. This completes Task 5—signaling.

You may note that each of the five tasks generally requires some header information. For example, the destination address must be included in the header for packets to be delivered to the correct destination. Each of the five layers in data communications performs one of the five tasks. Each of the next five chapters covers each of these layers and tasks in detail. At this time, try to get the overall picture: users pass commands and data, the data is packetized if necessary, and the packets are transferred to the destination without error. For reference, Table 2 shows the five networking layers, the tasks performed at each layer, and the important header information added at each layer. Please note that while the tasks listed in Table 2 are the most important tasks at each layer, most layers also do other tasks to improve network performance. These additional tasks will also be introduced when we look at each layer in detail in the next five chapters.

**Table 2** Network layer tasks and important header information

| Networking task | Supporting information in header |
|---|---|
| User needs | User commands |
| Segmentation and reassembly of packets | Sequence numbers |
| Identifying and locating destination | Address |
| Error control | Error check |
| Signaling | None |

After all the layers have added the required headers, at a high level, the packet structure looks as shown in Figure 11.

## TCP/IP stack

Since the five-layered network architecture of Table 2 is so widely used, each layer has been given a name that closely reflects the function of that layer. Often in industry, these layers are simply addressed by their position in the stack. Thus, the network layer is widely called Layer 3. These names and numbers are shown in Table 3 below.

Whereas various technologies are available for each layer, the five-layered networking software shown in Table 3 is called the TCP/IP stack in honor of the two core technologies used universally. TCP operates at Layer 4 and performs segmentation and reassembly of packets. IP operates at Layer 3 and identifies and locates the destination.

Common technologies used at the different layers are shown in Figure 12. In the most common implementation, TCP and IP are combined with another technology called Ethernet, which performs error control and signaling (Layers 2 and 1 respectively). This is the set of technologies you have used most of the time when connecting to the Internet.

Since the Ethernet and TCP/IP combination is so widely used and because both these technologies are publicly documented, this text focuses on Ethernet for the data-link layer (Chapter 3), IP for the network layer (Chapter 4) and TCP for the transport layer (Chapter 5).

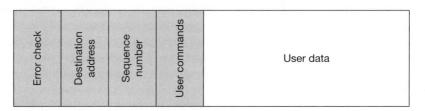

**FIGURE 11** Typical packet structure at a high level

**Table 3**    Network layer names and tasks in TCP/IP stack

| Layer number | Layer name | Networking task | Supporting information in header |
|---|---|---|---|
| | **Application** | User needs | User commands |
| 4 | **Transport** | Segmentation and reassembly of packets | Sequence numbers |
| 3 | **Network** | Identifying and locating destination | Address |
| 2 | **Datalink** | Error control | Error check |
| 1 | **Physical** | Signaling | None |

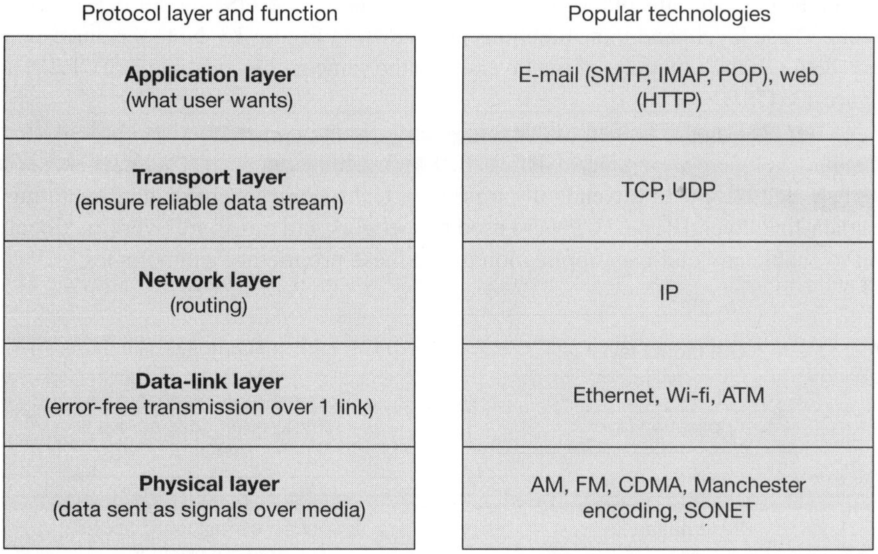

| Protocol layer and function | Popular technologies |
|---|---|
| **Application layer** (what user wants) | E-mail (SMTP, IMAP, POP), web (HTTP) |
| **Transport layer** (ensure reliable data stream) | TCP, UDP |
| **Network layer** (routing) | IP |
| **Data-link layer** (error-free transmission over 1 link) | Ethernet, Wi-fi, ATM |
| **Physical layer** (data sent as signals over media) | AM, FM, CDMA, Manchester encoding, SONET |

**FIGURE 12**    TCP/IP layers and technologies

## OSI model

What is missing from the neat five-layered network architecture introduced in the previous section is the tortuous path that led to the creation of the architecture. In the early days, many firms developed their own proprietary technologies for computer networking. Technologies such as SNA, DECnet, Appletalk, IPX/SPX were vying for popularity and commercial success. Each of these technologies was a complete networking solution, and was usually not properly layered. Unfortunately, all these technologies were proprietary and every vendor had an interest in locking in customers into their technology. As a result, IT managers had a hard time getting the different networking technologies to interoperate with each other. If a firm adopted the networking technology of one company, it was forced to buy all computer equipment from the same company. The result was that the choice of a networking technology often made organizations captive customers of the technology vendor, which could charge steep prices for subsequent sales.

Difficulties in interoperation between networking technologies created communication islands within organizations. Groups that adopted, say, SNA could not exchange information over the network with groups in the same organization that adopted, say, AppleTalk. The challenge, therefore, was to ensure interoperability between these competing technologies.

To overcome this challenge, the International Standards Organization (ISO) came up with the Open Standards Interconnect (OSI) model. *The OSI model is a logical structure for communications networks standardized by the International Organization for Standardization.* As the name suggests, this was a model, not a real technology solution for networking. However, for the first time in the domain of computer networking, the OSI model specified the concept of layers and defined the services to be offered at each layer. Compliance with the OSI model enables any system to communicate with any other OSI-compliant system. The OSI model defined seven layers. These layers and their functions are shown in Figure 13. Note the correspondence between the functions of the layers with the same names in Table 3 (TCP/IP) and Figure 13 (OSI).

The OSI model helped the development of computer networking because technology developers were able to define their technologies in terms of the layers served by their technology. In the end, all proprietary technologies were seen as operating at the data-link layer. IP and TCP were used for network and transport layer functionality and to enable any end-user application to use these proprietary technologies.

| OSI model layer | Layer function |
|---|---|
| Application layer | Request-reply mechanism for remote operations across a network |
| Presentation layer | Syntax conversion from host-specific syntax to syntax for network transfer |
| Session layer | Create and terminate connection; establish synchronization points for recovery in case of failure |
| Transport layer | Segmentation, reassembly of packets in one connection, multiplexing connections on one machine |
| Network layer | Routing and network addressing |
| Data-link layer | Error-free data transmission over a single link |
| Physical layer | Convert data to signals for transmission over physical media |

**FIGURE 13** Network layer names and tasks in OSI model

OSI model layers    TCP/IP stack layers

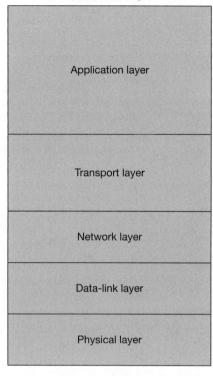

**FIGURE 14** OSI and TCP/IP

These days, the OSI model is used as an introduction to computer networking even though real-world technologies follow the TCP/IP architecture. TCP/IP may be seen as a simplified version of the OSI model. The correspondence between the layers of the OSI model and TCP/IP is shown in Figure 14. The figure shows that the lowest three layers in both stacks perform similar functionality. However, the TCP transport layer performs some of the functionality of the session layer in addition to the functionality of the OSI transport layer. The TCP/IP application layer performs all the functions of the OSI application layer. In addition, it also performs the functions of the OSI presentation layer and some functions of the OSI session layer.

---

### Gotchas

When asked to describe the functions of layers in the OSI model or TCP/IP stack, students sometimes write that the function of a layer, say the presentation layer, is to pass data from the session layer to the application layer. Please remember, no layer exists just to pass data from one layer to another. If that were the case, the layer in question could have been eliminated and the lower layer could have been modified to pass data directly to the upper layer.

  Every layer has a well-defined task.

## Principles of Internet Protocols (IP)

If you look at the names of the different technologies in Figure 12, you will note that most technologies have names that end in "p", e.g. HTTP, TCP, SMTP, UDP, IP, etc. So, what does this "p" represent? Is it some special feature of networking technologies? The "p" in these technology names stands for "protocol".

What is a protocol? *A protocol is a set of rules that permit information systems* (ISs) *to exchange information with each other*. Each protocol is designed to facilitate interoperation within a communication layer. For communication to occur, the communicators must have a common language with a shared interpretation of the words in the language. The protocol is the shared language. We have all heard cryptic conversations by taxi drivers, aircraft pilots, and police officers over the radio. You may have noticed that these radio conversations are very different from face-to-face conversations and mean little to the lay person. Yet, they obey well-defined rules, and words in the conversations have well-defined meanings to the operators. Speakers announce their names, deliver the messages, confirm reception, etc. The rules followed in these channels are an example of protocols. Since the communication channel is shared by many speakers, the messages are short and coded to quickly make way for other speakers.[13] Similarly, each layer in the network stack has a well-defined set of tasks, and the protocol software in each layer is capable of performing these tasks very efficiently.

The success of the Internet in general and TCP/IP in particular is based on some key design principles adopted by the designers of these protocols. Two of these stand out. The first is that at the very outset, the designers of TCP/IP visualized a federation of networks, where each network could adopt any arbitrary design or technology. This principle allows wireless Ethernet networks in homes to interoperate with fiber-optic networks in carriers. Interoperation can be expected even with networking technologies that do not exist yet. The second principle is that multiple applications, even those that have not yet been conceived, can use the Internet for network connectivity.

Together, these two principles led to the development of a common packet format that can be transferred by any network and that serves all applications. This common packet format is the IP packet format. Data from all applications is broken down into IP packets and all network technologies know how to transfer IP packets. This is shown in Figure 15, which shows that information from different applications such as the web and e-mail is transferred as IP packets. These IP packets may be carried by networks running on any underlying technology. A visual inspection of Figure 15 also shows why IP is sometimes called the "thin waist" of the network stack.

We experience the advantages of these two design principles of TCP/IP on a daily basis when we use the Internet for network connectivity. One computer, a laptop or PC, is able to run any network communication application because one packet format, IP, can serve all these applications and can be transferred across all networks. This contrasts with dedicated networks such as the phone and TV networks which can only serve one specific application. These two design principles have also led to the longevity of TCP and IP. When TCP and IP were created, the Internet had a few thousand users who connected to each other using phones lines, which offered data

---

[13] This example is from Pouzin, L. and H. Zimmermann, "A tutorial on protocols." *Proceedings of the IEEE*, 1978. **66**(11): pp. 1346–1370.

*File Transfer Protocol*

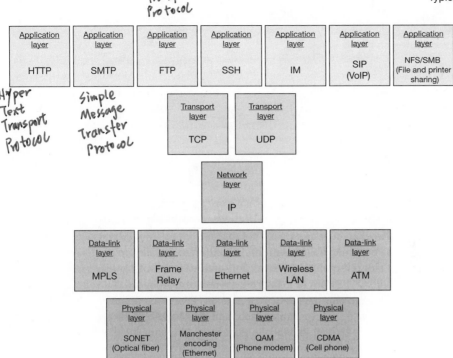

*Hyper Text Transport Protocol*

*Simple Message Transfer Protocol*

**FIGURE 15**   Technologies at TCP/IP architecture layers

rates of about 50 Kbps. Today, the Internet has over 500 million users connected using high-speed lines with data rates over 10 Gbps. While IT has evolved at a very rapid pace, all modern networks continue to run on TCP and IP, technologies that are largely unchanged since they were first defined almost 40 years ago.

## Typical computer network

Putting all the ideas in the chapter together and to set the stage for the remaining chapters, Figure 16 shows a typical computer network. Please refer to this figure anytime you are not sure where a specific technology fits in the overall network.

The figure considers a subscriber served by Verizon, an ISP (Internet Service Provider) connecting to a website at a university. A PC in the home is connected to the Internet through the home router. This router acts as the edge between the home network and the ISP network. A dedicated connection links the home router to the ISP network. Within the ISP network are a large number of routers that move the data packets successively closer to their destination by passing them on to the best neighboring router. Along the way, packets may be handed off to other networks at peering points. Finally, the packets are delivered to the destination network. For example, if you visit your university home page, the destination network is your university network. The destination network locates the web server hosting the web page and delivers these packets to the web server. The response from the web server takes the reverse path back to the home PC. The transaction is also shown in the inside cover.

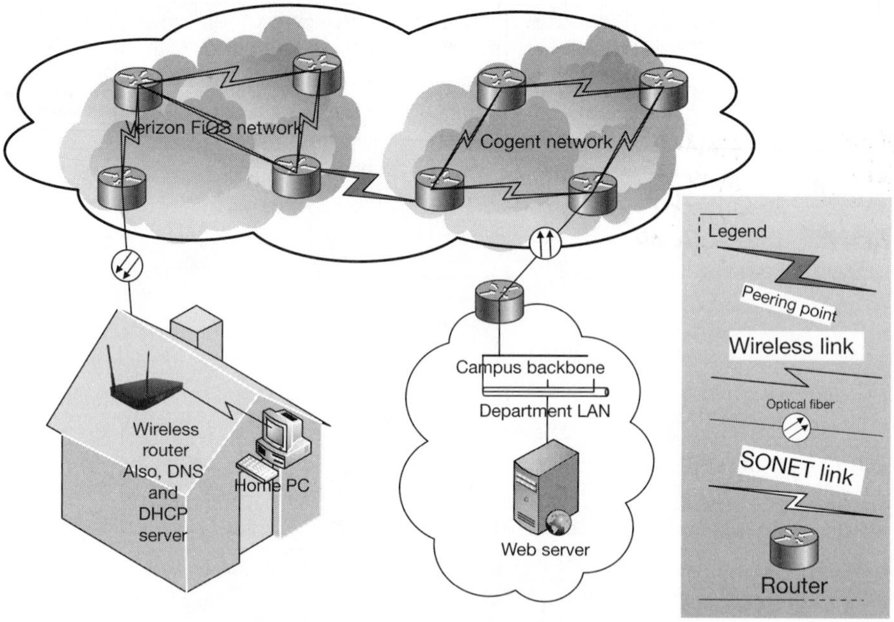

**FIGURE 16** A typical computer network

## SUMMARY

This chapter and the book began with a discussion of the utility of computer networks to demonstrate how computer networks are useful to individuals and businesses. We saw why it is to your professional advantage to understand the basics of how computer networks operate. We looked at the major milestones in the evolution of computer networks leading to the deployment of circuit-switched networks around the globe. We saw how modern networks are moving to packet switching because packet switching is very well-suited to handle the traffic patterns on the Internet. To set the stage for the later chapters, we introduced the idea of layering, using examples to show how layering is a common method to organize complicated functionality in computer software and hardware. The TCP/IP stack, which is the standard implementation of layering for packet switching, was also introduced. Finally, to place these ideas in context, we saw how multiple networks are connected together to form the Internet.

The rest of the book is organized by the layers of the TCP/IP stack. Since lower layers offer services to upper layers, we go bottom up on the stack. Chapter 2 covers the physical layer; Chapter 3 covers the data-link layer; Chapter 4 the network layer; the transport layer is discussed in Chapter 5, and the application layer in Chapter 6.

The next set of chapters looks at the technologies that support the TCP/IP stack. Chapter 7 covers important support services such as DHCP and DNS that enhance the capabilities of computer networks or make networks easier to use. Chapters 8 and 9 cover subnetting and routing. Two kinds of data-link layer technologies—WANs and wireless LANs—are covered in Chapters 10 and 11. Telephony is in Chapter 12. Finally, issues surrounding networks—security and legal issues—are covered in Chapters 13 and 14.

## ABOUT THE COLOPHON

Sir Arthur C. Clarke was a British science fiction author and futurist. He is most famous for the novel *2001: A Space Odyssey*. As a futurist, he attracted great fame for his proposal in 1945 for geostationary satellite communication systems. While it was considered a fantasy at the time, it became a reality within 20 years when Intelsat was launched in 1965, marking the beginning of satellite TV in the country.[14] Sir Clarke formulated three laws of predicting the future, the third of which is best known: any sufficiently advanced technology is indistinguishable from magic.

The Internet seems to fit this definition of an advanced technology very well. Pause to think about it. Isn't it magical that every time we use the Internet, our computers routinely break data down into packets; each of these packets independently locates its destination and finds its way there; and the receiver is able to reassemble all these packets of data back into a coherent whole as a web page, e-mail, instant message, speech, video, bank statement, or other artifact? Even better, isn't it wonderful that all these processes happen reliably day in and day out, and within milliseconds? We take all of this for granted, but isn't that part of the magic?

The rest of this book is dedicated to describing how this magic works.

---

## CASE STUDY | IS THE NETWORK THE WAY TO THE CUSTOMER'S HEART?: DOMINO'S PIZZA

---

*When we think of ways in which computer networks help businesses, the first thought that often comes to mind is e-commerce. Companies such as Amazon and e-Bay have made it commonplace for consumers to buy various categories of goods online. However, companies have had less success at selling food over the Internet. But people are becoming more comfortable with the Internet, and more people are online. Since 2005, Internet adoption has increased significantly in the United States, reaching almost 80% in 2009, compared to about 60% in 2005. This may finally be increasing our willingness to buy food online, beginning with a food category that people are already comfortable ordering for delivery—pizza.*

Domino's Pizza was founded in 1960 by brothers Thomas and James Monaghan who borrowed $900 to purchase a small pizza store in Ypsilanti, Michigan. Today, Domino's Pizza is the number one pizza-delivery company in the United States with a 17.5% share of the pizza-delivery market based on reported consumer spending. On average, over one million pizzas are sold each day throughout the system, with deliveries covering approximately ten million miles per week. Domino's Pizza pioneered the pizza-delivery business and has built the Domino's Pizza brand into one of the most widely recognized consumer brands in the world.

As of December 28, 2008, the company had 8,773 stores worldwide in more than 60 countries. Of these, 4,558 franchise stores and 489 company-owned stores were in the United States. At the end of 2008, the company had approximately 10,500 employees. Including those in franchises, an estimated 175,000 people worked in the Domino's Pizza system.

The company has three reportable business segments: (i) Domestic Stores (2008 revenues: $511.6 million and income from operations: $126.9 million), (ii) Domestic Supply Chain (2008 revenues: $771.1 million and income from operations: $47.1 million), and (iii) International Stores (2008 revenues: $142.4 million and income from operations: $63.9 million).

Domino's Pizza operates in the quick-service restaurant (QSR) industry. With sales of $33.9 billion in the twelve months ended November 2008, the U.S. QSR pizza category is the second largest category within the $230.3 billion U.S. QSR industry. The U.S. QSR pizza category is large and fragmented. The primary domestic competitors are regional and local companies as well as national chains: Domino's, Pizza Hut, and Papa John's. The three national chains accounted for approximately 47% of U.S. pizza delivery, based on reported consumer spending, with the remaining 53% attributable to regional chains and individual establishments.

Over the years, Domino's has developed a simple business model focused on its core strength of delivering quality pizza in a timely manner. This business model

---

[14] Arthur C. Clarke, "Extra-terrestrial relays," *Wireless World*, 1945, pp. 305–308, http://lakdiva.org/clarke/1945ww/ (accessed 11/09).

includes a delivery-oriented store design with low capital requirements, and a focused menu of pizza and complementary side items. The majority of its domestic stores are located in populated areas in or adjacent to large- or mid-sized cities, or on or near college campuses. The company believes that its pizza-delivery model provides a significant competitive advantage because most of its stores do not offer dine-in areas. As a result, they typically do not require expensive real estate, are relatively small, and are relatively inexpensive to build and equip. They also benefit from lower maintenance costs, as store assets have long lives and updates are not frequently required. The typical Domino's pizza store is relatively small, occupying approximately 1,000 to 1,300 square feet, and is designed with a focus on efficient and timely production of consistently high-quality pizza for delivery. The store layout has been refined over time to provide an efficient flow from order-taking to delivery. The entire order-taking and pizza-production process is designed for completion in approximately 12–15 minutes.

Competition in the pizza-delivery market is intense and is generally based on product quality, location, image, service, price, convenience, and concept. The industry is often affected by changes in consumer tastes, economic conditions, demographic trends, and consumers' disposable income. Apart from competitive pressures, during 2008, the company faced significant challenges in its domestic business, particularly rising commodity costs, a continued trend of negative domestic same-store sales growth and net negative domestic-store growth. These factors resulted in a revenue decline in 2008 of $37.8 million or 2.6%.

### Pizza Tracker

A large fraction of Domino's base is young. This customer base is increasingly connected to the network using cell phones and laptops and has a strong preference for using online search and Internet ordering for products and services. Internet ordering better fits the work flow of this audience than phone ordering. Therefore, strength in online order-taking can help quick-service restaurants reach this customer base.

Domino's introduced Pizza Tracker in 2007 to improve its online-ordering capabilities. Pizza Tracker has been integrated into PULSE, the company's new proprietary point-of-sale system. Customers access PizzaTracker through the build-your-own-pizza application on the company's home page. The application photographically simulates the pizza as customers select a size, choose a

sauce, and add toppings. Customers can add coupon codes and are shown the final price before they place their order. PizzaTracker also allows customers to track the progress of the pizza as it enters the oven, or when it leaves the store. At the time of its introduction, Domino's had the most feature-rich online pizza-ordering application among the three national pizza chains.

Installing the online ordering system costs approximately $20,000 per store. Many franchisees were initially hesitant to incur these costs. Resistance increased further when many of the bells and whistles in the online-ordering application did not work or were incompatible with the ways the franchisees operated their stores. In response, in developing the online-ordering system, Domino's CIO decided to focus on reliably executing core tasks such as taking orders, scheduling workers, and mapping delivery routes. This has helped overcome franchisee resistance.

Online orders are directly displayed to the right spot on the pizza-assembly line in the store. To provide status updates to customers, employees hit a button on their computer screens to update the status of the order. Another update can be generated when the delivery driver leaves the store with the pizza.

The online application makes it easy for connected customers to locate a nearby Domino's pizza and order their preferred pizza in a single visit to the company's website. The online-ordering system stores contact information and menu preferences for customers who have ordered online. This information can be used to simplify ordering for repeat customers and also to encourage adding items to orders.

The online-ordering system has proved quite popular. Almost 20% of all Domino's orders now come online. Anecdotal evidence from adopting franchisees suggests that online ordering has boosted overall orders and increased the average amount of each transaction.

## REFERENCES

Horowitz, B. "Where's your Domino's pizza? Track it online", *USA Today*, January 29, 2008.

Jargon, J. "Domino's IT Staff Delivers Slick Site, Ordering System", *Wall Street Journal*, November 24, 2009.

Pew Internet and American life project, "Internet adoption", http://pewinternet.org/Trend-Data/Internet-Adoption.aspx (accessed 12/31/2009).

# REVIEW QUESTIONS[15]

1. What is *business data communications*?

2. What are some of the ways in which computer networks are used in large businesses?

3. What are some of the ways in which small businesses can benefit from computer networks?

4. Look at the websites of some departments of your county government. What three services offered at these sites do you find most interesting?

5. Describe how the three online government services you chose could be helpful to you.

6. Describe the major trends in the growth of Internet traffic.

7. What is *packetization*?

8. Why is packetization useful in business data communication?

9. What are some of the factors that make packet switching more complex technologically than traditional phone circuits (circuit switching)?

10. Provide a high-level overview of the structure of a typical data packet. What are the kinds of information you are likely to find in the header of a typical packet?

11. Consider a typical office memo as a data packet. What information in the memo would be characterized as header information? What information would be characterized as the body of the packet?

12. Why is Internet traffic considered "bursty" compared to voice traffic?

13. What is *layering*?

14. Why is layering useful in organizations?

15. Why is layering useful in computer networking?

16. What are the five layers of the TCP/IP model?

17. What are the primary functions of each layer in the TCP/IP model?

18. TCP is often considered the most important layer of the TCP/IP model. What are the primary responsibilities of TCP?

19. What devices does a packet typically encounter?

20. What is the OSI model? What was the motivation for the development of the OSI model?

21. How has the OSI model been useful in the development of computer networks?

22. What are the seven layers of the OSI model?

23. What are the primary functions of each of the seven layers of the OSI model?

24. The packets used to transmit voice on the Internet are similar to the packets that are used to send e-mail. What are some of the advantages of this approach?

25. What are the two design principles behind Internet protocols?

# HANDS-ON EXERCISES

Figure 16 in the chapter showed a typical arrangement of networks that form part of the Internet. In this lab exercise, we will use a command-line utility called `traceroute` to view the networks that a packet crosses as it travels the network from your computer to some popular websites.

To use `traceroute`, open up the command prompt on your computer. On windows XP, you can do start → Run and type cmd in the dialog box. In Windows Vista, you can click start and type cmd in the "start search" dialog box. On the mac or on Linux desktops, you can open the terminal application to get a command prompt (On the mac, the terminal application is at Applications → Utilities → Terminal).

At the prompt, enter the command tracert followed by the URL of a website you want to trace. In the example of Figure 17, we use tracert to trace a route from our computer to the website of the Illinois Institute of Technology (www.iit.edu). Each row in the output has five columns. The first column is the serial count of the routers encountered in the path to the destination. This gives us a count of the number of hops required to reach the destination. For example, from Figure 17, we can see that there are 12 hops from the source to the destination. The next three columns provide the round trip times for three probe packets sent to the router at the location. For example, in Figure 17, we see that the round trip time for each of the three probe

---

[15] For your convenience, the companion website has a word document that includes all the questions.

```
C:\Windows\system32\cmd.exe

C:\Temp>tracert www.iit.edu

Tracing route to www.iit.edu [216.47.150.245]
over a maximum of 30 hops:

  1    51 ms    50 ms    50 ms  edu-vpn1-172-public.net.usf.edu [131.247.250.35]

  2    58 ms    50 ms    50 ms  131.247.250.62
  3    51 ms    50 ms    50 ms  vlan254.campus-backbone2.net.usf.edu [131.247.25
4.46]
  4    50 ms    50 ms    50 ms  131.247.254.242
  5    52 ms    50 ms    51 ms  tpa-flrcore-7609-1-te31-v1601-1.net.flrnet.org [
198.32.166.93]
  6    55 ms    55 ms    55 ms  tlh-flrcore-7609-1-te21-1.net.flrnet.org [198.32
.155.14]
  7    71 ms    74 ms    71 ms  hous-te0501-v513.layer3.nlr.net [198.32.155.254]

  8    97 ms    97 ms    97 ms  chic-hous-67.layer3.nlr.net [216.24.186.25]
  9   104 ms   107 ms   107 ms  74.114.96.13
 10    97 ms    97 ms    97 ms  216.47.141.25
 11    97 ms    97 ms    97 ms  216.47.159.5
 12    97 ms    97 ms    97 ms  www.iit.edu [216.47.150.245]

Trace complete.

C:\Temp>_
```

**FIGURE 17** Use of tracert command to find route to www.iit.edu

```
Windows PowerShell

PS C:\Temp> tracert www.u-tokyo.ac.jp

Tracing route to www.u-tokyo.ac.jp [133.11.114.194]
over a maximum of 30 hops:

  1    50 ms    49 ms    49 ms  edu-vpn1-172-public.net.usf.edu [131.247.250.35]
  2    50 ms    50 ms    50 ms  131.247.250.62
  3    50 ms    50 ms    50 ms  vlan254.campus-backbone1.net.usf.edu [131.247.254.45]
  4    50 ms    50 ms    50 ms  vlan256.wan-msfc.net.usf.edu [131.247.254.81]
  5    50 ms    50 ms    50 ms  atm900-128.enb-msfc.net.usf.edu [131.247.254.230]
  6    50 ms    50 ms    54 ms  tpa-flrcore-7609-1-te31-v1601-1.net.flrnet.org [198.32.166.93]
  7    55 ms    55 ms    55 ms  tlh-flrcore-7609-1-te21-1.net.flrnet.org [198.32.155.14]
  8    72 ms    71 ms    71 ms  hous-te0501-v513.layer3.nlr.net [198.32.155.254]
  9   102 ms   102 ms   102 ms  losa-hous-87.layer3.nlr.net [216.24.186.30]
 10   101 ms   101 ms   101 ms  transpac-1-lo-jmb-702.lsanca.pacificwave.net [207.231.240.136]
 11   216 ms   217 ms   216 ms  tokyo-losa-tp2.transpac2.net [192.203.116.146]
 12   217 ms   216 ms   217 ms  vlan53-cisco2.notemachi.wide.ad.jp [203.178.133.142]
 13   217 ms   217 ms   217 ms  ve-51.foundry6.otemachi.wide.ad.jp [203.178.141.141]
 14   217 ms   217 ms   217 ms  ve-42.foundry4.nezu.wide.ad.jp [203.178.136.66]
 15   218 ms   217 ms   217 ms  ra37-vlan566.nc.u-tokyo.ac.jp [133.11.125.237]
 16   217 ms   218 ms   217 ms  ra3a-gil-0-0.nc.u-tokyo.ac.jp [133.11.206.146]
 17   217 ms   217 ms   217 ms  ra39-vlan336.nc.u-tokyo.ac.jp [133.11.206.153]
 18   217 ms   217 ms   217 ms  ra35.nc.u-tokyo.ac.jp [133.11.127.41]
 19   217 ms   217 ms   217 ms  www.u-tokyo.ac.jp [133.11.114.194]

Trace complete.
PS C:\Temp>
```

**FIGURE 18** Tracing the route to the University of Tokyo

packets to reach the router on the 8th hop is 97 milliseconds. The last column gives us the name or numerical address of the router reached on the hop. For example, the router on the 8th hop in Figure 17 is chic-hous-67.layer3.nlr.net. Many ISPs give routers meaningful names that help network administrators quickly identify the location of the router on a map. For example, the tpa in the 5th router indicates that it is located in Tampa and the tlh in the 6th router indicates that it is located in Tallahassee, Florida.

The router names also indicate the networks the routers belong to, so that the names of the organizations operating the routers can be easily checked on the web. For example, routers 1 and 3 are located in USF, as seen from their usf.edu name. Routers 5 and 6 belong to the Florida Research and Educational Network, as can be checked by visiting the website www.flrnet.org. Routers 7 and 8 are operated by the National Lambda Rail, as can be checked by visiting the website www.nlr.net.

Figure 18 shows another route trace, this time to the University of Tokyo. We see that the packets take the path from USF → flrnet → nlr → pacificwave → transpac2 → Wide project (wide.ad.jp) → U. Tokyo.

The geographic names of the routers in Figure 18 also indicate the geographic path taken by the packets. Starting from the East Coast of the United States in Tampa, Florida, the packets travel via Tallahassee and Houston to reach Losa, California, in hop 9. Hops 10 and 11 take the packets to Tokyo, Japan, from Losa, California, over a transpacific route. In Japan, the Wide project routes packets to the University of Tokyo. Hops 15–19 are within the University of Tokyo as the packets take many small hops within the university to reach its web server.

When packets cross submarine routes (e.g. hops 10, 11 in Figure 18), they typically encounter relatively larger delays because of the longer distances that need to be covered. Delays may also be caused when the network on a hop is very busy handling other traffic.

Answer the following questions:

1. Briefly describe what traceroute does and how it is useful (you may find articles on traceroute on sources such as Wikipedia, useful).

2. Use traceroute to trace the route from your home or work computer to your university's website. Show the traceroute output. What networks were encountered along the way? What information about the geographic locations of the routers can you infer from the trace? What was the longest mean delay on any 1 hop along the way?

3. Use traceroute to trace the route from your home or work computer to the website of a university or company on another continent. Show the traceroute output. What networks were encountered along the way? What information about the geographic locations of the routers can you infer from the trace? What was the longest mean delay on any 1 hop along the way? What factors do you think caused this delay?

4. Visit the websites of the ISPs on one route. Show the network coverage map of any one ISP on the route that provides this information. (Note: This information is useful in marketing, therefore, most ISPs provide some graphical information about their coverage areas.)

# NETWORK DESIGN EXERCISE

We saw in this chapter that computer networks are useful to organizations in various ways. Subsequent chapters deal with the technology components used in these networks. To help you understand how the information in the book is used in the real world, the network design exercise will build the network for a company. Using an example of a fictitious multinational manufacturing firm headquartered in your town, in every chapter you will choose and configure the right technology from the available options in a manner that best meets the business needs of the firm.

Overall information about the company is presented here. Where required, the exercises in the chapters will provide more details specific to the chapter. You will be asked to draw network diagrams in many chapters. Visio is a popular software to draw networks. If you do not have access to Visio, the readings for this chapter at the companion website have a document that includes a world map and network icons that you can use to create the diagrams using word processors.

Coolco Inc. is a successful manufacturing company in your town. The company manufactures and sells widgets to other businesses around the world. As a result of its success, it has offices around the world. Since the company operates from multiple locations, it relies on a communications infrastructure to support business processes that are dispersed across these offices. As a consultant to Coolco's CIO, you are charged with designing the entire network infrastructure for the company.

## Firm details

Coolco maintains design, manufacturing, fulfillment, repair, and customer-service facilities around the world. The locations of these operations are shown in Table 4 and Figure 19.

The corporate offices have an assortment of mobile and stationary users. Mobile users are assigned laptops to conduct business from locations in the office and at customer sites or home offices. These users are usually connected to the network for 8–10 hours each day. The applications they access include e-mail and a wide host of resources, including marketing, human resources, R&D, product literature, and customer and vendor information. The call center and service center have stationary users. They typically access e-mail, product literature, and customer history.

**Table 4** Coolco office locations and staffing

| United States | Amsterdam, The Netherlands | Mumbai, India | Singapore, Singapore |
|---|---|---|---|
| • Building #1 with 4 floors, 300 employees: with 100 employees per floor on the first three floors and a lights-out data center on the fourth floor. | • Building #1 with 2 floors, 100 employees on the first floor. | • Building #1 with 2 floors, 200 employees: 100 employees on each floor. | • Building #1 with 3 floors, 200 employees: with 100 employees on the first floor and 50 employees each on the other two floors. |
| • Each floor has a dimension of 100 feet × 150 feet with a telecommunications closet located near the center of each floor. | • The first floor of this building houses a service center for the EMEA (Europe, Middle-East and Africa) region. | • The building houses the company's primary call center, operating 24 hours a day. | • The first floor is used by the marketing group for the AP (Asia-Pacific) region. The other two floors house a service center for the AP region. |
| • The two lower floors of this building are used for producing widgets. | • The firm's backup database is located on the second floor of the building. | | |
| • The remaining third floor has various corporate offices for HR, Finance, IT, and Marketing departments. | | | |
| • Data center hosts data from payroll, accounting, production, and other corporate functions. | | | |
| • The corporate website is also hosted here. | | | |

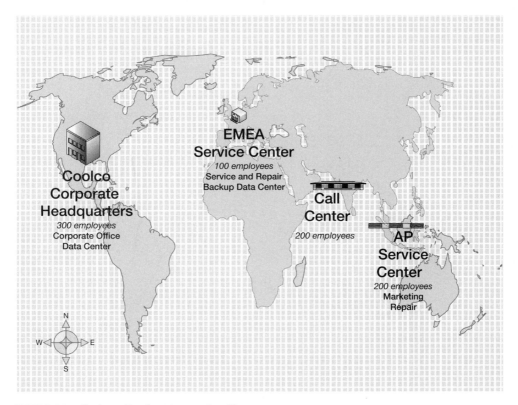

**FIGURE 19**   Coolco office locations and staffing

Answer the following question.

1. What are the ways in which computer networks can help Coolco in its business? Think of all the different ways in which the company can use computer networks at all its different offices.

## CASE QUESTIONS

1. Visit the websites of Domino's pizza and one other quick-service pizza restaurant. How long does it take for you to order a pizza of your choice from each of these restaurants? (Of course, you don't have to actually place the order for this exercise. Just get to the point where you are ready to place the order.)

2. If you haven't ordered pizza online before, to what extent has this exercise influenced the probability that you may consider online ordering the next time you decide to order pizza?

3. What features of the websites most influenced your decision?

4. Identify three of your friends who haven't ordered pizza online. What are the primary reasons these friends give for not ordering pizza online? To what extent have the pizzeria websites addressed these concerns?

5. (Optional) Find a friend who works at a restaurant that takes online orders, and gather the following information:

**a.** What fraction of the restaurant's revenues comes from the online-ordering system?

**b.** What are the common items ordered online?

**c.** What are the demographics of the customers who order online?

**d.** What features of the website are used the most?

**e.** How do customers find the website (e.g. local ads, search engines, etc.)?

# Physical Layer

## CHAPTER 2

*To accomplish almost anything worthwhile,*
*it is necessary to compromise between*
*the ideal and the practical.*
—FRANKLIN D. ROOSEVELT

## Overview

This chapter starts at the bottom of the TCP/IP technology stack that was introduced in Chapter 1 and describes the functions of the physical layer. The physical layer sends data as signals over a physical medium. At the end of this chapter you should know:

- the functions of the physical layer
- what a physical medium is and why copper and optical fiber are important physical media
- what signals are and why they are necessary
- an example of using signals to transfer data
- an example of multiplexing

## Functions of the physical layer

Chapter 1 described the function of the physical layer as *signaling* (Table 3 of Chapter 1). More formally, the function of the physical layer is defined as *providing transparent transmission of a bit stream over a circuit built from some physical communications medium.*[1] Both definitions convey the same idea about the functions of the physical layer—the physical layer gets data from the data-link layer in the form of a stream of data bits, and the physical layer is responsible for transmitting these bits as signals over a wire, optical fiber, wireless, or other medium. *Converting data to signals for transmission over physical media* is called signaling.

---

[1] Institute for Telecommunication Sciences (2007). "ATIS Telecom Glossary." Retrieved August 19, 2008, from http://www.atis.org/glossary/.

This is a good point to introduce the telecom glossary.[2] The telecom glossary is an American National Standard that is developed and maintained by the Alliance for Telecommunications Industry Solutions (ATIS). ATIS incorporates the expertise of the nation's largest communications companies. If you find yourself looking for definitions of technical terms related to networking for class or professional reports, the ATIS glossary would be an excellent starting point. Wherever possible, definitions in this text will be drawn from the ATIS telecom glossary.

Figure 1 shows the physical layer in operation. Recall from Chapter 1 that the physical layer is situated directly below the data-link layer in the TCP/IP stack. This position in the layered architecture means that when the data-link layer is ready to send data, it will pass the data on to the physical layer so that the physical layer can perform its service. Let's say that the data-link layer would like to send 8 bits of data (1 byte)— 10001100. What does the physical layer do with this data? What service does the physical layer perform? How does it add value?

The problem the physical layer solves is that data cannot be sent over a wire. The only known method of transferring data over a medium is to convert data into a signal and transmit the signal. We addressed this issue while describing the telegraph in Chapter 1 and noting why the telegraph was such a critical development for data communications. We cannot take a bit of data, pass it into one end of a wire and hope for the bit to somehow emerge at the other end as a data bit. The only known method of sending information over a wire is to convert the information into a form that can be transmitted over the wire. This converted form of information is called a signal. In simple terms, a signal is a change that can be detected at the receiving end. The telecom glossary defines a signal as *detectable transmitted energy that can be used to carry information.* In the telegraph example, the signal was created by the closing and opening of the switch, which caused the voltage on the line to rise or fall. This change in voltage was detected at the receiving end by the movement of the marker to one side. By interpreting the marks on the paper, the receiver could reconstruct the data sent by the sender.

Think of a more familiar example of the need for signals. Can you directly transfer thoughts and ideas that arise in your mind, even to your nearest and dearest ones? No. The only known method of transferring thoughts is to first convert thoughts and ideas into speech, signs (thumbs up, winks, etc.), or written text, and send the speech, signs, or text to the receiver. In this context, the thoughts in the mind are data, and the text or speech are signals. The receivers interpret the sound or text as thoughts in their own minds. Right now when you are reading this text, your eyes are receiving signals in the form of black and white patterns on this page. All your education allows your brain to interpret these black and white patterns (signals) as letters of the alphabet, words, sentences and paragraphs (data).

Figure 1 provides a visual description of the functions of the physical layer. The physical layer receives data in the form of numbers from the data-link layer and converts the data into signals that can be transmitted over a wire.

---

[2] http://www.atis.org/glossary/.

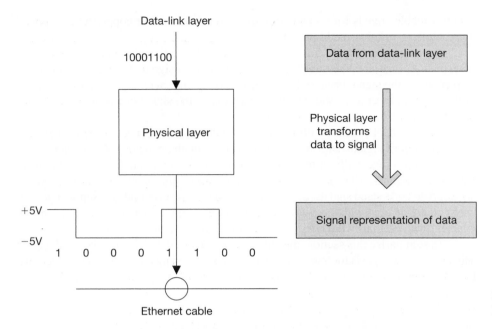

FIGURE 1  Physical layer function

## Special feature of the physical layer

So, the physical layer adds value to data communications by converting data into signals for transmission over media. Before we begin discussing media and signals, it is useful to note that one important characteristic distinguishes the physical layer from the other four layers of the TCP/IP stack. This characteristic is that the physical layer is the only layer in the stack that interacts with nature. The physical layer is the layer where the data finally hits the wire after being processed by the other layers. The physical layer, therefore, has to confront the limitations and capabilities of nature in a way that other layers do not. All other layers deal with data inside the computer. The physical layer deals with signals outside the computer.

In data communications, the properties of nature relevant to the physical layer are the signal-transmitting properties of the physical medium used. The physical layer has to generate signals that comply with the constraints specified by the medium. For example, if copper wire requires that data for transmission be passed to it in the form of electrical signals, the physical layer will send data as electrical signals over copper wire. If optical fiber requires that data be passed in the form of light signals, the physical layer will convert data to light signals for transmission over optical fiber. If copper has a bandwidth of about 100 MHz,[3] the physical layer has to satisfy itself with whatever data rates it can attain from this available bandwidth.

All the other layers add suitable header content to data packets to do their job. The physical layer does not add any header content. Rather, the physical layer converts

---

[3] Hz is an abbreviation for hertz, the unit of frequency. This is discussed a little later in the chapter. In general, the greater the bandwidth, the higher the data rates possible.

data to suitable signals for transmission to the destination over copper wires, optical fiber, wireless, or other medium.

We are, in fact, quite fortunate that it is possible to send information over a wire, even if it requires the transformation of data into a signal at the sending end and conversion of the signal back to data at the receiving end. Seen this way, the activities of the physical layer are a successful exploitation of the signal-carrying properties of transmission media.

This point of dealing with nature has been brought up because you may find the discussion of signals later in this chapter more mathematical than expected. Sine waves come up repeatedly in the section on signals because sine waves are the most elementary signals. The math is kept to a minimum, only to the extent absolutely necessary to understand signals. Later in this chapter, if you ever find yourself wondering why you are dealing with sine waves in a class on computer networks, please remind yourself that if signals were not used, data could not pass through a wire.

To summarize this section, the physical layer takes data from the data-link layer, and converts it to signals for transmission over transmission media. The next two sections look at transmission media and signals in more detail.

## Physical media and their properties

*A physical medium in data communications is the transmission path over which a signal propagates.* Common media include wire pairs, coaxial cable, optical fiber and wireless radio paths. Media used in data communications are often called physical media because media are generally physical objects such as copper or glass. A physical object is something you can touch and feel, and has physical properties such as weight and color. You can touch and feel copper and glass, and for a long time these were the only media used in computer networking. Hence, transmission media came to be known in the industry as physical media. A more recent communication medium in computer networking is wireless, and it has no physical properties. It is therefore not strictly appropriate anymore to use the term *physical media* to refer to all transmission media. However, the term *physical media* is commonly used in networking to refer to transmission media. Therefore, the terms *transmission media* and *physical media* will be used interchangeably in this text.

Not all materials are useful as media. From the previous section, it is clear that media must be good at carrying signals. Most plastics are not useful as media because there is no known way of sending signals through these plastics. Media must also be economical to use. Silver is the best known conductor of electricity. But it is not useful as a communication medium because it is prohibitively expensive. In any case, if you had network cables made of silver, you would need to guard them against theft.

Based on industry experience with various materials, copper and glass are common physical media used in computer networking. Both are economical and very efficient at carrying signals. Copper is commonly used in homes and offices to connect desktops to the network. Optical fiber is commonly used by ISPs in the core of the network to carry signals between networks. Optical fiber is also beginning to be used in office networks. In some parts of the country, ISPs are connecting homes directly with optical fiber, replacing the copper phone lines. Let's now look at these two transmission media.

## Copper wire as physical medium

Copper wire is one of the most common physical media used in networking. The entire phone network was built using copper wires. Almost every desktop is connected to the network using copper wire.

Copper has many properties that make it useful as a physical medium for data communications. Copper is the second best-known conductor of electricity, next only to silver. This allows copper wires to carry signals to great distances using relatively low amounts of power. In fact, copper is the industry standard benchmark for electrical conductivity. Further, copper is relatively abundant on earth. Of the known worldwide resources of copper, only about 12% have been mined throughout history.[4] Thus, copper provides an excellent combination of signal transmission capability and economy for use as a transmission medium.

> Copper industry resources point out some interesting trivia about copper. Copper is the oldest metal known to man. Its discovery dates back over 10,000 years. Wires are the only major use of copper that use newly refined metal. More than three-fourths of all other applications of copper use recycled metal.

The most common cable used in computer networking has eight strands of copper wire. The wires are organized in a manner called <u>unshielded twisted pair, or UTP.</u> As the name suggests, the eight wires are organized as four pairs. Generally, two of these pairs are used for information exchange. One pair of wires is used for the forward data path and another pair is used for the reverse data path. The other two pairs have traditionally been unused, though newer technologies are beginning to use all four wire pairs.

The term twisted in UTP refers to the fact that the two wires in each pair of wires are twisted around each other. This is seen in Figure 2. Twisting cancels electrical

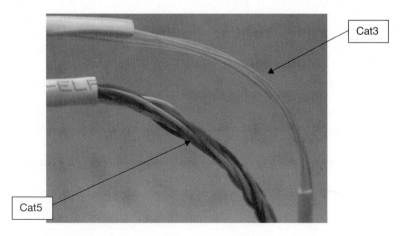

Cat3

Cat5

**FIGURE 2**   Cat5 and Cat3 cables

---

[4] http://www.copper.org.sg and http://www.copper.org.

noise from external sources such as electronic appliances and neighboring wire pairs. The tighter the twisting, the greater the noise resistance of the cable, and the higher the data rates the cable can support. In computer networking, the two wires in each pair carry signals that are the opposites of each other. This is called a balanced line, and, in a balanced line, the sender ensures that the voltage on one wire of the pair is the exact opposite of the voltage on the other wire of the pair. A balanced line further improves the noise resistance of twisted copper wires.

**FIGURE 3**  Shielded cable

The term *unshielded* in UTP refers to the fact that the wire pairs do not have a metallic shield as in cable TV wires. Figure 3 shows a picture of a shielded cable. Metallic shields block external interference and improve the signal-carrying capabilities of wires. However, shielding adds to the cost and weight of cables, and twisted balanced pairs provide sufficient noise resistance to eliminate the need for shielding in current networks. Therefore, shielded cables are losing in popularity for computer networks.

## Categories of UTP cables

*unshield twisted pair*

Since tighter twisting improves the data rates of copper cable, as computer networks have become faster, cables with tighter twisting have become available. The traditional phone system used cabling with three to four twists per foot of cable. This was adequate for slower computer networks as well, supporting data rates of up to 10 million bits per second (10 Mbps). As computer networks became faster, cables with three to four twists per inch (more than 10 times tightly wound than the previous generation) became common. These cables could support data rates of up to 100 Mbps.

Copper cables are specified by category. The older cable, with three to four twists *per foot*, is called category 3 cable. The newer cable, with three to four twists *per inch* is called category 5 cable. Category 5 has been further enhanced and is known as category 5e cable. Category is abbreviated as "Cat" for marketing purposes, so that category 5e cable is called Cat5e. Phone cable is called Cat3. Figure 2 shows Cat3 and Cat5 cables. Please note that cabling standards[5] do not specify the number of twists per inch on a cable. Standards only define the signal transmission properties of the wire. Cable manufacturers use the appropriate twist density to achieve the required signal-carrying specifications of the standard.

Each of the eight wires in a Cat5e cable is color coded to facilitate use. Four colors—blue, orange, green, and brown—are used to identify each of the four twisted pairs. Within each twisted pair, one of the wires uses the pure color, the other uses a colored band on a white background (Figure 4). This is commonly written as shown in Table 1.

Cat5e cables support gigabit speeds (1,000 mbps). Higher categories than Cat5e are now available. Category 6 supports data rates of up to 10,000 Mbps (10 Gbps). A relatively newer standard called Cat6a and category 7 supports up to 10 Gbps. Since Cat5e is already very tightly twisted, Cat6 and Cat7 do not increase the twisting rate

---

[5] TIA/ EIA-568-B: Commercial Building Telecommunications Cabling Standard, 2001.

**Table 1** Color codes for Cat5e wires

| Conductor identification | Color code | Abbreviation |
|---|---|---|
| Pair 1 | White-Blue | (W-BL) |
| | Blue | (BL) |
| Pair 2 | White-Orange | (W-O) |
| | Orange | (O) |
| Pair 3 | White-Green | (W-G) |
| | Green | (G) |
| Pair 4 | White-Brown | (W-BR) |
| | Brown | (BR) |

over Cat5e. Category 6 achieves higher data rates by using thicker wire and superior connectors. Category 7 achieves higher data rates by shielding the wires.

Copper cables for communication cost in the order of $1/foot. For normal installations, they are usually used in 5', 7', 15', and 25' sections. 1000' rolls of Cat6 cables cost about $0.25 per foot.

## Cable connectors

UTP cables are connected to computers and other communication devices through plugs called RJ 45 jacks. The term RJ stands for *registered jack* and RJ 45 is one of the many available cable connectors. Another common such connector, used in phone networks, is called the RJ 11 jack. Figure 4 shows the top and bottom views of a Cat5e cable ending in a RJ 45 jack.

To ensure that any cable may be used to connect any computer to a network, the placement of each of the eight wires on a RJ 45 jack has been specified as a standard

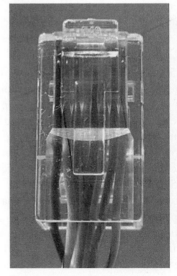
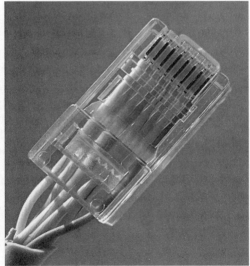

Top view of RJ 45 connector     Bottom view of RJ 45 connector

**FIGURE 4** Cat5e cable terminating in RJ 45 connector (jacket removed to show individual cables)

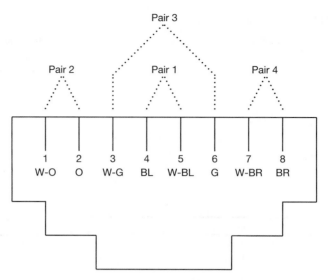

**FIGURE 5** Cat5e wire positions on RJ45 plug

called the EIA/TIA 568b standard color code. Figure 5 shows the positions at which each of the eight wires in a standard Cat5e cable terminates in a standard RJ 45 jack. When both ends of the cable are terminated as shown in Figure 5, we get a "straight-through" cable, which is appropriate for Ethernet use. The wire positions in Figure 5 may be compared to those in the bottom view of Figure 4. Table 2 shows the pin positions and functions of each wire.

The cable in Figure 4 has been exposed to demonstrate the wires in a Cat5 cable. Figure 6 shows the proper way of terminating the cable, with the jacket going all the way into the connector so that the wires are twisted till the very end to minimize interference.

**FIGURE 6** Cat5 cable showing proper termination

In commercial use, UTP cable with RJ 45 jacks has many advantages for desktop use. The cable is flexible and can be easily wired into any corner of any home or office. The cable is quite rugged and is not likely to break when stepped on, even in high traffic areas. In short segments, UTP cable is relatively light and can be carried by hand, without any heavy equipment. The RJ 45 plug uses an extremely simple press-and-click mechanism to connect to communication equipment. Since this design is extremely user friendly, even techno-phobic users can connect printers, home routers, and computers using off-the-shelf cables with RJ45 jacks.

Computer networks have traditionally used only two of the available four pairs of wires. These networks operate at speeds of up to 100 Mbps, and two pairs are adequate to provide these speeds. Table 2 shows how the wires in a Cat5e cable are typically used. It is seen that only two pairs are in use in most Ethernets (100 Mbps Ethernet). However, all four pairs become necessary to achieve even higher data rates of 1 Gbps and greater. The spare wires can be used to carry DC power and can power devices that consume up to 13 watts.

**Table 2**  Data transmission on Cat5e

| Conductor identification | Pin position | Color | Use (100 Mbps Ethernet) | Use (1 Gbps Ethernet) | Use (Power over Ethernet) |
|---|---|---|---|---|---|
| Pair 1 | 5 | White-Blue/ | None | Send/receive | +48Volts, <=13 Watts |
|  | 4 | Blue |  |  |  |
| Pair 2 | 1 | White-Orange/ | Transmit/Receive data | Send/receive | Receive data |
|  | 2 | Orange |  |  |  |
| Pair 3 | 3 | White-Green/ | Transmit/Receive data | Send/receive | Transmit data |
|  | 6 | Green |  |  |  |
| Pair 4 | 7 | White-Brown/ | None | Send/receive | −48Volts, <=13 Watts |
|  | 8 | Brown |  |  |  |

## Optical fiber as physical medium

Whereas copper is wildly popular on the desktop, it has serious disadvantages when used in the core or backbone of the network. The highest data rates that can be attained on a copper cable are limited to about 10 Gbps. Copper also experiences serious signal-reception problems at lengths beyond a few hundred meters. Therefore, long-distance copper cables require repeaters at frequent intervals, which add to the costs of the communication system. Finally, long copper cables can become very heavy, easily weighing a few tons. Optical fiber overcomes these obstacles and has emerged as the most commonly used transmission medium for long-distance communications.

*Optical fiber is a thin strand of glass that guides light along its length.* While copper is the most popular transmission medium for desktop connectivity, optical fiber is the dominant transmission medium for long-distance communications. Most large offices use optical fiber to bring network connectivity to a central location in buildings, and from there network connectivity is distributed to desktops over copper. Almost every long-distance phone call is carried over optical fiber between the central offices of telecom carriers. In many cities, optical fiber is beginning to replace the traditional copper link to the home. In fact, other than the end-user desktop, optical fiber is becoming the most common transmission medium for every other network link.

Four major factors favor optical fiber over copper—data rates, distance, installation, and costs. It is well-known that optical fiber can carry huge amounts of data compared to copper. Less well-known is the fact that, whereas signals need periodic amplification on copper links, optical fiber can be run hundreds of miles without the need for signal repeaters. This reduces maintenance costs and improves the reliability of the communication system because repeaters are a common source of failures in networks. Glass is lighter than copper and a single optical-fiber cable weighing a few hundred pounds can carry data equivalent to hundreds of copper lines. Therefore, there is less need for specialized heavy-lifting equipment when installing long-distance optical fiber. Finally, optical fiber for typical indoor applications costs approximately a dollar a foot, the same as copper.

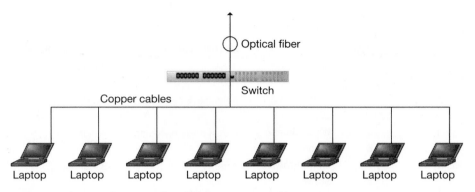

**FIGURE 7**   Aggregating network traffic from copper to fiber

Optical fiber may also be more earth-friendly. Whereas copper has to be mined from the earth, optical fiber is made out of glass, which is made out of sand, available in plenty in most parts of the world.

Copper continues to be favored on the desktop because it can better handle end-user abuse than fiber. Also, adapters to convert electrical signals inside the computer to light signals on the fiber cable cost in the range of $50. Given that most corporate PCs only cost in the range of $500–$1,000, fiber to the desktop adds 5%–10% to the cost of each desktop. Copper is therefore more economical for the desktop right now. However, it is economical to carry aggregated traffic from multiple desktops over fiber as shown in Figure 7.

Modern global communication depends upon vast lengths of optical fiber that have been laid out on the ocean floor to handle global information traffic. The map of submarine cables shown in Figure 8 was widely publicized after undersea cables were accidentally damaged in early 2008, causing Internet outage in parts of Asia.

### How optical fiber works—Total internal reflection

Optical fiber works on the principle of total internal reflection. You may recall, from experience or other classes, that light bends inward when it passes from air to water due to a phenomenon called refraction. The result is shown in Figure 9.

This is the conventional view of refraction because we generally care for the view of the world from air. This helps us understand why spoons appear bent in water, for example. To understand how optical fiber works, it is more useful to see the reverse path—what happens when light tries to leave water, or in the case of optical fiber, the glass. The glass used in optical fiber has a very high refractive index and bends the light inward very sharply. If light is bent very sharply at the glass edge going in, light cannot leave the glass edge going out, unless it hits the edge almost exactly at a right angle. The rest of the light is reflected back. This is called total internal reflection. It is shown in Figure 9. Seen from within water, this creates sunbeams as shown in Figure 11.

*two on one side, one for send, the other for receive* [handwritten marginalia]

*core* [handwritten annotation above "glass"]

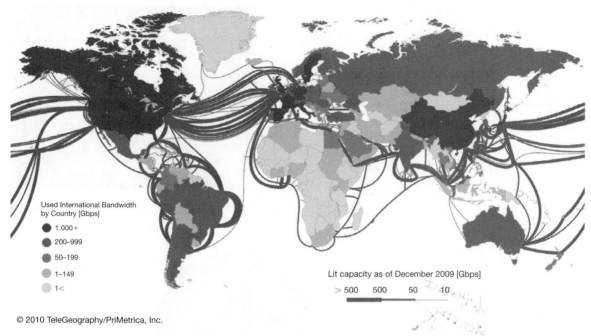

Used International Bandwidth by Country [Gbps]

- 1.000+
- 200–999
- 50–199
- 1–149
- 1<

Lit capacity as of December 2009 [Gbps]

> 500    500    50    10

© 2010 TeleGeography/PriMetrica, Inc.

**FIGURE 8**    Map of major submarine optical cables[6]

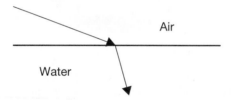

Air

Water

**FIGURE 9**    Total internal reflection (view from inside the fiber)

To summarize, total internal reflection makes glass very efficient at carrying signals over large distances because energy (in the form of light) sent into the glass medium is tightly contained within the glass. Unlike copper, which dissipates energy in the signals as heat, total internal reflection makes optical fiber a very efficient carrier of signals as light energy.

## Types of optical fiber

There are two types of optical fiber in common use—multimode and single mode. Multimode fiber uses LEDs as the light source and can carry signals over shorter distances, about 2 kilometers (1.2 miles). Multimode fiber is usually 62.5 microns in

---

[6] Courtesy of Telegeography.

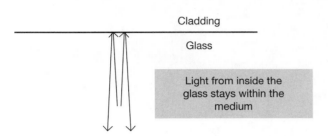

**FIGURE 10** Total internal reflection (conventional view)

Cladding

Glass

Light from inside the glass stays within the medium

**FIGURE 11** Sunbeam created from total internal reflection

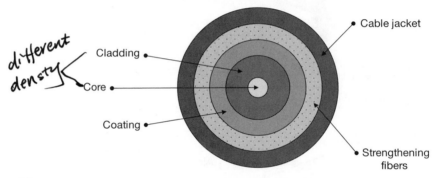

*different density*

Cladding

Core

Coating

Cable jacket

Strengthening fibers

**FIGURE 12** Cross-section of optical fiber

*lo micron vs 62.5 micron: the tinner the core, the more the light will be focus. straight and the long distance*

diameter (1 micron is a thousandth of a millimeter). Single-mode fiber is about 10 microns in diameter and can carry signals over distances of tens of miles. Both single-mode and multimode fibers cost approximately the same. Multimode is preferred for shorter distances because the LED light source used in multimode fiber costs less than the laser light source necessary for single-mode fiber.

### Construction of optical fiber

Optical fiber used in communication has a central light path surrounded by reinforcements to prevent wear and tear. A typical cross-section is shown in Figure 12.

At the center of the fiber is the core. This is the glass with a very high refractive index through which the light travels. The core is surrounded by a special glass coating called the cladding. The cladding has a very low refractive index. The high refractive index of the core together with the low refractive index of the cladding restricts the light signal so that it stays within the core and moves along the fiber. The coating and fibers cushion the glass. The jacket makes the fiber easy to handle, adds weatherproofing, and encloses the fibers.

Now that we have seen the media over which signals travel, let us turn our attention to the signals themselves.

---

**Gotchas**

I have seen students write on exams that optical fiber is faster than copper because fiber sends data at the speed of light. These students mean to say that since the speed of light is the maximum possible speed in the universe, signal speeds in copper wire are much slower than signal speeds in fiber, and as a result optical fiber has higher data rates than copper cables.

However, the electronic signal in the copper wire is also an electro-magnetic signal, just as light. Both travel at the speed of light. There are only very marginal differences in signal speeds between in copper and fiber.

Why then do we say that fiber is faster than copper? The more correct statement would be something like, fiber can carry more data than copper in the same amount of time.

Think of it this way: consider a two-lane expressway and a four-lane expressway, both with speed limits of 70 mph. Traffic in each lane moves at 70 mph in either expressway. But the four-lane expressway can carry much more traffic than the two-lane expressway in a given amount of time.

Think of copper as the two-lane expressway and fiber as the four-lane expressway. Fiber can transfer much more data in a given amount of time, though signals in both media travel at similar speeds. In fact, the analogy between the number of lanes on a highway and the data-carrying capacity of physical media is quite close. The data-carrying capacity of a medium is proportional to its band-width just as the traffic-carrying capacity of an interstate is proportional to its width in number of lanes. The bandwidth of optical fiber is thousands of times greater than the bandwidth of copper, allowing optical fiber to have data rates that are hundreds of times greater than data rates in copper.

---

## Data vs. signals

The physical layer converts data to signals for transmission over physical media such as copper wires or optical fiber. *Data are numbers, letters, or other representation of information that can be processed by people or machines.* For example, the text that you are reading right now is data. Our primary interest in using computer networks is to exchange data with other computer users. For example, we may want to inform colleagues about an upcoming meeting. This can be done by sending an e-mail to all meeting participants.

Unfortunately, data cannot be transmitted over wires. Take the e-mail above. Consider for a minute how you might send the e-mail over a wire. Perhaps you could print the e-mail. But how would you send the printed paper over a wire?

Consider another example that has been introduced earlier. Thoughts and ideas are the data in human communication. How do we exchange thoughts and ideas with colleagues? Unfortunately, as we all know; mind reading is just not possible, though wouldn't it be great if it were? If it were indeed possible, mind reading would be an example of transmission of raw data. Since such raw transmission of data is not possible, we use speech to share thoughts and ideas with listeners. Speech is a signal used in human communication.

Signals are detectable transmitted energy that can be used to carry information. Data is sent over wires as signals. Senders create changes in energy depending upon the data to be sent. When these changes in energy reach the receiver, the receiver interprets these changes as data. Signals are necessary because data cannot be transmitted directly.

Earlier in this chapter, we saw that the specific forms of energy to be used as signals depend upon the medium. When creating signals, the physical layer tries to best exploit the properties of the transmission medium used. Electrical energy is used for copper because copper is good at transmitting electrical energy. Light is used with optical fiber because glass is effective at carrying light but not electrical energy. We can now look at some common signals.

## Signals and their properties

*Signals are changes in energy that can be detected at the receiver.* We saw an example of the change with the telegraph. Turning the switch on or off created a change in voltage that could be detected at the receiver. Good signals have four desirable properties—easy reception, noise resistance, efficient utilization of bandwidth, and multiplexing.

The first desirable property, of course, is that a signal must be easily detectable at the receiver. Signals that require complicated detectors at the receiver increase system costs. Signals that are easier to detect also require less energy for transmission. The second property of good signals is that they should be good at resisting noise that gets added during transmission. Signals that are affected by noise are difficult to detect by the receiver and increase transmission errors. Third, good signals are efficient at using bandwidth so that more information can be sent within the available bandwidth of a transmission medium. Finally, good signals make it easy for signals to be multiplexed so that multiple channels of transmission can be created within the same medium.

Just as a surfaced road minimizes road bumps compared to a dirt road, good media such as copper and optical fiber help minimize noise in communication signals. Also, just as well-built cars resist damage from wear and tear, good signaling schemes resist the impact of noise on the signal. In this manner, good media and good signaling schemes combine to counter the impact of noise to the greatest extent possible and increase the data rates and distances over which signals can be transmitted.

Each of these four properties of good signals—easy reception, noise resistance, efficient utilization of bandwidth, and multiplexing—affects our daily lives. Some examples of the impact of each of these properties of signals on our daily lives are provided below to help you understand the vital role of signals in modern technology.

### Examples of the impact of improved signaling on our daily lives

Let us start with the impact of developments in signaling that have improved their detectability. Improvements in cell phones are almost entirely driven by improvements in signaling. The signals used by the earliest generation of cell phones were difficult to detect. As a result, cell phones had to transmit signals at very high power to be able to reach nearby cell phone towers. These cell phones needed large batteries to deliver this power and were therefore not very handy. CDMA signals used in modern phones are much easier to detect and cell phones can use smaller batteries. This has led to the development of extremely sleek cell phones in the last decade.

Now consider an example of the differences in noise resistance of signals. AM/FM radios illustrate the contrast in noise-resisting capabilities of different signals. FM is better at resisting noise than AM. As a result, you may have experienced that the sound quality on FM channels is far superior to the sound quality on AM channels. You may also have noticed that most music stations broadcast on FM. This is because music stations want to provide the best possible listening experience and prefer the superior noise resistance of FM. By contrast, AM channels are frequented by talk and news programs because on these stations, users don't mind an occasional streak of noise.

*(hz)*
*frequency modulation*
*amplitude modulation*

Improved efficiency in bandwidth utilization by newer signals has led to major changes in traditional media. The recent move by the government to mandate high-definition transmission is motivated by the development of signals that are very efficient at utilizing bandwidth. These signals can pack greater amounts of data than the signals currently used in broadcast TV. Modern signaling techniques combined with digital compression allow almost eight high-definition TV channels to be transmitted in the bandwidth used by one analog TV channel. The freed bandwidth can be sold to cell phone operators for other communication purposes.

Radio and TV illustrate the utility of multiplexing. Multiplexing allows all radio and TV stations in one geographical location to broadcast over the same general area and gives the audience the opportunity to tune to the desired station without interference from other stations. A demonstration of multiplexing is provided later in this chapter.

## Categories of signaling methods in data communications

All signals use energy to create change at the sending end that can be detected at the receiving end. As a simple example, consider the waves created on the surface of a lake when a pebble is dropped at one end of the lake. As the pebble is slowed down by the water, the kinetic energy of the pebble is transferred to the water, creating ripples on the lake. These ripples travel in all directions on the lake and can act as information-carrying signals.

In data communications, two generic kinds of signals are in common use—digital and analog. Digital signals are created when we turn a switch on or off depending upon whether the data to be sent is a 0 or a 1. Analog signals are created when we take a sine wave and modify some property of the sine wave. Figure 13 shows a simple digital signal and an analog signal.

### Digital signals   *computer only generate 0/1 digital data*

*Digital signals are signals in which discrete steps are used to represent information.* Digital signals are intuitively easy to visualize. For example, a positive voltage could signal a 1 and a negative voltage a 0.

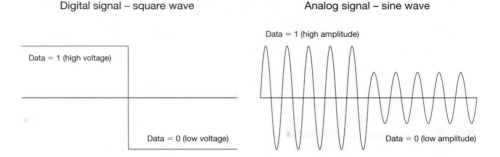

Digital signal – square wave

Data = 1 (high voltage)

Data = 0 (low voltage)

Analog signal – sine wave

Data = 1 (high amplitude)

Data = 0 (low amplitude)

**FIGURE 13** Digital and analog signals

In a simple digital signal, a high or low voltage could be used to indicate a 1 or 0. However, such a signal is not used in practice because it becomes difficult to detect bit boundaries. For example, if the data has 50 1s and a high voltage indicates a 1, we would have a high voltage on the line for a long duration. How is the receiver to know whether the sender wanted to send 49 1s or 50 1s or 51 1s? To avoid this confusion, when digital signals are used, a transition is forced in the signal for each data bit. Therefore, modern networks prefer to deal with changes in energy rather than with absolute energy levels. For example, a transition from a high voltage to a low voltage could mean a data bit of 0 and a transition from a low voltage to a high voltage could mean a 1. This is shown in Figure 14.

*A bit period is the amount of time required to transmit one bit of data.* When the signal includes transitions in every bit period, the sender and receiver do not have to synchronize clocks to count bits. The signals themselves identify when the data bit has been transmitted.

For this reason, modern signals force change in each bit period, as seen in Figure 1 and Figure 14. The receiver does not have to count bits; it can simply see if the signal

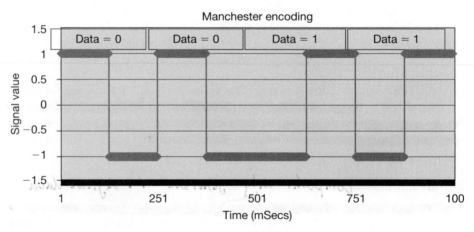

**FIGURE 14** Common digital signal (Manchester encoding, used in Ethernet)

is going from high to low, or low to high, and use this to decide if the sender was trying to send a 1 or a 0. Another common change-based signaling technique is to send information over sine waves. Both these schemes are discussed later in the chapter.

## Analog signals

*Analog signals are signals that have a (continuous) nature rather than a pulsed or discrete nature.* Analog signals are a little more difficult to visualize and understand than digital signals. Analog signals are created by manipulating sine waves. To begin with, we will address why we use a complicated-looking signal such as a sine wave for signaling. We will see what is so special about sine waves and why they are used for data communications.

It turns out that sine waves are remarkably easy to create. Sine waves are associated in various ways with any spinning object and are the most elementary signals in nature. For example, the height of a point on a spinning wheel is described by a sine wave as shown in Figure 15. The power that reaches your home is a sine wave (at 60 Hz) because it is generated by a turbine spinning inside a constant magnetic field. Computers use the electronic equivalent of a spinning wheel to generate sine waves for data communication.

Sine waves have three properties—amplitude, frequency, and phase. Figure 16 shows these properties. The amplitude is the height of the wave. The frequency of a wave is the number of complete cycles made by the wave in one second. In Figure 16, the wave completes two cycles in one second, and is said to have a frequency of 2 Hertz (Hz). The phase of the wave is the position of the wave at the start time. The wave in the example has a phase of $0°$.

To create analog signals, we start by generating a sine wave at the sender end. This wave is called a carrier wave, and it travels from the sender to the receiver over the medium. To transfer information using the carrier wave, we change one or more properties of the carrier wave in response to data. These changes are called modulation. Modulation is detected at the receiving end and is interpreted as data.

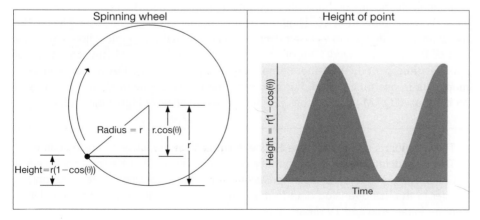

**FIGURE 15**  Sine wave generated from the height of a point on a spinning wheel.

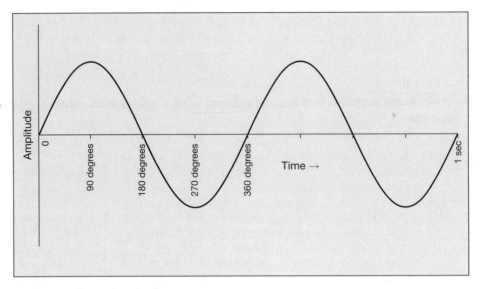

**FIGURE 16** Properties of a sine wave

Commonly used analog signals in data communication include amplitude modulation (AM) and phase modulation (PM). In amplitude modulation, a data bit of 1 may be sent as a wave of high amplitude and a 0 may be sent as a low amplitude wave (see Figure 17). In phase modulation, a wave starting with a phase of 0° may indicate a data bit of 0 while a wave starting with a phase of 180° could indicate a 1.

Another popular analog signaling technique is called quadrature amplitude modulation (QAM). QAM combines both amplitude modulation and phase modulation as seen in the final example in Figure 17. The figure shows how QAM could use two amplitudes and two initial phases to create four possible signaling levels. With four possible signaling levels, we can send 2 bits of data at a time. This is discussed in more detail in Chapter 4. In our example, a low amplitude signal starting with a phase of 0° could indicate the bit combination 00. High amplitude and starting phase of 180° indicates the bit combination 11. Though QAM is more complex than either AM or PM, its advantage is that it allows faster data transmission. In the examples shown, whereas AM or PM can only send 1 bit of data in one time period, QAM can send 2 bits of data per time period. With more amplitude and phase levels, QAM can send even more data in one time period. For reference, the fastest phone modems, operating at 56 kbps, used QAM to send 7 bits per time period to achieve higher data rates.

The waveforms shown in Figure 17 use digital data to modulate an analog carrier. These modulations are more formally called Amplitude Shift Keying and Phase Shift Keying. The terms *analog modulation* and *phase modulation* more commonly refer to the use of analog data to modulate analog signals. These were used in non-digital radio and TV broadcasts.

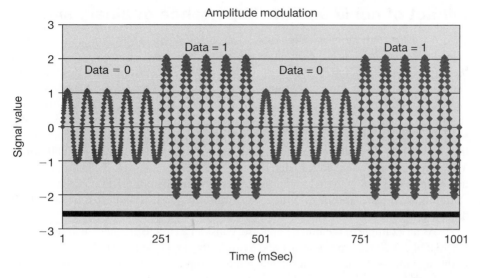

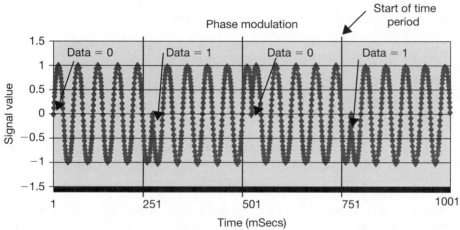

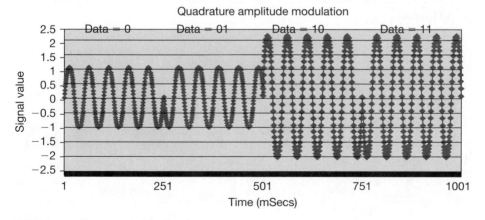

**FIGURE 17**  Common analog signals

## Impact of noise and the importance of binary signals

Before we leave the topic of signals, it is useful to spend a few moments to consider the impact of noise on signals. *Noise is any disturbance that interferes with the normal operation of a device.* Noise is one of the most important constraints in signaling. As the signal travels through the medium, noise keeps getting added to the signal. Noise comes from various sources such as cross-talk and heating of the wire from the signal flowing through it. The result is that, though the signal keeps getting weaker with distance, noise keeps accumulating. Eventually, at some distance from the source, it becomes very difficult to detect the signal from the background noise. You may have experienced this deterioration of the signal and the accumulation of noise while driving away from your home town while listening to one of your local stations on your car radio. Significant deterioration of the signal begins about 50 miles from your city.

As an example of the impact of noise, consider a simple digital signaling scheme where a high voltage represents a 1 and a low voltage represents a 0 (this is analogous to the signaling scheme used in the telegraph example of Chapter 1). Let us now add noise to this signal. Figure 18 shows how the original digital signal from the sender might appear to a receiver after the addition of noise. The figure shows 4 bit periods with the sender sending 1, followed by 0, 1, and then another 0. Observe how the sender has sent a clear signal but the received signal has only a slight resemblance to the transmitted signal.

Figure 18 shows the challenge receivers face when processing incoming signals. In the example, how will the receiver recover the data from the noisy signal it receives? A common technique is to average the signal value over the bit period. If the average is high, say any positive value, the receiver could interpret the signal as a 1 and if the average is negative, the receiver can interpret it as 0. Clearly, when the noise level becomes very high, the means for both 0s and 1s will become similar and it will be difficult to detect 0s from 1s in the signal.

The example also helps show why computers prefer to use binary numbers to represent data. Compared to other forms of representing data, such as decimal numbers, binary numbers help improve the reliability of reception in the presence of noise. To see why this is so, consider the example in Figure 19, this time using an AM signal.

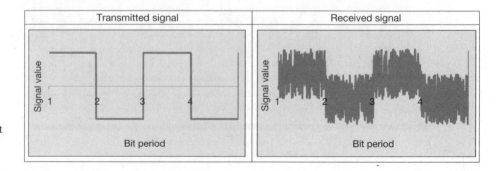

**FIGURE 18** Impact of noise on a digital signal

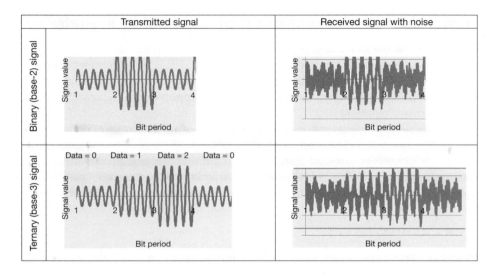

**FIGURE 19**   Binary and ternary signals

In Figure 19, the left column shows the transmitted data and the right column shows the received data. The received data includes the effect of noise. The first row shows a signal with two possible values (binary signal). The second row shows a signal with three possible values (ternary signal).

To convert the received signals back to data, we would apply a rule similar to the one used in the digital example. In the binary signal we might decide to interpret the signal as 0 if the mean amplitude in one bit period is less than some value (shown as a gridline in the top right cell of Figure 19) and 1 if the mean amplitude in a bit period is higher than the gridline.

If we use base 3, each data bit can have three values—0, 1, and 2. To represent these, the signal needs to take three values as well. We can implement these three values as low, medium, and high. To convert a ternary signal back to data, the rules get more complex. We need two separators now. We would use a rule such as: if the amplitude is less than the first gridline, we interpret the signal to be 0; if the amplitude exceeds the first gridline but is less than the second gridline, we will interpret the signal as 1; and if the amplitude exceeds the second gridline, the signal represents 2. This is clearly more complex than receiving a binary signal.

Which signal would you prefer to work with—the binary or the ternary signal? The advantage of the ternary signal is that it allows us to send more information in one bit period compared to the binary signal. However, it is also likely to lead to greater errors at the receiver end compared to the binary signal. This is because the differences between the signals representing the values of 0, 1, and 2 are less noticeable in the ternary signal than in the binary signal. For this reason, computers represent data in binary form. Binary representations are the most reliable form of representing data. The unit of information in a computer is called a binary digit or a bit. *A bit is a unit of information that designates one of two possible states of anything that conveys information.*

# Transmission and reception of data using signals

Before we close our discussion of signals, let us integrate all the ideas in this chapter to see how signals might be used in practice to send data. Let us consider a simple example. We will send the word, "hello" using a simplified version of amplitude modulation. In this simplified version of AM, high amplitude will represent 1 and a silent signal will represent 0.

Transmission and reception of data is performed in four steps. At the sender end, (1) the data is coded as binary numbers representing the data, and (2) the carrier signal is modulated as specified by the binary representation of the data. These steps are inverted at the receiving end where (3) the incoming signal is demodulated into the corresponding binary numbers and (4) the binary numbers are decoded into the data.

### STEP 1. CODING DATA

*Coding is the transformation of elements of one set to elements of another set.* For example, representing characters as numbers is a form of coding. There are two widely used schemes to code data as binary numbers. The simpler scheme is called the American Standard Code for Information Interchange (ASCII). ASCII is used to encode the characters in the English alphabet.[7] In the ASCII scheme, the numbers 48–57 represent the numbers 0–9; 65–90 represent the upper case letters *A–Z*; and the numbers 97–122 represent the lower case characters *a–z*. Other numbers represent punctuations and other characters.

The second scheme is Unicode. Unicode represents characters in almost all languages. At last count, it defined over 100,000 characters from languages including Chinese and Korean.[8] English characters are represented in Unicode by the same codes as ASCII codes. Other Unicode characters include 945–969 for the Greek characters α–ω.

For our example, we use the simple ASCII coding scheme. In ASCII, the letters in the word "hello" are coded as shown in the center column of Table 3. In the third column of the table, the decimal numbers are converted to the corresponding binary representation. If you are not familiar with decimal-to-binary conversion, do not worry about it now. It is covered in Chapter 4, in connection with IP addresses. For now, simply accept Column 3 of Table 3.

**Table 3** Binary representation of example data

| Letter | ASCII code | Binary representation |
|--------|------------|------------------------|
| h | 104 | 01101000 |
| e | 101 | 01100101 |
| l | 108 | 01101100 |
| o | 111 | 01101111 |

---

[7] http://www.asciitable.com/.

[8] A good site to search for Unicode characters is http://www.atm.ox.ac.uk/user/iwi/charmap.html.

So, if we want to send the word "hello", and both sides (sender and receiver) agree to use the ASCII code for encoding data, we could transmit the word "hello" as:

| 01101000 | 01100101 | 01101100 | 01101100 | 01101111 |
|:--------:|:--------:|:--------:|:--------:|:--------:|
| h | e | l | l | o |

## STEP 2. MODULATING CARRIER

After Step 1 of the four-step transmission and reception process is completed, it is relatively straightforward to modulate a carrier signal according to this binary data. The signal is shown in Figure 20. Note how the carrier is sent with a high amplitude when 1 is to be sent and nothing is sent (low amplitude) when a 0 is to be sent.

In Figure 20, the oscillating signal is the transmitted signal. This is the signal that will be carried by the medium to the receiver. For reference, the characters being transmitted (*h, e, l, l, o*) and the bit-level breakdown of each of these characters are shown near the axis. For example, *h* is represented as 01101000, and, in the first bit period, we send a signal with no amplitude for one bit period. For the next two bit periods, we send a sine wave with high amplitude to send the two 1s, and then a signal with no amplitude, and so on. This completes Step 2 of our four-step transmission and reception process.

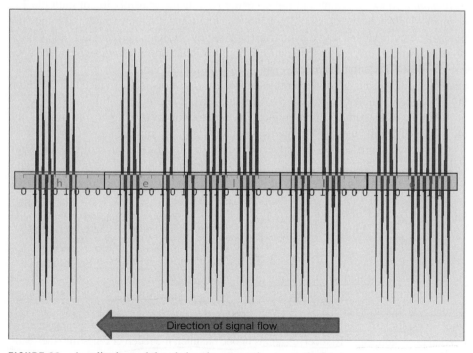

**FIGURE 20**  Amplitude modulated signal representing example data

### STEP 3. DEMODULATING SIGNAL

You probably can now see what the receiver will do. As the signal arrives at the receiving end, the receiver interprets the signal amplitudes for each bit period as either 0 or 1. If no signal is received for a bit period, the receiver interprets that as 0. If a wave is received during a bit period, the receiver interprets the signal as 1. This completes Step 3 of the transmission-reception process.

### STEP 4. DECODING DATA

Finally, in the last step, the receiver accumulates the bits in blocks of 8 bits each. When the first set of 8 bits is collected, the receiver compares the received bits 01101000 to the ASCII table and interprets the bits as the letter *h*. Similarly, it interprets the remaining bits as the characters '*e*, *l*, *l*, and *o*. This gives us the word "hello" at the receiving end.

Again, please remember, signaling is used only because direct transfer of data is not possible and energy in the form of signals is necessary to transport data over the air, wire, or fiber. The complex transformation of data to signals and back would not be done if somehow it were possible to directly transfer data over the medium.

## Multiplexing

*Edison*

Before we end the chapter, we consider an extremely useful property of signals—multiplexing. You may recall that multiplexing was introduced as a desirable property of signals. *Multiplexing is the combination of two or more information channels over a common medium.* Examples of multiplexing include the transmission of multiple TV channels over the same coaxial (TV) cable, or the transmission of multiple radio stations in the same air space over a metro area. As shown in Chapter 1, multiplexing is an extremely important milestone in data communication. Multiplexing is what made data communication economical because it allowed multiple phone, TV, and data signals to be combined for transmission over the same cable. This drastically reduced the need for laying out communication cables to homes and businesses. Since cabling costs are one of the biggest costs in data communication, a reduction in cabling costs significantly reduced the overall costs of setting up and maintaining a communication network.

Figure 21 provides a visual example of the usefulness of multiplexing and switching by showing a picture of the world before multiplexing and switching. The figure shows 150 cables over Broadway in NYC around the year 1900. Each cable provided one telephone connection. As telephony and telegraphy gained popularity, all major streets in all metro cities were blanketed by such cables. When we use multiplexing and switching, trunk lines such as this set of 150 cables, can be replaced by one cable, vastly reducing installation and maintenance costs.

In general, there are two categories of multiplexing. The first is used with analog signals and is called frequency-division multiplexing (FDM). As the name suggests, in this form of multiplexing, signals from one channel are sent at one frequency and signals from another channel are sent at another frequency. Fortunately, as a result of the properties of sine waves, signals at different frequencies do not interfere with each other even when they overlap geographically. To receive signals in one channel, the receiver tunes into the sender's frequency. This is what you do when you tune to a station on a car radio.

**FIGURE 21**   New York City, around 1900

The second category of multiplexing is called time-division multiplexing (TDM) and is used with digital signals. In this form of multiplexing, signals from different streams are sent at different time slots. Receivers scan the medium at their assigned time slots to receive their signals.

Though multiplexing sounds complex, it can be relatively easy to do. In the example that follows, we show an example of multiplexing two signals using amplitude modulation. For the rest of this section, it will be convenient to open the spreadsheet available at the link "multiplexing" in Chapter 2 on the companion website. You can open the charts on the spreadsheet to see the graphs in larger scale.

In the example, two stations wish to transmit signals. Each station has been allocated a carrier frequency. In Figure 22 below, the first column shows the activity at station 1, and the second column shows the activity at station 2. The rows show the signals, carriers, and modulated signals from the two stations. From the first row in the figure, observe that the two carriers are at different frequencies (the carrier wave in the first column has more waves than the carrier in the second column, though both cover the same amount of time). It is this difference in carrier frequencies that enables receivers to distinguish between the two signals.

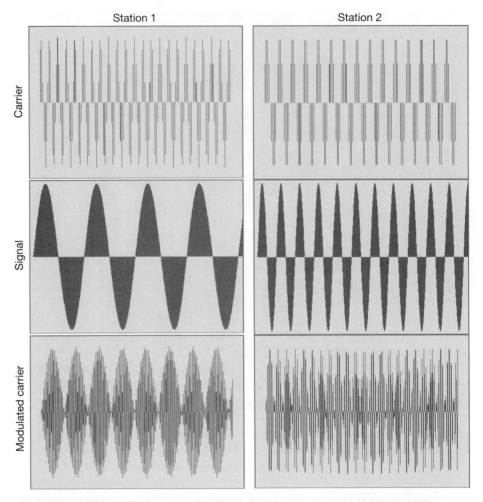

**FIGURE 22** AM multiplexing example

In the second row, we show the signals to be carried. Stations can transmit any information; however, for the purposes of this example, each station has a plain sine wave to transmit. The signals from the two stations are at different frequencies for easy reference in the example.

The third row shows the modulated signals. This is an example of AM using analog data. Compare the modulated carrier in Figure 22 to the AM signal in Figure 17. In Figure 17, digital data was used to modulate an analog carrier wave. Observe how the modulated signal is a sine wave with the frequency of the carrier wave, but with amplitude that varies with the amplitude of the transmitted signal.

Once each station has created the modulated signal, it simply transmits the signal into the shared medium. Here, all the signals get added up. The result for our example is shown in Figure 23. The signal in Figure 23 is just the sum of the two signals in the last row of Figure 22.

So, the signal seen in Figure 23 is the result of our attempt to transmit two signals in a shared medium. Look at the signal in Figure 23. Can you discern signal 1 or signal 2?

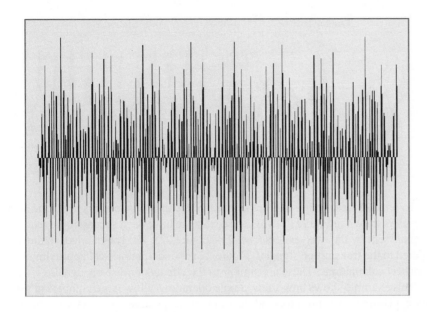

**FIGURE 23**   Resultant signal in the medium (modulated carrier from station 1 + modulated carrier from station 2)

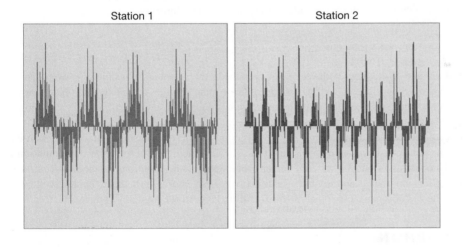

**FIGURE 24**   Result of demodulation at receiver end

Probably not. Though the constituent signals are not readily apparent in this figure, we will now see how they can be recovered quite easily.

The secret to recovering the original signals is to multiply the signal in the shared medium with a locally generated sine wave at the same frequency as the carrier. In a radio receiver, you do this when you tune your radio to a station. Your radio receiver generates a local sine wave at the selected frequency and multiplies it with the signal in the air. In the multiplexing spreadsheet, you see this in the columns titled "demodulated" of the "data" worksheet. As a result of the special properties of sine waves, this simple operation retains the modulated carrier from the selected station and eliminates all other signals. The results for the two stations are shown in Figure 24. Note how the result already approximates the signals sent by the two stations. The only task left is to remove the "rough edges" around the signals.

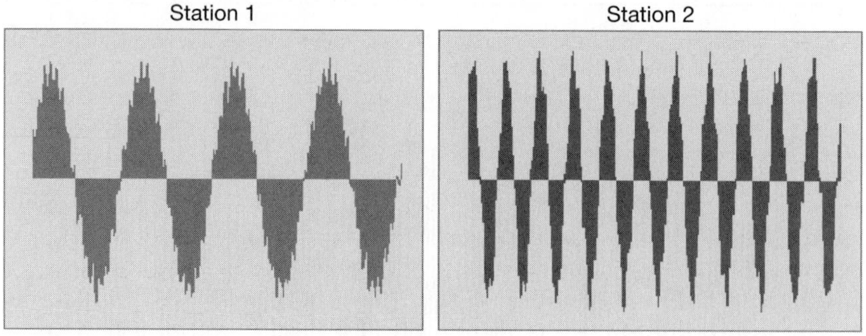

Station 1            Station 2

**FIGURE 25** Recovered signals after removing noise by averaging

To remove these rough edges, the standard technique is to average out the signal.[9] The result is shown in Figure 25. We can see that we have been successful in recovering the signals sent by the two senders (row 2 of Figure 22). The rough edges in the output compared to the transmitted signal in Figure 22 are due to numerical approximations in spreadsheet calculations. These are similar to the effects of noise on signals.

This example shows how a few simple operations allow large numbers of senders to share a common medium to send data to their respective receivers without mutual interference. Multiplexing is used in one form or another in almost every electronic communication—telephone, television, cell phones, Internet access, etc.

## SUMMARY

In this chapter we described the role of the physical layer in data communication. The layer is responsible for sending data as signals between adjacent devices on a communication network. Signals travel over a transmission medium such as copper wire. Signals are necessary in data communication because data cannot be transferred over wires. We described some reasons why copper and optical fiber are popular transmission media. Common analog and digital signals were introduced. The effect of noise on these signals was described. An example of transmitting a word demonstrated how coding schemes and modulation help transmit data as signals. Finally an example of multiplexing showed how different signals can be combined and separated.

The physical layer transmits data as best as it can over the physical medium. Nevertheless, transmission is error-prone. One of the functions of the data-link layer is to remove these errors. In the next chapter, we look at the data-link layer to see how this is done.

## ABOUT THE COLOPHON

Bismarck defined politics as the art of achieving the possible. The 32nd president of the United States, Franklin D. Roosevelt, put this idea in words when he said that it was necessary to compromise between the ideal and the practical to accomplish almost anything worthwhile.

The physical layer seems to embody this idea of compromising between the ideal and the practical. The ideal method to accomplish the worthwhile goal of data communications would be to transfer data without the need for complex transformations between data and signals.

However, the practical reality is that media cannot transfer data. Media can only transfer signals. And so, in data communications, as in politics, we compromise between the ideal and the practical and convert data to signals for just as long as is necessary for data transfer over physical media.

For most students learning about coding, signals, and modulation is not fun. But hopefully you appreciate that the practical realities of data communication force us to know at least the rudiments of coding, signals, and modulation.

---

[9] This is formally called low-pass filtering.

## CASE STUDY | THE PHYSICAL LAYER AS THE CONDUIT TO LOWER ENERGY COSTS: SMART GRIDS

*Everyone is acutely aware of rising energy costs and the prospect that the world may be running out of easy access to oil. One of the most promising solutions to the problem uses the power line as the physical medium of a computer network that links power producers and consumers in order to exchange information and optimize power utilization. It is estimated that the system has the potential to eliminate almost half of America's oil imports and hundreds of power plants. However, there are challenges to creating such a system. The challenges are centered primarily on the fact that the power grid was not designed to work as the physical layer of a computer network. Recent developments in physical layer technologies are helping overcome these challenges.*

To celebrate the beginning of the 21st century, the U.S. National Academy of Engineering carried out an exercise to identify the single most important engineering achievement of the 20th century. The Internet took thirteenth place on this list, and highways came eleventh. At the top of the list, as the most significant engineering achievement of the 20th Century, was electrification, as made possible by the grid. As summarized by the NAE, "*Scores of times each day, with the merest flick of a finger, each one of us taps into vast sources of energy—deep veins of coal and great reservoirs of oil, sweeping winds and rushing waters, the hidden power of the atom and the radiance of the Sun itself—all transformed into electricity, the workhorse of the modern world*".

The electric-power infrastructure of a country is often called "the grid." The United States' grid consists of more than 9,000 electric generating units with more than 1,000,000 megawatts of generating capacity connected to more than 300,000 miles of transmission lines. With rising population, bigger homes, and more and bigger appliances, even this infrastructure is running up against its limitations. Efforts to upgrade the grid are based on the idea of "smart grids." *The smart grid is the system that delivers electricity from suppliers to consumers using digital technology to save energy, reduce cost, and increase reliability and transparency*. The smart grid allows informed participation by customers; integrates all generation and storage options; and optimizes asset utilization. The smart grid will be capable of monitoring power generation, customer preferences, and even individual appliances. Bi-directional flows of energy and two-way communication and control capabilities on the smart grid will enable an array of new functionalities and applications. Figure 26 is the conceptual model for information and power flows among the key players in the smart grid.

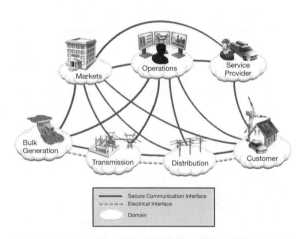

**FIGURE 26**  NIST smart grid conceptual model

How can the smart grid and data communications lower energy costs? Between 30%–50% of the typical power bill goes toward the transmission and distribution charge, which pays for the grid infrastructure. An estimated 10% of all generation infrastructure and 25% of distribution infrastructure is used less than 5% of the time, roughly 400 hours per year. By smoothing power demand, smart-grid technologies will eliminate the need for investments that are only marginally utilized. As an example, if all cars in the United States could run on batteries that were charged at night, the idle capacity in the power grid at night could meet 70% of the energy needs of cars and light trucks. This would improve asset utilization of generating stations and transmission lines. Improved asset utilization would lower energy costs for all consumers.

Smooth demand also means that power requirements can be met with lower-cost sources of power, such as nuclear power and coal. In addition, the smart grid will allow the integration of power-generating resources of every description: rooftop solar cells, fuel cells, and electric vehicles. In emergencies, communities will be able to generate sufficient electricity to keep essential services up and running even when the community is disconnected from the grid.

### The physical layer as a critical component of the smart grid

One of the primary challenges in making the smart grid work is to reliably transmit demand and price signals over power lines in the presence of the extremely intense and noisy power signal. In fact, of the five technologies identified by the Department of Energy as drivers of the smart grid (communications, sensing, components, controls, and interfaces), all technologies except components focus on the capture, transmission, and processing of information in real-time. All this information is transmitted over the power line, using the electrical wiring as the physical medium for data transmission. This takes advantage of the large installed base of electrical wiring in homes and businesses for signal transmissions.

To accomplish these goals, physical layer technologies such as multiplexing and modulation that were introduced in this chapter are key areas of R&D for the smart grid. To multiplex data signals along with power, power line communication technologies have been allocated two frequency bands on power lines: 3 kHz–148 kHz for low data rate applications and 2–28 MHz for high data-rate applications.

Since power signals are transmitted at considerably higher energy levels than data signals, electrical impulses (noise) generated when electrical appliances are switched on or off can overwhelm the low-power data signals. Further, the electrical meters and circuit breakers installed on power lines are not designed to facilitate data transmission and can degrade signals that pass through these devices. Therefore, as data-transmission functions are added to the power grid, these existing constraints have to be attended to. New modulation techniques such as differential quadrature-phase shift keying (DQPSK) and orthogonal frequency-division multiplexing (OFDM) are helping to overcome these constraints.

The National Institute for Standards and Technology (NIST) has been assigned primary responsibility to coordinate development of protocols and standards for interoperability of smart-grid devices. NIST is coordinating with a number of groups that have been working on physical layer technology standards for home automation, home networking, and related technologies. These technologies include Homeplug (data rates up to approx. 200 Mbps), Homegrid/ ITU G.hn (data rates up to 1 Gbps), IEEE 802.3 (Ethernet, covered in Chapter 3), and IEEE P1901 (data rates greater than 100 Mbps).

If successful, the smart-grid efforts will also lead to interoperability among home computing and entertaining devices. Unlike the media studied in this chapter (Cat5 cable, optical fiber, etc.), data transmission is not the primary function of electrical wiring, which is primarily designed to carry electrical power as 60 Hz (United States and Japan) or 50 Hz (Europe and Asia) signals. Yet, it is possible that as a result of developments in physical layer technologies, utility companies may someday become capable of offering high-speed Internet service using the same technologies that are being developed to help transmit power demand and price signals for the smart grid.

## REFERENCES

"Greatest Engineering Achievements of the 20th Century". http://www.greatachievements.org.

Kintner-Meyer, Michael, Kevin Schneider, and Robert Pratt. *"Impacts Assessment of Plug-In Hybrid Vehicles on Electric Utilities and Regional U.S. Power Grids Part 1: Technical Analysis."* Paper presented at the 2007 Electric Utilities Environmental Conference, Tucson, AZ, January 21–24, 2007.

National Institute of Standards and Technology. *"NIST Framework and Roadmap for Smart Grid Interoperability Standards"* Release 1.0 (Draft)." http://www.nist.gov/public_affairs/releases/upload/smartgrid_interoperability_final.pdf.

U.S. Department of Energy. *"The Smart Grid: An Introduction."* http://www.oe.energy.gov/DocumentsandMedia/DOE_SG_Book_Single_Pages(1).pdf.

U.S. Department of Energy. *"What the Smart Grid Means to America's Future."* http://www.oe.energy.gov/DocumentsandMedia/TechnologyProviders.pdf.

# REVIEW QUESTIONS

1. What is federal standard 1037C?

2. What is the primary responsibility of the physical layer in data communication?

3. The need to adapt to the physical world around us influences many details in the world around us. An example from sports is the dimples on golf balls. How do these dimples help golfers? Use the Internet to find the answer.

4. Define *physical medium* in the context of computer networking. What are the common physical media used in computer networks?

5. What properties are required for a material to be suitable for use as a physical medium in computer networks?

6. What is *UTP*? Why is the copper cable commonly used in computer networks called UTP?

7. What are the common categories of copper cable used in networks? Under what conditions would you prefer to use each category of cable?

8. What factors favor the use of optical fiber as a physical medium over copper?

9. What is *total internal reflection*? How does it help optical fiber transmit light signals efficiently?

10. What are the two categories of optical fiber? Under what conditions is each category preferred?

11. What are the components of optical fiber? What is the role of each component?

12. Define *data*.

13. Define *signal*.

14. What is the need to convert data to signals?

15. What are the properties of a good signal?

16. What is *modulation*? How does modulation help in data transmission?

17. What is *amplitude modulation*?

18. How does noise affect signals? What happens if the level of noise becomes too high relative to the strength of the signal?

19. Why is binary representation preferred in computers over common representations such as decimal?

20. Briefly describe the standard procedure used by the physical layer to send and receive data as a signal.

21. What is the ASCII code? Why is it useful in data communication? What is the ASCII code for the letter *a*? For the letter *A*?

22. What is *multiplexing*?

23. Why is multiplexing useful in data communication?

24. What are some examples of multiplexing in day-to-day life?

25. Describe how the interstate system may be seen as a multiplexed transportation system.

26. What are the two categories of multiplexing?

# HANDS-ON EXERCISES

In this exercise, we will use Excel to simulate amplitude modulation of an analog carrier wave using a digital signal. The process is called amplitude shift keying (ASK). We will consider one of the simplest cases of ASK, called on–off keying, in which the presence of a carrier wave indicates 1 and its absence indicates 0. A common usage scenario for on-off keying was to transmit Morse code. When the operator pressed a switch on, the signal would get transmitted and when the operator turned the switch

off, the signal would not be transmitted. A receiver could listen to these beeping signals and recover the text that was being sent.

The example in Figure 27, shows an on-off-keyed ASK signal for 1 second. During this time, the signal sends out 20 bits of data. The bit pattern sent is 01101100101101001100. The times on the *x*-axis are in milliseconds and the values on the *y*-axis are the signal amplitudes. Intervals of silence represent 0s being

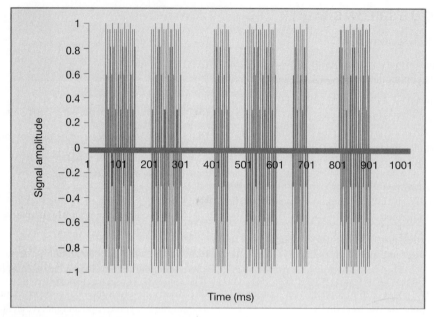

**FIGURE 27** Amplitude phase shift keying example

transmitted and the periods with the signals represent 1s being transmitted. For example, since the first bit transmitted is 0, the signal has 0 amplitude, from 0 ms–50 ms.

Answer the following questions using the "Exercise" worksheet in the Ch2_AM_multiplexing_example.xlsx spreadsheet, available on the companion website. Column A in the spreadsheet is the time, Column B is the data to be transmitted, Column C is the carrier signal and Column D will show the modulated signal. Each row is 1/1,000 of a second.

1. If the signal sends out data at the rate of 20 bits per second, how long does it take for the signal to send each bit? This time is called the bit interval or bit period.

2. If we send 25 bits per second, what will be the bit interval of the new signal?

3. Using a bit rate of 25 bits per second, modify the contents of Column B so that it represents the bit pattern 0011001011110001010101011. Show a graph of the data in Column B.

4. Sine waves have values Sin($2\pi$ft) where $f$ is the frequency of the wave. The carrier in column C of the example has a frequency of 150 Hz. Create a new column where the frequency of the carrier is 100 Hz. Plot both carrier signals on a graph.

5. The amplitude-modulated signal using on-off-keying is calculated as M = D*C, where M is the modulated signal, D is the digital data and C is the carrier signal. Compute the value of the modulated signal in the column titled "modulated signal." (Hint: you can look at Columns F and G in the "Data" worksheet to see how to compute the modulated signal). Do not report anything for this question, you will do that in the next question.

6. Plot the modulated signal as a function of time as in Figure 27.

7. Assume you are explaining your plot to a lay person. Describe how to interpret the signal in the question above to recover the data sequence of q3.

## CRITICAL THINKING QUESTION

We saw in this chapter how the limitations of our physical world force us to convert data into signals for communication. List any three other examples where the limitations of the physical world force us to do things the way we do them. The examples do not have to be related to IT.

## NETWORK DESIGN EXERCISES

Answer the following questions:

1. For each location, identify the most suitable physical medium to build the network. Make a rough estimate of the total quantity of the media that will be needed for each location. Use online or other resources to estimate the cost of purchasing enough quantities of the medium for each location.

2. Identify the most suitable physical medium to connect the different locations to each other (the long-distance links).

## CASE QUESTIONS

1. Visit the website www.greatachievements.org. Which of the top technologies of the 20th century could be categorized as a networking technology, if a network is defined in more general terms as an interconnection of three or more interacting entities?

2. For each of these technologies, briefly describe how networking (interaction) improves the utility of stand-alone components in the network.

3. Why should power be cheap at night and expensive during the day? You may find the Wikipedia article on capacity factors useful: http://en.wikipedia.org/wiki/Capacity_factor.

4. What changes in behaviors will be required of people to exploit the potential of the smart grid?

5. It is expected that smart meters will report the current price of power and smart appliances will be programmable to operate only when power prices fall below values you specify. How might you change your energy usage if smart meters and smart appliances were installed in your house?

6. It is expected that the smart grid will allow you to sell power stored in batteries (charged when power prices are low) or generated using solar, wind, and other means. What changes do you expect to see in your neighborhood if these technologies go mainstream?

7. Broadband over power line (BPL) may allow your local power company to compete as an Internet Service Provider (ISP). What advantages for the power company do you foresee over your current ISP if your power company decides to actually offer ISP service?

8. Using information from the Internet and other sources, write a short report (two to three paragraphs) about the smart-grid initiatives being undertaken by your local power company.

## CHAPTER 3

# Data-link Layer

*We may say that according to the*
*general theory of relativity space is*
*endowed with physical qualities; in this*
*sense, therefore, there exists an ether.*
—ALBERT EINSTEIN

## Overview

This chapter describes the functions of the data-link layer. The data-link layer interfaces with the network layer above it to transfer data reliably across one hop. To accomplish this goal, the data-link layer depends upon the physical layer below it for signaling. At the end of this chapter you should know:

- the functions of the data-link layer
- an overview of Ethernet, the primary technology used to connect corporate desktops
- error detection and correction using cyclic redundancy check (CRC)
- Ethernet frame structure
- MAC addresses and their organization
- switching

## Functions of the data-link layer

The physical layer sends signals between neighboring devices on a network. Using this service, the data-link layer sends data between neighboring devices on the network. To do this, it has two primary functions—addressing and error-detection. Addressing ensures that signals from the physical layer reach the correct device on the network. Once the signals are received, the error-detection function of the data-link layer detects if any errors were introduced during signal transmission. If any errors are detected, the data-link layer discards the data.

You might wonder what happens when you use a technology that discards data with errors. In these cases, the transport layer (layer 4 of the TCP/IP stack) recognizes the missing data and fixes the errors. However, every data-link layer technology ensures that errors are detected and acted upon. Data with errors is never passed on to the network layer from the data-link layer.

The data-link layer is the building block of the Internet. Many technologies are available that provide the functions of the data-link layer. When you use the Internet, information generally passes through multiple instances of the data-link layer before it reaches its final destination. Each instance of the data-link layer ensures that the data safely hops to the next device in the network. For example, referring to Figure 1 in Chapter 1 (shown here as Figure 1), the wireless link from the home PC to the home router is an instance of the data-link layer. The optical-fiber link from the home router to the carrier's router provides another instance of the data-link layer. Each link between the routers in the carrier's network is served by an instance of the data-link layer. In each case, the local instance of the data-link layer ensures that the data reaches the next device safely. It is common for large networks to mix and match different data-link technologies within the overall network depending upon network needs.

Thus, the physical and data-link layers together ensure that the data sent by one device on the network safely reaches the next device on the network without errors.

In the rest of this chapter, we focus on a very common data-link layer technology—Ethernet. Almost every corporate desktop is connected to the network 以太网 using Ethernet as the data-link layer technology. Anytime a desktop uses a connector like the one shown in Figure 2, it is using Ethernet. Therefore, Ethernet is a very relevant technology for IT professionals. Some other data-link layer technologies are discussed in Chapter 10 (WANs) and Chapter 11 (wireless).

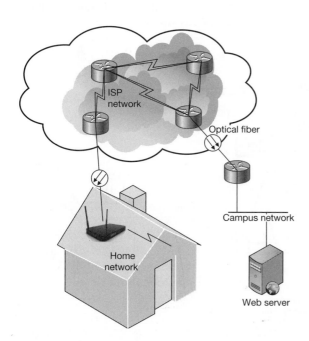

**FIGURE 1**    Data networks

**FIGURE 2**    Ethernet connector in the rear panel of a PC

For classroom purposes, Ethernet has another advantage over other data-link layer technologies. It is extensively documented and the documentation is publicly available.[1] Therefore, every aspect of Ethernet can be understood by referring to the formal technology specifications. The companion website has links to the important Ethernet specifications.

## Ethernet

*IEE 802.3 standard*

*局域网*

Ethernet is a technology for low-cost, high-speed communication in small networks. A network using Ethernet can be up to 100 meters in radius and have up to 250 devices. Because it covers a small territory, Ethernet networks are commonly called local area networks (LANs). Most departmental and small business networks use Ethernet for network connectivity. The technology was patented in 1977. The patent filing specified a maximum data rate of 3 million bits per second (3 Mbps). Technology has evolved considerably since then and most computers sold today support Ethernet data rates of up to 1 gigabit per second (1 Gbps = 1,000 Mbps), a speed increase of more than 300 times. Figure 3 shows the how the founder of Ethernet, Bob Metcalfe, visualized the technology.

Figure 4 is an early sketch of the Ethernet drawn by Bob Metcalfe and it provides an excellent visual overview of the technology. As seen in Figure 4, the core of Ethernet was a cable available throughout a building. This cable was called Ether, after the substance that was once believed to permeate the entire universe. Analogous to Ether, Ethernet was visualized as a technology that would be available anywhere in a building wired for Ethernet. Computers, called stations in Figure 4, obtained network

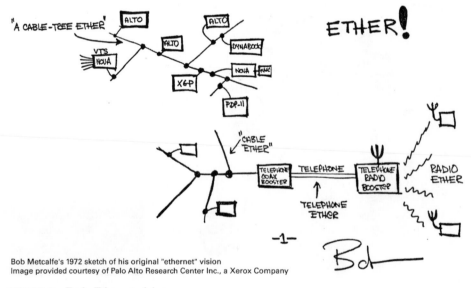

Bob Metcalfe's 1972 sketch of his original "ethernet" vision
Image provided courtesy of Palo Alto Research Center Inc., a Xerox Company

**FIGURE 3**   Early Ethernet vision

---

[1] http://standards.ieee.org/getieee802/portfolio.html.

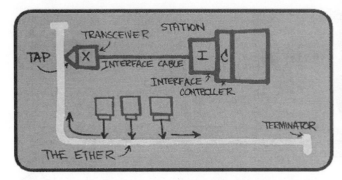

**FIGURE 4**    Early diagram of Ethernet (Robert Metcalfe and David Boggs, "Ethernet: Distributed packet switching for local computer networks," CACM, 19(7), pp. 395–404.)

**FIGURE 5**    Ethernet transmitter-receiver, early 1980s

connectivity by tapping into the Ether. Figure 5 shows the network interface used for Ethernet in the early 1980s.

When a station wanted to send data, it would simply send the data out into the Ether where the data would reach every other computer connected to the Ether. Though there was no privacy in Ethernet, since every station on the network received the data, this mechanism ensured that the data always reached its destination.

Ethernet traded privacy in favor of simplicity. Since any data sent on Ethernet is accessible to all other computers on the network, there is no privacy in Ethernet. However, the benefit is technical simplicity. No complex mechanism is needed to route data to specific computers. There are no controllers or other equipment to regulate which computer may transmit at any time. These simplifications greatly reduce the cost and complexity of networking, making Ethernet affordable for organizations of any size and budget.

Fortunately, the lack of privacy is not a major concern for the contexts in which Ethernet is used.[2] Recall that Ethernet is limited to short distances such as departments and small businesses. Within these small networks, it is safe to assume that all users have similar privileges to access and share data. Therefore, the loss of privacy is not a major concern in Ethernet and is an acceptable trade-off to simplify and economize the technology.

Ethernet operates a lot like a college classroom. As in Ethernet, anyone in the class can speak at any time. Every remark made by any speaker is heard by all other students in the class, even if the remarks are addressed to the instructor or a specific person. No formal rules are necessary to decide the sequence in which speakers are permitted to make comments in the class. When a participant has something to say, he simply waits for the appropriate moment when no one else is talking and speaks, and everyone can hear every comment. Just as in Ethernet, there is no privacy in the classroom, but this does not diminish the functionality of the classroom.

The Ethernet of Figure 4 has a major drawback. If the Ether failed, the entire network failed. And it was surprisingly easy for the Ether to fail. The Ether was a cable

---

[2] To address situations where privacy is a matter of concern, newer technologies such as 802.1ae have been created. They are considered beyond the scope of this text.

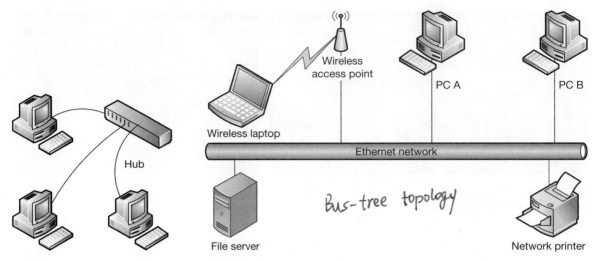

**FIGURE 6** Hub-based Ethernet    **FIGURE 7** Typical Ethernet

that usually ran through attics and closets in buildings. Here animals and workers could accidentally cut the cable in remote nooks that were difficult to locate. Therefore, later Ethernets placed the Ether in a box called the hub, with interface cables connecting individual computers to the hub from up to 100 meters away. Figure 6 shows such an arrangement. There is no difference in the basic operation of a hub-based Ethernet (Figure 6) and the early Ethernet shown in Figure 4 though they look very different. The advantage of the newer design (Figure 6) is that damage to a cable only hurts connectivity at the computer connected by the cable.

## Ethernet operation

We now look at the operation of Ethernet in a little more detail. A typical departmental Ethernet is shown in Figure 7. It includes the usual network elements such as a file server for shared files, a printer, a few desktops, and laptops accessing these resources wirelessly. We will consider the example where PC A wishes to send some data to PC B.

To accomplish the transfer, A can transmit the data on the wire. The transmission will reach all the devices on the network, including B. The basic elements of data transfer are therefore quite simple. There is just one hitch. When the data reaches B, how will it know that the data was being sent to it, and not to some other device on the network?

To overcome this problem, when A wants to send the data to B, it can add B's address to the data. This is analogous to putting a "To:" address on a letter before dropping it in the mailbox. To maintain the analogy with a small group discussion, this is also like addressing a specific participant in the group before making a remark. The address alerts the named member that the comments that follow are addressed to him, though everybody in the group can listen to those comments. With this refinement of adding an address to the data, Figure 8 shows a data packet sent from A and addressed to B.

This idea of adding a "To:" address to every block of data sent on the network is our introduction to packet headers. A packet of data contains data and some overhead, such as addresses, necessary for the data transfer to be successful. The "To:" address discussed here is called the destination address of the packet. As we proceed in this book, more overhead items will be introduced. With one exception, all the overhead in a packet is located in one place before the data. This location is called the packet header. Placing the overhead before the data facilitates packet processing. For example, as in Figure 8, if the receiver sees that a packet is not addressed to it, it does not have to worry about processing the rest of the packet. The only exception is error-detecting information, which is located at the end, as seen later in this chapter.

## Broadcast in Ethernet

We have seen how any data sent in Ethernet is received by all other computers on the network. This mechanism is fundamental to the operation of Ethernet. Ethernet is therefore called a broadcast network. *Broadcasting is the transmission of signals that may be simultaneously received by stations that usually make no acknowledgement.* Broadcast is a very important technique to simplify communication in small-scale networks.[3] We have already seen the example of broadcast in a classroom. In fact, all forms of shouting, use broadcast to send messages.

As another familiar example of broadcast, consider the ECRWSS service offered by the Postal Service. Local advertisers can use ECRWSS (Extended Carrier

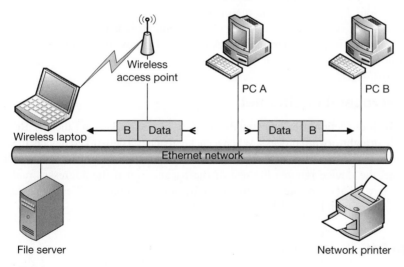

**FIGURE 8**    Packet in the medium

---

[3] Broadcast is so easy, even newborn babies know how to use it. Every time a baby cries, everybody within listening range knows that attention is required. From a data communications perspective, a newborn baby may be seen to communicate exactly one bit of information—1 (crying) and 0 (not crying).

facelogic®
essential skincare•spa

Call to schedule an appointment:

ECRWSS
POSTAL CUSTOMER

clubflyers.com•800.433.9298

**FIGURE 9**  Mail broadcast

Route Walking  Sequence Saturation) to cover the local area. You may have received such advertisements addressed to "ECRWSS postal customer." The mail carrier delivers such mail to every address along his route. Figure 9 shows an example of an ECRWSS letter.

ECRWSS simplifies work for everyone. Local advertisers do not have to address mail to individual customers and the postal service does not have to sort the mail. The trade-off is that the mail reaches a number of customers who are not interested in the specific advertisement. As a result, a lot of the ECRWSS broadcast mail you receive every day falls in the category of junk mail. The same thing happens in Ethernet as well. Most of the data a station receives in Ethernet is not of interest to the station. This suggests the major limitation of broadcast as a communication mechanism—it is simple, but also very inefficient. Broadcast is great for small networks, but unsuitable for large networks. After all, how large can a network be if everyone were to shout at each other?

## Packet receipt in Ethernet

In the previous section, we discussed the transmission of packets in Ethernet. Reception is a fairly straightforward process. When a packet reaches a networked device, the device compares its own address with the destination address of the packet. If they are not the same, the device ignores the rest of the packet. But if the addresses match, the device knows that the packet is addressed to it, and the device receives the packet. This process is shown in Figure 10.

## CSMA/CD

Broadcast is simple, but broadcast networks require courteous behavior from their users for efficient operation. This is because broadcast networks have a major limitation—they can only handle one transmission at a time. What happens to the data sent by A if B also transmits some data at the same time? The result is shown in Figure 11. In the figure, a packet is being sent to B at the same time that a packet is being sent to A. The result is called a collision. *A collision is the situation that occurs when two or more demands are made simultaneously on a system that can only handle one demand at any given instant.*

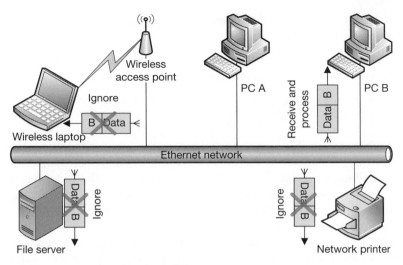

**FIGURE 10** Receipt of packet in Ethernet

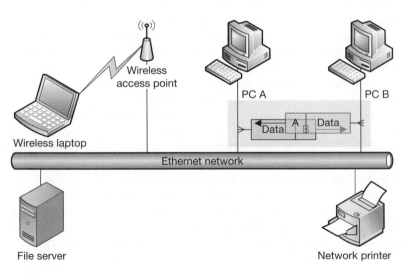

**FIGURE 11** Collision in Ethernet

Figure 11 shows that for efficient operation, Ethernet requires a mechanism that minimizes the possibility that two or more computers might send data over the medium at the same time. This is called medium access control (MAC). *Medium access control is the method used to determine who gets to send data over a shared medium.* The MAC mechanism used in Ethernet is called CSMA/CD, which is an acronym for <u>C</u>arrier <u>S</u>ense <u>M</u>ultiple <u>A</u>ccess with <u>C</u>ollision <u>D</u>etection. Though the term sounds complex, its operation is quite straightforward. Here is what each term in the acronym means:

Multiple Access: *A scheme that gives more than one computer access to the network for the purpose of transmitting information.*

Carrier Sense: *An ongoing activity of a data station in a multiple access network to detect whether another station is transmitting.*

Collision Detection: *The requirement that a transmitting computer that detects another signal while transmitting data, stops transmitting that data.*

Multiple access refers to the ability of Ethernet to serve multiple computers. Carrier sense requires computers that wish to send data on a multiple access network to first sense the medium for the absence of other data-carrying signals. Computers transmit only when they sense that the medium is silent. If the medium is busy, a computer with data to send waits for the current transmission to end before transmitting data.

Carrier sense greatly improves the efficiency of multiple access networks such as Ethernet. Unfortunately, collisions are possible even if transmitting computers confirm that the medium is silent before transmitting data. Consider what can happen if more than one computer gets ready to send data while a transmission is going on. As soon as the transmission ends, each waiting computer will sense that the medium is silent and decide that it is acceptable to transmit data. When all these waiting computers transmit data, the packets will collide with each other.

Therefore, to improve the efficiency of Ethernet, transmitting computers do more than just carrier sense. They continue to listen to the medium after beginning transmission. This is called collision detection. If all goes well, there is only one station transmitting data, and the signal this sender senses in the medium will be identical to the signal this sender transmitted into the medium. However, if another computer is also transmitting at the same time, a collision will occur. If a collision occurs, the signal the sender senses will be different from the signal it is transmitting. Once a computer detects a collision, it knows that further transmission is futile because the receiver will not be able to successfully decode the signal. The computer therefore immediately stops transmission.

One final challenge remains. Once a computer detects a collision and stops transmission, it still has data to transmit. The computer also knows that there is at least one other computer on the network that is also waiting to transmit, though it does not know the identities of the other waiting computers. Therefore, a mechanism is required to enable all these waiting computers to send data over the shared network, without colliding with other waiting senders.

The mechanism that is used to resolve collisions is called random back-off. Each computer that detects a collision waits for a random amount of time before sensing the medium again. If the medium is clear after the waiting period is over, the computer begins transmission; otherwise it waits for the ongoing transmission to end before sending again. If it detects a collision a second time, it waits even longer. Eventually, the transmission succeeds.

CSMA/CD is just a formal way of saying: do not interrupt. Bringing up the analogy with a classroom again, it is easy to see that a classroom is a multiple access (MA) channel. The instructor and students share the same transmission medium. In this environment, it is efficient to allow speakers to finish what they are saying without interruption. This is analogous to carrier sense. When two or more people start speaking at the same time, they immediately detect the collision and stop. This is analogous to collision detection. The colliding speakers then find a courteous way to decide who goes first, which is functionally equivalent to random back-off.

## Advantages and disadvantages of using CSMA/CD in Ethernet

The primary advantage of CSMA/CD is its simplicity. CSMA/CD does not require any additional equipment to work. It therefore greatly reduces the cost of networking. Further, since no configuration is required to make CSMA/CD work, Ethernet does not require any technical skills to set up. Additional computers can simply be plugged into the network. Home and small business networks are almost always Ethernets, and CSMA/CD is one of the reasons why it is so easy to add additional computers to home networks.

CSMA/CD however has some limitations. The primary limitation comes from the broadcast nature of a CSMA/CD network. Only one station can transmit at a time in a broadcast network. Collisions increase as the number of computers in a CSMA/CD network increases. Therefore these networks are not scalable. Experience suggests that delays caused by collisions become unacceptably large when about 100 users join the network.

Another potential disadvantage of CSMA/CD networks is that the maximum wait time to resolve a collision is undefined. There is no assurance that collisions will be resolved in a specified amount of time. As a result, CSMA/CD networks may not be suitable for applications that require guaranteed service. In its early days, this was considered a fatal defect of CSMA/CD networks. Modern networks resolve this limitation by over-provisioning—increasing the speed of the network so much that the likelihood of collisions is minimized. Also, as we will see later in this chapter, modern Ethernets have switching capabilities. Switching attempts to minimize the number of packets which reach devices other than their intended destination. It therefore minimizes the use of broadcasts and virtually eliminates collisions.

At this point, we have completed our discussion of the first function of the data-link layer—addressing and delivering data to the correct destination. The discussion was based on Ethernet. Other data-link layer technologies may operate differently, but they share many features with Ethernet. They all deliver data across one hop and they all use addressing to locate the destination.

We now begin our discussion of the second function of the data-link layer—error detection and possible correction. Again, the discussion will use the example of Ethernet, but the error-detection technique used in Ethernet, cyclic redundancy check (CRC), is used by virtually all data-link layer technologies for error detection.

# Error detection

It is easy to see that as the signal passes through the medium, it is likely to get corrupted due to noise and factors such as power outages and power spikes. When the corrupted signal is decoded, errors are introduced in the received data. For reliable operation of the network, these errors must be detected and corrected.

The standard technique used to detect errors at the data-link layer is called CRC. To motivate the need for a relatively complex error-detecting procedure such as CRC, it is useful to begin by seeing how errors are corrected in human communication. We will then see why error-correcting methods that work in human communication are unsatisfactory for computer communication. CRC overcomes these limitations in error-detection techniques that work so well in human communications.

To begin with, most human communication is social in nature and requires no error detection or correction. In most cases, we can tune out a conversation for long periods and still understand the information being conveyed. Where error detection or correction becomes necessary, contextual cues often help us to fix errors.

Where error correction is important in human communication, various techniques are popular. Three techniques are considered here. The first is echo, or reading back the information. If you have purchased goods over the phone, generally the customer service agent wants to make sure that the credit card information you have provided is correct. To do this, the agent reads back the credit card number and other details to you to confirm that he correctly copied the information you provided. The second technique is to provide redundant data to help reduce errors. For example, while fixing appointments, it is very useful to specify dates in detail. For example, instead of saying tomorrow, it is very useful to specify the day as: tomorrow, Thursday, November 15, 2000. Finally, the third technique is for the receiver to contact the sender in case he is in doubt about any piece of information.

The last two of the three techniques discussed above are obviously not suitable for computer communication. Computers cannot yet figure out how to use redundant information to fix errors. Or, be in doubt that some received information such as a name or address might possibly be incorrect. The first technique, *echo*, seems promising. The receiver can echo back the information it receives from the sender. If the echo does not match what was sent, the sender knows there is a problem. However, echo has a major flaw. As Figure 12 shows, errors may get cancelled in the two-way exchange. In the example, the sender sent the word "hello" to the receiver. However, due to a transmission error in 1 bit of data, this was received as "gello." When the receiver echoed it back for confirmation, unfortunately, a second transmission error caused another 1-bit error to reverse the effect of the error introduced during onward

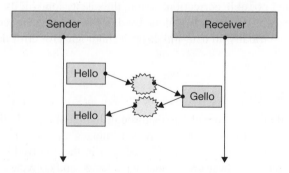

**FIGURE 12** Error cancellation in echo

transmission. This caused the word to be received back as "hello", leading the sender to believe that the transmission was successful. This kind of error cancellation may not happen every time, but the example shows that echo is not a very reliable method for error detection.

The above discussion suggests that informal methods that succeed in removing errors in human communication are inadequate to remove errors in computer communication. Whereas human communication is quite tolerant of errors, modern networks are used for shopping, banking, and other commercial transactions that are highly intolerant of errors. Therefore, extremely reliable methods of error detection are necessary in data-communication networks.

The general approach used for error detection in computer communication is to help the receiver determine on its own that the data it has received has errors, without seeking confirmation from the sender. This is done by adding some meta-data[4] to the transmitted data. The sender computes this meta-data from the transmitted data and adds it to the packet. At the receiving end, the receiver re-computes the meta-data from the received data and compares its own computation of the meta-data with the meta-data sent by the sender. If the two meta-data match, the receiver accepts the data as correct. Otherwise, it rejects the data.

## Simple example of error correction

Let us consider a simple example of using meta-data for error-detection. The method used in the example is too simple to be useful in practice. However, it illustrates the basic ideas behind using meta-data for error-detection.[5]

Say we wish to transmit the word HELLO. To keep things simple, instead of using ASCII, we choose a simple coding scheme where we transmit each letter as its position in the alphabet. Thus, the letter $A$ is coded as 1, $B$ as 2, and so on. With this coding scheme, the data to be transmitted is: 8 5 12 12 15.

Let us calculate our error-detecting meta-data as follows: We will add up the digits to be transmitted until we get a single digit. Thus, we get $8 + 5 + 12 + 12 + 15 = 52$, we repeat to get our meta-data $5 + 2 = 7$. We can then transmit 8 5 12 12 15 7.

If there are no transmission errors, the receiver will get 8 5 12 12 15 7. The receiver knows that the last number received is the error-detecting meta-data and 8 5 12 12 15 is the data. It can calculate $8 + 5 + 12 + 12 + 15 = 52$ and $5 + 2 = 7$. Since the calculated meta-data matches the received meta-data, the receiver can conclude that the data was received without errors.

Let us see what happens if an error is introduced during transmission and the receiver gets 7 5 12 12 15 7. When the receiver repeats the error-detection computation, it obtains $7 + 5 + 12 + 12 + 15 = 51$ and $5 + 1 = 6$. Since $6 \neq 7$, the receiver can discard the received data as defective (note that 7 5 12 12 15 in our scheme was the code for GELLO).

So far, so good. The scheme will detect the error when one error is introduced during transmission. However, the proposed scheme is too naïve and error-prone. For example, this scheme will not detect errors in the above example if the receiver gets 8 5

---

[4] Meta data is any data about data, it is usually used to provide definition or documentation.
[5] The scheme presented here is a variant of the parity scheme used on hard drives.

11 13 15 7 or 2 2 11 13 15 7. Clearly, there is a need for an error-detecting scheme that can detect arbitrary kinds of errors. This is provided by CRC, which is why commercial data-link layer technologies use CRC for error-detection.

## Cyclic redundancy check (CRC)

*CRC is an error checking algorithm that checks data integrity by computing a polynomial algorithm based checksum.* CRC used in Ethernet can detect all errors in data that affect 32 or fewer bits.[6] It can also detect any errors affecting any combination of an odd number of bits. Errors affecting some combination of an even number of bits are also highly likely to be detected. The overall detection rate is 99.99999998% of all errors that affect 33 or more bits in the data. This is considered satisfactory for commercial use. For these reasons, CRC is preferred over simpler error-detection methods.

At a high level, CRC uses modulo-2 division, which may be called lazy division. The dividend in the division is the data for which the meta-data is to be calculated, along with a few zeros added as required by the procedure. The divisor is specified by the technology being used. When the division is completed, the remainder is the error-correcting meta-data.

Modulo-2 division is done the same way as regular division. The only difference is that while subtracting numbers, we use the following rules instead of conventional subtraction:

$$0 - 0 = 0 \qquad 1 - 1 = 0 \qquad 0 - 1 = 1 \qquad 1 - 0 = 1$$

**FIGURE 13** Modulo-2 subtraction rules

Only the third rule above is different from conventional division. In conventional division, it is not possible to subtract a smaller number from a larger number. However, this is possible in modulo-2 division. These rules may be called lazy division because you do not really have to subtract. If the numbers are the same, the difference is 0, otherwise it is 1.

At the sender end, the CRC meta-data is computed using a four-step process. These steps are summarized here before being explained by example.

Step 1: The technology specifies the divisor. The data to be transmitted is the dividend.

Step 2: Add specified number of 0s to the tail end of the dividend. The number of 0s to be added is one less than the number of bits in the divisor.

Step 3: Complete the modulo-2 division till the remainder has fewer bits than the divisor.

Step 4: The remainder is the CRC meta-data. Add 0s to the head of the remainder till it has one less number of bits than the divisor. The resulting number is called the frame-check sequence (FCS).

---

[6] Recall from Chapter 2 that a bit is a unit of information that designates one of two possible states of anything that conveys information.

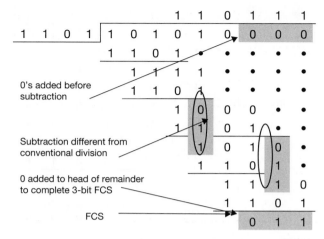

**FIGURE 14**    CRC—Sender operation

The receiver's operation reverses the sender's operations. It performs a modulo-2 division using the data as the dividend with the same divisor as used by the sender (this divisor is specified by the technology). In place of the 0s added by the sender, the receiver places the FCS received from the sender. If the remainder is 0, the receiver accepts the data as correct, otherwise it rejects the data.

Let us now consider a simple example. In the example, the divisor specified by the technology is 1101. The data to be transmitted is 101010. The calculations are shown in Figure 14.

## CRC example

Step 1: The divisor is 1101, the dividend is 101010.

Step 2: Since the divisor has 4 bits, we add 3 0s to the tail of the dividend; this gives us 101010 000 to use as the dividend.    *why ?*

Step 3: Perform modulo-2 division. This is shown in Figure 14. It is quite similar to regular division. The only difference is that the subtraction operation uses modulo-2 rules instead of regular subtraction. The instances where this happens in the example have been highlighted in the figure.

Step 4: When the division ends, we have a remainder of 11. However, since the divisor has four digits, we need a three-digit remainder for the FCS. We therefore add a 0 to the head of the remainder to get an FCS of 011.

The sender will now send the data (1010101) and the FCS (011) to the receiver. The receiver performs a modulo-2 division using the data and FCS as dividend with the technology-specified divisor. The operation is shown in Figure 15.

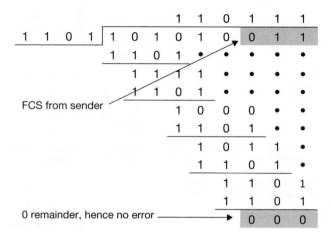

**FIGURE 15**   CRC—Receiver operation

Since the remainder is 0, the receiver accepts the data as error-free. The receiver is confident that there are no errors affecting any combination of three or fewer bits in the data or any combination of odd number of bits. It is also convinced that there is only an extremely small chance that there are any errors affecting some combination of more than four even numbers of bits.

The error-detection capability of CRC depends upon the choice of divisor and the length of the divisor. Ethernet uses a divisor of 1 00000100 11000001 00011101 10110111. This is 32 bits long and is judged as providing the required level of error-detecting capabilities.

Whereas the destination address field helps the data-link layer perform its first function, delivery, the FCS field introduced in this section helps the data-link layer perform its second function—error detection and possible correction. The FCS field is placed in the data packet at the tail end of the data. This is done because the FCS is appended to the tail end of the data in the CRC computation at the receiving end. Locating the FCS at the tail end (called the packet trailer) eliminates the need for the receiver to rearrange data from different parts of the packet before performing the CRC verification. The data packet of Figure 8 can now be modified to also include the FCS, and it is shown in Figure 16. The FCS is the only overhead item in a packet among all layers in the TCP/IP stack that is placed in the trailer.

If an error is detected, how does Ethernet fix these errors? It doesn't because it doesn't have to. It simply discards the frame. Upper layers (specifically TCP) are capable of detecting this lost frame and have it re-transmitted. Therefore Ethernet can simply focus on making sure that no bit-level errors occur during transmission.

Just like Ethernet, all data-link layer technologies in use today ensure that errors are detected, and most make no attempt to fix these errors. In Chapter 5 (transport layer), we will see why it is perfectly fine for data-link layer technologies to not attempt to correct errors.

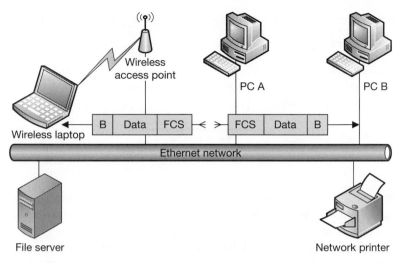

**FIGURE 16**    Packet with FCS in the medium

---

### The etymology of "algorithm"[7]

CRC is an algorithm. The word algorithm comes to us from al-Khowârizmî, who created the earliest known work in Arabic arithmetic. Al-Khowârizmî lived around 800 AD. He was the first mathematician to publish rules for addition, subtraction, multiplication and division using the (then) newly developed Hindu numerals. Speak the word al-Khowârizmî fast. It sounds a lot like algorithm, and the word algorithm means "rules for computing," in reference to the rules for computing developed by al-Khowârizmî.

---

## Ethernet frame structure

The packet at the data link is called a frame. This is because the preamble and FCS fields are seen as framing the packet from both ends. This is a unique feature of the structure of the data-link layer packet in Ethernet. Other layers (IP and TCP) have neither a preamble nor a field that tails the data.

We can now look at the structure of an Ethernet frame. The complete Ethernet frame is shown in Figure 17.

Of the overhead items in an Ethernet frame, shown in Figure 17, we have already seen two—the destination address and the frame-check sequence (FCS). Another obvious required item of information is the source address. Just like the sender address in a letter, this field tells the receiver where to send a reply.

---

[7] Peter L. Bernstein, *"Against the gods: The remarkable story of risk,"* New York: Jonh Wiley & Sons, 1996.

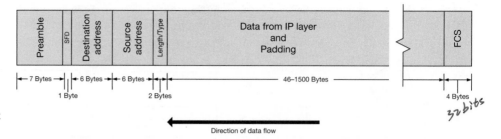

**FIGURE 17** Ethernet frame structure

There are three fields in the Ethernet frame we have not discussed yet—the preamble, start-of-frame delimiter (SFD) and length/ type. We can take them up now.

The preamble and start-of-frame delimiter (SFD) help the receiver locate the beginning of an incoming data-link layer frame, much like the whistle of an arriving train. Since the exact bit pattern is known in advance, these bits also help the receiver synchronize itself with the receiver and know exactly how long it takes the sender to transmit each bit. These fields are necessary because in normal operation, there are stray signals in the medium even if there is no network traffic. When signals from a new frame arrive at a receiver, it is extremely helpful to the receiver if it gets a clear indication that these signals represent data, and are not random noise in the medium. Therefore, at the beginning of a frame, the data-link layer transmits a well-defined sequence of 7 bytes[8] (56 bits) called the preamble:

10101010 10101010 10101010 10101010 10101010 10101010 10101010

The bit sequence in the preamble is long enough and regular enough that it is extremely unlikely to be produced by random noise. At the end of the preamble, one more byte is sent to alert the receiver about the beginning of the frame. This is called the start-of-frame delimiter (SFD) and is the bit sequence 10101011. At the end of these 64 bits (56 in preamble and 8 in SFD), the useful information in the frame begins.

The field that immediately follows the SFD is the destination address which, as described earlier, helps computers on the network determine whether the frame is addressed to them. After the destination address is the source address field. The source address field is required when creating a response to a frame. Upon processing a frame, if a computer determines that a response is required, it uses the source address of the incoming frame as the destination address of the response frame.

After the address fields is the length field. The length field specifies the length of the data in the data-link layer frame. Ethernet specifies that the total length of the frame should not exceed 1,518 bytes.[9] The length field is required because,

---

[8] A sequence of 8 bits is called a byte. A bit is usually abbreviated using the lower case *b* (1 Mbps = 1 megabit per second), while a byte is usually abbreviated using an upper case *B* (1 MB = 1 megabyte).

[9] Many large organizations use an updated version of Ethernet. In this version, the length field is also interpreted as a "type" field. To keep the discussion simple and focus on the essential properties of Ethernet, this alternate use of the length field is considered beyond the scope of the text.

unlike the beginning of the packet which is clearly marked by the preamble and SFD, there is no field that explicitly defines the end of the frame. Instead, the length field helps the receiver identify the end of the frame. The receiver counts bytes till it gets "length" number of bytes. It then knows that it has accounted for the entire frame. Once the receiver identifies the end of the frame from the length field, it knows that the last 4 bytes in the frame constitute the FCS. It then knows that the remaining information in the frame (between the length and FCS fields) is the data in the frame. After error-check, this data is passed to the receiver's network layer.

## Ethernet addresses

All the fields in the Ethernet header are automatically calculated by the host without any end-user administration or configuration. Of these fields, the address fields (source address and destination address) have a well-defined structure that may be of interest to network administrators. Every computer with a network interface as in Figure 2 has an Ethernet address. Some computers even have two or more such interfaces for redundancy or to increase network capacity. Each such interface has its own Ethernet address. In the industry, Ethernet addresses are commonly called MAC addresses or physical addresses. The term *MAC address* comes from the fact that the address is associated with the data-link layer, which also performs medium access control (MAC). The term physical address comes from the fact that the data-link layer is commonly implemented in hardware called the network interface card (NIC).

Ethernet defines the address field to be 48 bits in length. The 48 bits are split into two parts of 24 bits each as shown in Figure 18. The first 24 bits determine the organizationally unique identifier (OUI) or manufacturer ID. Manufacturers are assigned OUIs[10] by the IEEE.[11] The first 24 bits of every network interface card address are the

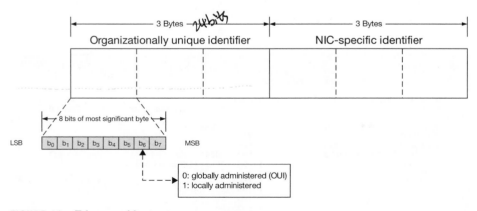

**FIGURE 18** Ethernet address

---

[10] OUI records can be searched at http://standards.ieee.org/regauth/oui/index.shtml.
[11] IEEE is the Institute for Electrical and Electronics Engineers.

OUI of the manufacturer. No two manufacturers have the same OUI. The remaining 24 bits are assigned by the manufacturer such that no two NICs made by a manufacturer have the same NIC-specific ID. Together, the OUI and NIC-specific ID ensure that every NIC card made in the world has a unique ID.

Some modern virtualization technologies allow administrators to assign more than one physical address to a NIC. When this is done, the complete 48-bit MAC addresses are assigned by the local network administrator. As shown in Figure 18, Ethernet allows administrators to use one bit in the OUI part of the MAC address to indicate that the address is locally assigned. This is just mentioned here for reference. You don't have to worry about virtualization in this course.

You can view the physical address of a Windows computer by typing in the command ipconfig/all on your DOS prompt (Start → Type cmd in the Start Search box). An example is shown in Figure 19. You may find it interesting to confirm the OUI allocation to the manufacturer of your NIC card at the IEEE registration authority website.

As seen in Figure 19, the physical address is usually displayed in hexadecimal format. Since most students are unfamiliar with the hexadecimal notation, an introduction is provided here. The hexadecimal notation is a way of representing binary numbers in 4-bit blocks. Thus, 48-bit MAC addresses are represented using 12 (48 ÷ 4) hexadecimal characters.

Table 1 shows how each possible block of 4 bits is represented using the hexadecimal notation. For example, the bits 1100 are represented as C. The hexadecimal notation is very common in data communications. You can refer to Table 1 for the hexadecimal representation when necessary in later chapters.

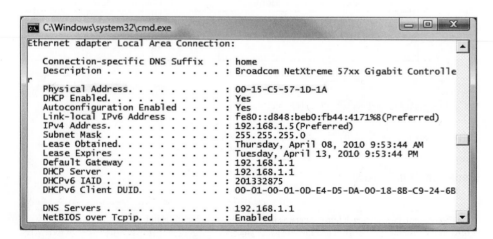

**FIGURE 19**   Ethernet address example

**Table 1**   Hexadecimal notation

| Bits | Hex representation | Bits | Hex representation |
|------|-------------------|------|-------------------|
| 0000 | 0 | 1000 | 8 |
| 0001 | 1 | 1001 | 9 |
| 0010 | 2 | 1010 | A |
| 0011 | 3 | 1011 | B |
| 0100 | 4 | 1100 | C |
| 0101 | 5 | 1101 | D |
| 0110 | 6 | 1110 | E |
| 0111 | 7 | 1111 | F |

| 48 bit MAC address | 0000 | 0000 | 0001 | 0101 | 1100 | 0101 | 0101 | 0111 | 0001 | 1101 | 0001 | 1010 |
|---|---|---|---|---|---|---|---|---|---|---|---|---|
| 12 dig HEX representation | 0 | 0 | 1 | 5 | c | 5 | 5 | 7 | 1 | d | 1 | a |

**FIGURE 20**   Binary representation of physical address shown in Figure 19

Based on Table 1, we can decode the binary representation of the physical address in Figure 19 as shown in Figure 20.

## Ethernet—State of the market

Modern Ethernet networks largely follow the operational principles described in this chapter. There has been one additional development that we have not covered yet. This is the replacement of hubs (shown in Figure 6) with switches. Switches greatly increase the data transmission efficiency of hub-based CSMA/CD Ethernets. Almost all Ethernets designed in recent times use switches instead of hubs.

Whereas hubs broadcast all data to every computer on the network, modern high-speed electronics makes it possible to create switches that read the destination addresses of incoming frames and send the frames only to the correct targets. By limiting broadcast, switches greatly reduce collisions. Switches can simultaneously transfer data between multiple pairs of ports.

With the evolution of technology, basic switches now cost about the same as hubs. There is therefore very little incentive today to use hubs instead of switches. Basic switches are very easy to use and require no configuration. Switches automatically discover the MAC addresses of computers connected to the different ports. Switches maintain this information about the computers connected to the different ports in a forwarding table. Switches look up the forwarding table to determine the port on which an incoming frame should be sent out.

Switches use a very interesting mechanism to discover MAC addresses. To populate their forwarding tables, switches monitor the source addresses of incoming packets on each port. If the source MAC address of a frame coming into port 3 is 00:18:8B:c9:24:6B, the switch automatically knows that the computer with MAC address 00:18:8B:c9:24:6B is connected to port 3. The switch can add this information to its forwarding table. Now, if an incoming frame has destination address 00:18:8B: c9:24:6B, the switch knows that the frame should be forwarded on to port 3. This way, the forwarding table is automatically created and updated in real time with no manual intervention.

Switches cannot eliminate broadcasts. Even in switched networks, a lot of support traffic continues to be broadcast. For example, if a switch hasn't yet learned about the location of a particular destination MAC address and receives a frame to be sent to this address, it floods the traffic out of all ports in the hope of finding the correct destination. This effectively makes the switch revert back to the standard hub operation for the frame. The important categories of this traffic are covered in Chapter 7, Support Services.

## From Ethernet to the outside world

Ethernet LANs are great for applications such as file and printer sharing on small networks. In the next chapter we will see how individual Ethernets are connected to other Ethernets and larger networks to create even more useful networks—Internets. At a very high level, Ethernets connect to Internets in the manner shown in Figure 21.

The shaded network is a departmental Ethernet LAN. The LAN is connected to the carrier network by a device called a router. Traffic directed to computers

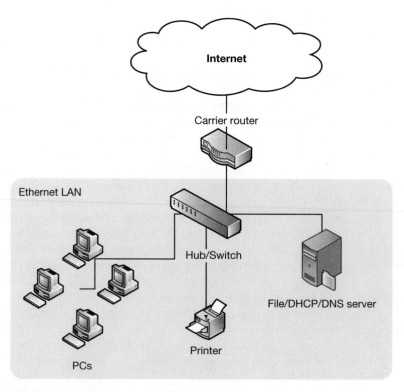

**FIGURE 21** Ethernet as part of larger network

outside the LAN is sent to the router. The router determines the next hop for the packet among its neighboring routers. This process continues through the maze of other networks until the packet reaches its final destination on the other network.

Outside the Ethernet, traffic is no longer sent by broadcast for reasons of efficiency. The alternate mechanism is called point-to-point and is used everywhere outside LANs. This is covered in later chapters.

---

## CASE STUDY | LOCAL AREA NETWORKS HELP SERVE WORLD-CLASS HOSPITALITY: THE VENETIAN AND HARRAH'S

---

*Local area networks help businesses share information and computer resources efficiently. Though these local area networks are invisible to customers and employees, used correctly, they can be more important and profitable to the business than dazzling sights. Here we see how two of the leading casino resorts in Las Vegas—The Venetian and Harrah's—use local area networks to run their operations and distinguish themselves from the competition.*

The Venetian in Las Vegas is one of the largest resorts in the world, with over 7,000 guest rooms, over 70 restaurants, almost 2 million square feet of convention space, and over 120,000 square feet of casino space. Supporting these services are over 65,000 networked devices including approximately 7,000 printers and 2 devices in each guest room that provide wired and wireless Internet access to the room. All these devices are connected by an Ethernet infrastructure with over 700 switches. Devices used in each application, such as front desk registration, security cameras, point-of-sale, and Internet telephony, are connected by a network  (called a virtual LAN) dedicated to the application. Figure 22 provides a representative diagram of a part of the Ethernet at the resort, showing how guest registration and floor operations are networked.

The LAN enables resort operations in various ways. As an example, the IT leadership at the resort believes that the LAN saves 10–15 seconds during each guest check-in and check-out. Networking capabilities at slot machines enable customer-friendly features, such as electronic funds transfers for bets and winnings, and improve revenues at the resort.

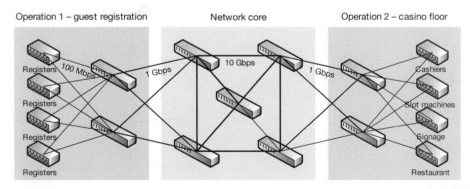

**FIGURE 22**  Part of Ethernet LAN at The Venetian casino resort

As shown in Figure 22, it is common for networks to transfer traffic between parts of the network through a central core. As a result, traffic volumes are higher in the core of the network. To support these higher traffic rates, the core of the network has higher speed links, and switches capable of handling higher data rates.

Ethernet is a very reliable technology and the network has not experienced any major failure in over 10 years of operation. Yet, for safety, network administrators try to plan for device failures. Figure 22 shows how enterprise networks commonly use redundancy to improve the reliability of the network. Each sub-Ethernet (VLAN) in the

LAN is connected to two different switches. The network can continue operating even if one switch in a pair fails. The network also enables the resort to combine all kinds of information—voice, data, and video—on a single infrastructure.

When the organization gets bigger and establishes business operations at different sites, the LANs can be interconnected, using technologies called wide area networks, to create even greater business value. A company in the industry that is well-known for doing this successfully is Harrah's. Harrah's Entertainment is a nationwide casino resort chain widely admired for obtaining business advantage from the nation's first national reward network in the industry. It began investing in its computer network in the mid-1990s at a time when its competitors were investing in glitz and glamour to attract customers. Instead of investing in glamour, Harrah's wanted to distinguish itself from its competition by using IT to learn more about its customers and develop appropriate marketing campaigns based on this knowledge.

At the core of Harrah's strategy was winner's information network (WINet), the company's national customer database. Over a period of three years, the company invested in networking all its slot machines, event reservations, and customer relationship applications across all its resorts nationwide, to WINet.

Once WINet became usable, all customer activity at all Harrah's resorts was stored in the company's central database. Harrah's resorts in the country were able to use WINet to access the common central database to keep track of all customer activities across all of its resorts in the country. This allowed the company to design customized promotional campaigns and rewards programs for customers based on each individual customer's spending patterns.

Since the slot machines are connected through LANs to the company's central database, customers can check their rewards points from any slot machine at any of the company's resorts. Customers also appeared to like the ability of customer service agents to pull up their transaction history and ask them about their trips. High-spending customers appreciated the gifts the company would place in their suites at any Harrah's resort in the country on birthdays, anniversaries, and other special occasions without any reminders. The occupancy rate at the company's hotels exceeded 90% compared to an industry average of about 60%. The company is able to attract more of its customers' gaming budgets—43% in 2002, compared to 36% in 1997.

In 1999, the company had an annual profit of $594 million. According to Harrah's estimates that year, WINet and associated programs saved the company over $20 million. The number of customers playing at more than one resort has increased by over 70%, contributing almost $50 million in annual profits. Almost twice as many casino players carried Harrah's rewards cards as cards from any competitor.

## REFERENCES

Duffy, Jim, "10G Ethernet powers glitzy casino," *Network World,* May 26, 2008.

"Make every customer more profitable: Harrah's Entertainment Inc," *CIO Insight,* December 1, 2003.

Heun, Christopher T. "Harrah's bets on IT to understand its customers," *Information Week,* December 11, 2000.

Levinson, Meredith "Harrah's knows what you did last night," *CIO*, June 6, 2001.

Levinson, Meredith "Harrah's Entertainment—Jackpot! Using IT to manage customer information," *CIO,* Feburary 1, 2001.

## SUMMARY

This chapter covered the data-link layer. This layer transfers data over one network link, or hop, for example between a laptop and the wireless router at home. The data-link layer helps senders and receivers identify themselves on the local network (addressing). The layer also ensures that any errors in data transmission over the physical medium are detected. We used the example of Ethernet to discuss the advantages and disadvantages of using broadcasts as a mechanism for data transfer. The use of CRC for error-detection was described. The concept of headers was introduced for the first time in the book with a description of the Ethernet header. The two parts of Ethernet addresses were discussed. We also examined switches and how they improve the efficiency of Ethernets over hubs.

# ABOUT THE COLOPHON

For a long time physicists used the concept of Ether to explain how light could travel through space where no physical medium existed. Ether was thought of as an omnipresent, undetectable medium that could propagate magnetic waves such as light waves.[12] The colophon shows how Einstein saw parallels between Ether and physical matter.

When Bob Metcalfe and David Boggs were building the first network at PARC, their plan was to run a cable through every corridor in the building to create an omnipresent medium for the propagation of electronic signals carrying data packets. Seeing the parallels between Ether and their network, Metcalfe and Boggs named their network Ethernet on May 22, 1973. Prior to getting this name, their network was called the Alto Aloha network because it connected Alto computers using ideas developed for a wireless network at the University of Hawaii.[13]

Though modern Ethernets are significantly different from Metcalfe and Boggs' network, the Ethernet name survives.

# REVIEW QUESTIONS

1. What are the primary functions of the data-link layer?

2. Ethernet is the most popular end-user technology at the data-link layer. What is *ether* in the context of computer networking?

3. What are the components of a typical Ethernet? What are the functions of each component?

4. What is *broadcast* in the context of Ethernet?

5. What are the advantages of broadcasting data in Ethernet? What are some other examples of communication in day-to-day life that use broadcast?

6. What are the limitations of broadcast as a method of sending data to the intended receiver of communication?

7. What is *carrier sensing* in Ethernet? What is *multiple access*? What is a collision and what is collision detection? How are collisions detected in Ethernet?

8. Describe some techniques you have used in the past to ensure error-free communication over the telephone.

9. Provide a lay person's overview of CRC.

10. What is CRC used for in data communication?

11. Why is CRC preferred over simpler computational techniques?

12. With a divisor of 1101, perform the sender-side computation and calculate the CRC when the data is 1001011.

13. Check your computation by performing the receiver-side computation.

14. What is the size of the smallest Ethernet frame? The largest frame?

15. List the fields in the Ethernet header. What are the roles of each of these fields?

16. The start-of-frame and preamble fields are unique to the data-link layer in that they do not carry any useful information. What is the role of these fields?

17. The SFD field alerts the receiver about the beginning of a data frame. How does the receiver know when the frame ends?

18. What is the structure of a MAC address? What information can be gathered from a MAC address?

19. What is the MAC address of your computer? You can get this information by typing ipconfig/all in Windows, or ifconfig on mac/ linux (Figure 23).

---

[12] Albert Einstein, "*Ether and the Theory of Relativity*," address delivered on May 5, 1920, in the University of Leyden, http://www.tu-harburg.de/rzt/rzt/it/Ether.html (accessed 02/27/10).

[13] Cade Metz, "Ethernet—a name for the ages," *The Register*, March 13, 2009, http://www.theregister.co.uk/2009/03/13/metcalfe_remembers/print.html (accessed 02/27/2010).

**20.** What is the hexadecimal notation? How is the number 14 represented in hexadecimal?

**21.** Write the binary number 01010000 in hex (Hint: break the number into two four-bit blocks and represent each four-bit block in hexadecimal notation).

**22.** What are *hubs*?

**23.** What are *switches*?

**24.** What are the advantages of switches over hubs in Ethernets? Under what conditions may you prefer to use a hub instead of a switch?

**25.** What are the common data transfer speeds in Ethernet? What is the maximum possible speed of the network card on your computer? In Windows Vista, you can right-click on the network adapter to check its speed (Control panel → Network connections → <select adapter>).

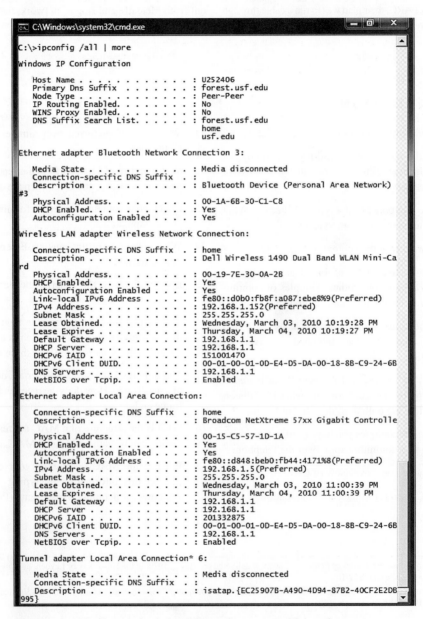

```
C:\Windows\system32\cmd.exe

C:\>ipconfig /all | more

Windows IP Configuration

    Host Name . . . . . . . . . . . . : U252406
    Primary Dns Suffix  . . . . . . . : forest.usf.edu
    Node Type . . . . . . . . . . . . : Peer-Peer
    IP Routing Enabled. . . . . . . . : No
    WINS Proxy Enabled. . . . . . . . : No
    DNS Suffix Search List. . . . . . : forest.usf.edu
                                        home
                                        usf.edu

Ethernet adapter Bluetooth Network Connection 3:

    Media State . . . . . . . . . . . : Media disconnected
    Connection-specific DNS Suffix  . :
    Description . . . . . . . . . . . : Bluetooth Device (Personal Area Network)
#3
    Physical Address. . . . . . . . . : 00-1A-6B-30-C1-C8
    DHCP Enabled. . . . . . . . . . . : Yes
    Autoconfiguration Enabled . . . . : Yes

Wireless LAN adapter Wireless Network Connection:

    Connection-specific DNS Suffix  . : home
    Description . . . . . . . . . . . : Dell Wireless 1490 Dual Band WLAN Mini-Ca
rd
    Physical Address. . . . . . . . . : 00-19-7E-30-0A-2B
    DHCP Enabled. . . . . . . . . . . : Yes
    Autoconfiguration Enabled . . . . : Yes
    Link-local IPv6 Address . . . . . : fe80::d0b0:fb8f:a087:ebe8%9(Preferred)
    IPv4 Address. . . . . . . . . . . : 192.168.1.152(Preferred)
    Subnet Mask . . . . . . . . . . . : 255.255.255.0
    Lease Obtained. . . . . . . . . . : Wednesday, March 03, 2010 10:19:28 PM
    Lease Expires . . . . . . . . . . : Thursday, March 04, 2010 10:19:27 PM
    Default Gateway . . . . . . . . . : 192.168.1.1
    DHCP Server . . . . . . . . . . . : 192.168.1.1
    DHCPv6 IAID . . . . . . . . . . . : 151001470
    DHCPv6 Client DUID. . . . . . . . : 00-01-00-01-0D-E4-D5-DA-00-18-8B-C9-24-6B
    DNS Servers . . . . . . . . . . . : 192.168.1.1
    NetBIOS over Tcpip. . . . . . . . : Enabled

Ethernet adapter Local Area Connection:

    Connection-specific DNS Suffix  . : home
    Description . . . . . . . . . . . : Broadcom NetXtreme 57xx Gigabit Controlle
r
    Physical Address. . . . . . . . . : 00-15-C5-57-1D-1A
    DHCP Enabled. . . . . . . . . . . : Yes
    Autoconfiguration Enabled . . . . : Yes
    Link-local IPv6 Address . . . . . : fe80::d848:beb0:fb44:4171%8(Preferred)
    IPv4 Address. . . . . . . . . . . : 192.168.1.5(Preferred)
    Subnet Mask . . . . . . . . . . . : 255.255.255.0
    Lease Obtained. . . . . . . . . . : Wednesday, March 03, 2010 11:00:39 PM
    Lease Expires . . . . . . . . . . : Thursday, March 04, 2010 11:00:39 PM
    Default Gateway . . . . . . . . . : 192.168.1.1
    DHCP Server . . . . . . . . . . . : 192.168.1.1
    DHCPv6 IAID . . . . . . . . . . . : 201332875
    DHCPv6 Client DUID. . . . . . . . : 00-01-00-01-0D-E4-D5-DA-00-18-8B-C9-24-6B
    DNS Servers . . . . . . . . . . . : 192.168.1.1
    NetBIOS over Tcpip. . . . . . . . : Enabled

Tunnel adapter Local Area Connection* 6:

    Media State . . . . . . . . . . . : Media disconnected
    Connection-specific DNS Suffix  . :
    Description . . . . . . . . . . . : isatap.{EC25907B-A490-4D94-87B2-40CF2E2DB
995}
```

**FIGURE 23**   Viewing configuration information on network interfaces

# HANDS-ON EXERCISE

We saw in this chapter that Ethernet specifies a 48-bit address for network cards. This address is popularly called the MAC address or the physical address of the interface. Recent laptop computers usually have three such interfaces—one for the wired network card, another for the wireless LAN card, and a third for the Bluetooth interface. In this exercise, you will identify the Mac addresses of the interfaces on a computer, convert the hexadecimal representations to the 48-bit binary addresses, and identify the manufacturers of the network cards.

`ipconfig` is a convenient utility on Windows computers to see the configuration information of all these interfaces on Windows. On Macs and Linux machines, the equivalent utility is `ifconfig`. To use `ipconfig`, you need to open up the command prompt (start → run → type "cmd" on the search field). At the command prompt, you can type the command `ipconfig/all` to view the configuration of all network information. If you have a number of such interfaces, you can paginate the output using the command `ipconfig/all|more` as shown in Figure 23.

The output in Figure 23 shows that the Mac address of the Bluetooth interface is 00-1A-6B-30-C1-C8; of the wireless adapter is 00-19-7E-30-0A-2B; and of the wired Ethernet card is 00-15-C5-57-1D-1A. We can look up the hexademical table in the chapter to convert each hexadecimal digit to binary and obtain the 48-bit Mac address of

the Bluetooth interface as 0000 0000 0001 1010 0110 1011 0011 0000 1100 0001 1100 1000.

Looking up the OUI 00-1A-6B of the Bluetooth adapter card in the public OUI listing (http://standards. ieee.org/regauth/oui/index.shtml and http://standards.ieee. org/regauth/oui/oui.txt), we find that the Bluetooth adapter is manufactured by USI, located in Taiwan, Republic of China. Similarly, the wireless card is manufactured by Hon Hai Precision Ind. Co., Ltd, Taiwan, Republic of China; and the OUI of the wired Ethernet interface card is owned by Dell.

Do the following on a computer you use at work or at home.

1. Show the output of the command `ipconfig/all` or `ipconfig/all|more` (if there are numerous adapters on your computer).

2. From q1 above, what are the Mac addresses of the different interfaces on your computer?

3. Express each of these Mac addresses as 48-bit binary addresses.

4. Look up the OUIs of each of these Mac addresses and list the names and locations of the manufacturers of these Mac cards.

# NETWORK DESIGN EXERCISE

Answer the following question.

1. Assume that all locations use Ethernet for local connectivity within the buildings. Typically, each floor in each building will have its own Ethernet, and these Ethernets will be connected to other Ethernets in the same building through a switch. Draw the Ethernet diagram for the second floor of the AP service center.

# CASE QUESTIONS

1. What are some of the ways in which computer networks helped the resorts in the case improve their business operations?

2. What changes in attitudes of the managers of individual Harrah's resorts were necessary to exploit the potential of the chain-wide rewards program? (You

may need to read the articles in the references. They can be Googled).

3. A leading competitor to Harrah's on the Vegas strip is Mirage, which is famous for its volcano show. If you haven't seen the glittery show yourself, view a video of the famous volcano at Mirage on the Internet.

What do you think are the business benefits of the investment in the spectacle? Compare the costs and benefits of investing in spectacular shows such as the Volcano to the costs and benefits of investing in computer networking, based on the example of Harrah's Entertainment.

4. Consider a nationwide resort chain with computers, but without computer networks. Briefly describe how you would implement a rewards program for the chain. In your description, include ideas on how you would collect data about guest activities; how you would store and update such data in your records; and how you would inform guests about their current rewards status.

5. Consider any one organization you have worked for. What ideas could you use at this organization from the ways in which the two resorts have used computer networks to improve their business?

6. What are some of the ethical questions that arise when companies tap into customer psychology to encourage them to spend more on slot machines in order to earn rewards points?

7. What are some financial impacts (revenues, profits) of computer networking for the two resorts—Venetian and Harrah's?

8. (Optional) Report on yet another company in the hospitality industry that has used computer networks to improve its business operations. In the report, include information on the business processes affected and the financial impacts.

# Network Layer

*The journey of a thousand miles begins with a single step.*
—CHINESE PROVERB

## Overview

This chapter covers the network layer. The network layer transfers data from a source computer to a destination computer via one or more networks. Each network in the path uses the data-link layer technology of its choice to transfer data to the next network. The standard protocol used by all networks at this layer is the Internet protocol (IP). IP assigns an address to every device on the network, and every IT professional and most computer users need a working knowledge of IP addresses. At the end of this chapter you should know:

- the functions of the network layer
- an overview of the Internet protocol (IP)
- the IP header
- IP addresses
- the CIDR notation for IP addresses
- obtaining IP addresses
- IP version 6

## Functions of the network layer

The network layer is responsible for transferring packets of data from the source computer to the destination computer via one or more networks. The data-link layer is responsible for transferring data within a network. In general, though, the source and destination of a data packet can be located on different networks. For example, when you visit your school's home page from your home PC, the source is on your home network and the destination is on the university network. The data-link layer cannot exchange data between these two computers, and the network layer becomes necessary to transfer data across networks. This function of the network layer may be summarized in one word—routing.

Routing is performed in networks by devices called routers. Routing is examined in Chapter 9. This chapter focuses on the tasks performed by the source and destination computers to help routers perform their routing function.

Figure 1 provides an overview of the role of routers. Routers connect networks. For example, when a network grows to the point where it is too large for an Ethernet, the network can be divided into multiple Ethernets. A router can be used to connect the Ethernets, creating a network of networks.

To help routers perform their routing function, every device on the network is assigned a unique network layer identifier. This identifier also serves as the address of the computer on the Internet. Since this address is defined by IP, the network layer protocol, this address is popularly called the IP address of the computer. Before sending a data packet out on the network, the sender adds the destination's IP address to the header of every data packet.

In Chapter 3, we saw that networked computers also have MAC addresses. You might wonder how data-link layer addresses are related to IP addresses. If you simply want to identify a computer on the network, why do you need two different addresses for every computer? The relationship between data-link layer addresses and IP addresses is clarified in Figure 2. The data-link layer address allows the packet to be delivered correctly within each individual network on the path to the destination. The IP address retains the address of the actual source and the final destination. Note in Figure 2 that the destination IP address does not change throughout the packet's

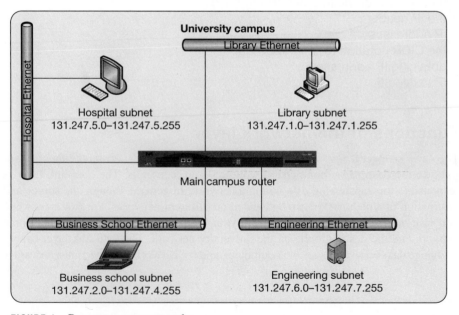

**FIGURE 1** Routers connect networks.

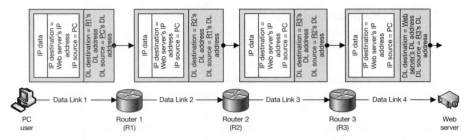

**FIGURE 2**    IP addresses and their relationship to data-link layer addresses

journey from the source (PC) to the destination (web server). However, the data-link layer addresses keep changing as the packet gets transferred from network to network. Thus, immediately as the packet leaves the PC, the data-link destination address points the packet to the nearest router. The data-link layer technology on this hop uses the data-link layer destination address to deliver the packet to router 1. On the 2nd hop, the data-link layer destination address is router 2, and so on. All this time, the destination IP address maintains the address of the final destination.

On its way to the destination, the packet encounters its first router (R1) when it reaches the outer edge of its local Ethernet. This router is connected to one or more other routers. The router looks at the destination address of the packet, and determines the best neighboring router to hand the packet over to. In the example of Figure 2, it is R2. With each successive hand-over, the packet moves closer to its target until it is finally delivered to the correct destination (web server).

It is amazing that this process works. But it is one of the miracles of modern technology that billions of data packets are delivered in this manner on the Internet every day and they all reach their destinations almost instantaneously without incident.

There is a very direct analogy between routing and a typical road trip. Say you want to travel from your home in Arlington, Texas, to Busch Gardens, Tampa, Florida. The final destination address is Busch Gardens, Tampa. Busch Gardens, therefore, corresponds to your IP destination address. However, your route map will point to several intermediate destinations along the way. For example, exit 53B on I-30E to U.S.-80, left on N56[th] Street, and so on. Each of these intermediate destinations is analogous to a data-link layer destination address. All the while, you never forget your final destination address—Busch Gardens. However, at each point on the trip, your goal is always to get to the next exit. As long as you get all the intermediate destinations right, you are guaranteed to get to the final destination.

A related issue is—why is it necessary to use a different address format, such as the MAC address, to identify intermediate destinations? Why can't intermediate destinations also be identified by IP address? One reason is that some of these technologies (e.g. Ethernet) were developed independently of IP, and already had their own address formats before being integrated with IP. Another reason is that allowing data-link layer addresses to be independent of IP addresses provides great flexibility in technology design at the data-link layer. It also allows the data-link layer to be independent of the network layer. Upgrades to IP, whenever necessary, will not require simultaneous upgrades to data-link layer technologies.

The designers of the Internet deliberately designed the network layer in such a way that all the complexity of routing is located in specialized devices called routers. The source and destination hosts do not have any routing responsibilities. The only thing senders have to do is to label packets with the correct source and destination addresses. Routers take care of the rest to deliver the packets to the correct destination. This design allows even simple devices, such as handheld computers and inexpensive security cameras with limited processing capability, to be connected to the Internet. These devices do not have to be capable of performing the complex operations required to route packets. Any device that can label packets with source and destination IP addresses can access the wonders of the Internet, without worrying about routing.

## Overview of the Internet protocol (IP)

The most common protocol used at the network layer is the Internet protocol, also known by its acronym, IP. A number of technologies have competed for dominance at the network layer in the past. However, IP has emerged as the clear winner at the network layer with virtually no viable competition at this time. Therefore this book focuses on IP when discussing the functioning of the network layer.

IP was specified in 1981 in RFC 791. A major factor that helped popularize IP was its use to enable networking in the BSD UNIX distribution. At that time, though few large communities of users had access to computers, the computer science academic community was already using BSD UNIX for its day-to-day computing needs. The incorporation of TCP and IP in BSD UNIX dispersed these protocols among the leading-edge users of the time, paving the way for further adoption of TCP and IP among other communities and, eventually, by all major operating systems.[1]

IP is highly adaptable. This adaptability has helped IP maintain its popularity for over a quarter of a century, even as the applications being used on the Internet have changed dramatically since the introduction of IP in the early 1980s. Most applications that make the Internet popular today were not even envisioned when IP was first introduced. The web was created almost 10 years after IP, in the early 1990s, bringing network interactivity to the masses. Real-time applications such as instant messaging emerged even later. Early in this century, bandwidth-hungry media applications such as video became popular. IP has successfully handled the routing needs of all these new applications. The success of IP at meeting the evolving needs of the Internet so far gives us confidence that IP will continue to be successful in the future at the network layer.

When defining the functions of IP, its designers deliberately limited the capabilities of IP in one important respect. IP does not provide end-to-end reliability. In other words, if there are problems such as defective routers along the path from source to destination, IP will not worry about ensuring that data packets will actually reach their destination. Instead, reliability is provided by the transport layer. In other words, once a router dispatches a data packet on to a neighboring router, the packet is left to its own fate and the router does not worry about the packet any more. If the neighboring router is unable to process the data packet for any reason, the packet can get lost, but routers

---

[1] http://www.isoc.org/internet/history/brief.shtml.

do not worry about recovering lost packets. Instead, routers focus on routing the next packet. For this reason, the service provided by IP is also called best-effort delivery. *Best-effort delivery is a network service in which the network does not provide any guarantee that data will be delivered.* Limiting IP functions to best effort greatly simplifies the design of routers.

## IP Header

Before proceeding further to examine the IP header, it is useful to integrate what we have learned so far. When a packet is in the medium, the location of the data-link layer header, the IP header, and the data passed to IP from the transport layer is as shown in Figure 3. Leading the packet is the data-link layer header. Immediately behind it is the IP header. The data-link layer FCS is at the trailing end of the packet. The IP header and transport-layer data together constitute the IP data for the data-link layer. A comparison between Figure 3 and Figure 17 of Chapter 3 would help to further clarify how IP packets fit into the data-link-layer frame.

A very effective way to learn about a protocol is to look at the protocol header and examine the functions of each field in the header.[2] The IP header is shown in Figure 4.

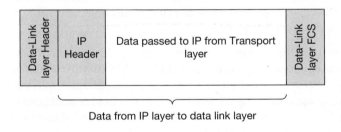

**FIGURE 3**   Data-link and IP headers in relation to packet

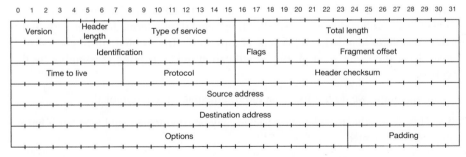

Note: Each tick mark represents a bit position

**FIGURE 4**   IP header

---

[2] RFC 791 is a great resource for this section. A reading of the RFC is highly recommended for readers of this chapter. The RFC is available from many sources, e.g. http://www.rfc-editor.org/rfc/rfc791.txt. Figure 4 is from RFC 791.

The IP header adds information that enables IP to do its job. The information in the various fields of the IP header is used primarily by routers to perform routing. The information in the fields and their functions are briefly described below.

*Version:* The version field tells routers the version of IP being used. Having a separate field to identify software versions simplifies upgrades.[3] Most of the Internet currently runs version 4 of IP. The upgrade to IP is numbered version 6. The primary motivation for upgrading IP is to increase the potential size of the Internet. More details on version 6 are provided in a later section of this chapter.

*Header length:* This field specifies the length of the IP header. This field is necessary because IP allows the header to include various options, which means that the length of the header can be variable. The IP header specifies where the header ends and the data begins. Note that the header length of IP only specifies the length of the IP header, not the length of the entire frame. This field would not be needed if the IP header had a fixed size.

*Type of service:* The designers of IP allowed the source to specify the desired service priority. This field is colloquially called the TOS field. A higher number in the TOS field signifies a higher desired priority. Implementing TOS requires that routers be able to maintain different queues for packets with different TOS values. This is analogous to high-occupancy-vehicle (HOV) lanes in some busy parts of the interstate system. Carriers implementing TOS may want to charge more for higher priority delivery. Since implementing multiple queues is difficult, at this time, networks are not required to honor the desired service priority.

*Total length:* This field specifies the size of the packet, including the header information and data. The maximum possible value of this field is 65,535 (the discussion on binary numbers later in the chapter will show why this is so). This field therefore limits the size of IP packets to approximately 65 KB. Note that this field is analogous to the frame-length field of Ethernet. Interestingly, initially the recommended size limit was 576 bytes to accommodate the limited processing capability of computers.

*Identification:* IP allows packets to be fragmented if necessary. Fragmentation allows packets to be broken down into smaller fragments if an intermediate network in the path is unable to handle large packets. If a packet is fragmented, all fragments of a packet have the same value in the identification field, enabling reassembly by the receiver.

In this book, we do not focus on the fragmentation function of IP.

*Flags:* This field indicates whether a packet may be fragmented, and whether it has in fact, been fragmented.

*Fragment offset:* If an IP packet is fragmented, this field specifies the position of the current packet with respect to all other fragments with the same identification.

---

[3] Ethernet does not have a version field. Therefore as new features such as VLANs got added to Ethernet, the interpretation of the length field was changed to mean length/ type to provide information analogous to the IP version field. Had Ethernet had a version field, it would have been much easier to define newer versions of Ethernet, with different features, without resorting to these hacks.

*Time to live:* As the name suggests, this field specifies the remaining life of the packet on the network. When a packet is sent out, the source puts some value in this field, usually 128 or 256. Each time a packet passes a router, the router decrements the value of this field by 1. If the value of the TTL field of a packet ever reaches 0, the router discards the packet. This mechanism ensures that no packet can live on forever on the Internet even if poorly configured routers send packets on endless circular routes. This field therefore acts as a safety valve on the Internet.

Note that this field also implies that there can be no more than 256 routers between any source and destination on the Internet. In practice today, packets usually pass through a maximum of about 15–20 routers.

*Protocol:* Many transport-layer technologies have been defined as potential users of IP. The protocol field in IP identifies the transport-layer technology that is sending and receiving the packet. The values in the protocol field for familiar transport-layer technologies include 6 (TCP) and 17 (UDP). These numbers are defined in RFC 1700.

*Header checksum:* This field carries error-detection information for the packet header. The IP header checksum is only calculated over the IP header, not over the packet data. Unlike the CRC checksum that is used to ensure data-integrity in the data-link layer, the error-detection procedure used in the IP header is very limited in its error-detection capability. However, the most vital information in the IP header is the source and destination IP addresses, and the IP header checksum provides some protection against errors to these addresses. The IP header checksum therefore gives a certain amount of assurance that IP packets will only get delivered to the correct destination. The header checksum is recalculated at each node.

Thus, there are two major differences between the IP header checksum and Ethernet CRC. CRC is for the entire frame whereas the IP checksum is only computed over the header. Also, while CRC is very robust at error detection, the IP header checksum is less reliable. Since the Ethernet data also includes the IP header, the Ethernet CRC also checks for errors in the IP header. In fact, in the newest version of IP, IP version 6, the header checksum has been eliminated since the Ethernet CRC was deemed sufficient.

*Source and destination addresses:* As indicated in Figure 2, these fields identify the originating source and ultimate destination of the packet. The next section of this chapter focuses on these two fields. In fact, these two fields are a major focus of this chapter.

At the end of this course, you are likely to use two items of information from the course the most—the names and functions of the OSI layers and IP addresses.

*Options:* This field allows the source of the packet to specify various kinds of optional information for use in routing. For example, one early option was to define source routing, whereby the source could specify the path from source to destination and insist that routers only send packets along that route. This option was considered necessary for military users of the Internet who would wish to specify a route that avoided routers in hostile countries. As the name suggests, options are optional, a source is not required to specify any options. Options are generally not used any more.

Padding: This field consists of a string of 0s to ensure that the IP header is a multiple of 32 bits in size. Padding becomes necessary if options are used.

Thus far, we have seen the protocol headers at two layers—the data-link layer and the network layer. This introduction to protocol headers demonstrates a very interesting feature of protocols. End users care only about the data in the packet, and treat the protocol header as overhead. But the hardware and software implementing the protocol only know how to interpret the fields in the header. On the receiving side, as soon as a layer interprets the header information inserted by its counterpart on the sender side, it runs into information that it does not understand. For example, see Figure 3. As soon as the data-link layer processes the data-link header, it encounters the IP header. The data-link layer software has no idea how to interpret the IP header. So, the data-link layer passes all this information to the IP protocol at the network layer for processing. This process is repeated at every layer until eventually, the application layer passes usable data to the end user.[4]

## IP addresses

Of all the fields in the IP header, the source and destination address fields get the most attention. As a matter of fact, these two fields are probably the best known fields among all protocol headers. In this section, we examine the IP address fields in more detail. Given the attention given to IP addresses, it is important that every IT professional has a good working knowledge of IP addresses and their organization. IP addresses may be the most important networking-related operational detail for any IT professional.

*An address is a unique label that helps locate an entity on a network.* As Figure 4 shows, IP address fields are 32 bits in length. Every network connection of a computer connected to the Internet is assigned a unique 32-bit number as an IP address. For example, a laptop with a wireless connection and a wired connection will have one IP address for the wireless connection and one IP address for the wired connection. This number serves as the network layer source address for all packets leaving the computer from the connection. This is also the destination address for all packets arriving at the connection.

The importance of IP addresses in packet routing is reason enough to learn about IP addresses. There is, however, an even more important reason for you to spend time learning about IP addresses. By design, network administrators have tremendous flexibility and discretion in allocating IP addresses to computers within their organizations. Therefore, an understanding of the organization of IP addresses will help you leverage this flexibility when required.

A working knowledge of binary numbers is essential when working with IP addresses. The following overview provides the information necessary to be comfortable working with binary numbers involved in computer networking in general, and IP addresses in particular. If you are comfortable working with binary numbers, you can skip the overview of binary numbers below.

### Binary numbers overview

This overview provides everything you need to know about working with binary numbers for computer networking. We know from Chapter 2 that all computer data is stored as binary numbers. It becomes particularly important to be comfortable with binary

---

[4] John Day, "Patterns in Network Architecture: A Return to Fundamentals," Prentice Hall (2008), 464 pp.

numbers when working with computer addresses. IP addresses, like all other protocol header fields, are binary numbers. Working knowledge of binary numbers helps network administrators compute the best possible organization of IP addresses, and calculate the maximum possible sizes of computer networks and other network details.

One particularly important skill is the ability to convert from binary numbers to decimal and vice-versa. Fortunately, in most cases, you will only deal with binary numbers that are 8 bits in length. You should therefore be very comfortable working with 8-bit binary numbers.

Our primary interest in binary numbers in this book is to use binary numbers to assign computer addresses. An address is essentially a unique label that locates a computer on the network. Larger numbers allow more computers to be identified. Therefore, our primary goal in this overview is to be able to determine how many computers can be identified, given the size of binary numbers used as identifiers.

Before using binary numbers to calculate the number of possible addresses, let us use decimal numbers and a simple example to understand what we are trying to do. Say you are asked to use one-digit decimal numbers to label computers in a student lab. How can you proceed? You can label the first computer as 0, the second computer as 1, and so on, until you label the 10th computer as 9. At this point you will run out of unique labels. If the labels are not unique, they cannot serve as addresses. For example, if two computers have the label 0, there would be conflicts and confusion to determine which computer really had the label 0. Therefore, even if you have more computers in the lab, but can only assign one-digit labels, you will only be able to use 10 computers in the lab. If you use two-digit labels, you will be able to assign labels to 100 computers (0–99) before you run out of labels.

Therefore, we see that the number of possible labels depends upon the size of numbers used to assign the labels. In general, using n-digit decimal numbers, we can assign $10^n$ labels.

Binary digits are called bits. Each bit can take two values—0 and 1. Continuing the idea in the previous paragraph, when using binary numbers to assign labels, if we have 1-bit binary numbers, we can assign two labels. The first label will be a 0; the second label will be a 1. If we have 2-bit binary numbers, we can assign four labels—00, 01, 10, and 11. With 3-bit binary numbers, there can be 8 labels—000, 001, 010, 011, 100, 101, 110, and 111. With $n$-digit binary numbers, we can have $2^n$ labels.

These relationships are shown in Table 1. The first row of the table shows the labels that are possible with 1-bit binary numbers. We can have two such labels as

**Table 1**  Labeling with binary numbers

| Bits | Labels | Number of labels | Formula for number of labels |
|---|---|---|---|
| 1 | ID:0  ID:1 | | $2^1$ |
| 2 | ID:00  ID:01  ID:10  ID:11 | 4 | $2^2$ |
| 3 | 000, 001, 010, 011, 100, 101, 110, 111 | 8 | $2^3$ |
| n | | | $2^n$ |

shown in the first row. The table shows one computer being assigned label 0 and the other computer being assigned label 1.

The second row uses 2-bit labels. We can have four computers with 2-bit labels. Computers with these labels are shown. The labels are 00, 01, 10, and 11. Similarly, if we have 3-bit labels, we can label eight computers. For brevity, these computers are not shown in the table, though the labels that would be used are shown. In general, with $n$-bit labels, we can label $2^n$ computers. This means that if we have $n$ bits to label computers in a network, the network can accommodate at most $2^n$ computers if every computer on the network requires a unique label to serve as its address on the network. More address bits imply more possible computers on the network. Every additional address bit doubles the potential size of the network.

Network administrators specify the number of address bits available on a network in a standard format called the subnet mask (subnet masks are discussed in Chapter 8). The subnet mask expresses the number of address bits in a network as a binary number. To deal with these representations as a network administrator, you will need to be able to convert numbers from decimal form to binary as well as in the reverse direction—from binary form to decimal.

As a network administrator, you will need to be comfortable with numbers in the range 0–255. These correspond to binary numbers that are up to 8 bits long. Before discussing the conversion process between binary and decimal, let us quickly recapitulate how decimal numbers are represented. A number such as 358 represents the number $3*100 + 5*10 + 8*1$. We say that the place value of 3 is 100, the place value of 5 is 10 and the place value of 8 is 1. This is shown in Table 2. Since the place values are increasing powers of 10, decimal numbers are called base-10 numbers.

The same idea is used in binary numbers. The only difference is that the place values are powers of 2 and the possible digits are 0 or 1. Thus, the place value of the right-most digit is 1; the place value of the next digit is $2^1 = 2$, followed by $2^2 = 4$, and so on. An example is shown in Table 3. We can use a procedure similar to the procedure used with decimal numbers in Table 2 to calculate the number represented by the binary number 101 as shown in Table 3. The binary number 101 represents $1*4 + 0*2 + 1*1 = 5$, as can be verified from Table 3. Table 4 extends Table 3 to 8 bits.

With this background, we can begin converting from decimal to binary. I find it convenient to start with the template shown in Table 5 (taken from Table 4) and then use the following three-step procedure to convert a number from decimal to binary:

**Table 2**  Example of decimal number

| 3 | 5 | 8 | **Digit** |
|---|---|---|---|
| 100 | 10 | 1 | **Place value** |
| $(10^2)$ | $(10^1)$ | $(10^0)$ | |

**Table 3**  Example of binary number

| 1 | 0 | 1 | **Digit** |
|---|---|---|---|
| 4 | 2 | 1 | **Place value** |
| $(2^2)$ | $(2^1)$ | $(2^0)$ | |

**Table 4**  Template to convert from decimal to binary

| 128 | 64 | 32 | 16 | 8 | 4 | 2 | 1 |
|---|---|---|---|---|---|---|---|
| $(2^7)$ | $(2^6)$ | $(2^5)$ | $(2^4)$ | $(2^3)$ | $(2^2)$ | $(2^1)$ | $(2^0)$ |

**Table 5**  Template for converting from decimal to binary

| — | — | — | — | — | — | — | — |
|---|---|---|---|---|---|---|---|
| 128 | 64 | 32 | 16 | 8 | 4 | 2 | 1 |

**Table 6** Converting 133 to binary—using 128

| 1 | | | | | | | |
|---|---|---|---|---|---|---|---|
| 128 | 64 | 32 | 16 | 8 | 4 | 2 | 1 |

**Table 7** Converting 133 to binary—using 4

| 1 | | | | | 1 | | |
|---|---|---|---|---|---|---|---|
| 128 | 64 | 32 | 16 | 8 | 4 | 2 | 1 |

**Table 8** Converting 133 to binary—using 1 and completing

| 1 | 0 | 0 | 0 | 0 | 1 | 0 | 1 |
|---|---|---|---|---|---|---|---|
| 128 | 64 | 32 | 16 | 8 | 4 | 2 | 1 |

**Table 9** Example to convert from binary to decimal—11100011

| 1 | 1 | 1 | 0 | 0 | 0 | 1 | 1 |
|---|---|---|---|---|---|---|---|
| 128 | 64 | 32 | 16 | 8 | 4 | 2 | 1 |

1. Starting from the left, put 1 in the largest place value that is less than or equal to the number

2. Subtract the place value from the number. The remainder is the new number

3. Repeat until the remainder is 0. Fill all remaining places with 0.

We can use an example to see how this works by converting 133 to binary. We start with the template in Table 5. The largest number in the template that is less than or equal to 133 is 128. So we place a 1 above 128. The result is shown in Table 6.

The remainder is $133 - 128 = 5$. The largest number in the template that is less than or equal to 5 is 4. So, we place a 1 above 4. The result is shown in Table 7.

The remainder is $5 - 4 = 1$, so we place a 1 over 1 and fill the remaining positions with 0, giving the binary representation of 133 as 10000101 as shown in Table 8.

To convert from binary to decimal, use the same template as before (Table 5). Start by writing the digits of the binary number in the appropriate places and add up the place values with 1. For example, if we are interested in finding the decimal equivalent of the binary number 11100011, we start by filling the template of Table 5 with the digits of the binary number as shown in Table 9. The decimal representation of 11100011 is then the sum of all place values with 1, giving $1*128 + 1*64 + 1*32 + 1*2 + 1*1 = 227$.

A good value to remember is the largest possible 8-bit binary number. This number is $128 + 64 + 32 + 16 + 8 + 4 + 2 + 1 = 255$. You will run into this number quite often when you work with IP addresses, particularly with subnet masks.

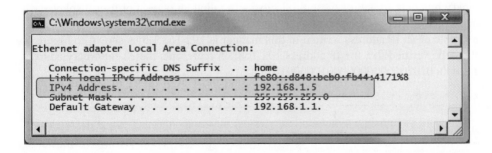

**FIGURE 5** Network configuration of your computer

---

### Number systems have implications[5]

Number systems have implications. The earliest numbering system was developed by the Greeks in about 450 BC. The Greek system used alphabets to represent numbers, much as Roman numerals, that are popular even today (these are the numbers such as i, v, x that are often used for page numbering). Though these numbering systems were useful, they had many limitations. Most importantly, though these numbers could be used to easily represent the results of computations, they could almost never be used to perform computations in the head (for example, try subtracting iv from xiii using mental math). Therefore, these numbers were generally used to record results computed by other methods, usually an abacus. The Greek and Roman numbers did not include 0, and could not represent negative numbers. This made it difficult to use these numbers to represent losses in commercial transactions.

Almost a thousand years later, in about 500 AD, the Hindu number system we use today was developed. This system included a 0, and used only 10 symbols, from 0 to 9, to represent all conceivable numbers using the concept of place values. This created the required regularity so that commercial computations could be performed mentally without the use of an abacus. Until this system became popular in the western world in around 1,000 AD, all but the most elementary computations required the use of an abacus, seriously constraining commerce.

---

11000000  10101000  00000001  00000101

192.      168.      1         5

**FIGURE 6**  Example of dotted decimal representation of IP addresses

## Dotted decimal notation for IP addresses

With this background of binary numbers, we can look at the standard manner in which IP addresses are written. Recall that IP addresses are 32-bit binary numbers. For convenience of representation, the 32-bit IP addresses are broken down into four blocks of 8 bits each. (This is why we emphasized 8-bit binary numbers in the introduction to binary numbers.) Each of these 8-bit blocks is called an octet. For user display, each octet is converted to decimal and the four decimal numbers are separated by dots. An example of an IP address written in this manner is 192.168.1.5 as shown in Figure 6. It can be verified that the IP address 192.168.1.5 represents the 32-bit binary address 11000000101010000000000100000101.

---

[5]This remark is drawn from Peter L. Bernstein, *"Against the Gods: The Remarkable Story of Risk,"* New York: John Wiley & Sons, 1996.

You can view the IP address of your computer by opening up a command shell (Start → cmd in Windows, or Applications → Utilities → Terminal on a Mac) and viewing your network configuration (`ipconfig /all` in Windows or `ifconfig` on a Mac). You will see information similar to Figure 5. Every time you see an IP address in dotted decimal notation, you are seeing a human-readable representation of an underlying 32-bit binary number.

## Structure of IP addresses

IP addresses are organized in a manner that makes them very friendly toward network administrators. This is extremely helpful because network administrators deal with IP addresses all day long. Unlike MAC addresses that are assigned in a factory, IP addresses are assigned by network administrators. This is why it is very important to understand the structure of IP addresses so that you can leverage the potential of IP addresses to your benefit.

Broadly speaking, IP addresses are broken down into two parts. The left part of the IP address represents the network (organization or ISP) to which the IP address belongs. This is called the network part of the IP address. The remaining bits of the IP address identify the computer within this network. This is often called the host part of the IP address. For example, in the IP address 131.91.128.84, the first two octets (131.91) are the network part. Later you will see that these numbers indicate that this address belongs to the network of the Florida Atlantic University. The remaining two octets (128.84) identify a computer within the FAU network.

Students often take time to understand the multi-part addressing scheme used in IP. However, this method of breaking down addresses into two parts where the left part identifies a larger organization and the right part identifies a user within the organization is very common. Three other analogues come to mind and are briefly described below.

The most familiar multi-part addressing scheme is the numbering scheme used in phone numbers. The phone network uses a three-part addressing scheme where the first part identifies the geographical area; the second part identifies the local exchange within the geographical area, and the remaining digits identify the specific user. For example, in the phone number (813) 974-6716, the digits 813 indicate that the number is in Tampa, Florida. The next set of three digits, 974, indicates USF within Tampa, and finally the remaining digits, 6716, are the phone number within the USF network in Tampa.

While the organization of phone numbers into multiple parts is very familiar, there are two other examples of multi-part addressing that we all use every day but that are less familiar—credit-card numbers and zip codes (Figure 7).

Credit cards also use a multi-part addressing scheme. You may have noticed that most Discover credit cards begin in 6011; all Visa cards begin with 4; all MasterCards

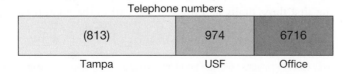

**FIGURE 7**   Multi-part addressing in phone numbers

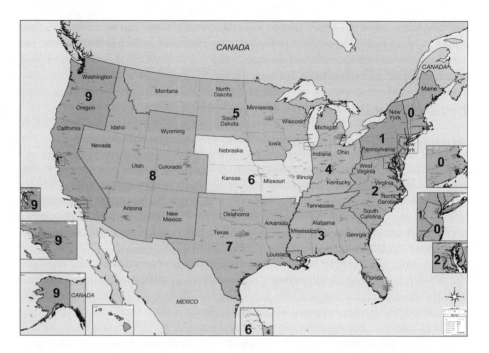

**FIGURE 8** Zip codes—by the left-most digit

begin with 51, 52, 53, 54, or 55, and so on. It turns out that credit cards have a three-part structure. The left-most six digits of a credit card number identify the issuer—the network and bank that issued the card. (Therefore the issuer ID is itself a two-part number.) The remaining digits identify the account number within the issuer.[6] Interestingly, the last digit of the credit card account number is actually an error-detection digit (analogous to the FCS in the data-link trailer).

Zip codes are also multi-part numbers. As seen in Figure 8, the left-most digit of a zip code identifies the national region. All zip codes beginning in 1 are in New York or Pennsylvania. The second digit further narrows down the location of a zip code as shown in Figure 9.[7] For example, zip codes beginning in 10 are in Manhattan, New York City, New York. An excellent animation of multi-part addressing in zip codes is available at http://benfry.com/zipdecode/.

All these instances of multi-part addressing—phone numbers, credit-card numbers, and zip codes—serve the same purpose, which is to simplify delivery. Multi-part addresses are not just labels assigned to objects; these labels specify *where* the object is located to increasing degrees of precision.

This is particularly useful in networks which contain a large number of objects that need to be located. For example, when you dial a phone number, the local exchange does not need to figure out the exact location of the dialed number. All it needs to do is to look at the first three digits and transfer the call to the appropriate metro area.

---

[6] Wikipedia has a very nice description of the credit-card numbering system at http://en.wikipedia.org/wiki/Credit_card_numbers.

[7] Wikipedia also has a good description of the structure of zip codes at http://en.wikipedia.org/wiki/Zip_codes.

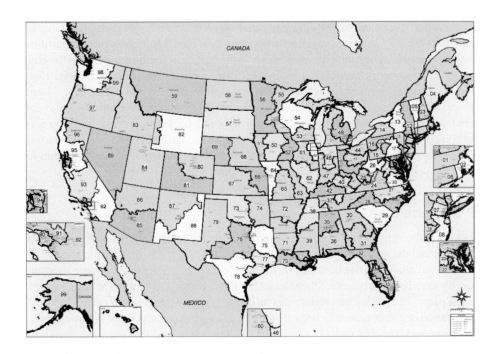

**FIGURE 9**  Zip codes—by two left-most digits

At the metro exchange, the next three digits are used to transfer the call to the appropriate local exchange. Only the local exchange needs to know the exact location of the phone, and it only has to do so by looking at the last four digits. Similarly, when you swipe a credit card at the grocery store, the card reader looks at the first few digits and selects the appropriate card network—Visa, MasterCard, Discover, American Express, etc. The selected network uses the remaining digits of the issuer ID to send the customer request to the appropriate bank. The bank uses the remaining digits of the credit card number to identify the account within its network and sends back the appropriate credit authorization. Finally, when you drop a letter in the mail-box, the local post office does not have to locate the exact street address of the addressee on the map. All it needs to do is to create 10 bins and drop each letter into the appropriate bin by looking at the left-most digit of the zip code. Each of these 10 bins can then be sent to the distribution center in the appropriate geographical area. For example, the bin for zip codes beginning with 1 can be sent to the NY/ PA area. At the distribution center, the mail can be sorted further by the remaining digits of the zip code until it reaches the mailman at the addressee's post office. The mailman of course, is expected to know all street addresses on his route, so he can deliver the letters to the correct home. But only the mailman needs to know exact locations on his delivery route. And, other than the mailman, nobody in the USPS is required to locate a street address.

Multi-part addressing simplifies the work at each location of the network. With three digits in the area code, we can have 1,000 ($10^3$) exchanges. Each exchange only needs to know how to connect to these 1,000 exchanges in order to be able to connect all its users to any destination within North America. This is a much simpler task than knowing how to connect to each of the 10 billion possible phone numbers. (With 10 digits, we can have $10^{10}$, or 10 billion, phone numbers.)

As in these examples, IP addresses are broken into two major parts. The left part is the network part and the remaining bits are the host part. The reason for this partition is also the same as in the examples above—the partition facilitates delivery of data packets. The network part identifies the network to which the address belongs. Usually, this is a telecom carrier such as AT&T or BellSouth. But it could also be a large organization such as a metropolitan university. The larger Internet only looks at the network part of the destination IP address of incoming packets and transfers packets to the correct networks. When the packet reaches the destination network, the destination network looks at the remaining bits of the IP address to locate the computer within its own network and delivers the packet to the computer.

## IP address classes

Looking at the structure of IP addresses and recalling the relationship between the size of a number and the number of addresses it supports, it is easy to see that organizations with more bits available in the host part of the IP address can address more computers and thereby have larger networks. Since the size of the network part + the size of the organization part = 32 bits, we can restate this as follows: organizations with smaller network parts can have larger networks because they have larger host parts in their IP addresses.

Recognizing that networks come in different sizes, and that one size would not fit all organizations, in the early days of the Internet, the network parts of IP addresses were classified into three address classes—A, B, and C. Class A addresses were for the largest organizations, Class B was for medium-sized organizations, and Class C was for the smallest organizations. Organizations could request an address block of the size that best suited its needs. The address classes are shown in Figure 10.

In Class-A networks, the first 8 bits identified the network ID and the remaining 24 bits identified hosts within the network. Of the 8 bits identifying the network, the first bit identified the fact that this was a Class-A network. Therefore, $7 (8 - 1)$ bits uniquely identified each Class-A network. Recalling from Table 1 that n bits allow $2^n$ labels, with 7 bits, we could label $2^7 = 128$ Class-A networks. Therefore, we could

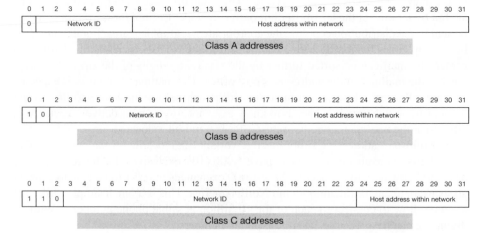

**FIGURE 10** IP address classes

have 128 Class-A networks, and each Class-A network could have $2^{24} = 16,777,216$ hosts. The first octet in all Class-A networks was in the range $0 - 127$, giving 128 possible Class-A networks.

In Class-B networks, the first 16 bits of IP addresses identified the network ID and the remaining 16 bits identified hosts within each network. Within the network part, the first 2 bits identified the address as a Class-B network, leaving 14 bits to identify each network. We could therefore have $2^{14} = 16,384$ Class-B networks and each Class-B network could have $2^{16} = 65,536$ hosts. The first octet of all Class-B networks was in the range 128–191.

Finally, in Class C, the first 24 bits were the network part, leaving 8 bits for the host part within each network. Each Class-C network could, therefore, have $2^8 = 256$ hosts. Of the 24 bits identifying the network, 3 bits were used to label the network as a Class-C network, leaving 21 bits to identify each Class-C network. Therefore $2^{21} = 2,097,152$ Class-C networks were possible. The first octet of IP addresses in Class-C networks was in the range $192-223.$

Figure 10 shows the organization of IP addresses in this scheme. By convention, bit positions start from 0, so the 32 bits go from position 0–31. The figure shows how the 32 bits of an IP address are assigned to network and organization parts in the three address classes. The figure shows the boundaries of the network and organization parts of the different address classes. Observe that as we go from Class A to Class B to Class C, the host part of the IP address class gets smaller, leading to smaller supported networks.

In the addressing scheme described above, the class of an address is identifiable from the first octet of the address. If the first octet is in the range $0-127$, we know that the IP address belongs to a Class-A network. If the 1st octet is in the range $128-191$, we know that the IP address belongs to a Class-B network; and if the 1st octet of an IP address is in the range $192-223$, we know that the IP address belongs to a Class-C network. For example, 97.166.26.237 is a Class-A address and 219.23.46.78 is a Class-C address.

An interesting exercise is to look at the distribution of all available IP addresses among the different address classes. This is shown in Figure 11. The entire figure represents all available IP addresses ($2^{32} = 4,294,967,296$ IP addresses). Of these, half

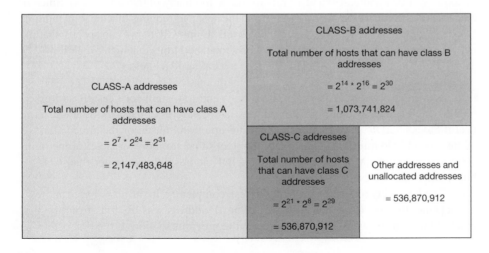

**FIGURE 11**
Available addresses in each class

are Class-A addresses ($2^7 * 2^{24} = 2{,}147{,}483{,}648$). One-fourth are Class-B addresses, and one-eighth are Class-C addresses. The remaining one-eighth of the address space is either unallocated or consists of other address types.

If you observe Figure 11, the defects of the IP address allocation scheme discussed so far and used in the early days of the Internet become apparent. One hundred twenty-eight networks own half the addresses on the Internet. Surely this is unsustainable. Which will be these 128 lucky networks? What happens when an organization with a Class-A address block shrinks in size, for example, if the owner goes out of business? CIDR was created to address these concerns.

## Classless inter-domain routing (CIDR)

The addressing scheme described in the previous section is called a class-based addressing scheme because there are three distinct sizes of address pools—Classes A, B, and C as shown in Figure 10. Figure 10 also indicates a significant problem with the class-based addressing scheme—there are only three possible sizes of address blocks. If you need 2,000 addresses, you can either get eight Class-C blocks or one Class-B block. Handling eight blocks is complex, and the Class-B block wastes a lot of IP addresses. What if you are a global bank and need 500,000 addresses? Should you be given a Class-A address block? What happens to the 15.5 million IP addresses you will not use? Neither of these solutions is satisfactory. Managing multiple Class-C address blocks adds to network complexity, and using a larger address block is inefficient.

CIDR (classless inter-domain routing) was introduced in 1993 to address the problem of unavailability of address blocks of reasonable size. As the name suggests, CIDR is an address allocation scheme that eliminates the concept of address classes and allows address blocks of arbitrary length. Whereas the network part of class-based addresses could only be 8 bits (Class A), 16 bits (Class B) or 24 bits (Class C), in classless addressing, the network part can be of any length. Thus address-block sizes of any power of 2 are possible with CIDR.

For example, say we need 2,000 IP addresses. We can get the required number of addresses if we have 11 bits in the host part of the IP address ($2^{11} = 2{,}048$). 10 bits would be too few (1,024 addresses) and 12 bits would be too many (4,096 addresses). Since IP addresses are 32 bits in length, using 11 bits in the host part requires that the remaining 21 bits be used as the network ID. CIDR enables this. Using CIDR, we can specify that the network part of the address in this organization should be 21 bits in length ($32 - 11 = 21$). Thus, CIDR enables near-surgical precision in allocating IP addresses.

The primary beneficiaries of CIDR are medium-sized organizations. These organizations are too big for Class-C address blocks and too small for Class-B addresses. CIDR enables the aggregation of multiple Class-C address blocks into larger, more useful blocks. CIDR also enables the splitting up of an unused or reclaimed Class-A address block into multiple smaller address blocks that are more suitable for medium-sized organizations. Most large ISPs have CIDR address blocks larger than Class B but smaller than Class A.

The flexibility of CIDR introduces a fresh complexity. In the class-based addressing scheme, the size of the network part of an IP address was obvious from the first octet of the address, as we have discussed in the previous section. If the first octet was in the range $0-127$, it was a Class-A network, $128-191$ was Class B, and $192-223$ was Class C. There is no such regularity in CIDR. Therefore, it becomes necessary to specify the size of the network part of CIDR addresses. Accordingly, CIDR addresses are specified by two numbers—the network part of the address and the size of the network part. Routers need to know the network part of an IP address because they use this information to direct the packet to the correct destination network.

In CIDR, the size of the network part is specified by a number that accompanies all network addresses in CIDR notation. The number specifies the number of bits in the network part of the IP address. For example, the CIDR address 73.5.0.0/17 indicates that the network ID for this organization has 17 bits. This leaves $32 - 17 = 15$ bits for the host ID in the organization.

To complete the implications of CIDR, once we know the CIDR network address, we can calculate the number of computers that can be supported by the network. In our example, if 17 bits are taken up by the network part, the remaining 15 bits $(32-17)$ can be used to identify hosts within the network. This means that a /17 network can have at most $2^{15} = 32,768$ computers.

You can view examples of network address at any network registry (discussed in the next section). As an exercise, visit www.arin.net and type in the following IP addresses in the WHOIS search box on the page. Confirm that the IP addresses belong to the organizations listed. What are the CIDR addresses of these organizations? How many computers can each of these networks support?

129.107.56.31 (University of Texas at Arlington)

204.154.83.103 (Shenandoah University)

## Obtaining IP addresses

Now that you know about IP addresses, you are probably curious about the procedure for getting an IP address for yourself or your organization. Initially, IP addresses were allocated directly by Jon Postel, who managed number assignments on the Internet.[8] But as the Internet has evolved and taken on commercial importance, formal procedures have been developed for allocating network addresses.

At the top level, the Internet Assigned Numbers Authority (IANA) is responsible for managing all the available IP addresses. There are 4 billion IP addresses as we have calculated earlier. IANA distributes this pool of IP addresses among regional registries. There are five such registries at this time—ARIN for North America; RIPE for Europe, Middle East, and Central Asia; APNIC for the Far East; LACNIC for Latin America; and AfriNIC for Africa. Users contact the registries within their respective continents to obtain IP addresses. Organizations can use their IP address blocks to assign IP addresses to hosts on their network anywhere in the world.

---

[8] To see how far we have come, please read the first paragraph of RFC 790 (http://tools.ietf.org/rfc/rfc790.txt) to see how easy it was to get network addresses in the early days.

The distribution of the overall IP address space among these registries is available from the IANA website.[9,10] Distributing IP addresses among registries has played a major role in democratizing the Internet by reducing American influence in the operation of the Internet.

For administrative convenience, the registries have adopted a policy of allocating addresses only to large telecom carriers. This limits the number of organizations the registries have to deal with. It also provides the registries with some assurance that organizations with address allocations will have suitable technical expertise to manage these address allocations. Finally, allocating IP addresses in large blocks also simplifies the global routing of packets by limiting the growth in the size of routing tables. This is discussed in Chapter 9.

Formally, the policy adopted by the registries for address allocation is specified in RFC 2050. Only networks that are connected to two or more networks are allowed to apply to the registries to obtain a network address.[11,12] Most organizations that need IP addresses will therefore contract with their local ISPs to obtain network addresses. The registries actively try not to allocate IP addresses directly to individuals and very small organizations.

You may note that unlike phone numbers, IP addresses have limited geographic significance. An IP address block will identify the network, but the network can expand globally. This is because the phone networks in most countries were government monopolies or state-regulated utilities. As a result, phone networks were organized along national boundaries. However, the Internet has developed in a more entrepreneurial environment where intellectual-property based boundaries are better recognized than national boundaries. As a result, IP network addresses identify networks (organizations), but not geographies.

# IPv6

The current version of IP has served network needs very well thus far. The primary focus of the book is therefore IPv4, the current version of IP. However, as the Internet gains popularity, one bottleneck of IP has come to the fore. This is the lack of availability of IP addresses. Many short-term solutions have been developed to deal with this problem. These are addressed in Chapter 7. The long-term solution to this problem is an upgrade of IP from version 4 to IP version 6. A brief discussion of IPv6 follows.

When IP was originally designed, the IP address space was expected to meet the needs of the Internet for the foreseeable future. The 32-bit IP address fields allowed more than 4 billion ($2^{32}$) IP addresses. This equated to about one IP address per human being on earth at the time. Given the relatively low penetration of telephones a generation ago and the exorbitant costs of computers in those days, allocating one IP address per human being was considered quite generous and adequate to meet the needs of the Internet.

However, the allocation of IP addresses has turned out to be quite inefficient. Some experts have expressed fears that the highest efficiency that will be attained in using IP

---

[9] A very good overview of IANA's role is at http://www.iana.org/numbers/.

[10] The distribution of IP addresses is available at http://www.iana.org/assignments/ipv4-address-space/.

[11] The guidelines for obtaining an initial address allocation from ARIN are at https://www.arin.net/resources/request/ipv4_initial_alloc.html.

[12] The prerequisites for such allocation are at http://www.arin.net/policy/nrpm.html#four.

addresses will be about 15%, which suggests that we will run out of IP addresses once about 600 million computers are connected to the Internet. We are getting quite close to that number and there is increasing concern about the shortage of IP addresses. At last count, there were about 625 million computers connected to the Internet.[13] However, others are optimistic about the availability of IPv4 addresses in the future.[14]

This problem of lack of availability of IP addresses is particularly acute outside the United States. The Internet originated in the U.S., and organizations in the U.S. were quicker in realizing the potential of the Internet. They also had relatively easier access to the Internet registry, which was located in California in its early days. Most large American organizations and telecom carriers therefore secured the required blocks of IP addresses.

As organizations and telecom carriers in other countries come online, they have to make do with the limited blocks of IP addresses that remain available. For example, most state universities in the United States have /16 IP addresses (65,536 addresses). By contrast, Tsinghua University, one of the top-ranked universities in China, the world's largest country by population, shares a /16 address pool with its ISP (211.151.0.0/16). As another example, BSNL, the national Internet backbone of India, the world's second largest country by population, has 131,072 IP addresses (61.0.0.0–61.1.255.255[15]). By contrast, one of the many address pools available to RoadRunner, a mid-sized ISP in the United States, has 712,704 IP addresses (97.96.0.0/13, 97.104.0.0/15, 97.106.0.0/17, 97.106.128.0/18, 97.106.192.0/19).[16] This is more than 5 times the size of the BSNL address pool which covers all of India.

As a result, many networks outside the United States are being forced into using IPv6 due to their huge populations and growing demand. In fact, more IPv6 address blocks have been allocated outside the U.S. than to the U.S.[17] IPv6 is also being used on a growing number of cellular networks to provide per-handset addressing because IPv4 simply doesn't have enough available addresses.

IP version 6 was defined in RFC 2460 in 1998 to expand the IP address space. The source and destination address fields in the upgraded version of IP are 128 bits in length, giving $2^{128}$ possible IP addresses. During the upgrade, the IP header was also simplified to take advantage of the highly robust network infrastructure available today. Recall that in the current version of IP, the header checksum of every packet is recalculated by every router, since each router decrements the time-to-live by 1. This adds computational complexity to routers, which is difficult to manage since many routers handle tens of thousands of packets each second. IPv6 relies on the robustness of the data-link layer and the inherently low error rates of modern networks. It eliminates the header checksum to greatly simplify the task of routers because there is no checksum to be computed by routers. Finally, IPv6 also adds header fields that can potentially allow telecom carriers to offer value-added services to customers.

The IPv6 address space is very large. With 128-bit IP addresses, IPv6 has $2^{128}$ addresses. $2^{128}$ is 340,282,366,920,938,463,463,374,607,431,768,211,45 (340 * $10^{36}$).

---

[13] http://ftp.isc.org/www/survey/reports/current/.

[14] http://www.cisco.com/web/about/ac123/ac147/archived_issues/ipj_6-4/ipv4.html.

[15] Verified 04/15/2010.

[16] RoadRunner also has other address pools including 24.24.0.0/14, 24.28.0.0/15, 24.92.160.0/19, 24.92.192.0/18, 24.93.0.0/16, 24.94.0.0/15.

[17] http://www.ipv6actnow.org/info/statistics/.

At first sight, this number seems large, but not particularly impressive. To get an idea of the magnitude of the number of IP addresses available in IPv6, consider that the surface area of the earth is 510 million square kilometers ($510*10^6*10^6$ m$^2$). Do the math and you get 600 billion trillion IP addresses for each square meter of the earth's surface. Since one square meter is approximately 10 square feet, this is 60 billion trillion IP addresses per square foot of the earth's surface—including the oceans, deserts, and other inhospitable areas. A typical home with about 1,000 square feet can therefore have 60 trillion trillion IPv6 addresses. It would be very surprising if we ever run out of IP addresses in IPv6.

Figure 12 shows the IPv6 header. Whereas the IPv4 header has fourteen fields, the IPv6 header only has eight fields, leading to a simpler protocol. The main change is the noticeable increase in the size of the address fields. The functions of the other fields are summarized below:

Version: This number is 6 for this version of IP.

Traffic class: This field is similar to the Type-of-Service field in IPv4. It allows senders to specify a class of service for the packet. This field is useful if routers are capable of offering different classes of service for different packets.

Though it sounds very promising, differentiating between service classes is quite complicated. As a familiar example of what it takes to offer differentiated services, consider high-occupancy vehicle (HOV) lanes on highways. These lanes enforce different classes of service to different users of the highway network. Since HOV lanes are typically empty, cars with more than one occupant can move faster. But implementing HOV lanes adds the complexity of lane designation, driver education, fine enforcement, etc.[18,19] Similarly, implementing traffic classes on computer networks requires that routers be capable of selecting packets belonging to each traffic class and rearranging their sequence in outgoing traffic according to priority. This is clearly a very complex task. Therefore, traffic class is quite difficult to implement in practice.

Flow label: This field is similar to the traffic-class field. It allows senders to designate a few packets for special handling. Again, this field is useful only if routers are capable of handling different packets differently.

Payload length: This field is similar to the total-length field in IPv4 and specifies the size of the packet data.

Next header: Again, this field is like the protocol field of IPv4 and specifies the transport-layer protocol that is using IP to deliver this packet. As in IPv4, the protocol numbers are defined in RFC 1700.

Hop limit: Finally, the hop-limit field is like the time-to-live field in IPv4. Each router decrements this field by one. When the hop limit reaches 0, the packet is discarded. As in IPv4, this field acts as a safety valve, removing damaged packets from the network.

---

[18] Emergency vehicles are another example of a differentiated multiple class. Again, it is not enough for these vehicles to flash lights and blow horns, it is also necessary that the rest of the traffic on the road allows quick passage to emergency vehicles.

[19] Fast-Pass offerings at theme parks are yet another example of differentiating between traffic classes. As you may have experienced, it is not enough to issue fast passes (traffic labeling), it is also necessary to create a separate fast-pass queue and enforce pass restrictions on this queue.

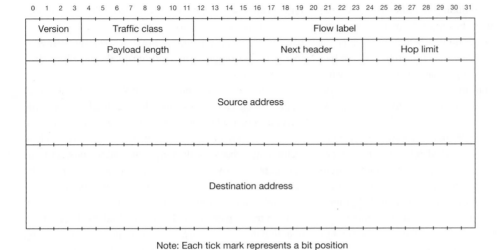

Note: Each tick mark represents a bit position

**FIGURE 12**   The IPv6 header

---

## CASE STUDY | WHO IS MINDING THE STORE, THE NETWORK OR THE MERCHANDISER?: WALMART

---

*Supply-chain management is the flow of information from cash registers to an order-entry system to ensure that product replenishment matches store needs. Walmart trucks are a familiar sight on America's highways, replenishing over 75,000 different items from over 145 distribution centers in over 4,000 stores around the country. What is not so visible is the computer network that carries sales and inventory data from point-of-sale systems back to headquarters, and which gives the company its unique competitive advantage. This data and its strategic use has been the key to the company's success in keeping costs low, while ensuring that the products are always stocked. While Walmart is the best known user of computer networks in the retailing industry, every large retailer now depends upon computer networks to manage inventory and distribution. Retailers that try to compete based on the expertise of merchandizing managers have a high performance bar.*

Sam Walton was driven from a young age, becoming the youngest boy in the state's history at that time to become an Eagle Scout. After running franchised variety stores in his early career, Sam and his younger brother James L. (Bud) Walton opened their first Discount City store in Rogers, Arkansas, in 1962. Sam Walton invested 95%, his brother 3%, and the store manager 2% in the store. The same year, Sebastian S. Kresge opened his first

Kmart store in Garden City, Michigan. Interestingly, Target started this same year, opening its first four branches around Minneapolis in 1962. Even more interestingly, Carrefour, the leading European grocer also opened its first hypermarket in 1962.

Kmart expanded rapidly at first. The second Walmart opened two years later in 1964, and five years after opening their first stores, Walmart had 18 stores with annual sales of $9 million. By this time, Kmart had 250 stores with total annual sales exceeding $800 million. Thus, in the 1960s, each Kmart store had over 6 times the sales of each Walmart store. During the 1960s, Sam Walton made many changes in the way he operated his stores, inspired largely by what Kmart was doing.

Move forward to 2000. Both Walmart and Kmart had slightly over 2,000 stores each. But Walmart's revenue for the year exceeded $200 billion, compared to less than $40 billion for Kmart. Not only did Walmart have higher revenues, it also earned over 10 times the profit margins that Kmart earned. How did the two chains reach these widely divergent outcomes from similar origins and goals? How did Kmart lose its huge early lead?

A big differentiator between the two companies is the way they use computer networks to manage information. By the mid-1960s, when he had just five to six stores running, Sam Walton was finding it difficult to track the inventory in his stores from the reports he received from his store managers. He understood that better record-keeping would help him figure out how much merchandise he had in each store, what was selling, what was not selling, what to mark-down to push out the store, and what to reorder. If shelves were empty less frequently, store sales would go up.

Based on this insight, Walmart first entered the computer age in 1969, by leasing an IBM 360 computer to manage inventory at its distribution center. Stores increasingly began to use electronic cash registers to transmit sales data back to distribution centers and headquarters for prompt inventory refills. The company built its first computer network using phone lines in 1977. The network was used to transmit information, such as orders, messages from buyers, and payroll data, speeding up restocking of merchandise in the stores. In 1979, the company built its first data center. In 1987, Walmart created its own satellite network. The increased bandwidth of this network compared to the telephone network speeded up credit-card authorizations and cut processing time in half from 14 seconds to 7 seconds, speeding check out and reducing the number of cashiers needed at check-out counters.

Once the network and computer systems were in place, Walmart adopted technologies such as EDI and developed a system called RetailLink to computerize the creation and exchange of documents, such as purchase orders, invoices, and receipts, between Walmart and its suppliers. The result was that suppliers such as Procter and Gamble could check on store inventory levels and sales data at Walmart in real time to determine their own manufacturing and delivery schedules. The system would aggregate sales of products from each vendor throughout the entire store chain and streamline payments to suppliers. Eventually these suppliers forced Kmart to also develop a system similar to RetailLink, called Kmart Information Network.

Another component of Walmart's success was its process of cross-docking at its distribution centers. In this procedure, manufacturers send full-trucks of merchandise to distribution centers. At these centers, goods are quickly repacked and loaded to trucks for delivery to stores, often within 48 hours of arrival. There is no storage of goods at warehouses. For this system to be successful without inventory accumulation or stock-outs, it was critically necessary that information about store demand be transmitted as far back in the supply chain as possible. Walmart's investments in its computer network enabled this information transmission.

The company's founder, Sam Walton, was famously frugal, flying coach class and sharing hotel rooms while traveling even when he was wealthy enough to afford a personal jet. Given this frugality, he was believed to hate technology because of its high costs, and to consider IT as very expensive overhead. The reality however, was that he scouted nationwide, pursuing experts in distribution, logistics, and technology to work for him. He even spent time at an IBM training center in 1966 to find talented executives to automate his company. He spent over two years wooing David Glass, who led the installation of the company's first computer network in 1977, and who later succeeded Sam Walton as the CEO of the company. Sam Walton has been quoted as saying, "It's only because of information technology that our store managers have a really clear sense of how they're doing . . . they get all kinds of information transmitted to them over the satellite on an amazingly timely basis: . . . up-to-the-minute point-of-sale data that tells them what is selling in their own store. . . ."

Walmart's computer network and distribution system began to give it an important cost advantage. By the mid-1980s, compared to industry average distribution costs of 5%, Walmart's distribution costs were 2%, giving it a 3% cost advantage over all other retailers, including Kmart.

### Meanwhile at Kmart

Whereas Walmart invested heavily in computer networks and other information technologies to identify what was selling at each store and what did not, Kmart always believed that the store manager had the best knowledge about the store's neighborhood. It was part of the company's belief system that a good store manager could accomplish anything. In 1973, when the almost-700 Kmart stores were sending almost 40,000 invoices daily to headquarters, that took weeks or even months to process, Kmart considered setting up a computerized system to collect and centralize all this information. But the plan was met with fierce opposition from store managers and merchandisers at the company who did not want to give up control. The computerization plan was dropped as a result of this opposition. Such was the faith of Kmart in the ability of its store managers and merchandisers that in the early 1990s, when IT developed store-wide reports identifying which products were not selling, store managers and senior managers chose to ignore the reports and ultimately asked IT to stop producing those reports. As late as 2002, Kmart gave store managers the authority to tailor the store's inventory.

Without a computer network and technology to provide a clear picture of what was selling and what was not selling, eventually, it was common at Kmart stores to see piles of unsold merchandise alongside hundreds of bare shelves of hot-selling and basic items. We know from personal experience that once a busy customer returns empty handed from a store, it is difficult to motivate the customer to return to the store. Kmart was beginning to fall behind.

When new management took over in 2000, they located and disposed of 15,000 trucks of unsellable inventory gathering dust over the years behind stores, more than 7 trucks per store. Even more interestingly, because of the poor information systems at Kmart, all this merchandise was unaccounted for. It was later discovered that what was happening was that when the company found good deals, they would buy large quantities of the product and unsold units were pushed into trucks behind stores.

By contrast to Kmart, which depended upon store managers to decide what to stock in a store, Walmart depended largely on combining sales data with publicly available information such as zip code profiling to decide what to stock in a store.

Without a clear vision for the role of IT in the company, between 1994 and 2002, Kmart had six CIOs. Each CEO/CIO threw out parts of systems developed by their predecessors and started building a new system from scratch. The systems that resulted were often incompatible with each other, limiting opportunities for integrating reports and data. When Kmart first installed computers in stores, it did not link cash registers to the computers, so it could not collect sales data in real time as Walmart could do. In 1987, the same year that Walmart invested $20 million on its satellite network, Kmart announced a $1 billion investment in IT. Even with this investment, Kmart developed one system for apparel and another system for the rest of the store, with no possibility of information exchange between the systems. In the meantime, Walmart systematically built a network that gave its executives a complete picture at any point in time, of where goods were and how fast they were moving in the entire chain.

Even in the 1990s, Kmart analysts did not have automated systems to generate chain-wide reports on supply and demand and had to use spreadsheets to integrate information from multiple data sources to gather this information. Most Kmart buyers did not know how to use computers to track sales and orders.

In 2002, Kmart filed for bankruptcy protection. That same year, for the first time, Walmart topped the Fortune 500 list as the biggest company in America, measured by annual revenue, earning $219.8 billion in revenue in 2001. The magazine noted that Walmart was the first service company to top the list.

## REFERENCES

"How Kmart Fell Behind." *Baselinemag,* December 10, 2001. http://www.baselinemag.com/c/a/Projects-Supply-Chain/How-Kmart-Fell-Behind/ (accessed 1/8/2010).

Ortega, Bob. *"In Sam We Trust: The Untold Story of Sam Walton and How Wal-Mart Is Devouring the World".* New York: Random House, 1998.

Piliouras, Teresa C. Mann. *"Network Design: Management and Technical Perspectives,"* 2nd ed. Auerbach Publications, 2004.

Public Broadcasting Service *"Is Wal-Mart Good for America? The Rise of Wal-Mart"* http://www.pbs.org/wgbh/pages/frontline/shows/walmart/transform/cron.html (accessed 12/31/2009).

Turner, Marcia Layton. *"Kmart's Ten Deadly Sins."* New York: John Wiley & Sons, 2003.

Vance, Sandra S., and Roy V. Scott. *"Wal-Mart: A History of Sam Walton's Retail Phenomenon."* New York: Twayne Publishers, 1994.

"Wal-Mart Timeline." http://walmartstores.com/AboutUs/7603.aspx (accessed 12/31/2009).

## SUMMARY

The network layer routes packets between networks. IP is used almost universally at the network layer and we briefly described the roles of the different fields of the IP header. Given their importance to network administrators, the chapter paid particular attention to IP addresses and the breakdown of IP addresses into a network part and an organization part. The relationship between the length of an address field and the number of computers that can be connected on the network was described. The CIDR notation to improve IP addressing flexibility was introduced. Finally, a brief description of IPv6 was provided.

## ABOUT THE COLOPHON

What is good for people can be good for networks. The quote in the colophon is attributed to Chinese philosopher Laozi in the 6th century BC. It is widely used as a motivational instrument in books and movies to help people move progressively towards their goals. Many significant goals seem unattainable at first. However, if people take even small steps that bring them successively closer to their goals, the goals can often be achieved.

As we saw in this chapter, this quote is an excellent visualization aid to describe how packet-switched networks route packets. Most routers are not directly connected to the final destination. Yet, they can pass each packet to a neighboring router that is one step closer to the destination. Eventually, all packets reach their destinations.

Maybe the next time you see a seemingly difficult goal, pause and think of how routers are successfully able to deliver billions of packets each day. They do this simply by helping packets take one well-directed step at a time. You might be able to do so the same with the tasks required to help you reach your goals in life.

## REVIEW QUESTIONS

1. Briefly describe routing—the primary function of the network layer.

2. How are IP addresses similar to MAC addresses? In what ways are the two addresses different?

3. What is the need for a computer address at the IP layer when computers also have a MAC address?

4. What are the advantages of designing the Internet in such a way that specialized devices called routers handle all the details of routing? What may be the possible disadvantages?

5. What are the advantages of designing IP as a best-effort protocol?

6. What were the primary motivations for the development of IP version 6?

7. Which, in your opinion, are the three most important fields in the IP header? Briefly describe the functions of these fields.

8. What is the need for the time-to-live field in the IP header?

9. What is the size of the largest possible IP packet?

10. How many objects can be uniquely labeled with 10-bit address labels?

11. You wish to assign unique labels to 200 objects using binary numbers. What is the minimum number of bits needed?

12. How would you represent 217 in binary? 168?

13. What decimal number does the binary number 10001101 represent? 11011001?

14. What is *dotted decimal notation*?

15. What information is conveyed by each part of a three-part IP address?

16. How are the 32 bits of an IP address organized in a typical large network?

17. Find the IP addresses of any five department websites at your school. Do you observe any patterns in the IP addresses of the websites? (You can find the IP addresses for URLs in many ways. Many websites

will give you the IP address if you provide a URL. An example is http://www.selfseo.com/find_ip_ address_of_a_website.php. Alternately, you can open a command prompt or terminal window and type in nslookup, for example, nslookup www.msu.edu.)

18. In what way are the 32 bits of an IP address organized similarly to the 10 digits of phone numbers? In what way are they different?

19. What were the three address classes in early IP networks? How many hosts (computers) could be accommodated in a network in each address class?

20. What are the disadvantages of using address classes? How does CIDR overcome these disadvantages?

21. What is *registry* in the context of IP addresses?

22. What are *regional registries*? What is the need for regional registries?

23. What requirements must an organization satisfy in order to obtain IP addresses directly from a registry?

25. On your home computer, what is the IP address reported by ipconfig/all (Windows) or ifconfig (MAC/ Linux)?

26. From your home computer, go to www.whatismyip .com and make a note of your IP address. Type this address into the search box at www.arin.net. Who is the owner of that address block?

## HANDS-ON EXERCISES

This chapter introduced IP addresses. The hands-on exercise in this chapter will use two handy utilities that are very useful to gather network layer information—ipconfig and ping. While ipconfig was introduced in Chapter 3, ping will be introduced here.

### ipconfig

In the hands-on exercise in Chapter 3, you used ipconfig (or ifconfig) to obtain information on the MAC addresses of the network interfaces on your computer. In this exercise, you will continue the same exercise to get information about the IP addresses assigned to these interfaces. You have already seen a preview of this information in Chapter 3 because ipconfig provides information on both the MAC addresses and IP addresses. Figure 13 shows an example ipconfig output on Windows XP. The IP address of the Ethernet interface in the example is 131.247.95.118. (Note that the ipconfig output shown in Chapter 3 was from Windows Vista and the output here is from Windows XP. We see that whereas Windows Vista lists all interfaces in the ipconfig output, including those that are not connected, Windows XP only shows the configuration information for connected interfaces. Software vendors regularly update utilities based on user feedback).

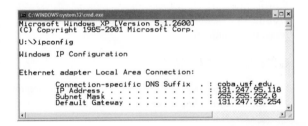

**FIGURE 13**  ipconfig output showing IP address of Ethernet interface

Use ipconfig (or ifcfg on the MAC/ Linux) to answer the following questions:

1. What are the IP addresses assigned to the interfaces on your computer?

2. We have seen in this chapter that the network parts of IP addresses identify the owners of IP address blocks. Use the WHOIS search facility at the American Registry for Internet numbers (http://www.arin.net) to search the WHOIS database and identify the owner of the address block to which your IP address belongs. You can do this by visiting http://www.arin.net → typing in your IP address into the search WHOIS field on the site → press enter or click the button next to the search field. (Please see Figure 14 for reference.) Follow the link to the "related organization's POC

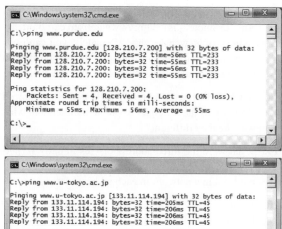

**FIGURE 15** Using ping

**FIGURE 14** Searching the ARIN database for IP address block ownership

records" just below the table to gather information on the following fields associated with your IP address:

*where is 'c'?*

a. OrgName
b. NetRange
d. NetType
e. NameServer
f. OrgTechName
g. OrgTechPhone

3. Is the OrgName the same as your ISP's name? (If not, we will explore the main reason for this in Chapter 7).

## Ping

The network layer is responsible for host-level routing, i.e., the layer makes sure that packets are delivered to a remote computer if the remote computer is connected to the Internet. This role of IP can be reverse-engineered to detect whether a remote computer is connected to the Internet and networking has been properly configured on the remote computer. If the IP software on your computer can

deliver a packet to the remote computer, we know that the remote computer must be connected to the Internet and its networking software must be properly configured. If IP cannot deliver packets to the remote computer, there must be some problem in network connectivity between the two computers.

Ping is the utility that is used to check for network connectivity. Ping sends a special form of IP packets called ICMP ECHO packets to the target host. When the target host receives these IP packets, it sends back a reply. Ping reports the round-trip time for the packet request-response cycle, giving an indication of the network connectivity between the two computers. Ping is extremely simple to use as can be seen from the examples in Figure 15. In the example, we use the ping command to check for connectivity to the web server at Purdue University and the University of Tokyo.

The ping output also reports on the average packet round-trip times. The two examples in Figure 15 show that packet round-trip times depend upon the destinations. The ping requests originated from Tampa, Florida. It takes 4 times as long for a reply to be received from Tokyo (205 ms) as it takes for a reply from Purdue (55 ms). This is understandable since Tokyo is much farther from Tampa than is Indiana (where Purdue is located).

The `ping` utility can also be used to confirm network connectivity and configuration at your own computer. If you encounter network connectivity issues, you can `ping` a remote computer that you know is connected to the Internet. If you do not hear a `ping` response, it is likely that the problem is at your end. You may need to check a few sites because many sites do not respond to `ping` requests for security reasons.

Answer the following questions.

1. How does ping work? Use Wikipedia or other resource to write a brief description of how ping works.

2. Use Wikipedia or other resource to write a brief description of the Internet Control Message Protocol (ICMP) and its use.

3. Ping the website of your university. Show the output. What is the average round-trip time?

4. Ping the website of a university in a neighboring city or town. Show the output. What is the average round-trip time?

5. Ping the website of a company located abroad. Show the output. What is the average round-trip time?

6. You wake up one day to find that you are unable to connect to the Internet from home. You make some calls to your friends and neighbors and find that they have no issues connecting to the Internet. You conclude that the fault is within your home. As seen in Figure 16, there are two networking components within your home—your computer and your home router. As seen in Figure 17, the IP address of the home router is the IP address of the default gateway in your `ipconfig` output, and home routers typically respond to `ping` requests. How can you use `ping` to determine whether the network

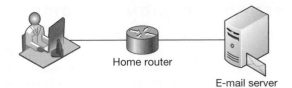

Home router

E-mail server

**FIGURE 16**   Home network connection

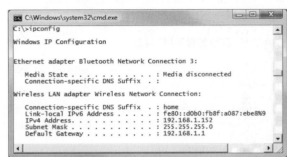

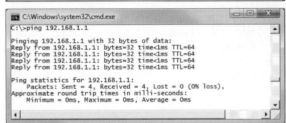

**FIGURE 17**   Pinging the local home router

connectivity problem is at the home router or at your computer?

7. The creator of ping has an interesting description of its creation at http://ftp.arl.army.mil/~mike/ping.html. What is the most interesting story narrated by the author of the use of ping for network trouble-shooting?

## CRITICAL THINKING QUESTION

The genetic code uses three-letter DNA-words, where each letter can take four values—A, C, G, and T. How many words are possible in the DNA dictionary?[20]

---

[20]This is from Richard Dawkins, "The greatest show on earth: The evidence for evolution," 2009, Free Press. The genetic code is universal, all but identical across animals, plants, fungi, bacteria, archaea, and viruses, and is believed to provide strong evidence of evolution. The 64 DNA words are translated into 20 amino acids and one punctuation mark, which toggles reading. The 64-word dictionary is universal across the living kingdoms.

## NETWORK DESIGN EXERCISE

In this exercise, we estimate the CIDR address block requirements for Coolco. For example, if Coolco needs about 8,000 IP addresses, you would say that Coolco needs a /19 CIDR block. This is because a /19 address block uses 19 bits for the network part of the IP address, leaving $32 - 19 = 13$ bits available for the host part. This allows unique labeling for $2^{13} = 8,192$ hosts. Answer the following questions:

1. If each computer on Coolco's network is allocated an IP address, how many IP addresses is Coolco likely to need?

2. Based on this estimate, what is a CIDR address-block size suitable for Coolco?

## CASE QUESTIONS

1. Based on the case, what computer networking technologies do retailers like Walmart use?

2. Based on the case, how do retailers like Walmart use computer networks to lower the costs of goods sold?

3. What is *cross-docking*?

4. Among the processes at a retailer that can be managed using IT are merchandise planning, sourcing, distribution, and store operations. Briefly define each process using any information source available to you (such as Wikipedia or Google).

5. For each of these processes, give an example of how IT can be used to manage the process. If your example uses computer networks, highlight the role of the network.

6. Based on the case, what are some reasons that Kmart did not achieve the same benefits from IT investments as Walmart?

## CHAPTER 5

# Transport Layer

*I view the fundamental problem*
*of resource sharing to be the*
*problem of inter-process communication.*

—D.C. WALDEN, RFC 62

## Overview

This chapter covers the transport layer. The network and lower layers deliver packets between computers across networks to the best of their capability; the transport layer provides all the remaining bookkeeping functions necessary for reliable data transfer between applications on these computers.

At the end of this chapter you should know about:

- the need for a transport layer
- Transmission Control Protocol (TCP), the popular transport-layer protocol
- TCP functions, including segmentation, reliability, flow-control, multiplexing, and connection-establishment
- the fields of the TCP header
- UDP, a simpler protocol at the transport layer

## The need for a transport layer

We saw in Chapter 4 that the network layer does best-effort delivery of packets between any two computers located anywhere on the Internet. Since computer networks are used for data transfer, and the network layer already performs the task of data delivery, what is the need for yet another layer of software for data communication? What value can the transport layer add?

It turns out that some additional processing is required before the data-transfer capability offered by the network layer can become useful for computer applications. Three tasks are vital. (1) The network layer can accept at most 65,535 bytes of data per packet. If an application has a bigger block of data to transfer (audio and video files come to mind), some entity needs to chop the larger block of data into smaller segments before handing the segments to the network layer. This task is called segmentation. If the transport layer did not perform segmentation, the application developers would have to do it while developing their applications. (2) The network layer only provides best-effort delivery and may drop packets or duplicate packets. Some entity needs to resolve these losses and duplications. Again, if the transport layer did not do this, the applications would have to do it. This task is called reliability. (3) The network layer does not distinguish between applications on the computer. It simply sends data from one computer to the other. Once the packets reach the destination computer, some entity needs to distribute incoming data packets to the appropriate application on the computer. This task is called multiplexing because it allows multiple applications on a computer to share a common network link.

Therefore, the transport layer has to perform many functions to ensure reliable data delivery. At the sending end, the transport layer receives data from the application layer and breaks down the application data into segments. The transport layer keeps track of these segments to account for packet loss or duplication by the network layer. The transport layer also provides a mechanism to distinguish between data segments created by each individual application on the computer. Finally, the transport layer provides for graceful use of network resources by allowing receiving computers to specify the data transfer rate.

Figure 1 shows the placement of the transport layer relative to the network layer (IP) and the application layer. The transport layer receives data from applications and performs all the bookkeeping functions described above to make the inherently unreliable computer networks (network layer) appear reliable to applications. The result is that, as far as computer applications are concerned, apart from network delays, there is no difference between accessing data from the local hard drive and from across the network.

The most popular transport layer protocol is the Transmission Control Protocol (TCP). The TCP/IP stack derives its name from this protocol. *TCP is a highly reliable host-to-host transport-layer protocol over packet-switched networks.* Most end-user

↳ *end-to-end*

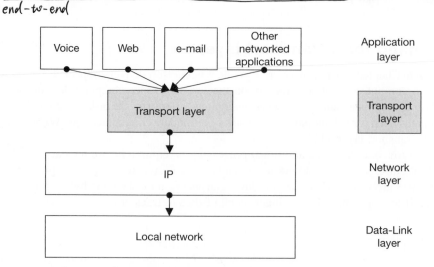

**FIGURE 1**  Transport layer relative to applications and the Network layer

applications such as e-mail and the web, use TCP. However, many applications do not need the segmentation and reliability offered by TCP. For these applications a simpler transport-layer protocol called the User Datagram Protocol (UDP) has been defined. UDP eliminates almost all the computational processing associated with TCP. Most of this chapter focuses on TCP. The last section of the chapter looks at UDP, in particular, the various scenarios where UDP is preferable to TCP.

UDP was defined in RFC 768 in 1980. TCP was defined in RFC 793 in 1981.

# Transmission Control Protocol (TCP)

At a very high level, the operation of TCP may be explained as follows. At the sending end, computer applications generate the data that needs to be transmitted over the network. Examples of such data include e-mail, a web page from a web server, or a movie stream by a media server. The application hands this data off to TCP for transmission over the network. If the data to be transmitted is large, TCP first breaks the data into segments smaller than 65 KB (the data limit for IP). TCP then assigns sequence numbers to each segment and hands over the numbered segments to IP. IP transmits these segments over to the receiving computer.

At the receiving end, when TCP gets the segments from IP, it uses the sequence numbers assigned by the sender TCP to reassemble the data into its original form. TCP then passes the reconstructed data to the application. For example, if a web server sends an image that is about 100 KB in size, the sender TCP could break the image into two segments and label the segments as segment 1 and segment 2. At the receiving end, TCP would use the segment numbers 1 and 2 to reassemble the fragments in the correct order. The reconstructed image would then be passed to the browser. Neither the sending web server nor the receiving web browser (user applications) would be aware of the segmentation of the image into fragments by TCP during transmission.

To summarize, TCP provides a reliable communication service between applications over networks of arbitrary complexity and any level of unreliability. The only thing computer applications have to do to use the network is to pass data to TCP. TCP takes care of all communication complexities on behalf of the applications. TCP delegates the task of best-effort routing to IP, but performs all other bookkeeping required for reliable communication.

# TCP functions

We have already seen that TCP has to perform three essential functions to resolve the imperfections of IP—segmentation, reliability, and multiplexing. In addition, as you will see, TCP also performs two more useful tasks—flow control and connection establishment. We now look at each of these tasks in detail.

## Segmentation

The segmentation function of TCP allows IP, which has a maximum packet size of 65,535 KB, to transfer application data of arbitrary size. TCP assists IP by breaking application data into segments of manageable size for IP. These segments are called datagrams.

A note on packet names. We have seen three names for data packets so far—frames, packets, and datagrams. The data created at the data-link layer is called a frame. At the network layer, IP creates packets and at the transport layer, TCP and UDP create datagrams. Using these names consistently instead of the generic name—packet—facilitates professional discussion. If you are talking about frames, everyone understands that you are talking about the data-link layer.

TCP adds a sequence number to every datagram before transmission. Sequence numbers help the receiving TCP to reorder datagrams even if they are received out of order from the network. TCP assigns a sequence number to each byte of data and places the sequence number of the first byte of data in a datagram as the sequence number of the datagram.

Figure 2 shows an example of segmentation by TCP. In the example, the application is trying to send 930 bytes of data over the network. In real life, such a small data block would not be segmented; however, using small numbers keeps our example simple.

Say the transport layer decides to segment the data into three segments of similar sizes—300 bytes, 320 bytes, and 310 bytes. The first segment is numbered 1 as expected. The sequence number of the second segment also accounts for the length of the first segment and is assigned sequence number 301. This number is calculated as the sequence number of the first segment + the length of the first segment. Since the second segment has a length of 320 bytes, the third segment has a sequence number of 621 (301 + 320). This is shown in Figure 2.

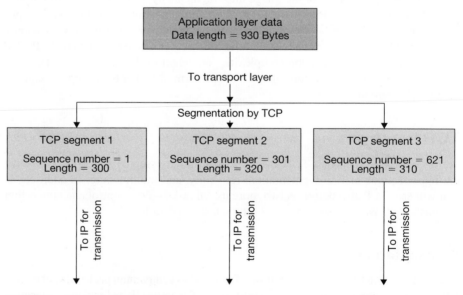

**FIGURE 2**  Segmentation by TCP

Therefore in general:

Sequence number of a TCP segment = sequence number of the previous segment +
length of previous segment

What is the advantage of using a scheme that assigns sequence numbers by data bytes and not by datagram? In other words, do we have any advantage in using the numbering scheme shown in Figure 2 instead of the simpler scheme where the segments would be numbered 1, 2, and 3? The primary advantage of the numbering scheme shown in Figure 2 and used by TCP is that the scheme makes acknowledgments easier. Since every data byte in TCP gets a sequence number, the receiver has the flexibility to acknowledge by data byte rather than by segment boundary. The receiver is not constrained to acknowledge complete segments. In other words, in our example, it is possible for the receiver to acknowledge that 400 bytes or 600 bytes have been received successfully. TCP generally acknowledges datagrams by datagram boundary, but TCP can acknowledge partial datagrams because of the sequence numbering scheme used in TCP.

Segmentation has both advantages and disadvantages. Let us start with the advantages. If every data byte has equal likelihood of being delivered in error, smaller segments are less likely to encounter errors during transmission. Therefore segmentation reduces the chances of error. In case a segment does get corrupted during transmission, only the corrupted segment needs to be retransmitted. Without segmentation, the entire data block would have to be retransmitted if even a single byte of data encountered a transmission error. Therefore, segmentation reduces the need for reprocessing in case of error. Finally, with segmentation, it is easier for routers to handle segments. Imagine sending an entire DVD movie as one data segment. A regular DVD has about 4 GB of data. If we were to send out a 4-GB data segment, every router along the path would have to dedicate 4 GB of memory to store the packet before forwarding it to the next router. Clearly, this would make routers extremely expensive. Therefore, segmentation simplifies packet handling.

You may now better appreciate the analogy between packetization and knock-down kits that was introduced in Chapter 1. A lot of furniture is shipped as knock-down kits. These kits are easy to handle, take less space and can be transported in any general-purpose truck, lowering costs. The trade-off is that customers need to reassemble the furniture at home. The knocking down and labeling of each furniture part is akin to what the sending TCP does. Reassembly of furniture based on part labels by end users at home is akin to the TCP receiving function. In the DVD example above, the DVD is like the table that is difficult to ship. The data segments of the DVD are like the kits that are easy to ship, though slightly complex to reassemble.

The primary disadvantage of segmentation is the additional complexity introduced by segmentation and reassembly. The sending TCP needs to compute sequence numbers and the receiving TCP needs to reassemble the segments based on sequence numbers. It is possible for segments to get lost or duplicated and these duplicates and losses need to be identified and processed appropriately.

## Reliability

TCP makes the network reliable. The basic mechanism for getting reliability is for the receiver to periodically acknowledge received datagrams. If an acknowledgment is not received within a reasonable amount of time, the sender assumes the worst and resends the datagram. This basic mechanism is illustrated in Figure 3.

In the example of Figure 3, the sender begins transmission and the first segment is acknowledged successfully. When the first segment is acknowledged, the second segment is transmitted. Unfortunately, a router on the return path loses power and the acknowledgment is lost, even though the segment was received successfully by the receiver. After waiting for some time (called the time-out interval), the sender resends the segment and this time the acknowledgment successfully reaches the sender.

As the example shows, it is possible for segments to be duplicated. Note how the receiver gets two segments with sequence number 301 indicating that these segments have duplicate data and the receiver can discard one of them. The TCP software takes care of handling duplicate datagrams.

In addition to keeping track of datagrams, there is a second dimension of reliability offered by TCP. This is in ensuring that the received datagrams are complete. Recall that the maximum frame size in Ethernet is about 1,500 bytes, but the maximum IP packet size is 65,536 bytes. The fragmentation function of IP allows further fragmentation of packets to fit Ethernet frames. It is possible that some Ethernet frames may get lost during transmission. Since IP does not detect packet-data errors (it only detects header errors), when the receiving TCP attempts to reassemble such a segment,

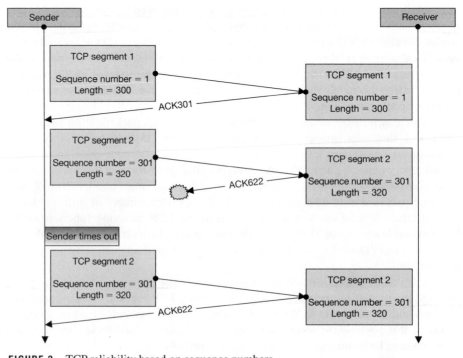

**FIGURE 3**　TCP reliability based on sequence numbers

it needs a mechanism to know that the segment is incomplete. For this purpose, TCP also computes a checksum to each datagram. This checksum is not as robust as the data-link layer CRC, but it is good enough to detect damaged segments.

When a TCP segment is identified as being damaged, the receiving TCP does not have to do anything. It can simply discard the segment and wait for the sender to timeout and resend the segment.

## Multiplexing

The third essential function of TCP is multiplexing. *Multiplexing is the combining of two or more information channels onto a common transmission medium.* Multiplexing at the transport layer allows multiple applications to share the same network interface card and network link. This is a good place to highlight an important capability of computers as communication devices. You may have noticed this difference between computers and telephones. Telephones can only help in one (albeit, highly useful) communication task—talk. You pick up the phone, dial a number, and talk. More interestingly from the point of view of multiplexing, you can only carry out one telephone conversation at a time. But computers can multitask. You can browse the web (with multiple browser tabs open simultaneously, even streaming different video channels on each tab), chat on an instant messaging client, listen to streaming music, monitor a stock quote service, and watch live traffic updates. And, you can do all these simultaneously on your computer. This is where multiplexing comes in.

Each of these applications is sending and receiving data segments. All these data segments go out of the same Ethernet or other network link. Yet, we never see computers displaying information in wrong windows. So, clearly the computer has a mechanism to distinguish between packets coming to each application on the common link. This is accomplished by the multiplexing function of TCP. In the context of TCP, the information flowing to and from each individual application is an information channel and the common transmission medium is the network connection of the computer.

TCP enables multiplexing by providing multiple port addresses within each host. Each application that needs a network connection, a browser tab for example, is assigned a port number. Each port therefore identifies a communication channel on the host.

If you have developed network applications, you may be familiar with the concept of a "socket." A network (IP) address and a port address together constitute a communication socket. The application can send data over the network using the socket. Each network connection is then identified by a pair of sockets: the port and IP addresses of the sender are the socket at one end of the connection and the port and IP addresses of the receiver are the socket at the other end of the connection. Together, the two sockets make up the network connection.

Figure 4 shows an example of various applications on a client PC simultaneously connecting to applications on various computers on the Internet. Each application on the PC is assigned a separate port by the client operating system. Network traffic related to the application leaves from and arrives at the assigned ports. When packets come to the client PC, the computer can use the port numbers to identify what application to pass the packets to.

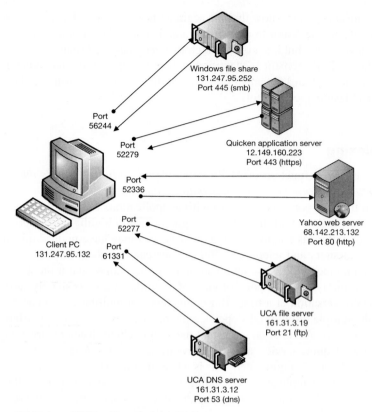

**FIGURE 4**    TCP ports and multiplexing

In Figure 4, the web browser is using port 52336 to connect to the Yahoo web server. The Yahoo web server is running on port 80. Packets leaving the client PC have a source port address of 52336 and a destination port address of 80. Similarly, packets going to the Windows file sharing have a source port address of 56244 and a destination port address of 445. These port numbers uniquely identify the applications running on the respective computers.

From a networking point of view, there are two very interesting questions here: (1) How does the client PC know the IP address of the UCA file server because, after all, no end user ever types in IP addresses into any application? (2) How does the client know that the UCA DNS server is running on port 53 because again, after all, nobody ever specifies a port number while using the Internet?

We will address the first question in Chapter 7 when we discuss DNS. DNS is a service that translates site names such as www.uca.edu to IP addresses such as 161.31.3.35. The second question is addressed later in this section.

Computer port numbers are a lot like airport gates. The runway at the airport is analogous to the computer's network cable. Just as all aircraft landing at an airport share the runway, all network traffic related to the computer is carried by the cable. The airport code is analogous to the computer's IP address—just as aircraft identify an airport on the air-traffic network by its airport code, packets identify a computer on

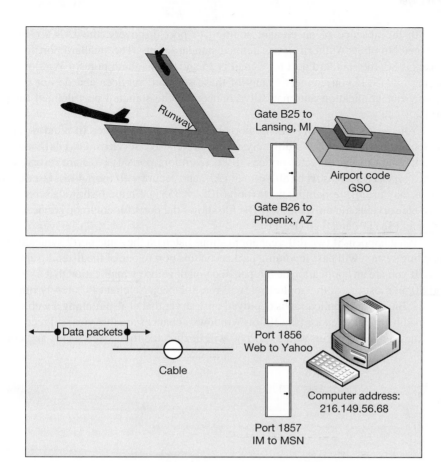

**FIGURE 5**    Analogy between TCP ports and airport gates

the computer network by its IP address. Port numbers are like airport gates. A single airport can serve multiple destinations and airlines simultaneously by parking different aircrafts at different gates. Similarly, a single computer can serve multiple applications connecting to multiple destinations. Figure 5 shows this analogy.

In Figure 5, the aircraft at gate B25 might be a USAIR Airbus A320 leaving for Lansing, Michigan, arriving at gate 7 of the Capital Region International Airport in Lansing. The aircraft at gate B26 might be a Southwest Boeing 737 going to Phoenix, Arizona arriving at gate D7 of Phoenix Sky Harbor airport. Similarly, packets leaving port 1856 on the computer might carry web traffic to port 80 at yahoo.com, while packets leaving port 1857 might carry IM traffic to port 1863 at MSN.

We can now turn our attention to the question raised earlier. And, this is the last issue that needs to be resolved to make port addressing work—how do we know what port to connect to? The client's port number is assigned by the local operating system and this information is available to the receiver in the incoming datagram. But how do we know what number to put in the destination port address field? How do we know that the web server is listening on port 80? If we want to access a Windows file server, how do we know what port to connect to?

In the absence of an elegant solution to port discovery, the IANA (Internet Assigned Numbers Authority)[1] has defined standard ports. The standard port for web servers is 80, the standard port for e-mail is 25 and the standard port for Windows file sharing is 445. If you connect to any of these standard services and do not specify a port, your application automatically connects to the standard port defined for the service.

You can see the list of standard ports known to your computer. In Windows, they are defined in the file C:\Windows\System32\drivers \etc\services. On UNIX derivatives, they are in the file /etc/services. By convention, ports 1–1023 are reserved for defined services such as web (80), e-mail (25), and secure web (port 443). User applications may use the remaining ports (ports 1024–65535). Figure 6 shows a screenshot of the etc\services file on Windows. The file shows the ports for common services such as e-mail (SMTP) and web (HTTP).

What happens if two different applications listen on the same port? Typically, the operating system will pass incoming packets on this port to one of the listening applications. If you are an application developer, and you develop an application that listens on port 80, in most cases, the application will run fine because client PCs rarely run web servers. But if your application is deployed on a server that is also running a web server provided by the OS vendor (say IIS on Windows), chances are that you will receive an error message and packets sent to port 80 will be directed to the web server and not to

*[handwritten: TCP : port 80 UDP = port 23]*

```
services - Notepad
File  Edit  Format  View  Help
# copyright (c) 1993-2004 Microsoft corp.
#
# This file contains port numbers for well-known services defined by IANA
#
# Format:
#
# <service name>   <port number>/<protocol>   [aliases...]   [#<comment>]
#

echo             7/tcp
echo             7/udp
discard          9/tcp        sink null
discard          9/udp        sink null
systat          11/tcp        users                     #Active users
systat          11/udp        users                     #Active users
daytime         13/tcp
daytime         13/udp
qotd            17/tcp        quote                     #Quote of the day
qotd            17/udp        quote                     #Quote of the day
chargen         19/tcp        ttytst source             #Character generator
chargen         19/udp        ttytst source             #Character generator
ftp-data        20/tcp                                  #FTP, data
ftp             21/tcp                                  #FTP, control
ssh             22/tcp                                  #SSH Remote Login Protocol
telnet          23/tcp
smtp            25/tcp        mail                      #Simple Mail Transfer Protocol
time            37/tcp        timserver
time            37/udp        timserver
rlp             39/udp        resource                  #Resource Location Protocol
nameserver      42/tcp        name                      #Host Name Server
nameserver      42/udp        name                      #Host Name Server
nicname         43/tcp        whois
domain          53/tcp                                  #Domain Name Server
domain          53/udp                                  #Domain Name Server
bootps          67/udp        dhcps                     #Bootstrap Protocol Server
bootpc          68/udp        dhcpc                     #Bootstrap Protocol Client
tftp            69/udp                                  #Trivial File Transfer
gopher          70/tcp
finger          79/tcp
http            80/tcp        www www-http              #World Wide Web
hosts2-ns       81/tcp                                  #HOSTS2 Name Server
hosts2-ns       81/udp                                  #HOSTS2 Name Server
kerberos        88/tcp        krb5 kerberos-sec         #Kerberos
```

**FIGURE 6** etc/services file on Windows

---

[1] This is the same agency that has ultimate responsibility for IP addresses.

your application. Your application will appear unresponsive as a result. As an application developer, therefore, it is a good idea to avoid the reserved ports (0-1023).[2]

All operating systems provide a utility, netstat, to view port usage. On Windows, you can run netstat by typing netstat on the command prompt (start → Programs → Accessories → Command prompt → netstat). Some useful options require netstat to run with administrative privileges. To run the command prompt with administrative privileges, right-click the command prompt application in the Accessories program group and select "Run as administrator". Figure 7 and Figure 8 show the output of the netstat utility with some useful options.

netstat–b is an excellent way to identify potential network security weaknesses on a computer. This utility identifies all applications on your computer that are

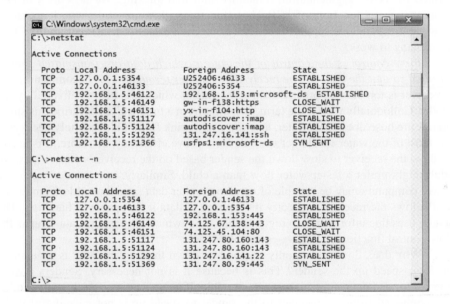

**FIGURE 7** Viewing used ports with the netstat utility

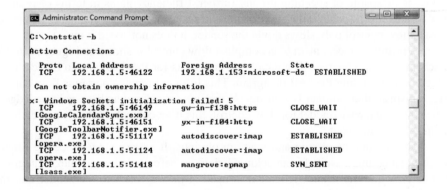

**FIGURE 8** netstat–b to show the executables that are using ports

---

[2] Also, in Linux and UNIX systems, root privileges are sometimes necessary to listen on the reserved ports. Hence, as a developer, avoid the reserved ports when possible.

communicating on the network (ESTABLISHED state) or have the potential to communicate (LISTEN state), and the ports on which they are expecting packets. When you look at the output of netstat–b, all applications you see listed should be known or expected applications. Any unexpected application needs to be investigated as a potential security hazard. You can use this information to stop unnecessary applications or use a firewall to block packets coming from unsafe locations on the Internet to these open applications.

## Flow control

In the last three parts of this section, we have looked at the three critical tasks performed by TCP—segmentation, reliability, and multiplexing. We now look at two additional useful functions of TCP. These functions allow graceful network operation (flow control) and one support function (connection establishment) required for TCP sequencing to work.

*Flow control is the control of the rate at which data are transmitted from a terminal so that the data can be received by another terminal.* This becomes useful if a receiver is too slow to process data at the rate at which it is being delivered by the sender. Colloquially we use the term "drinking from a fire hose" to describe this situation. A fire hose does serve water, and you could drink from it if absolutely necessary, but most of the water would get wasted. To improve efficiency, therefore, it is useful to allow the receiver to slow down the sender based on the receiver's capabilities. An adult might prefer a faster water flow than a child. Similarly, in computer networks, newer computers may be capable of handling higher data rates than older computers. TCP allows the receiver to specify the amount of data it is capable of handling. The sender uses this information to regulate the rate at which it transmits data. This is the flow-control function of TCP.

Why does flow control only try to slow down the sender? Why is no attempt made to speed up the sender? This is because it is not necessary. Senders always attempt to send data at the highest rate possible. If a receiver is faster than the sender, any command from the receiver to the sender to speed up is not meaningful if the sender is incapable of speeding up any further. Efficiency gains in terms of reduced loss of data are possible only by allowing the receiver to reduce the sender's speed. Hence, flow control only slows down the sender, it does not speed it up.

A primitive mechanism to accomplish flow control is shown in Figure 9. In this mechanism, the sender sends a datagram, and waits for the datagram to be acknowledged before sending the next datagram. This is an extremely courteous flow control mechanism in that no data is sent unless the previous data has been acknowledged. Since this is the basic model for flow control, this flow-control mechanism even has a name—"stop-and-wait."

The limitations of stop-and-wait are obvious. It is very slow. Once the sender sends a datagram, it waits for an acknowledgment before sending the next datagram. Similarly, while the acknowledgment is making its way back to the sender and the next datagram is reaching the receiver across the network, the receiver sits idle. Therefore, this flow control mechanism is not particularly useful. Clearly, there is room to improve efficiency in terms of increasing data-transfer speeds.

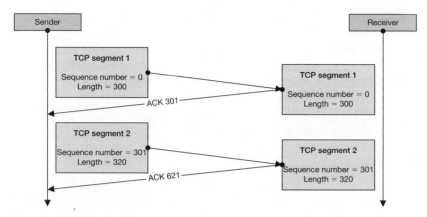

**FIGURE 9**    Stop-and-wait flow control, a very simple flow-control mechanism

TCP improves upon stop-and-wait flow control by allowing the receiver to indicate a "window size" with every acknowledgment. *The window size is the amount of data the receiver is capable of processing.* This is therefore the amount of data that the sender may send without waiting for an acknowledgment from the receiver. Using the window-size information, the stop-and-wait flow control of Figure 9 may be improved as shown in Figure 10. In the figure, the receiver begins by announcing a window size of 700 bytes. Assuming that the sender has 620 bytes of data to send, since 620 < 700, it sends all the data at once, without waiting for an acknowledgment from the receiver for the first datagram. Please note that it is unlikely that such a small amount of data would be split into two datagrams, but the figure illustrates how multiple datagrams might be sent without waiting for an acknowledgment. TCP acknowledgments are cumulative. The receiver acknowledges this data by sending a datagram, labeled ACK 621 in Figure 10. ACK 621 (value of 621 in the acknowledgement number field) mean s that all data up to byte 620 has been received successfully.

Figure 10 is the basic mechanism used by TCP to implement flow control. Figure 11 shows how this mechanism works when the sender has larger quantities of data to send. When the sender receives the window size from the receiver, it transmits the permitted quantity of data. The transmitted data may be said to be in the "sent window" of the sender. The data in the "sent window" has been transmitted but has not yet been acknowledged by the receiver. The "width" of the "sent window" is equal to or less than the advertised window size. The sender holds on to the data in the "sent window" because it is possible that there could be transmission errors which may require some data within the "sent window" to be resent. If the sender sends more data, it might overwhelm the receiver, leading to lost packets and wasteful use of network resources. When the sender reaches the limit on transmission permissions, it waits for an acknowledgment from the receiver.

When an acknowledgment is received (datagram with ACK 601; window size 900 in Figure 11), the sender is free to send more data. In our example, the receiver has advertised a higher window size and so the sender can now send up to 900 bytes of data starting from sequence number 601. The example shows how the sender sends

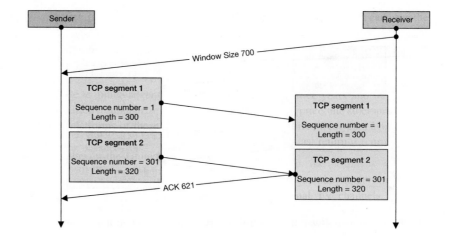

**FIGURE 10** Using TCP window size to refine stop-and-wait flow control

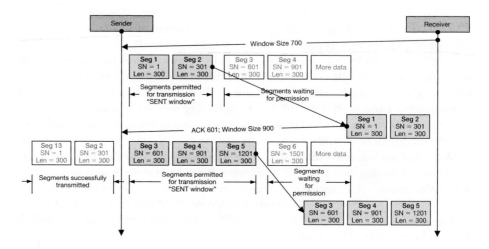

**FIGURE 11** Sliding-window flow control

this data, places the data in the "sent window" and waits for acknowledgments before sending more data.[3]

Since the "sent window" keeps sliding over the data to be sent, the flow-control mechanism is called sliding-window flow control. *Sliding-window flow control uses a variable-length window that allows a sender to transmit a specified number of data units before an acknowledgement is received.*

## Connection establishment

We now come to the last function of TCP. This relates to the initialization of sequence numbers for a TCP connection and exchange of this initialization information between sender and receiver.

---

[3] There are a number of good online animations to demonstrate TCP. One of these is linked from the companion website.

We have thus far used a sequence number of 1 for the first byte of data in all our examples. While this is intuitive to understand, the problem with this simple scheme is that it becomes difficult to identify duplicate datagrams, particularly if a user revisits a network destination in quick succession from the same client. If a receiver gets two datagrams with sequence numbers of 1 from the same computer, it becomes difficult to determine whether the datagrams are duplicates or two different connections.

To overcome this confusion, TCP ensures that TCP numbers are not repeated in quick succession. This is done by generating the initial sequence number (ISN) for connections from a continuously advancing number generator. Once the initial sequence number has been generated for a connection, sequence numbers for all subsequent datagrams in the connection are sequentially numbered by data bytes as discussed before. With this refinement, Figure 9 can be modified as in Figure 12. In the figure, the ISN is 1620789.

Since data communication is usually bidirectional, TCP always creates a bidirectional connection to facilitate bidirectional transfer of data. For example, when you visit a website, you send the name of the web page you are interested in browsing and the website sends the contents of the page to you. In a bidirectional connection, each time two computers communicate, two TCP streams of data are generated—one from the sender to the receiver and the other from the receiver to the sender. Therefore, two ISNs are generated. Each side generates an initial sequence number for outgoing data from its side.

One final task now remains. If the two sides are not going to start with a sequence number of 1, each side has to inform the other side of the initial sequence number it will use for the connection. For this task, TCP defines a procedure in which three special packets are exchanged between the two computers before any data exchange takes place. This is called the three-way handshake and is shown in Figure 13.

The three-way handshake is really a simple procedure. Say the sender generates an initial sequence number (ISN) of 83441 and the receiver generates an ISN of 2713867. The sender begins by sending its ISN to the receiver in a blank datagram (no data). This is the transfer labeled 1 in Figure 13. The receiver acknowledges

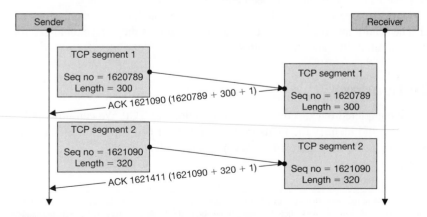

**FIGURE 12**　Stop-and-wait flow control with ISN

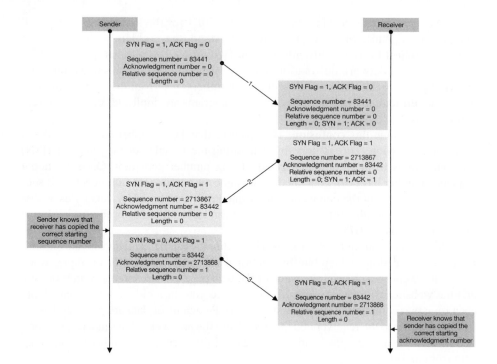

**FIGURE 13** Three-way handshake to exchange initial sequence numbers

the sender ISN by putting the 83442 in the ACK field of its response as expected.[4] In addition, it also inserts its own ISN of 2713867 in the sequence number field of the acknowledgment. This transaction is labeled 2 in Figure 13. When the sender receives this acknowledgment from the receiver, it knows that its ISN has been copied correctly by the receiver. It also knows the ISN selected by the receiver. In the final datagram of the three-way handshake, the sender acknowledges the receiver's ISN and places the expected acknowledgment number of 2713868 in the acknowledgment number field of its response. This is labeled 3 in Figure 13. When the receiver gets this datagram it knows that its own ISN has also been correctly copied by the sender.

Once the two ISNs have been successfully copied, data transmission can proceed. The sender and receiver use the sequence numbers they just exchanged for segmentation, reliability, and flow control.

## TCP header

We have completed our discussion of the functions of TCP. We can now look at the TCP header and identify the fields in the TCP header that support the TCP tasks discussed in this chapter. Figure 14 shows the TCP header.

---

[4] The careful student may note that the formula for calculating the ACK field isn't quite followed in the 3-way handshake. The ACK is usually sequence + length. However, in the handshake, the ACK is actually sequence + length + 1 (since length is zero). In both cases, the ACK tells the other end "this is the byte I want next".

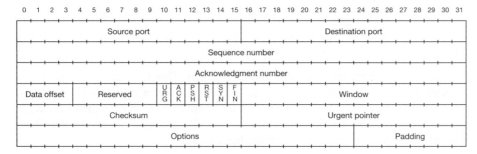

Note: Each tick mark represents a bit position

**FIGURE 14**    TCP header

The roles of the important fields in the TCP header have already been discussed. For reference, a quick summary of each field is provided below:

*Source and destination port addresses*: These are the port numbers on the two sides of the data transfer.

A useful point to note in the TCP header is that the port address fields are 16 bits in length. This means that 65,536 ($2^{16}$) port numbers are possible on each computer. If the computer has sufficient processing power to manage the data on all these connections, a computer running TCP can uniquely label 65,536 separate communication channels simultaneously to a given remote machine on a fixed port. As has been pointed out before, it is useful to compare this capability of TCP with the limited capability of the telephone which can only support one connection at a time.

*Sequence number:* The sequence number of the first data byte in the datagram.

*Acknowledgment number:* The next sequence number expected by the sender of the datagram.

*Data offset:* Size of the TCP header. This field identifies where the data begins in the datagram. This is necessary because a TCP datagram may have variable-sized options.

*Reserved:* These bits have no current use, but may be used to add new functionality in the future.

*Control bits:* Six bits indicating special information. Control bits indicate changes in TCP state, such as whether a new connection is being opened, or an existing connection is being closed.

*Window:* This is the window size, and it indicates the number of data bytes the sender of the datagram is willing to accept beyond the acknowledgment number field of the datagram.

*Checksum:* A checksum on the entire datagram and the IP header. This is used for error detection.

*Urgent pointer:* Used to indicate that the data in the datagram must be processed immediately. This feature is not generally used anymore, but was popular in earlier applications.

*Options:* Potential options that can be defined, such as maximum receivable datagram size.

*Padding:* 0 or more bits to ensure that the TCP header length is a multiple of 32 bits. This field is useful if options are used.

The TCP checksum is a very interesting field. This field includes information from the IP header in its computations. Layering requires that each layer be independent of other layers.[5] The TCP checksum is therefore the one field in the technologies we have discussed so far that explicitly violates the principles of layering by being dependent upon the value of fields in another layer.

# UDP

This chapter has shown how TCP is very reliable. But the reliability comes at the cost of a fairly complex protocol. TCP requires the generation and exchange of ISNs, checksum, sequence numbers, and reassembly of datagrams. TCP is very useful when ordered and reliable data delivery is required for an application. Examples of such applications include the web, e-mail, and any application carrying financially sensitive information. However, there are many applications where reliable and ordered delivery is not required. In these cases, much of the complexity of TCP can be eliminated in favor of a simpler transport protocol.

An example of a situation where reliable, ordered delivery is not required is sensor data. Sensors usually send out very small amounts of data (e.g. time = 9:30 a.m., or temperature = 43°F). Such small transmissions do not require segmentation. Sensors also generally send data at frequent intervals, say every minute, which creates a lot of redundancy to handle lost datagrams. Thus, even if an occasional sensor reading is lost, it does not significantly affect applications using this data. These applications therefore do not need the reliability of TCP.

Another situation where reliable, ordered delivery is not useful is real-time communication, such as voice or video. If a data packet from a video frame is lost, there is no point in receiving a retransmitted datagram once the video frame has advanced and the TV is displaying the next scene. It is therefore best to ignore lost datagrams in video feeds, tolerate the occasional loss, and move on.

For situations such as these, or where application developers might be interested in enforcing their own flow control, an alternate transport-layer protocol has been defined. This protocol is called UDP, which stands for User Datagram Protocol. UDP was defined in RFC 768 in 1980.

The UDP header is shown in Figure 15. Comparing the UDP and TCP headers, we see that UDP eliminates all sequencing and acknowledgments, but preserves port

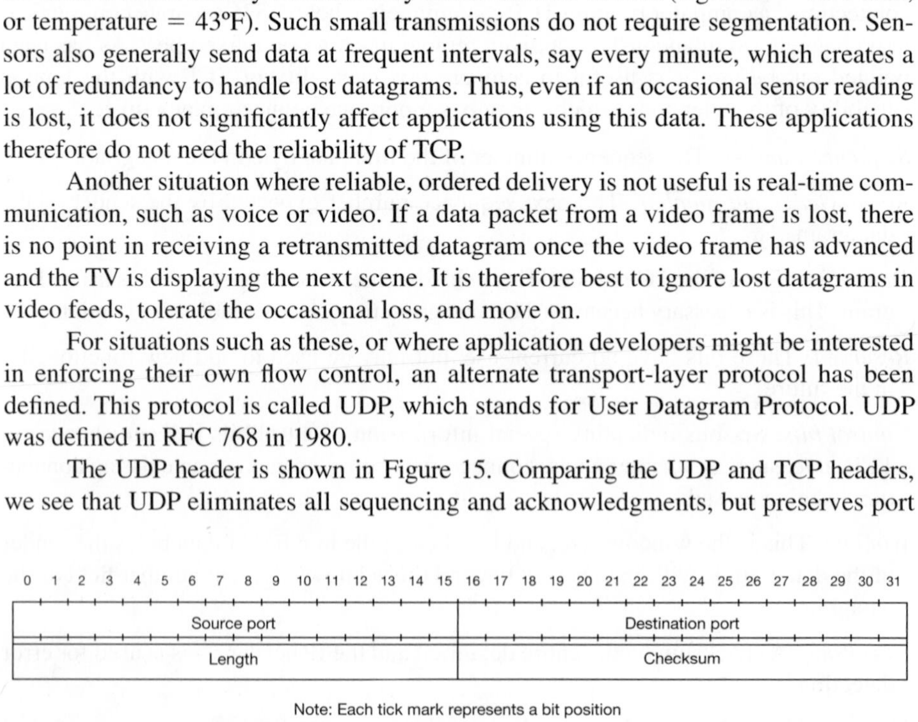

```
0  1  2  3  4  5  6  7  8  9  10 11 12 13 14 15 16 17 18 19 20 21 22 23 24 25 26 27 28 29 30 31
```

| Source port | Destination port |
|---|---|
| Length | Checksum |

Note: Each tick mark represents a bit position

**FIGURE 15**  UDP header

---

[5] What happens to the checksum when IPv6 is used? See section 8.1 of RFC 2460 (IPv6).

numbers for the multiplexing function. UDP essentially adds port addresses to the IP header. Since the function of UDP (multiplexing) is a subset of the functions of TCP, there is no additional description provided here to understand the functioning of UDP.

For reference, the fields of the UDP header are described below:

*Source and destination ports:* These fields perform the same functions as TCP ports.

*Length:* This field defines the length of the entire datagram.

*Checksum:* This field is computed in a manner similar to the TCP checksum, though it is often not used in computer-intensive applications such as video streaming.

---

## CASE STUDY  |  SHOW ME THE MONEY: THE FINANCIAL INDUSTRY

---

*What is money? Is it the cash in your pocket? Or, perhaps, the cash in all the pockets of the world combined? Facts suggest otherwise. As a result of fractional reserve banking, most of the world's money exists as accounting entries in the databases of financial institutions worldwide. In fact, it may not be an exaggeration to say that the entire world's money is data in a distributed database.*

The numbers bear this out as well. The total volume of U.S. currency in circulation at the end of November 2009 was $860.9 billion. A more general measure of money is called M1 and includes deposits in checking accounts and travelers checks. At the end of November 2009, M1 was $1,679.8 billion. This quantity of money supports bank assets worth $11,865.5 billion (reported as H.8 by the Federal Reserve), i.e., more than 6 times the amount of cash in circulation. More interestingly, the total volume of transactions on the securities markets in 2008 was $1,880 trillion, or approx $6.8 trillion each business day. In other words, each business day, the value of securities transactions in the United States is worth over 4 times the total amount of M1 money in circulation in the world.

If you have worked in any job, chances are that you received your salary in the form of a check which you deposited in your bank account. In fact, other than the occasional fund-raiser for charitable causes, there was probably no cash transaction between you and your employer. If the job was in a corporate setup, your salary was probably deposited electronically into your bank account, without even the paper check.

For most of your shopping, you probably use a credit card or debit card. When the monthly payments on these cards come due, you probably mail a paper check, or increasingly, ask the card company to withdraw payments directly from a designated bank account. Just as you don't see cash for most of your income sources, you probably don't use cash for most of your household expenses either. In fact, the most common use for cash may be expenses such as payments at toll booths, charges that are too small for electronic-payment systems to process.

You may notice that a common feature of both income and expenses in the typical household is that the transactions take the form of debits and matching credits in the databases of your employer's bank, your bank, and your credit-card company. All of these databases are networked using extremely reliable computer networks.

Financial transactions take the form of data exchange between networked databases in all parts of the financial system. For example, if you buy stocks in a brokerage account, your brokerage firm debits the cost of the transaction from your account and transfers the money to the brokerage firm of the seller of the stock, which then credits the payment to the seller's account. No paper cash changes hands. In fact, no paper stock certificates change hands either. Since the early 1970s, stock ownership in the United States is recorded exclusively in the form of bookkeeping entries at a company called the Depository Trust and Clearing Corporation (DTCC). When the stock sale is settled, DTCC records a change in the ownership of the stock in its databases.

Indeed, transactions cannot happen at the required speeds if money in the form of cash and securities in the form of paper certificates needed to physically change hands in each transaction. Without computer networks helping automate the settlement of trades, securities markets could not exist in their current form.

### Latency in the financial services industry

A special feature of computer networks in the financial industry is their need for low latency. Almost 50% of all trades in many securities markets are now electronic, where computerized platforms match orders received from computerized algorithmic engines at buyers and sellers. Trading algorithms on these exchanges try to profit from split-second price imperfections. Buyers and sellers who can trade faster have an advantage in these markets. As a result, improvements in computer networking technologies now play a central role at the core of the financial services industry. In response, technology vendors in the financial services sector are engaged in what is called a "low-latency arms race."

When latency becomes critical, the reliability functions of TCP become expensive because they can slow the transmission of data. Among the measures taken to reduce latency are minimizing router hops, optimizing the TCP/IP stack, disabling Nagle algorithm, and tuning TCP Window and datagram sizes. Some architectures even avoid TCP in favor of protocols such as sockets-direct protocol (SDP) to reduce latency. Improvements in data storage are also helping to reduce latency. Solid State devices can provide access times that are hundreds or thousands of times faster than hard disks.

Even the speed of light can be a limiting factor in reducing latency. Data travels at about 100,000 miles per second in optical fiber, leading to latency of about 10 microseconds per mile. Algorithmic traders cannot afford to wait that long to execute their trades. In response, trading exchanges are increasingly offering proximity services which allow trading firms to locate their electronic trading systems physically close to the exchange order-matching systems, sometimes even within the premises of stock exchanges.

Reflecting these recent developments in the financial services industry, a recent job posting (12/09) in the *Wall Street Journal* read as follows (all abbreviations are from the original post):

Sr Anlyst/Dev w/Goldman Sachs in NY, NY. Wrk w/clnts to gthr sftwr reqs for PETS systs, which use C++, Linux, Sybase, and Java. Req: Mstrs Deg (U.S. or equiv) in Comp Sci or rel fld + 3yrs exp in the job offrd or in rel Sftwr and Dev pos. Prior wrk exp must incl 3yrs: C++, Java Dev in Linux and Solaris; perfrmng ntwrk prgrmmng usng socket oriented prgrmmng, TIBCO etc.; dsgning and dvlpng multi-threaded srvr systs w/lo latency usng C++ Pthreads; dsgning and dvlpng prcsses w/multi-tier architctr usng technlgies usng Java's distrbtd technlgies such as remote mthd invocatn, and J2EE. NO PHONE CALLS PLEASE.

## REFERENCES

Board of Governors of the Federal Reserve System. *"H.8—Assets and Liabilities of Commercial Banks in the United States."* http://www.federalreserve.gov/Releases/h8/Current/ (accessed 12/31/2009).

Depository Trust and Clearing Corporation. *"An Introduction to DTCC."* http://www.dtcc.com/downloads/about/Introduction_to_DTCC.pdf (accessed 12/31/2009).

Depository Trust and Clearing Corporation. *"Following a Trade."* http://www.dtcc.com/downloads/about/Following%20a%20Trade.pdf (accessed 12/31/2009).

Depository Trust and Clearing Corporation. *"Transaction Statistics and Performance."* http://www.dtcc.com/about/business/statistics.php (accessed 12/31/2009).

Federal Reserve Bank of New York. *"The Money Supply."* http://www.newyorkfed.org/aboutthefed/fedpoint/fed49.html (accessed 12/31/2009).

Federal Reserve Statistical Release. *"H.6—Money Stock Measures."* http://www.federalreserve.gov/releases/H6/Current/ (accessed 12/31/2009).

*"U.S. Currency in Circulation."* http://www.visualeconomics.com/the-value-of-united-states-currency-in-circulation/.

## SUMMARY

This chapter discussed the transport layer. The transport layer provides segmentation, reliability, and multiplexing functions in data communications. Where necessary, it also provides flow control. The layer receives raw data from the end-user application and delivers it to the receiving computer reliably, without errors. For purposes of network transport, the layer may segment the data into datagrams. The segments are labeled with sequence numbers before transmission to facilitate reassembly of the data at the receiving end. Before delivery to the application at the receiving end, the data is reassembled in the correct sequence. The enduser application is completely unaware of the segmentation and reassembly performed by the transport layer for data transfer.

Data segments at the transport layer are called datagrams. The primary protocol at the transport layer is TCP. For applications that do not need reliability or ordered delivery of data, an alternate protocol, UDP, has also been defined. Application developers are often interested in specifying an appropriate value for the port address fields of TCP or UDP to ensure that their applications do not interfere with other applications on computers where their applications are installed.

An interesting pattern may be observed in the placement of protocol layers. The physical layer does best-effort information transmission across a single link. This transmission can introduce bit-level errors. These errors are removed by the data-link layer. The network layer does best-effort routing across networks. Some packets can be lost during routing. The transport layer removes these errors. Thus, protocol layers alternate best-effort transmission and error correction.

With this chapter, we have completed discussion of the technologies that reliably transfer any amount of data across any two computers located anywhere on the Internet and interconnected by networks of arbitrary complexity and unreliability.

In the next chapter we will see some standard network applications that make these network services useful for end users.

## ABOUT THE COLOPHON

This book has focused on data communication between applications on different computers. However, the problem is more general. Anytime two or more applications wish to share any computing resource, even if the applications are running on the same computer, the sharing mechanism uses most of the principles discussed in this book. Computer scientists use the term *process* to refer to running programs. Processes need to define rules for cooperation with each other. These rules are called protocols. To send and receive data, operating systems allocate ports to processes. These are the same ports that we have seen in detail in this chapter. This idea is described very well in RFC 62, from which the quote has been taken. Thus, the ideas introduced in this chapter describe the standard method by which computers share resources.

## REVIEW QUESTIONS

1. What are the functions of the transport layer?

2. Why are two protocols, TCP and UDP, defined at the transport layer instead of just TCP?

3. What is *segmentation*?

4. Why is segmentation useful?

5. What is *reliability* in the context of the transport layer?

6. What are the important potential problems with reliability that are handled by the transport layer?

7. How does TCP provide reliability?

8. What is *flow control*?

9. Why is it more useful to allow the receiver to control flow speed, rather than the sender?

10. How is flow control implemented?

11. What is *sliding window* in the context of flow control? Describe its operation.

12. What is *multiplexing* in the context of the transport layer?

13. How is the multiplexing at the transport layer different from the multiplexing at the physical layer?

14. What is a socket?

15. What is a port?

16. Why is it necessary to define port numbers at the receiving end for network services (such as web, e-mail, etc.)?

17. From the /etc/services file on your computer, list any five standard ports not listed in the text.

18. If you were developing an application that provided services over the network, could you have your application listen to client requests on port 80 (the port for web servers)? If yes, do you think it would be a good idea? Why, or why not?

19. What is *connection establishment* in TCP? Why is it necessary?

20. Describe the three-way handshake used in TCP.

21. What is the maximum number of possible TCP ports on a machine?

22. Why is the initial sequence number for a connection chosen at random?

23. A receiver sends an acknowledgment packet with the number 2817 in the acknowledgment number field. What inference can the sender draw from this packet?

24. What is the function of the window-size field in TCP?

25. What are some application scenarios where UDP may be more useful than TCP? Why?

## HANDS-ON EXERCISE

The utility used to gather information about open ports on a computer is netstat. By default, netstat shows all the open ports on the local computer and the ports on remote computers that they are connected to. The first output in Figure 16 shows the use of netstat to list open ports on the local computer. We see three open ports.

**FIGURE 16** Output from netstat before and after connecting to www.stu.edu. Netstat –f can identify the remote computers.

The various options available with netstat can be seen using the DOS help for netstat using the command netstat/?. Without any options, netstat shows the network connections open on the computer. The –n option shows IP addresses instead of computer names.

Netstat can be used to infer how networked applications work. For example, we can use netstat to see the connections opened by web browsers to display web pages. An example is shown in Figure 16, which shows a second invocation of netstat a few seconds after the first call to netstat. The main activity performed during this interval was a visit to the home page of St. Thomas University, (www.stu.edu). From a comparison of the first two outputs of netstat, we see that the visit to www.stu.edu opened five ports on the local computer. These ports allow the browser to quickly gather all the different pieces of information required to assemble the web page from different sources on the Internet. Netstat has an option, –f, to view the URLs of the remote computers. This option is handy to identify the remote computers. Output from netstat –f is also included in Figure 16.

Answer the following questions:

1. Show the output of netstat on your computer.

2. netstat has an option, –b, that shows the applications on the computer that open each port. Using the –b option requires that netstat be run with administrator privileges. You can do this by right-clicking

the Command Prompt icon and selecting "Run as Administrator"). What applications have opened each open port on your computer?

3. Visit your university or college website. Then run `netstat` again. Show the output.

4. How many new ports were opened by the browser to gather all the information on the page?

5. How does opening multiple ports simultaneously speed up the display of the web page on your browser?

# NETWORK DESIGN EXERCISE

There isn't much configuration that network administrators have to do at the transport layer. However, since the transport layer is the primary location for segmentation, this is a good place to estimate data-rate requirements for the long-haul network links. In this exercise you will estimate the data-rate requirements for the link from Amsterdam to Mumbai.

Assume that the traffic on the link from Amsterdam to Mumbai primarily consists of data required to support the call center in Mumbai. Traffic from the Mumbai call center has two components:

a) Database transactions to pull customer data from the data center in Amsterdam. Each customer transaction takes an average of 3 minutes, during which time the agent typically makes three queries to the database. Each query generates about 3,000 bytes of data.

b) Customer support calls to a 1-800 number routed to Mumbai from Tampa through Amsterdam. The calls

use a G.728 codec and each call requires a 31.5 Kbps bit rate.[6]

Answer the following questions:

1. What is the average data rate in bits per second required to support the database queries with no unnecessary delays? To do this, you would like to have enough capacity so that all agents can run queries simultaneously. Remember that 1 byte = 8 bits and carriers report data rates in bits per second because this gives a larger number, which is useful for marketing purposes (10 mega-bits-per-second is more marketable than 1.25 mega-bytes-per-second).

2. What is the data rate required to support the voice traffic?

3. Adding both the above, what is the total data rate required on the Amsterdam–Mumbai link? What fraction of this traffic is data, and what fraction is voice?

# CASE QUESTIONS

1. Watch your personal expenses for a week. What fraction of your total expenses is in the form of cash? What fraction is in the form of network data exchange (credit and debit cards, online payments)? For privacy reasons, please do not report actual amounts, just report fractions.

2. Do a similar exercise for your net worth. What fraction of your net worth is in the form of cash or cash equivalents (checking and savings accounts)? What fraction is in the form of networked data (retirement

assets, brokerage account assets)? Again, please only report fractions. Hint: you may find websites such as mint (www.mint.com) helpful in gathering this information from multiple financial institutions in which you have accounts.

3. What is the sequence of actions in settling a trade in securities markets? How many of these actions are completed over computer networks? How many by manual transfer? Hint: Look at the broker-to-broker trade in the DTCC publication, "Following a Trade".

---

[6] http://www.ciscosystems.to/en/US/tech/tk652/tk698/technologies_tech_note09186a0080094ae2.shtml (accessed 3/19/2010).

For the following questions, please use online sources to gather the required information. Anwer each question in not more than 4–5 sentences each.

4. What is the Nagle algorithm? Why is it useful in TCP? Why might it be a good idea to disable the use of the algorithm when TCP is used in the financial services industry?

5. Specialist firms have emerged to help organizations reduce latency. One such firm is Corvil. Visit the firm's website and write a brief report on the services offered by the firm. If you prefer, you may report on another firm that focuses on helping organizations reduce latency in the financial services industry.

6. What is an Internet socket? What is socket-oriented programming or network programming? Why do you think financial services firms are interested in experts in computer network programming?

7. The ad on page 142 mentions *pthreads*. What are *pthreads*? Why are they useful? Hint: You may find this site very useful: https://computing.llnl.gov/tutorials/pthreads/.

## CHAPTER 6

# Application Layer

*There's my . . . network.*
— STEVE JOBS

## Overview

This chapter covers the application layer. The application layer helps end user applications to use the data communications service provided by TCP and UDP. At the end of this chapter you should know about:

- the services provided by the application layer
- the Hypertext Transfer Protocol (HTTP), used to retrieve web pages
- the Simple Mail Transfer Protocol (SMTP), used to exchange e-mails
- the File Transfer Protocol (FTP), used for transferring large amounts of data
- the Secure Shell Protocol (SSH), used to securely connect to remote computers
- Instant Messaging and presence services

## Application-layer overview

The application layer enables end-user applications to use TCP and UDP in meaningful ways, for example to send e-mail or to download web pages. The application layer hides TCP and IP from the end user. The application layer provides functions that greatly simplify the development of networked end-user applications. For example, the HTTP application-layer protocol retrieves web pages. Developers of web browsers can focus on creating a pleasant end-user interface and use the HTTP protocol to retrieve content to populate the web pages.

The application layer deals with all the idiosyncratic requirements of each individual application. For each specified end-user activity, there is a specific application-layer protocol suitable for the activity. For example, there is HTTP for web transfers and SMTP for e-mail. Application-layer protocols define commands that are appropriate to accomplish the specified end-user activity and are, therefore, unique to the activity. For example, the HTTP application-layer protocol has commands to retrieve web pages. But since e-mail is not used to retrieve web pages, the SMTP application-layer protocol does not define commands to retrieve web pages. Instead, SMTP has commands to locate the receiver on the target mail server.

There is a very clear analogy between the ways in which end users interact with computer networks and transportation networks, such as the U.S. Postal Service (USPS). The USPS can transport any cargo for end users. All this cargo is transported in the same USPS trucks. However different items are treated differently. Books are shipped in boxes, get media mail rates, and are transported with the lowest priority. Liquids are packaged in water-tight containers. Fragile objects are mailed in specially labeled containers and receive special handling. The key point to observe is that different items may be packaged differently though they are all shipped using the same trucks. The Internet uses the same principle. The application layer provides the required support for each application. However, all traffic is transported over the same TCP/IP network.

The application layer is therefore unique among the five layers of the TCP/IP stack. The lower layers do not distinguish between end-user applications. Any physical-layer and data-link-layer technology can be used in combination with IP and either TCP or UDP to transport data for any application. However, the application-layer protocols are customized to each application. This is shown in Figure 1. All differences between applications are reflected in the differences among the various application-layer protocols.

There is yet another difference between application-layer protocols and the lower-layer protocols. All application-layer protocols interface with computer resources external to the communication system, typically the file system. The file system on the computer is where you store all your documents and programs. For example, the HTTP protocol reads files from the web server's file system and writes

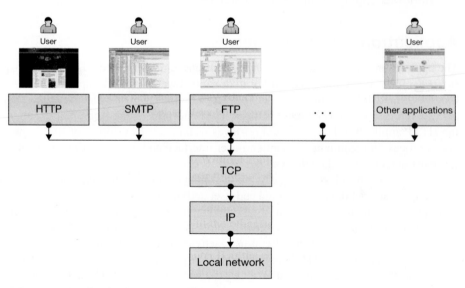

**FIGURE 1** Application layer in TCP/IP stack

the contents of the file on the web browser's local file system. Therefore, the file system is outside the communication system. The lower-layer protocols deal only with communication entities and have nothing to do with the rest of the computer that is not involved in communication.

The TCP/IP design of using a common data-transport mechanism to support any arbitrary application has greatly contributed to the popularization of the Internet. The architecture greatly improves efficiency in terms of lower costs. End users just have to buy one computer capable of running TCP/IP and can be assured that the computer will be capable of running all network applications, including those that haven't yet been developed. For example, voice-over IP (VoIP) is a relatively new application. Yet, using VoIP on a computer only requires installing a VoIP application such as Skype. No upgrades to TCP/IP, Ethernet, or the physical layer are necessary to add VoIP functionality to a computer.

The architecture of using common transport protocols is particularly economical for network carriers. Carriers can deploy one common TCP/IP network infrastructure to support all networking applications, including voice, video, and data. Contrast this with the earlier generation of networks where each city had one network for telephones and another network for television.[1]

An initial set of application-layer protocols (SMTP, FTP, and Telnet) to use TCP/IP was defined in RFC 1123 in 1989. You may note that this list does not include one of the most popular application-layer protocols today, HTTP, which is used for retrieving web pages. HTTP was only defined in 1996 in RFC 1945. Many other interesting applications have been defined in recent years, including instant messaging, file sharing, and even video streaming. The ability of the Internet to accommodate all these diverse applications with no changes to TCP/IP demonstrates the versatility of TCP/IP. It also reinforces our belief that TCP/IP should be capable of handling other network applications that may emerge in the future.

In the following sections of this chapter, we will discuss some common application-layer protocols in more detail. Where possible, we will also relate these protocols to contemporary business practice.

# HTTP

The simplest protocol to understand is the Hypertext Transfer Protocol (HTTP). *HTTP is a protocol that facilitates the transfer of files between local and remote systems on the World Wide Web.*

*The World Wide Web (web for short) is an information system that displays pages containing hypertext, graphics, and audio and video content from computers located anywhere around the globe.* The web is only a small fraction of the Internet, yet is so important that lay users treat the web and the Internet as synonyms.

---

[1] Of course, unified networks were not possible 50 years ago because the cables available then were incapable of handling the large volumes of network traffic in a unified network. Modern fiber-optic cables can handle virtually unlimited quantities of data.

### internet vs. Internet vs. web

Lay users often use these three terms interchangeably. But there are slight differences in meanings that you should be aware of. Figure 2 shows the relationships between the three terms. The term internet (spelled with a lower case *i*) is distinguished from the Internet (spelled with an upper case *I*). *An internet is any interconnection among or between computer networks.*

*The Internet is a worldwide interconnection of individual computer networks that provide access to all other users on the Internet.*

*The web is the part of the Internet where information is accessed using HTTP.* Information on the web is typically accessed using web browsers.

If you setup LANs in two neighboring homes and connect the LANs together, you get an "internet." If you connect one of these LANs to "the Internet," this internet becomes part of the Internet. If you run a web server on one of the computers in the LANs, the information on your LANs, accessible through the web server, becomes part of the web.

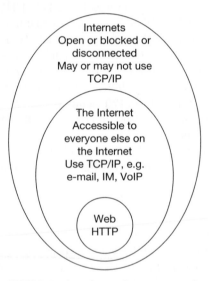

**FIGURE 2**   internet vs. Internet vs. web

Over the last few years, users have found innumerable uses of the web. One of the earliest exciting developments was the ability to shop online. This was soon followed by comparison-shopping online. Today, most people do not buy any expensive item before researching it online.

The web has transformed traditional business models in a wide range of industries. Stock brokers have been impacted because investors can place their own trades online and do not have to call share brokers to trade on their behalf. As a result, brokerage fees have come down from over $70/trade to as low as $7/trade. The travel agent industry has almost been decimated because most travelers now make their

**Table 1**    Evolution of web traffic

| Rank | December 31, 2005 | April 2008 | April 2009 |
|------|-------------------|------------|------------|
| 1 | Yahoo.com | Yahoo.com | Google.com |
| 2 | msn.com | Youtube.com | Facebook.com |
| 3 | Google.com | Live.com | Yahoo.com |
| 4 | Ebay.com | Google.com | Youtube.com |
| 5 | Amazon.com | Myspace.com | Live.com |
| 6 | Microsoft.com | Facebook.com | Wikipedia.org |
| 7 | Myspace.com | msn.com | Blogger.com |
| 8 | Google.co.uk | Hi5.com | Baidu.com |
| 9 | Aol.com | Wikipedia.org | msn.com |
| 10 | Go.com | Orkut.com | qq.com |

own vacation arrangements. Amazon has become a formidable competitor in many retail categories. Wikipedia has emerged as a popular reference encyclopedia online. A recent class of applications is social networking, where people with shared interests can interact over the Internet. You have probably registered a profile on at least one of these social networks. You probably also check your assignments and grades from home using a web-based system.

Just as traditional business models are evolving in response to the web, the use of the web has been evolving as well. A few years ago (2005), the most popular websites were information-providing websites such as Yahoo and AOL. In 2008, of the top 10 most popular websites, 4 were social networking sites (Table 1).[2] Just one year later, in 2009, search sites seemed to be the most popular. Table 1 shows that it is not easy to maintain popularity on the web. A famous map called the Web Trends Map[3] shows the most popular websites, organized by category.

## Evolution of the web

The web is useful because web servers allow many of these users to make information on their computers available on the web. People have different motivations for making information publicly available. Some are interested in selling things, others like to share personal interests, and many are just interested in expressing themselves. A common feature, however, is that most people making information available online have a great interest in providing the right information and in a form that engages viewers. Therefore, the web has become an effective and useful information filter that is attractive to viewers.

The popularity of the web began around 1993. At this time, commercial ISPs were beginning to sell Internet connections to individuals. The ability to browse the web was a major motivation for individuals to pay a monthly subscription fee for Internet access. In 1992, AOL went public with about 150,000 paying subscribers.

---

[2] http://www.alexa.com/topsites.
[3] http://informationarchitects.jp/start/ (accessed 04/17/2010).

| | A | B | C |
|---|---|---|---|
| 1 | | **AOL subscriber growth rate** | |
| 2 | | | |
| 3 | Date | Subscribers | Growth rate |
| 4 | 33604 | 150000 | =(B5/B4)^(1/((A5-A4)/365))-1 |
| 5 | 36891 | 26700000 | |
| 6 | | | |
| 7 | | | |
| 8 | Date | Subscribers | Growth rate |
| 9 | January 1 1992 | 150000 | 77.78% |
| 10 | December 31 2000 | 26700000 | |

**FIGURE 3**   Calculating AOL's subscription growth rate

In its last public filing before merging with Time Warner, AOL had 26.7 million ISP customers. These numbers mean that AOL sustained an annual subscription growth rate of almost 80% for over 9 years! (Figure 3). There are very few contemporary examples of businesses that sustained such high growth rates for such a long time.

The web browser was a major driver of the growth in popularity of the Internet. Netscape Navigator was released to the public in 1994. For the first time, non-technical users could access the wealth of information on the Internet. The most captivating feature of the browser was its ability to display images alongside text. It should be remembered that at this time (1994), very few computer applications were capable of displaying text alongside images on the same page. Therefore, the multimedia web page was itself a novelty. Further, the blue hyperlinks had almost magical powers and could instantly take users to web pages in other countries and even other continents.[4] By 1998, however, Internet Explorer became the dominant web browser, and on January 23, 1998, the Netscape source code was released to the open source community where the Mozilla project was born. We now see Mozilla as the Firefox browser.

The current size of the Internet can be estimated using various metrics. We will look at three—number of hosts, web servers, and web pages. According to the Internet Systems Consortium (ISC),[5] there are approximately 500 million hosts (computers) on the Internet. Netcraft[6] estimates that there are approximately 170 million websites on the Internet, of which about 70 million are active. Public websites have approximately 50 billion pages.[7]

---

### Estimated size of the text on the Internet

500 million hosts
170 million websites
50 billion pages

---

[4] The website www.dejavu.org recreates the web experience of the time, including the user interfaces of the early web browsers.
[5] ISC is the authoritative source for counting the number of hosts connected to the Internet.
[6] Netcraft has been conducting surveys of websites for a long time and is the standard resource for this statistic.
[7] This information is based on the announcement by a new search engine, Cuil, in July 2008.

We can use the above information to estimate the sizes of search-engine databases. If we assume that each web page has approximately 10,000 characters (for a size of 10 KB/page), the text content of the public web is approximately 500 TB in size.

Netcraft also reports on the market shares of web servers. As of April 2010, the open source Apache web server had the highest market share, accounting for almost 55% of all web hosts. Microsoft's Internet Information Server (IIS) was second with almost 25% of web hosts.

## Web marketing

A big part of the commercial importance of the web is its role in marketing.

The role of the web in marketing comes from its ability to target marketing to the individual. Of the traditional forms of marketing, print media (newspapers and magazines) allow some localization of advertisements through local print editions. TV also allows some localization by broadcasting ads that are relevant to an entire metro viewing area. Billboards offer a little more localization. (Hungry? Food Exit just 1 mile away.) But the web enables unprecedented levels of localization. Not only can web ads be localized to your neighborhood, they can also be customized to your tastes and needs as revealed by your browsing or shopping behavior. Partly for this reason, the web is witnessing the highest growth rate among all advertising media (Table 2). While the overall growth rate in advertising is 3%, about the same as the growth rate of the U.S. economy, web advertising is growing at 26%.

A very popular model of advertising on the web involves search advertising. *Search advertising is the placement of advertisements on web search results.* Search advertising addresses a major limitation of the web as an advertising medium. The web offers a "pull" model of communication. People have to choose to "pull" a web page to their browsers by typing the URL into the browser's address bar. Creating a website leads to no benefits unless the target audience becomes aware of its existence.

Search offers a way around this problem. If a web surfer is searching for a product or service that a business offers, and is located in the coverage area of the business, he is a potential customer. It is useful to attract his attention. This makes the web a powerful marketing medium, and search engines are becoming a powerful intermediary

**Table 2** Growth rates of advertising media (2007 estimates from Morgan Stanley)

| Medium | 2007 spend ($ billions) | Y/Y growth | Households reached | Ad spending/household |
|---|---|---|---|---|
| Direct phone | $110 | 7% | 107 | $1,032 |
| Newspapers | $116 | 5% | 115 | $818 |
| Internet/online | $21 | 26% | 71 | $288 |
| Yellow pages | $16 | 1% | 114 | $141 |
| Total | $469 | 3% | | $4,774 |

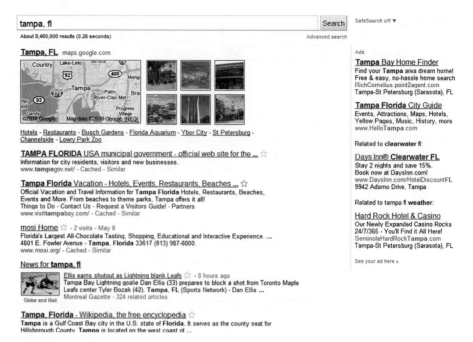

**FIGURE 4** Example of search advertising

in web marketing. Google earned 99% of its revenues in 2006 and 2007 and 97% of revenues in 2008 from online advertising.[8]

Search advertisements are related to the keywords used in the current search. Figure 4 shows an example of search advertising. Search ads derive their utility from their relevance to what the user is looking for at that very moment.

Advertisers can specify search keywords and the prices they are willing to pay when users click their ads. Ads are sorted by willingness to pay—those who bid the highest appear on top of the list of ads. Clients pay only when someone clicks on their ads. Therefore, advertisers incur no expense until their ads draw potential customers to their websites. Since search advertisements can be so effective, costs per click for the ads can get quite high. In 2004, lawyers were bidding up to $45 per click for the term "Mesothelioma" to solicit clients affected by a form of cancer caused by exposure to asbestos.[9]

> Strange as it may seem, marketing is a very powerful force in the U.S. economy. Estimates vary and range from Morgan Stanley's estimate of $450 billion in marketing expenditures 2007 to Blackfriar group's estimate of $1,000 billion in 2005. With a U.S. GDP of $14,000 billion in 2008, these estimates suggest that marketing accounts for about 5% of the U.S. economy. While retailers spend the most on marketing as a percentage of revenues, manufacturers incur the highest total marketing expenditures.

---

[8] Google form 10-K for 2008.
[9] Bialik, C. "Lawyers Bid Up Value of Web-Search Ads." *Wall Street Journal*, 2004.

# Web pages

Let us now turn to the technology behind the web. The web consists of web pages. Web pages are special in that they are connected to each other through hyperlinks on the pages. Figuratively, web pages linked to each other through links create a web of pages. Each of these pages can be located anywhere in the world. The two ideas are combined to get the name World Wide Web,[10] a map of which is shown in Figure 5.

Authors of web pages link to other pages that they determine are relevant to the content on their pages. *Links on other web pages that point to a page are called inlinks (or backlinks).* Therefore, the more inlinks to a page, the more likely it is that the page contains relevant information. Information about inlinks can be useful. If you have your own page on the web, the inlinks to your page provide a measure of interest on the web in your page. Inlinks can help you identify other websites that link to your site. Google provides an easy way to search for inlinks to a page. For example, a search for link: http://www.washington.edu/ will list the inlinks to the home page of the University of Washington.

Web pages are created using a simple language called Hypertext Markup Language (HTML). Figure 6 shows an example of a simple web page written in HTML. Figure 7 shows this page as it appears on a web browser.[11] USF is a hyperlink on the page. Clicking on USF on the page takes you to the home page of the University of South Florida.

**FIGURE 5**   Map of World Wide Web

```
<html>
      <head>
      <title>HTML 101</title>
      </head>
      <body>
      <h1>Welcome to html page at
      <a href = "www.usf.edu">USF</a></h1>
      <p>Please check back later</p>
      </body>
</html>
```

**FIGURE 6**   Example web page written in HTML

# Welcome to html page at USF

Please check back later

**FIGURE 7**   Example web page as displayed in a browser

---

[10] Figure 5 is from http://www.vlib.us/web/worldwideweb3d.html (accessed 04/17/2010).
[11] To learn HTML, the companion website has a cached copy of the NCSA HTML tutorial. For a long time, this simple-to-follow tutorial, which took about three hours to complete, was the authoritative reference to learn HTML. I learned HTML using this tutorial.

As indicated in the example, unlike programming languages, HTML does not have conditions, loops, or methods. It simply defines how a certain piece of text should be displayed on the screen and what the browser should do if the user clicks on a hyperlink.

HTML pages have some special features that are not present in book pages. The most important feature is the idea of hypertext. *Hypertext is text that includes navigable links to other hypertext.* This allows web-application developers to create web pages that provide viewers with immediate access to related information elsewhere. For example, on a merchant website, you can tempt customers with links to other items they may be interested in. (These items may be identified using prior shopping history.) On social networking sites you can provide links to the profiles of common friends. The result is that though the page structure of a merchant site may look the same to everybody, the contents of the page can be customized to each visitor.

## The HTTP protocol

HTML pages may be viewed in many ways. The most common method is to store them on web servers and transfer them to browsers using the HTTP protocol. The HTTP protocol is a simple request/response protocol used to transfer raw data. HTTP was first defined in RFC 1945 in 1996. The current version of HTTP was specified in RFC 2616 in 1999. After SMTP, FTP, and Telnet, which were defined in the early 1980s, HTTP was the first new application-layer protocol that gained importance. Though HTTP is newer than FTP or SMTP, and newer technologies are usually more complex to understand than older technologies, HTTP is the simplest application-layer protocol to understand. This is why this chapter begins with HTTP.

In using HTTP, the client sends a request for a file to the web server. The requested file is usually an HTML page. The web server responds to the request by sending the requested file over TCP. In addition, the server provides a status code that indicates the extent to which the server was successful in fulfilling the client's request. The server also provides meta-data that indicates the nature of the content to the client. The client can use the meta-data to decide how to process and display the content. The HTTP transaction for the example web page (Figure 7) is shown in Figure 8.

We can now examine salient features of the HTTP request/response cycle shown in Figure 8.

The HTTP transaction began with the client's request:

```
GET /index.html HTTP/1.1
```

The request also included the following supplemental information:

```
User-Agent: Opera/9.27 (Windows NT 6.0; U; en)
Host: www.ismlab.usf.edu
Accept: text/html, application/xml;q=0.9, application/xhtml+xml,
image/png, image/jpeg, image/gif, image/x-xbitmap, */*;q=0.1
Accept-Language: en-US,en;q=0.9
Accept-Charset: iso-8859-1, utf-8, utf-16, *;q=0.1
Accept-Encoding: deflate, gzip, x-gzip, identity, *;q=0
Cache-Control: no-cache
Connection: Keep-Alive, TE
TE: deflate, gzip, chunked, identity, trailers
```

```
GET /index.html HTTP/1.1
User-Agent: Opera/9.27 (Windows NT 6.0; U; en)
Host: www.ismlab.usf.edu
Accept: text/html, application/xml;q=0.9, application/xhtml+xml, image/png, image/jpeg, image/
gif, image/x-xbitmap, */*;q=0.1
Accept-Language: en-US,en;q=0.9
Accept-Charset: iso-8859-1, utf-8, utf-16, *;q=0.1
Accept-Encoding: deflate, gzip, x-gzip, identity, *;q=0
Cookie: __utmz=118619277.1227574991.6.4.utmcsr=coba.usf.edu|utmccn=(referral)|utmcmd=referral|
utmcct=/departments/isds/faculty/agrawal/index.html;
__utma=118619277.2614276856621331000.1212003453.1226937862.1227574991.6
Cookie2: $version=1
Cache-Control: no-cache
Connection: Keep-Alive, TE
TE: deflate, gzip, chunked, identity, trailers

HTTP/1.1 200 OK
Date: Sun, 25 Jan 2009 19:58:26 GMT
Server: Apache/2.2.6 (Unix) PHP/5.2.4
Last-Modified: Sun, 25 Jan 2009 19:37:03 GMT
ETag: "3e021-b9-bf1755c0"
Accept-Ranges: bytes
Content-Length: 185
Keep-Alive: timeout=5, max=100
Connection: Keep-Alive
Content-Type: text/html

<html>
.<head>
.<title>HTML 101</title>
.</head>
.<body>
.<h1>Welcome to html page at
.<a href = .www.usf.edu.>USF</a> </h1>
.<p>Please check back later</p>
.</body>
</html>
```

**FIGURE 8**   HTTP transaction for example web page

It is convenient to start looking at this request from the third line. In this line, the client specifies that it is trying to connect to the web server named www.ismlab. usf.edu. In the first line of the request, the client has asked for a file called /index.html. This is specified using the HTTP command: GET /index.html.

This command means that the client wants the file called index.html located at the top of the web server's directory for the site. In the second line, the client has specified that it is using the Opera 9.27 web browser. This is a useful piece of information in case the website customizes responses for specific browsers. In the fourth line, the client has specified that it is capable of processing HTML text and various image formats. In the remaining lines the client has specified some other capabilities such as language and compression.

When the server receives this request, it knows what file the client is requesting, and what its capabilities are. We see from Figure 8 that the web server sends the following in response:

```
<DM>HTTP/1.1 200 OK
Date: Sun, 25 Jan 2009 19:41:12 GMT
Server: Apache/2.2.6 (Unix) PHP/5.2.4
Last-Modified: Sun, 25 Jan 2009 19:37:03 GMT
Accept-Ranges: bytes
Content-Length: 185
Keep-Alive: timeout=5, max=100
Connection: Keep-Alive
Content-Type: text/html

<html>
     <head>
     <title>HTML 101</title>
```

```
              </head>
              <body>
              Welcome to html page at
              <a href = "www.usf.edu">USF</a></h1>
              <p>Please check back later</p>
              </body>
       </html>
```

In the very first line, the server provides a status code for the response. In this example, the status code is 200. We can look up the code in RFC 2616 and see that status code 200 means that "the request has succeeded". For human readability, HTTP also allows the server to include a reason phrase "OK" following the status code (i.e., that code 200 means "OK"). In line 3, the server identifies its version (Apache 2.2.6). In line 6, the server indicates that the response is 185 bytes in length. The content type is text/ html, which means that the browser can display the text as regular HTML text. After providing this background information, the web server sends the file we saw in Figure 6, and which the browser can display as shown in Figure 7.

In the example in Figure 8, the web page was sent as plain-text. Pages can also be compressed before transmission. Google provides a very interesting example of the use of this feature. Figure 9 shows a Google search for the term "USA" (http://www. google.com /search?q=usa). Google sends the search results in zipped format and alerts the browser of the compression by specifying content-encoding: gzip as highlighted

```
GET /search?q=usa HTTP/1.1
User-Agent: Opera/9.27 (Windows NT 6.0; U; en)
Host: www.google.com
Accept: text/html, application/xml;q=0.9, application/xhtml+xml, image/png, image/jpeg, image/
gif, image/x-xbitmap, */*;q=0.1
Accept-Language: en-US,en;q=0.9
Accept-Charset: iso-8859-1, utf-8, utf-16, *;q=0.1
Accept-Encoding: deflate, gzip, x-gzip, identity, *;q=0
Cookie: SS=Q0=dxNh; S=calendar=OBG1FoRwrO_eQUU2czrnJA; rememberme=true;
PREF=ID=f6b16990b6b77aab:FF=4:LD=en:NR=100:TM=1190041332:LM=1223006335:GM=1:WF=5:S=mTCrrvSY6arT2
SID=DQAAAHgAAABnSOHyrHIwPBty1O_T9rwlhCyOz5Uqn8K1NZ1GM6z_HPK8eA_VSTxNHjKfORPxgoJm1ffyAaeSGAZuCdJB
DH3lszqt8M4dkx-b6d6JSGHTUm9lrWMSA;
NID=19=kgFeS1umO0yLye0HhDMxS6nd8BDwzeTT7O-2DnP1ThAZRL1BwmJH7Td3nM2v_4F8tykE97k6QnDI-
jC123WuPYxcxaA6roZYMFJYcIMbGpqzThUWIHlSyiOUsAlNfA3I
Cookie2: $Version=1
Connection: Keep-Alive, TE
TE: deflate, gzip, chunked, identity, trailers

HTTP/1.1 200 OK
Cache-Control: private, max-age=0
Date: Sun, 25 Jan 2009 21:12:41 GMT
Expires: -1
Content-Type: text/html; charset=UTF-8
Set-Cookie: SS=Q0=dxNh; path=/search
Server: gws
Transfer-Encoding: chunked
Content-Encoding: gzip

d7a
..........Z{s.6...../..LQ..."r.6M3.f2M..M...$H"..&@...~..).1.f...A`......95b...".$X.
$...KA...:."N....~.........bX..../......DEV...$........8.3OH..t6...i~.9.<R.c..X....n..
`i4.4..  .#/..#X{Y..b .|
6..",ON...U8..Y*...MqMm..:.<.L.,....6..........X ...q...........16.LO.q&.g1.......4.w..Q.
+....y*t.9....}..G.U...8.....%/.2kFW...K...$..U."m.3i.
[....mB.F......!....m......&4...B2...,Jg...i.3"g....1^.L....<..._j5f..&.}A.
Q2.s.>`....m-..Z..N...g.qfI..*6.Y..b.;.....I;..X7.$.tV.p..A.....f.....H...
#.1..R.R..V...x..B>../.??.......7.Z\Y`y!...J..~
$.d...oZ......N<...Mv...Fd.mj..tA....EME^8....Zi/.2.4.z...ZG.9.........-....4.@m .G$q....d...-
_.........n=...1....6...{.\.. .|...&..a8......
q..e..H........{..O.........X>.o..g..QA!]..a
.7...7.].G.H.xde|].c.8%gvda..0.[......x..N.....$a.~F
F.%H*..8X.y.Ee.ZW!
<8....P&.`d.9I..A,.g...;......1.&....n9...2......n........!..C........o....9%....%.A`ym...
[wr....m..
.....b..L[..6Eit..,..QM.[...C:..6cp5.M.XL.f.|6o..OSI.......w..+('.Cj./.F...f..R*.5..%
```

**FIGURE 9** Google results are zipped before transmission

**FIGURE 10**    Google results (compressed above) displayed in a browser

in Figure 9. For reference, the page as it appeared on a browser is shown in Figure 10. This is one way of improving the performance of websites over slow links.

Please note that whereas the HTTP application-layer protocol facilitates web browsing, the protocol is not the web-browsing application. The web-browser application and web pages are not a part of the TCP/IP stack. The browser application uses commands from the HTTP protocol to retrieve web pages from web servers.

## URLs

Before leaving the section on the web, let us take a look at the information conveyed by familiar addresses, such as http://www.slu.edu, that are used to get pages in web browsers. These addresses are called URLs. *A URL, or uniform resource locator, is a character string describing the location and access method of a resource on the Internet.* URLs were defined in 1994 in RFC 1738 as a way to represent any resource available through the Internet.

Though URLs are mostly used to get web pages from web browsers, and we typically don't pay much attention to their structure, URLs have been designed to be a general method to access any resource on the Internet. It is useful to know about the components of URLs. All URLs use the following general form:

```
protocol://host [:port ]/[abs_path]
```

The URL begins with the protocol used. The most familiar example is of course, `http`. When the receiver sees a URL beginning with http, it knows that the rest of the URL is to be interpreted in the manner specified for `http`. `Http://www.slu.edu` is an example of a familiar Internet resource being accessed using the HTTP protocol.

Another example URL is `ftp://128.197.27.121`, which uses the FTP protocol to access a resource at the host 128.197.27.121.

The second part of the URL is the host. The host specifies the IP address or domain name of the computer on which the client is trying to access the Internet resource. Thus the URLs http://www.slu.edu or http://165.134.39.20 specify that the client is trying to access a resource using the HTTP protocol on the computer with IP address 165.134.39.20 (or domain name www.slu.edu).

The third part of a URL is the port address. The port address is separated from the host address using a ":". An example could be ftp://ftp.bu.edu:21. This would indicate an FTP resource running on port 21 on the computer ftp.bu.edu. As we saw in Chapter 5, port numbers are generally unnecessary because services typically run on default ports. We could have accessed the FTP resource above with the URL ftp://ftp.bu.edu.

Once we access the Internet service running on a port on a computer, the last part of the URL allows navigation through the directory structure of the service. If a web server at www.example.com has the page today_prices.html at the top level, we can access it using the URL: http://www.example.com/today_prices.html. As another example, if the FTP server in the previous paragraph has a top-level directory called *etc*, its contents can be accessed using the URL: ftp://ftp.bu.edu/etc. A file in this directory, called *group,* can be accessed by FTP using the URL ftp://ftp.bu.edu/etc/group.

Just as default ports have been defined at the transport layer for convenience, web browsers and web servers recognize some default values for the convenience of end users. For example, if you do not specify the HTML file name of the home page of a website, the server assumes by default that you are looking for a file called index.html or index.htm.

Web applications allow users to send application parameters through the URL. For example, a URL such as http://www.example.org:8080/grades?fName=john could be used to send the value "john" as the value of the variable "fName" in web application "grades" listening on port 8080 on the host www.example.org. Google allows users to specify the search term as the value for the "q" variable to the search application. For example, you can directly type in the following URL in your browser to obtain the results of a Google search for "TCP": http://www.google.com/search?q=tcp.

URLs can be used to access any resource on the Internet. A common use of URLs by application developers is to specify database connections. For example, a MySQL database called ism4220 running on host ismlab.usf.edu can be accessed using the URL `mysql://ismlab.usf.edu:3036/ism4220 ?user=testuser&password=tes tpass`. This causes the client to use the MySQL protocol (using the MySQL driver installed locally) to connect to port 3036 on the host ismlab.usf.edu and attempt a connection to the ism4220 database using the username and password specified.

In the next section we cover e-mail, one of the oldest Internet applications. E-mail was the primary use of the Internet for more than two decades, the 70s and the 80s. The web only became popular in the latter half of the 1990s.

## E-mail

E-mail is widely considered to be the "killer app" on the Internet. Figuratively, a killer app is a computer application to die for. It is an application that is so useful that it causes people to buy a larger, more expensive system just to get the functionality of the killer app.

*E-mail is an electronic means for communication in which information—including text, graphics, and sound—is sent, stored, processed, and received. Messages are held in storage until called for by the addressee.*

At the time of the creation of the Internet in the late 60s, e-mail and FTP were visualized as the two major Internet applications. E-mail was designed for short messages, and FTP was designed to transfer bulk information. Though HTTP has supplanted most of the functionality of FTP, e-mail continues to be one of the most popular applications on the Internet. Businesses have a high regard for e-mail because e-mail can be used in various ways to improve business productivity. As a measure of e-mail's integration into daily life, note how the contact information of almost every professional now includes an e-mail address along with a phone number.

E-mail has changed how we communicate. E-mail has played such a dominant role in modern business that e-mail now has a place in financial history as the leading cause of one of the greatest financial manias of all time. In his famous book on market manias, Charles Kindleberger has attributed the dot-com bubble to e-mail and related technologies.[12] The book states that "*events that lead to a [financial] crisis start with a 'displacement', some exogenous, outside shock to the macroeconomic system.*" In other words, a financial mania begins with some unanticipated event that has great economic impact. Further, to describe the dot-com mania, the book states that "*the shock in the United States in the 1990s was the revolution in information technology and new and lower-cost forms of communication and control that involved the computer, wireless communication and e-mail*".[13] Though we now take e-mail for granted, this vignette is intended to show that the business community was so wonderstruck about the possibilities created by e-mail when e-mail first became available to a wider audience, that an entire financial bubble developed as a result.

The popularity of e-mail is based on its unique ability to meet the human need to communicate. Where HTTP allows information dissemination to a wide audience, e-mail allows communication with targeted individuals. E-mail should continue to be extremely popular in the near future because the human need to communicate has not diminished. Even in 2008, the most popular applications on Facebook, the popular social networking site, were communication applications. As seen in Table 3, even young and trendy users seem to seek communication on social networking sites more than activities, such as

**Table 3**   Facebook applications—top categories (2008)

| Category | Usage | Sample applications |
| --- | --- | --- |
| Communication | 26% | Superwall, Superpoke! |
| Social comparison | 12% | Hot or not, likeness |
| Social games | 11% | Zombies, pirates |
| Social selection | 10% | Top friends, social circles |
| Profile enhancement | 10% | Sketch me, Books iRead |

[12] Kindleberger, C.P. and R. Aliber, *Manias, Panics, and Crashes: A History of Financial Crises*. 5th ed. Hoboken, NJ: Wiley, 2005.
[13] E-mail has been underlined here for emphasis.

social comparison and games. Not only is communication popular among young users, all other application categories are a distant second to communication applications.

There are, however, some changes happening on the e-mail front. Among young users, e-mail seems to be losing some ground to more fast-paced technologies such as text messaging, chat, and social networks. In response, e-mail providers have improved the technology to offer "push-e-mail" in which incoming mail arriving at a mailbox located on the server is "pushed out" almost instantaneously to a mobile device. Also, as we will see when we examine the technology behind e-mail, e-mail is a very expensive technology to support. As a result, to manage costs, colleges and universities are now increasingly partnering with larger companies, such as Google, Microsoft, and Yahoo, to offer e-mail service to their users.

## E-mail as a communication medium

Every communication medium has its own unique properties. If we know some of the unique properties of e-mail as a communications medium, we can use this information to identify situations where the use of e-mail is appropriate and where it is not.

A key property of e-mail as a communication medium is that e-mail uses a *push* form of communication. This means that the sender decides who to send the message to and when to send the message. This may be contrasted with the web's *pull* nature. On the web, it is the receiver who decides which web page to read and when. While there is no guarantee that the audience will ever visit a web page, e-mail is a mechanism to reach the recipient's mailbox.

The push nature of e-mail makes it an extremely cost-effective measure for organization leadership to instantly disseminate information to everybody in the organization. In the traditional method of pushing information down through direct reports, not only do managers have no control over whether the information is being disseminated at all, they also have no control over the actual message being passed on. Print flyers are useful, but very expensive and time consuming to print and mail. Putting up a website is easy, but employees need a way to know what site to visit. Therefore, CEOs now routinely use e-mail to directly send vital information to all employees.

E-mail has helped reduce communication barriers created by organizational hierarchies. E-mail also eliminates cues about age, gender, and appearance. These cues sometimes influence communication on other channels such as the telephone and face-to-face conversations.

For its convenience and capabilities, e-mail is now an essential part of project communication plans. Before projects begin, project managers develop communication plans that define the stages of a project when status updates will be sent out, and the people who will get these updates. In many project communication plans, e-mail is now the primary communication channel.

E-mail also has other advantages as a communication medium. Unlike the telephone, e-mail is an asynchronous[14] medium. This means that the sender and the receiver do not have to be on their computers at the same time to communicate. A sender can send the message at his convenience and receivers can reply at their

---

[14] Asynchronous = not required to occur at the same time.

convenience. E-mail therefore eliminates the game of phone tag. Within organizations, e-mail eliminates hierarchical barriers.

E-mail also makes it very easy to locate expertise in remote locations of the organization. E-mail is particularly useful in obtaining the opinions of introverted people or people who are hesitant to speak before large groups. Many of these people are quite comfortable expressing themselves over e-mail. In groups where some individuals have the tendency to dominate conversations, e-mail can be effective in extracting the opinions of the less vocal group members.

From an economic perspective, e-mail eliminates the costs of communication. Once the Internet connection is paid for and the e-mail account is set up, there are no marginal costs to sending e-mail. This generally increases the supply of e-mail. An unfortunate consequence has been the rise in spam e-mail. It is just as easy to send a mass e-mail to 20 million recipients as it is to send an e-mail to one recipient. Even if just 0.001% of all the receivers make purchases following the e-mail, spamming can be profitable. As a result, it is a very challenging problem to stop spam.

The low marginal cost of sending e-mail introduces other problems. E-mail is often copied to more people than necessary to keep them "in the loop." Each of these receivers must spend precious time deciding how to act on the mail. The low cost of sending e-mail encourages people to "shoot" e-mails before thinking enough. Also, unlike organized meetings, there is often no clear leader in e-mail discussions and discussions can drift toward unrelated topics.

Overall, the benefits of e-mail have made it the communication medium of choice in the professional workplace. E-mail is so important that even without realizing it, e-mail is central to how many professionals conduct their business. Some of the most important business communications are now sent and received only by e-mail. As a result, organizations are now required to develop formal retention policies for e-mail to comply with rule 34 and rule 26(f) of federal civil procedure.[15,16] These rules require companies to make information relevant in legal proceedings available to courts of law. Many large companies now save all e-mail for at least one month. If an e-mail is required in a legal matter, it is retained until the matter is settled.

## E-mail system architecture

The technology components and protocols that make e-mail work are shown in Figure 12. Each e-mail user has access to an e-mail client and a mailbox on an e-mail server. The mailbox provides long-term storage for e-mail. In industry parlance, the e-mail client is called a mail-user agent (MUA). The e-mail server is called the mail-transfer agent (MTA). Common mail-user agents include Outlook and Thunderbird, and most users are familiar with their use. These clients provide a familiar interface for users to compose e-mail and to read and delete e-mail in their mailboxes. Common MTAs include Exchange, Sendmail, and Postfix. Since MTAs act behind the scenes and end users don't deal with MTAs, many e-mail users are not familiar with MTAs. However, MTAs are commercially very important, with Microsoft Exchange generating over $1 billion in annual sales. Figure 11 provides a breakup of the market shares of the popular MTAs and MUAs as of 2008.

---

[15] http://www.law.cornell.edu/rules/frcp/Rule26.htm.
[16] http://www.law.cornell.edu/rules/frcp/Rule34.htm.

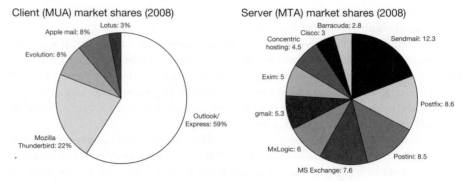

**FIGURE 11** Market shares of popular MUAs and MTAs

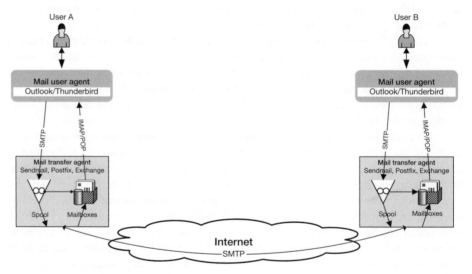

**FIGURE 12** E-mail system architecture

## E-mail protocols

E-mail is a relatively complex service to set up. Two sets of protocols are employed to use e-mail. *SMTP, or Simple Mail Transfer Protocol, is the protocol used to transfer e-mail between mail servers.* Figure 12 shows how SMTP is used to deliver e-mail between MTAs. Mail access protocols such as IMAP or POP are used to retrieve e-mail from mailboxes located on the mail servers. Figure 12 also illustrates how users use POP/IMAP to manage mail boxes. It may be noted that outgoing e-mail does not go to the mailbox.

SMTP was one of the earliest application protocols created. It was defined along with FTP and Telnet in RFC 821 in 1982. At that time, users typically ran e-mail servers on their workstations and directly interacted with their mailbox. There were no mail clients or mail access protocols such as POP/IMAP. SMTP was used to send e-mail messages to other e-mail users running SMTP on their own workstations. This was fine as long as the workstations were located on university networks and could be left online 24/7, ready to receive incoming e-mail at any time of the day.

As e-mail proliferated, many users who joined the Internet only had dial-up connectivity and could not be expected to be online 24/7 to receive incoming e-mail. It then became necessary to create a mechanism so that e-mail servers running SMTP could be hosted on University or ISP networks where they would be online 24/7 under the watchful eyes of a trained system administrator. These e-mail servers would be ready to receive incoming e-mail at any time of the day. Whenever convenient, end users could access e-mail that had been delivered to their mailboxes since the last access. POP and IMAP were therefore developed as protocols for users to access e-mail from their mailboxes. POP was developed in 1996 and IMAP in 2003. IMAP added features that allowed multiple e-mail clients (possibly at work and home) to maintain synchronization with each other and the mailbox.

The older e-mail system where SMTP was the only e-mail protocol and all users ran mail servers directly on their PCs is analogous to the system used by carriers such as FedEx and UPS that require users to sign off on packages upon receipt. If there is no one to receive the package (which would be analogous to the mail server not being online when an e-mail message is to be delivered), these carriers return a second time, possibly even a third time. If the carriers fail to find the receiver after multiple attempts, delivery fails and the package is returned to the sender. SMTP operates in a similar manner and makes multiple attempts to deliver e-mail; if it fails after repeated attempts, it informs the sender of the failure.

The newer e-mail system that separates mail delivery to the mailbox from mail clearance out of the mailbox is analogous to the way the postal system works. All users have a mailbox that is available 24/7 for a mailman to deliver mail. The mailman can deliver mail to this mailbox even when residents are not at home. The mailman's operation is analogous to the working of SMTP. Like the mailman, SMTP performs only one task—delivery of mail to the mailbox. Residents typically check their mailboxes when they return from work in the evenings. Residents' operations are analogous to the operations of POP/ IMAP. Residents perform various actions on each mail: open mail, throw some mail in the trash, stack some mail for later action, and save some mail in special folders for later reference (e.g. bank statements). POP/IMAP actions such as read, delete, move, create folder, etc. are analogous to these actions.

## SMTP

As illustrated in the mailman example, SMTP delivers e-mail messages to mailboxes. SMTP does this in three steps. In the first step, SMTP initiates a connection with the receiving SMTP server and informs the receiver of the sender's e-mail address. In the second step, the sender SMTP provides the receiving SMTP with a list of recipients of the message on the receiver's system. Finally, the sender sends the message. This sequence of steps may be seen in the sequence of SMTP transactions shown below. These transactions show a user, John, on the system *example.com*, using SMTP to send an e-mail to users Joe, Jane, and Jill on the system *example.net* about the wonders of Business Data Communications.

In the example, SMTP commands are in UPPERCASE.

Step 1: Sender initiates the communication and informs the receiver of the sender's e-mail address.

> Sender: MAIL FROM john@example.com
> Receiver: OK

At this point, the receiving e-mail server knows that an e-mail message is coming in. It also knows the e-mail address of the sender. If necessary, this information is used to send notifications of delivery failures.

Step 2: The sender provides the receiving SMTP (e-mail) server with a list of recipients on the server.

> Sender: RCPT TO joe@example.net
> Receiver: OK
> Sender: RCPT TO jane@example.net
> Receiver: FAILURE
> Sender: RCPT TO jill@example.net
> Receiver: OK

In this step, the receiver knows the mailboxes to which the message is to be delivered. Also, the sender has been informed of receivers who do not have mailboxes on the server. These could simply be typos, or they could be users whose accounts have been deleted.

Step 3: The sender provides the data that will be delivered as e-mail messages to the two receivers (Joe and Jill) with mailboxes on the receiving SMTP server.

> Sender: DATA
> Receiver: START MAIL INPUT
> Sender: Business Data Communication technologies are great
> Sender: for business and personal communications
> Sender: .
> Receiver: OK

In this step, the sender sends a message of arbitrary length and ends it with a pre-specified end-of-file indicator (.). When the receiver sees the end-of-file indicator, it knows that the message has been completed. The message is then delivered to the INBOX of each user's mailbox. At this point, the responsibilities of SMTP are over.

The e-mail message will stay in the two inboxes until the receivers use POP/IMAP to delete or move them to other folders. Figure 13 shows a Wireshark capture of an SMTP mail transmission.

**FIGURE 13**  SMTP Wireshark capture

## POP (Post Office Protocol)

*The Post Office Protocol (POP) is a protocol that allows a user to access a mailbox on an e-mail server and perform useful actions on the contents of the mailbox.* The most common use of POP is to retrieve new e-mail messages that are stored in the mailbox since the last time the mailbox was accessed. After the download is successful, the mail is usually deleted from the mail server. IMAP (discussed in the next section) allows more complex operations on the mailbox.

The POP transaction is performed in a sequence of three states. The POP transaction begins with the AUTHORIZATION STATE where the user identifies himself to the mail server to get access to his mailbox. The AUTHORIZATION STATE is followed by the TRANSACTION STATE where the user retrieves messages that are waiting to be read. As each message is retrieved, it is marked for deletion. When the TRANSACTION STATE is completed, POP enters into the UPDATE STATE where all messages marked for deletion in the transaction state are deleted.

We can continue our e-mail example that was introduced in SMTP. User Jill now has at least one message in her mailbox. When she opens her POP e-mail client (such as Thunderbird or Outlook) to check her mail, the operations are as follows. POP commands are in BOLD.

The transaction begins with Jill's e-mail client opening a connection to the server on a TCP port waiting for POP connections. By default, this is port 110. When the connection is established, the POP software sends an OK message to indicate that it is ready to accept POP commands. POP then enters the AUTHORIZATION STATE. In the example below, gthyf5675rder45srgafde5 is Jill's password.

```
POP server: +OK
Jill: APOP jill gthyf5675rder45srgafde5
POP server: +OK jill's mailbox has two messages (400 bytes)
```

At this point, Jill has provided her credentials (username and password) to the POP server. Satisfied with this information, the POP server provides a status report indicating that two messages with a total size of 400 bytes are waiting to be read. The AUTHORIZATION STATE ends and the TRANSACTION STATE begins.

```
Jill: RETR 1
POP server: +OK 200 Bytes <POP server sends message>
Jill: DELE 1
POP server: +OK message 1 marked for deletion
<repeat for message 2>
```

At this point, Jill has retrieved both her messages and these messages are marked for deletion on the POP server. The TRANSACTION STATE is over because the transaction is over as far as Jill is concerned. All that is left is some bookkeeping to prepare the mailbox to receive subsequent messages. To do this, the POP server enters the UPDATE STATE.

```
Jill: QUIT
POP server: +OK (mailbox empty)
```

When the UPDATE STATE ends, the mailbox is empty and ready to receive more e-mail. Jill can now read her downloaded messages locally.

The term "Post Office Protocol" makes a lot of sense when it is viewed in terms of the operations performed by a customer of a Post Office (PO) box. The postal service drops mail at the PO box just as SMTP drops e-mail in the inbox. Customers are given keys they can use to come into the Post Office at any time of the day, open the PO box, and retrieve the mail delivered since the last time the PO box was emptied. The PO box becomes empty once again when the mail is retrieved by the user. You may note that POP works exactly the same way.

## IMAP (Internet Mail Access Protocol)

As e-mail became popular and people began accessing e-mail from home and work, a major limitation of POP emerged. Since POP deletes e-mail upon retrieval, it was difficult to access the same e-mail from home and work. IMAP was developed to overcome this limitation. IMAP also allows multiple e-mail clients to synchronize with the contents on the server. *The Internet Message Access Protocol is a protocol that allows a client to access a mailbox on an e-mail server and manipulate messages located on the server as conveniently as they could be manipulated locally.* IMAP includes operations for creating, deleting, and renaming mailboxes, checking for new messages, permanently removing messages, setting and clearing flags, and searching for and selective fetching of messages and portions of messages.

IMAP differs from POP in that IMAP adds two information fields to every message on the server: flags and message IDs. Flags are a user-friendly feature that allows users to mark each message with 0 or more flags: seen, answered, flagged, deleted, draft, recent.

Message IDs are the key field that makes IMAP more capable than POP. Every message on the server has a unique 64-bit ID called a UID. No two messages on an IMAP server (across all mailboxes on the server) can have the same UID. With 64 bits, a mailbox can have $2^{64}$ (more than 18 billion billion) unique messages, which is sufficient today, even with the GB-sized mailboxes offered by many service providers. In addition, messages within a mailbox have message sequence numbers (MSN) that indicate the relative position of messages within the mailbox. The oldest message in the mailbox has an MSN of one. IMAP messages are accessed using either the UID or the MSN. UIDs allow multiple clients to check the contents of a mailbox and resynchronize with the server upon connection to the server.

IMAP transactions pass through four states—NOT AUTHENTICATED, AUTHENTICATED, SELECTED and LOGOUT. These states roughly correspond to the POP states with the IMAP, NOT AUTHENTICATED, and AUTHENTICATED states mapping to the POP AUTHORIZATION STATE, IMAP SELECTED to POP TRANSACTION, and IMAP LOGOUT to POP UPDATE states. As in the POP example, we can continue the SMTP example to show how Jill may read her e-mail using IMAP.

The e-mail client begins by establishing a TCP connection with the e-mail server listening on an IMAP port. (By default, this port is 143.) When the connection is successful, the IMAP server indicates that it is ready to accept commands, and the transaction begins:

IMAP Server:   * OK IMAP4rev1 Service Ready

Note: The server is now in the NOT AUTHENTICATED STATE, and Jill has to provide her credentials to get access to her mailbox

Jill:   a001 login jill fgjf5656kjhfjhfg456jhgcv5654jhv
       IMAP Server:   a001 OK LOGIN completed

At this point, the NOT AUTHENTICATED STATE is over, and Jill gets access to her mailbox with the server in the AUTHENTICATED STATE.

Jill:  a002 select inbox
  IMAP Server:    * 18 EXIST
  IMAP SERVER:  * FLAGS (\Answered \Flagged \Deleted \Seen \Draft)
  IMAP SERVER:  * 2 RECENT
  IMAP SERVER:  * OK [UNSEEN 17] Message 17 is the first unseen message
  IMAP SERVER:  * OK [UIDVALIDITY 3857529045] UIDs valid
  IMAP SERVER:  a002 OK [READ-WRITE] SELECT completed

In the AUTHENTICATED STATE, Jill selects the folder she is interested in working with. The IMAP server responds with information about the contents of the selected folder, indicating that the folder has 18 messages, of which 2 (messages 17 and 18) are new. After providing this status update, the server enters the SELECTED state where Jill can manipulate the messages in the folder.

Jill:  a003 fetch 17 full
  IMAP SERVER:   * 17 FETCH (FLAGS (\Seen) INTERNALDATE "17-Jul-2008" ....... <mail contents>)
  IMAP SERVER:   a003 OK FETCH completed
Jill:  a005 logout

In this example, Jill is only interested in reading message 17. (We would like to think that this is the message delivered by John about the wonders of data communications). In the SELECTED STATE, she asks for the message to be delivered to her e-mail client for offline reading. When she logs out, the IMAP server enters the LOGOUT STATE for graceful closure.

IMAP SERVER:   * BYE IMAP4rev1 server terminating connection
IMAP SERVER:   a005 OK LOGOUT completed

In the LOGOUT STATE, the IMAP server closes the connection, performing any background tasks on the contents of the mail folder.

As you can see, e-mail is a very complex service to provide. It requires multiple protocols (SMTP and POP/ IMAP) in cooperating to provide end-user functionality. Provision of e-mail also requires technical skills and resources to maintain hardware that operates 24/7 indefinitely, even in the presence of disk failures. For this reason, many large organizations, particularly universities, are handing over e-mail functionality to service providers with the required expertise. This provides considerable savings in hardware and personnel costs. The service providers attempt to monetize the service through advertising, cross-selling, and other activities.

At the beginning of this chapter, we mentioned that application layer protocols define appropriate end-user commands. We saw earlier how HTTP uses the GET command. In this section we saw that e-mail does not have a GET command. Instead,

SMTP has MAIL FROM, POP has RETRIEVE, and IMAP has FETCH. All these commands transfer data using TCP/IP. Whereas it makes sense to have a GET command in HTTP to retrieve web pages, it does not make sense to have GET in SMTP because SMTP does not "get" anything. SMTP only sends e-mail. So SMTP does not have the GET command.

## Web mail

An increasing number of users use web mail (e.g. gmail) instead of traditional e-mail clients. Web mail retains all the components of the e-mail system shown in Figure 12. In addition, to provide the web interface, web mail introduces a web server between the mail server and the end user. An application running on the web server accepts user commands to manipulate e-mail and executes the commands on the user's behalf on the SMTP and POP/IMAP servers. This is shown in Figure 14.

# FTP (File Transfer Protocol)

FTP was developed along with SMTP to enable end users to exchange information using the Internet. *FTP is an Internet protocol for transferring files from one computer to another, regardless of the hardware and software configurations of the two computers*. While e-mail was intended to send small messages, FTP was intended for large messages. Whereas e-mail continues to be popular, FTP has now largely been replaced by HTTP for downloads. Among young users, FTP also competes with Bit Torrent for sharing extremely large volumes of data. The Filezilla open-source project has created a very popular FTP client.

Though many end users are not aware of FTP, FTP is routinely used by web developers who need to upload web pages to web servers. If you have worked as a web developer, chances are that you are very familiar with FTP. HTTP can be used to download information from web servers, but FTP continues to be one of the simplest ways to upload content to web servers. FTP is also more convenient than HTTP when multiple files have to be transferred. In the last few years, file transfer has reemerged in a different form. Photo sharing and printing sites such as Shutterfly and Flickr, and video sharing sites such as Youtube allow users to perform file-transfer operations. Finally, if you are a web-applications developer, though it is not immediately apparent, deploying web applications to remote servers is essentially the use of FTP to transfer the packaged application file to the remote application server.

Figure 15 shows the operation of FTP. FTP essentially allows files to be transferred between any two computers. The operation of FTP is quite similar to the operation of HTTP in the sense that the client uses FTP commands to specify the files to be transferred and these files are transferred between the client and server.

However, there are two major distinctions between HTTP and FTP. The first difference is the bidirectionality of FTP. Whereas the natural direction of file movement in HTTP is unidirectional—from the web server to the web browser, files can be moved in either direction in FTP—from the client to the server (upload) or from the server to the client (download). Since HTTP is inconvenient for file uploads, FTP is needed for file uploads.

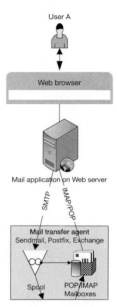

**FIGURE 14**   Web mail

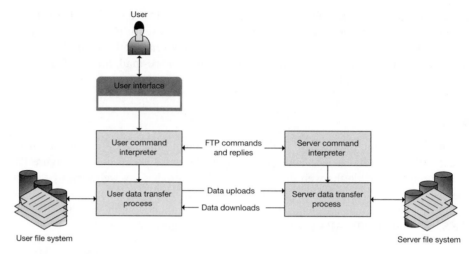

**FIGURE 15** FTP operation

The second major difference between HTTP and FTP is the presence of a control channel in FTP. HTTP uses a single channel to transfer HTTP commands and HTTP data. FTP uses one channel for commands and another channel for data transfer. The additional channel does not necessarily make FTP faster than HTTP because most of the delay in data transfer is caused by network latency. However, the control channel ensures that commands do not get delayed by getting trapped behind large data transfers.

For students interested in reading about the evolution of Internet technologies, RFC 959 describes the evolution of the FTP protocol. Though FTP is a relatively simple protocol, it passed though many steps before arriving at its final form. The earliest FTP protocol (RFC 114) accomplished the goal of specifying a common set of end-user commands independent of end-user technologies (such as differences in directory structures and control characters). The protocol accomplished these goals on two specific computers at MIT and used the proprietary transport protocols of these two computers for data transfer. By RFC 354, the idea of separating FTP commands (from the client to server) and FTP data (from server to client) had been clarified. New commands such as "Make Directory" and "Remove Directory" were added to FTP in RFC 959. RFC 1123 described FTP as a core Internet application-layer protocol to interface with TCP and IP.

## SSH (Secure shell)

SSH is a protocol for secure remote login and other secure network services over an insecure network. SSH is a relatively recent protocol. It was defined in 2006 in RFC 4250–RFC 4254. Of these five documents, I find RFC 4253 to be the most useful in understanding the protocol.

SSH is a very interesting protocol to examine for two reasons. First, unlike all the protocols we have discussed so far in this chapter, SSH is a protocol for direct usage. As described in RFC 114, direct usage implies that users are "logged into" a remote computer and execute commands on it just as local users. The Windows remote desktop is another example of direct usage. Protocols such as HTTP, e-mail, and FTP allow indirect usage since users do not log into the remote system and do not need to know how to use the remote system. Users of indirect protocols may not even be aware of the specific hardware and software running on the remote computer (do you know what operating system your university web server runs on? Even if you knew, would that knowledge affect your usage of the university website?)

The second interesting aspect of SSH is its use of encryption. Most technologies for secure communication, including SSH and SSL, follow a common sequence of steps to exchange information securely. We can use SSH to get a broad overview of the procedures used to encrypt information sent over a network.

To enhance security, SSH also provides for a mechanism to authenticate computers. The first time a computer is used to log in to a remote computer, the local computer remembers the address and some secret information associated with the remote computer. Later, if the user tries to use the same IP address and its secret information does not match the stored secret information about the remote computer, the client computer will detect the mismatch and report it to the user for necessary action.

Since we have not yet discussed encryption protocols (discussed in Chapter 13), at this point, it is adequate to get an overview of how SSH secures data using encryption. SSH operation may be seen as advancing through five stages: (1) connection establishment, (2) protocol identification, (3) key exchange, (4) shift from public to private keys, and (5) secure data exchange. There follows a brief overview of these five stages.

Like all network communication, SSH remote login begins with a TCP connection to a computer waiting to receive SSH connections. SSH typically listens on port 22. After connection establishment, the two computers negotiate the method used for encryption.

To account for differences in computational capabilities between local and remote computers, many secure technologies are available for use in SSH, each offering different levels of security, but with higher security coming at the cost of increased computational complexity. Therefore, before data communication can begin, the two computers decide on which of the available security technologies to use for the current connection.

At this point, a very interesting combination of security technologies is used. Chapter 13 will introduce public and private key encryption. For our purposes, it is enough to know that (1) public key encryption allows secrets to be exchanged openly, at the cost of heavy computation, and (2) private key encryption allows known secrets to be used for privacy in communication. The advantage of private key encryption is low computational overhead.

With this in mind, in the third stage, public key encryption is used by the two computers to openly exchange a secret key that will be used in private key encryption for the rest of the communication. Now the two computers simultaneously switch to private key encryption in the fourth stage.

Finally, in the fifth stage, secure data communication can occur using private key encryption. At this point, the remote user has a direct "logged on" connection to the remote system to an account on the remote system. The user can execute applications, write documents, and perform any actions on the remote computer that he could have performed if he had direct access to the computer. All information is hidden (encrypted) during transmission over the network.

## IM

The last application-layer protocol we discuss in this chapter is <u>instant messaging</u> or IM. *IM is an application-layer protocol that allows users to send short, quick messages to each other.* The primary difference between IM and e-mail is the absence of a mailbox in IM. Since there is no mailbox in IM, messages cannot be sent to offline clients. (Services may allow you to send a short "hello" but no more than that.) If you wish to keep a record of an IM conversation, you are required to do that by saving the communication after it is completed.

Instant messaging was defined in RFC 2778 in 2000. In addition to message exchange, instant messaging protocols also support *presence. Presence is the ability of users to subscribe to each other and be notified of changes in state such as being online or busy or away.* When a user changes state, all users who choose to be notified of that user's state are informed of the change.

1997 was a red-letter year for instant messaging. That year was the first time that AOL (the dominant ISP of the time) sent more instant messages than the total volume of mail handled by the U.S. Postal Service.

---

**CASE STUDY** | WILL THE NETWORK SILENCE THE PRINT MEDIA?: GOOGLE ADS

---

*The print media has traditionally been the most effective check on the misuse of power of the ruling elite. In the past, efforts by the print media have even forced a U.S. president to leave office. In recent years though, the print media seems to have met an opponent as formidable as itself—online news sources. The print media has been unable to resist the defection of its audience to online news sources. The Internet may turn out to be the most formidable adversary the print media has ever faced.*

In 1972, an investigation by the *Washington Post* culminated in the resignation of U.S. President Richard Nixon two years later. Possibly out of fear for the power of expression, in 1968 in Romania, Nicolae Ceausescu made owning an unregistered typewriter a crime punishable by death. Other prize-winning examples of investigative journalism in the print media have exposed corruption in governments at all levels and have led to many social reforms. While the print media has attacked some of the most powerful sectors of modern society, the print media may itself be under attack from the Internet in the coming years.

Newspapers reached their peak daily circulation in 1984 at 63 million subscriptions. Since then, circulation has been falling at approximately 1% each year. Coinciding with the rapid rise in the online population in 2005 (case study Chapter 1), newspaper circulation has fallen sharply since 2004. In 2009, daily newspaper circulation fell almost 10% from the previous year, reaching 44 million copies per day, a level last seen in the 1940s. At the same time, prime-time network TV viewing also fell 10% in 2008.

The drop in circulation has been accompanied by a drop in advertising revenues for the print media. Newspapers typically earn over 75% of their revenues from advertising, and only about 25% from subscriptions. The Newspaper Association of America reported that newspaper advertising revenues fell 16.6% in 2008 and were likely to fall by more than 25% in 2009. Newspapers, which have put up with open hostility from powerful governments, have been unable to withstand this onslaught of change in reader preferences. The *Tribune*, owner of the *Los Angeles Times*, has sought bankruptcy protection. *Business Week*, the popular magazine that published the widely followed MBA rankings, was sold to Bloomberg for only an estimated $2–$5 million. In 2008, *U.S. News and World Report*, publisher of the famous college rankings, went from a weekly publication schedule to bi-weekly and, finally, to a monthly publication schedule. In early 2009, one of the nation's leading newspapers, the *New York Times*, mortgaged its headquarters building to borrow a mere $250 million at a steep interest rate of 14%. This was at a time when home mortgages could be obtained at an interest rate of approximately 5%.

What is causing this pain in the print media? Very simply, the Internet. As we saw in the case study in Chapter 1, since 2005, there has been a dramatic rise in the number of people online. There has also been a corresponding increase in the amount of time people spend online. According to an estimate, people spend 8% of their time with newspapers, and 29% of their time online.

There is a logical explanation for this change in user behavior. Paraphrasing a senior Google executive, in traditional media, the audience has to go where the content is— a movie theater, or Channel 298 at 8 p.m. on Thursday. On the Internet, content providers have no choice but to go where the audience is. Accordingly, TV shows are now on Hulu, and movies are on Netflix, available for viewing at any time of the day. Advertising dollars have chased this shift in audience tastes and have been diverted to online channels. Since total advertising expenditures have remained virtually constant, most of the online ad revenues have come at the cost of traditional media.

Online channels are much more advertiser-friendly than traditional media. As stated by Mel Karmazin, the CEO of Viacom, which owns channels such as CBS, "You pay $2.5 million for a spot on the Super Bowl . . . you pay your money. You take your chances." By contrast, Google has developed highly measurable advertising mechanisms. Where traditional media cannot tell advertisers what works and what doesn't, Google can state with a high degree of precision that $100 spent on advertising through its platforms will lead to $X in revenues. It can report revenues

for each customer and create separate reports for advertisers from different industries. It is therefore not surprising that advertisers also prefer the Internet over other advertising channels.

There is no surprise that, with its rising popularity and better measurability, online media are growing while the print media is shrinking.. While the newspaper industry shed over 33,000 jobs between 2007 and 2009, Google added over 150 employees each week during 2008. While newspaper ad revenues fell from $18 billion in 2005 to $9 billion in 2008, Google earned $22 billion in revenues in 2008, almost entirely from advertising.

Newspapers missed many chances to develop online platforms, probably because they were late to take the online medium seriously. Newspapers always had great faith in the power of their "storytelling." In 1995, Craig's List was founded. This website gave users the opportunity to post classifieds by city and by category and was clearly a threat to newspaper classifieds. But newspapers did not take this threat seriously at that time. Newspapers also do not seem to have considered the tiny text ads next to Google searches as a serious competitive threat. Only in 2008, CBS became the first traditional media company to open an office in Silicon Valley.

Though Google has benefitted from the shift in audience tastes, it clearly needs the newspapers to create interesting content. Google CEO Eric Schmidt has said, "There is a systemic shift going on in how people spend their time . . . We have a shared problem. We need newspapers' content. And it is critically important that they continue." At the current time, when a reader follows a news story to a newspaper's website, the newspaper gets the opportunity to display ads to the reader. Google serves newspapers by increasing traffic to their websites, but it is still not clear whether this will be sufficient for newspapers to survive in their current form. Expect a lot of changes in how the print media structures its business.

Do you recall the statistic that people spend 8% of their time with newspapers and 29% of their time online? Well, that is not the complete story. Advertisers still spend 20% of their ad budgets on newspapers and only 8% on the Internet. If advertising expenditures become proportional to the time we spend with each medium, there could be even more pain ahead for newspapers.

## REFERENCES

Ahrens, F. "Mexican Billionaire Gives Loan to New York Times Co." *Washington Post,* January 21, 2009. http://www. washingtonpost.com/wpdyn/content/article/2009/01/20/ AR2009012003988.html (accessed 1/2/10).

Auletta, K. *"Googled: The End of the World as We Know It."* New York: Penguin Press, 2009.

Crovitz, L.G. "China's Web Crackdown Continues," *Wall Street Journal,* January 11, 2010, A17.

Lowry, T. "Bloomberg Wins Bidding for *Business Week,"* BusinessWeek, October 13, 2010. http://www.businessweek .com/innovate/FineOnMedia/archives/2009/10/bloomberg_ wins.html (accessed 1/2/10).

Meeker, M., C. Boyce, M. Masurekar, and L. Wu. *"Economy + Internet Trends."* Morgan Stanley report, March 20, 2009.

Perez-Pena, R. "U.S. Newspaper Circulation Falls 10%," *New York Times,* October 26, 2009. http://www.nytimes.com/2009/10/27/ business/media/27audit.html (accessed 1/2/10).

Smith, E. *"Paper Cuts."* http://graphicdesignr.net/papercuts/.

"The Watergate Story." *Washington Post* http://www.washington post. com/wp-srv/politics/special/watergate/ (accessed 1/2/10).

## SUMMARY

This chapter introduced the most common application-layer protocols—HTTP, e-mail (SMTP, POP, IMAP), FTP, SSH, and IM. These protocols provide convenient commands that end-user applications can use to exploit the data-transport services offered by TCP/IP.

While discussing these protocols, we discussed how HTTP offers a *pull* form of communication whereas e-mail offers a *push* form of communication. We presented ways in which these differences can influence how the two protocols are used in business. We also discussed how most application-layer protocols support indirect usage whereas SSH supports direct usage. Finally, it was pointed out that the key technological difference between e-mail and IM is the availability of a mailbox in e-mail and of *presence* in IM.

The protocols discussed in the chapter are not the only application-layer protocols available. An example of an application-layer protocol not discussed in this chapter is SIP (session initiation protocol) for voice. However, the protocols covered here are the most widely used, and demonstrate how application-layer protocols specify user commands that exploit TCP/IP to provide meaningful services to the end user. Information about the other protocols can be obtained from the RFCs for these protocols.

## ABOUT THE COLOPHON

Apple has been a pioneer at introducing most of the common networking technologies in desktop computers. Wireless networks, USB, and Gigabit Ethernet are some communication technologies that first reached critical mass in consumer adoption because they were available on Apple computers.

However, Steve Jobs, the founder of Apple, is also very picky about the technologies the company actually uses in its computers. He is often quoted as saying, "I'm as proud of what we don't do as I am of what we do." Networking was one of the technologies that initially did not make the cut for inclusion in Macs.

A story that is reported[17] is that when Steve Jobs first went to see a demonstration of the technologies at Xerox PARC (where the Ethernet was invented and which had been deployed by the time of Steve Jobs' visit), he was so infatuated by the capabilities of the graphical user interface that he completely missed noticing the other phenomenon on display there—computer networking. Later, when Steve Jobs was asked how he would network his new computers, he flung a floppy disk at the engineer asking the question and yelled, "There's my . . . network."

That goes to show, even one of the most forward-thinking leaders in the computing industry could not recognize the importance of computer networks when he first saw them.

## ADDITIONAL NOTES

Important tips on e-mail etiquette and a popular recommendation for managing e-mail are provided here.

---

[17] Hiltzik, M. A., *Dealers of Lightning: Xerox PARC and the Dawn of the Computer Age.* (New York: Harper Paperbacks, April 2000).

# E-mail etiquette

This is a text on the technology, but it is very useful to point out a few tips on e-mail etiquette. It is very important to remember that e-mail does not change the rules of effective communication. E-mail does make it easy for you to get your message to the receiver's inbox, but it is just as easy for the receiver to delete the message. Precision, courtesy, language, and background information together increase the likelihood that the receiver will read and act on the e-mail.

An excellent article by Horowitz[18] that dates back almost 15 years provides simple, timeless advice for anyone using e-mail. The advice is based on the heritage of e-mail as an alternate to business memos. Memos are business communication designed to be saved in an organized filing system.[19] Suggestions include:

Make the subject line descriptive—The subject line should help the receiver in deciding on how to act on the message or file it.

Discuss one subject per message—This facilitates forwarding and replies. If someone needs to be brought into the discussion, there is less danger of unwanted information leakage if every message deals with just one subject.

Keep the message short and to the point—Where possible, fit the entire message into one screen so the user does not have to use the mouse or keyboard to scroll down.

Scrutinize the addressees every time—E-mails are notorious for going to more people than necessary. Make sure an e-mail to your boss does not include criticism of the same boss!!!

Use smileys—One major limitation of e-mail is its lack of emotion. Add the emotional touch using smileys. Smileys are keystroke combinations that indicate emotions. For example :-) indicates happy news whereas :-( indicates sad news.

AVOID ALL CAPS—This is interpreted to mean shouting. Do not jump to conclusions however, if you receive e-mail in ALL CAPS. Many senior citizens find it easier to use ALL CAPS when composing e-mail.

Be extra polite—Even with the best of intention, written criticism appears harsher than verbal criticism.

Be calm—Do not "shoot off" an e-mail in anger. Most long-time users of the Internet have at least one unpleasant memory of an occasion when they sent off an angry e-mail to a friend over an issue that seems trivial in retrospect.

Avoid flaming—Sending nasty or insulting messages is called flaming. Avoid this. If something seriously bothers you, try resolving it over the phone or in person.

And finally, a summary rule:

Do not send anything by e-mail that you would not want your mom to see on page 1 of the *Wall Street Journal*—It is useful to remember that almost all the e-mails exchanged by Enron executives are available in research databases online. The companion website of the book also has some select messages extracted from the database. None of these executives anticipated that their e-mails would be publicly displayed in such manner.

---

[18] Horowitz, R.B. and M.G. Barchilon, "Stylistic Guidelines for E-mail." *IEEE Transaction on Professional Communications*. **37**(4), (1994): 207–212.
[19] Yates, J., "The Emergence of the Memo as a Managerial Genre." *Management Communication Quarterly*. **2**(4), (1989): 485–510.

## Personal e-mail management

There are two schools of thought regarding personal e-mail management. One school of thought believes that ideally, users should maintain an empty Inbox. This is popularly called the Inbox zero method. A leading proponent of this school of thought is Merlin Mann whose lecture on the topic is very popular. Another believer of this method was Prof. Randy Pausch of Carnegie Mellon Univ., who led the creation of the Alice programming environment. On the other end of the spectrum is the view held by Google, that e-mail should never be deleted or even managed. Rather, e-mail should be searched.[20] Below is a summary of the Inbox zero method.

Everybody has to comply with the storage limitations of their mail service providers. There is, however, an emerging school of thought that the ideal way to manage e-mail is an empty inbox: Inbox zero. This has been popularized by Merlin Mann's *Inbox zero* video and by Prof. Randy Pausch in a popular lecture on time management. Links to both videos are available through the companion website and are very highly recommended.

The central principle of *Inbox zero* is to define a small number of actions which you will use to process every incoming e-mail. These actions should be designed to liberate the information content in each e-mail to its correct permanent location in a calendar, files, tasks, or even well-designed mail folders. Managing e-mail is then the act of managing these actions. Instead of reacting to each incoming e-mail in real time, it is recommended that you process incoming mail only when you are prepared to process your inbox to zero.

Merlin Mann provides an excellent set of five (and only five) actions that work for him. His actions on e-mail, in decreasing order of priority are:

1. Delete (or if useful, archive to some large local folder).
2. Delegate—this applies to e-mails that require follow-up work. Before the end of the day, such e-mails should leave the inbox and go into an appropriate location with appropriate labels.
3. Respond, if a response is required, and then delete.
4. Defer, act during the day, and then delete.
5. Do, (what is suggested in the e-mail), and then delete.

Apart from #2, all are relatively simple to manage. You may need to develop your own procedure to manage e-mails that fall in the "delegate" category.

## REVIEW QUESTIONS

1. What are the functions of the application layer? How were the earliest application-layer protocols defined? What application do you spend the most time on?

2. How has the web been most useful to you?

3. What are the three most popular websites in the world today? What primary service does each site offer?

4. Describe some changes in the patterns of Internet usage based on changes in the list of most popular websites globally.

---

[20] Douglas Merrill and James A. Martin, *Getting Organized in the Google Era: How to Get Stuff out of Your Head, Find It When You Need It, and Get It Done Right*, (New York: Crown Business, 2010).

5. Why is the web gaining popularity as a marketing tool over traditional methods such as yellow pages?

6. What is a hyperlink? What is an inlink? What information about a web page can be inferred from inlinks to the page?

7. What is *HTML*?

8. What is *search advertising*? Why is it a powerful method of advertising compared to traditional media such as newspapers?

9. What is *AdWords*?

10. What is *URL*? Describe the parts of a typical web URL.

11. What is a killer application?

12. In what ways do you use e-mail in your daily life? When do you prefer to use e-mail over the postal system? When do you prefer the postal system over e-mail?

13. Describe the differences between pull and push forms of communication, using the web and e-mail as examples.

14. Using examples from your own life, describe some advantages of e-mail as a communication medium

compared to your other choices (such as cell phones, meetings).

15. What are some potential disadvantages with e-mail as a communication medium? Can you describe some occasions when you have run into these disadvantages of e-mail?

16. What is *flaming*?

17. Describe the high-level structure of the e-mail system.

18. What are an MTA and an MUA in the context of e-mail?

19. What is the role of SMTP in e-mail?

21. What is the role of POP/IMAP in e-mail?

22. What are some important differences between POP and IMAP?

23. What is *FTP*? How is FTP different from HTTP?

24. What is *SSH*?

25. What is *instant messaging*? How is IM different from e-mail?

26. What is *presence* in the context of IM?

## HANDS-ON EXERCISE—WIRESHARK

In this exercise, we will use Wireshark, the leading packet-analyzing application. We will use Wireshark to explore all the protocol header fields described in Chapters 2–6. Wireshark is open source and is available for most of the popular operating systems. Wireshark provides a graphical user interface to assist users in probing the various protocol header fields in packets. Wireshark recognizes a large variety of packet formats. To assist users, Wireshark also interprets the meanings of header fields and reports special packets such as TCP-handshake packets.

While the introductory content in this exercise will help you get started with Wireshark, the Wireshark website also has a number of useful resources, including short training videos. These are available from the "Learn Wireshark" link at the Wireshark website.

### Installing and using Wireshark

Wireshark is available for download from http://www.wireshark.org.

Wireshark works in conjunction with packet-capturing utilities, which go by names such as WinPcap. These

utilities access the lower network layers and capture packets. The captured packets are interpreted and displayed by Wireshark.

Download Wireshark from the Wireshark website. For reference, the download page appears as shown in Figure 16. The application installs like any other application. Save the installer file to your desktop (for ease of locating later). After the file has downloaded, double-click the file to install the application. During the installation, Wireshark also installs the WinPcap utility and prompts you to confirm the installation of the utility. During installation, Wireshark also adds entries to the Programs menu in Windows.

The Wireshark application window is shown in Figure 17. The three columns show the three most important activities you are likely to perform with Wireshark. In the leftmost column, Wireshark displays the network interfaces it detects on your computer. In this example, Wireshark has detected two active interfaces—the Broadcom NeXtreme Gigabit Ethernet driver and the adapter for the VPN connection. When you click on one of these adapter names, Wireshark begins to capture packets on the selected interface using the default options. After starting a capture,

**FIGURE 16** Wireshark's download page

if you use a networked application such as a web browser, Wireshark will capture all the packets generated by the application. The captured packets are displayed on the capture window as shown in Figure 19. This is the window in which we will spend most of our time in this exercise.

To stop a capture, click on the "Stop the running live capture" button in the packet-capture window. It is the fourth button from the left in the main toolbar, as of Wireshark 1.2.6.

The second column in the main Wireshark application window (Figure 17) shows recently saved files and also allows users to download sample captures from the Wireshark wiki. The third column in the Wireshark window takes users to online resources including documentation.

The packet-capture window (Figure 18) has three panes. From top to bottom, the panes show increasing levels of detail in the captured data. The packet-list pane at the top shows all the captured packets, one packet per line. The info column in the packet-list pane shows summary information about the packet, based on Wireshark's interpretation of the protocol-header fields. Clicking on a line in the packet-list pane selects the packet. For example, line 8 has been selected in Figure 19. A very useful feature of this pane is that it highlights packets using protocol-specific colors. For example, web packets are highlighted in green.

When a packet is selected in the top pane (packet-list pane), the packet-detail pane shows a protocol layer-wise breakup of all the header information in the packet. For example, in Figure 19, the packet-detail pane shows header information for the Ethernet, IP, TCP, and HTTP layers of the selected packet (packet 8 in the packet-list

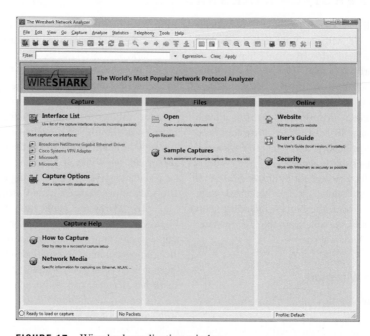

**FIGURE 17** Wireshark application window

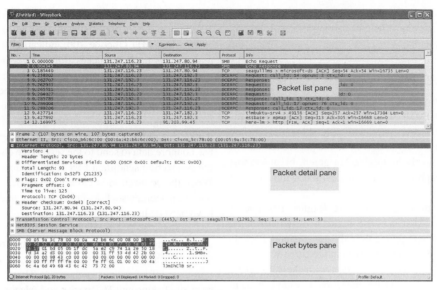

**FIGURE 18**   Wireshark packet-capture window

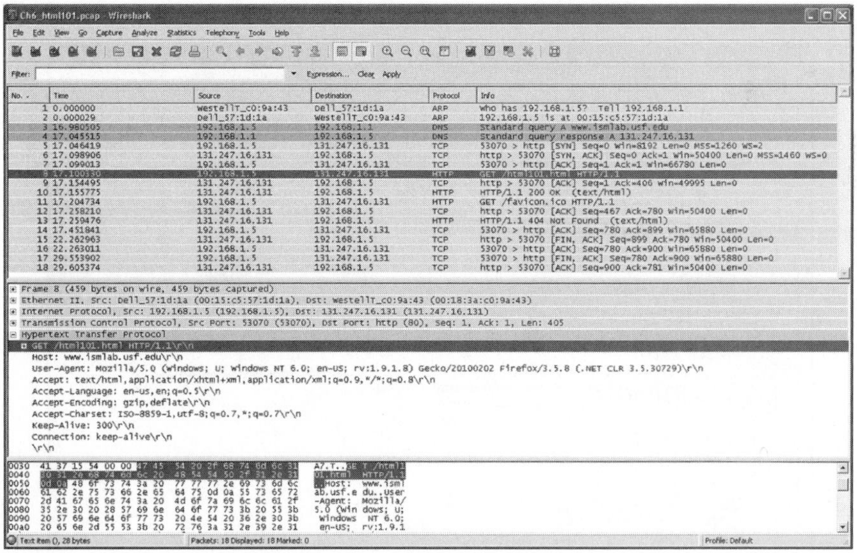

**FIGURE 19**   Wireshark packet-capture for html101.html

pane). By default, Wireshark shows the important summary information for each layer. Clicking on the ⊞ sign next to a protocol layer expands the layer-header information, showing information about all fields at that layer for the packet. For example, in Figure 19, the HTTP header has been expanded displaying all HTTP header fields, such as host and GET.

The third pane, the packet-bytes pane, shows the byte-level view of the selected packet. If a field is selected in the packet-detail pane, the packet-bytes pane highlights the bytes containing that information in the packet. For example the HTTP header has been selected in Figure 19, and the HTTP-header bytes have been highlighted in the packet-bytes pane.

Thus, starting from the top pane, the three panes in Wireshark allow us to drill into captured packets to any desired level of detail.

## Viewing and analyzing a capture

The companion website includes a packet-capture while the html101.html web page used in the chapter was downloaded. Since the web page was very short, only a few packets were necessary to download the page. Predictably, the capture is mostly highlighted in green, because most packets in the capture are associated with downloading the web page.

Walking through the capture (Figure 19), packet numbers 1–4 are ARP and DNS packets. We will examine the functions of these protocols in the next chapter. Packets 5–7 are the three packets involved in the three-way handshake to establish a TCP connection with the web server (Chapter 5). Once the TCP connection is established, in packet 8, the client uses HTTP to send a GET request to the web server asking for the html101.html page. In packet 10, the web server sends back the web page. The response also includes HTTP code 200, indicating that the client's request was handled successfully. Once the web page is transferred completely, the web server sends a TCP FIN (final) packet to the client, indicating that the server has no more data to send and is ready to close the connection. This is analogous to the way we generally close phone conversations using phrases such as "talk to you later." If the client has no more data to send to the server, the client also closes the connection sending a FIN packet (packet number 17). When the connection is closed, the operating system can release resources such as port numbers and memory that have been dedicated to the connection.

Since TCP connections are very common, Wireshark has a very convenient view to strip out lower-level protocol-header information and aggregate all the application-layer information into one view. This view is accessed by right-clicking any TCP packet and selecting "Follow TCP Stream." This brings up the window shown in Figure 20.

**FIGURE 20** Follow TCP Stream window

This window is an excellent tool to understand the operation of application-layer protocols. The HTTP transaction begins with the HTTP GET request from the browser. The server responds with the status code and the HTML page. When the browser asks for the favicon image, the server responds with error code 404 and a formatted page, displaying the code in an error page. For the convenience of users, Wireshark highlights client requests and server responses in different colors.

To answer the questions for this exercise, install Wireshark, start Wireshark, begin capturing packets on an active interface and then use a web browser to visit the website of your university. Stop the capture after the page has downloaded completely. Scroll through these packets until you reach the web packets in your capture. Answer the following:

1.  Using online and any other resources, write a brief summary of how Wireshark is used to manage computer networks.

2.  What are the sequence and acknowledgement numbers of the three TCP packets performing the three-way handshake? These packets were exchanged just before the GET request for the web page.

3.  Right-click an HTTP packet and select "Follow TCP stream." What are the HTTP header fields in the first client request and the first server response? What are the values in these fields? As an example, in Figure 20, one of the client fields is "Host" and the value of the field is "www.ismlab.usf.edu."

4.  How many different GET requests did your browser have to make to download the entire page? What were the arguments to these GET requests? For example, in Figure 20, the browser made two GET requests. The first request asked for "/html101.html" and the

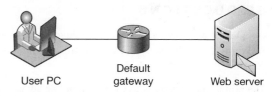

**FIGURE 21**   Typical network setup

second GET request asked for "/favicon.ico." If there are more than five GET requests, only list the arguments for the first five GET requests.

5.  What is the IP address of your default gateway? This is obtained from `ipconfig`.

6.  What is the MAC address (physical address) of the default gateway identified above? This is obtained from `arp -a`.

7.  Select an HTTP packet. List its source and destination IP addresses as well as source and destination Ethernet addresses.

8.  Referring to Figure 21 and the information collected in questions 5 and 6 above, what machines does each of these addresses (MAC and IP) refer to? You may be able to relate this to the idea that whereas MAC addresses are hop-by-hop addresses, IP addresses are end-to-end addresses.

9.  What are the source and destination port addresses in the selected packet?

10. Look up your `etc\services` file (in Windows, this file is usually located in C:\Windows\System32\ drivers\etc). Which of these ports is a standard port? Paste the entire line from the `etc\services` file that contains information about this port.

## NETWORK DESIGN EXERCISE

In Chapter 1, you identified different ways in which Coolco could use computer networks at its different offices. Answer the following question related to these uses of computer networks:

1.  For at least five of these uses of computer networking, use the Internet or other sources to identify the market-leading software applications used to obtain the required functionality (for example, to serve web pages, the market-leading software is the Apache web server). In a table, provide the following information for the five uses: the application (use) category, the market-leading software application in the category, and a paragraph or two about the strengths of the selected software application. (You can use the marketing information from the application's website to describe the strengths of the application.)

## CASE QUESTIONS

1. Google offers two channels for advertising—AdWords and AdSense. What is AdWords? What is AdSense?

2. The principal competitors to Google in online advertising are Yahoo and Microsoft. Briefly summarize the capabilities of the advertising platforms of these two firms.

   The largest newspaper publisher in the United States is Gannett (ticker symbol: GCI), the publisher of *USA Today* and other magazines. Open its latest 10K statement and search for "Publishing operating revenues" to answer the next four questions. You may search for the company's SEC filings directly at the SEC website (http://www.sec.gov/edgar/searchedgar/companysearch.html) or through financial websites such as http://finance.yahoo.com. On Yahoo Finance, you can enter the ticker symbol of the firm and follow the link to SEC Filings on the results page.

3. What are the sources of revenues of the company from its publishing business?

4. What fraction of the company's revenues in its printing business come from advertising?

5. What fraction of the company's revenues in its printing business come from circulation?

6. Ignoring dividends, how has the company's stock performed in the last three years and five years? Hint: Find the latest stock price, the stock price three years ago, and the stock price five years ago. Then simply calculate the returns as: return = (current price – old price)/old price.

7. Spot Runner is a company that integrates online media with traditional TV channels. Write a brief description of the services offered by the company. In the write-up, describe how the company can benefit small businesses such as local pizza parlors trying to advertise on local TV stations.

8. Take a leading national newspaper or your leading local newspaper. Briefly describe its online presence. Include information such as the following: What are the major news categories on the publication's website? What are the main products or services advertised? What customization options does the site offer? Does it charge a subscription fee for online content? What do you think is the newspaper's target audience?

# Support Services

## CHAPTER 7

*What's in a name? That which we call a rose*
*By any other name would smell as sweet;*
— JULIET TO ROMEO

## Overview

In the previous chapters, we have examined each layer of the TCP/IP stack. To make these technologies easy to use, the designers of the Internet also created some supporting technologies. One of these services, DHCP, automatically assigns IP addresses to computers that join networks. Another service, DNS, allows users to address hosts using names such as www.uta.edu instead of IP addresses such as 129.107.56.31. At the end of this chapter you should know:

- what DHCP is and how it works
- what non-routable addresses are and how they are used
- what NAPT is and how it works
- what ARP is and why it is useful
- what DNS is and how it works
- how all the above services are put together in your home network

## DHCP (Dynamic Host Configuration Protocol)

We saw in Chapter 4 how every computer on the network is uniquely identified by its IP address. Comparing the computer addresses at the MAC layer (Chapter 3) and IP addresses at the network layer, we saw that the great advantage of IP addresses over MAC addresses is that network administrators can assign IP addresses according to the needs of the network.

But the flexibility of IP address assignment introduces a new chore for network administrators. They must find a way to assign IP addresses for every computer that joins a network. This works fine if there are very few computers on the network and if these few computers remain connected to the network forever. Examples of such networks include public computing labs at most universities and corporate data centers. In these cases, the network administrator can permanently assign an IP address for each computer manually.

Unfortunately, most networks do not meet these criteria of limited size or relative stability. University wireless networks are an example. Students enter the network at all times of the day, stay connected for some time during class, and then return home. In these networks, manual IP address assignment can get very cumbersome and error-prone.

Pause for a moment to think how you might provide IP addresses manually to these mobile wireless users on a typical college campus. Perhaps each student could be given an IP address when they register as a student at the university. Unfortunately, most schools do not have enough IP addresses to do this. If students cannot be allocated an IP address for the whole year, perhaps students could obtain an IP address for the day on entering campus, perhaps by logging into a secure kiosk. In this case, we would only need as many IP addresses as the number of students who visit campus during the day.

But then, in the rush to return home after class, many students are likely to forget to return their allocated IP addresses at the end of the day. Periodically, when all IP addresses available to campus IT are lost in this manner, some kind of reset procedure will be necessary to reclaim all addresses lost since the last reset. Hopefully, this example has convinced you that it is not easy to manually assign IP addresses in large networks.

Another problem with manual IP address assignment is that if IT is not careful while handing out IP addresses, they might occasionally assign duplicate addresses, causing network connectivity problems to the users assigned these duplicated addresses.

Manual assignment of IP addresses also makes the organization vulnerable in case the network administrator quits without notice. If the departing administrator did not keep good records, the new administrator would have no easy way to collect information about all IP addresses already allocated in the organization.

DHCP, or dynamic host configuration protocol, addresses these issues by automating the allocation of IP addresses in networks. _DHCP is a technology that enables automatic assignment and collection of IP addresses_. Almost every network has a DHCP server to allocate IP addresses. On your home network, the wireless router typically acts as the DHCP server.

Besides making it easier to use IP addresses by automating their allocation, DHCP is also designed to improve the efficiency of allocating IP addresses. We have seen in Chapter 4 how the 32-bit size of the IP address field limits the number of available IP addresses to about 4 billion. Unfortunately however, since these addresses are allocated in blocks by the registries, the available IP addresses are not used very efficiently. According to some estimates, only about 5%–15% of the available IP pool of 4 billion addresses would actually get used.[1] This meant that when we reached about 200–600 million hosts on the Internet, we would run out of IP addresses to assign to new computers joining the network. As of January 2010, there were already over 700 million hosts online. Thus, we have already reached the point where, until recently, experts believed that new computers would not be able to join the Internet, limiting the growth of the Internet.

---

[1] Lawton, G. "Is IPv6 Finally Gaining Ground?" _IEEE Computer_ (August 2001): 11–15.

The long-term solution to remove the shortage of IP addresses is to increase the number of IP addresses available. IPv6 accomplishes this by using a 128-bit IP address field. As we have seen in Chapter 4, IPv6 provides trillions of IP addresses per square foot of the earth's surface, ensuring that we will never run out of IP addresses.

However, since introducing IPv6 requires significant investments on the part of network operators, a short-term solution has been devised until such time that IPv6 becomes more prevalent. This solution is expected to allow IPv4 addresses to meet network needs for some more years. The solution is implemented using three technology components—DHCP, reusable IP addresses, and address translation. DHCP is the first of these three components of the IP-address reuse mechanism that we will examine.

To understand the role of DHCP, it may be noted that most computers that are allocated IP addresses do not use the addresses efficiently. Only a small fraction of the computers that have been allocated IP addresses are actually performing any network activity at any given time. We could greatly improve the efficiency of IP address utilization if we could allocate an IP address to a computer only when the computer needed network connectivity.

DHCP was introduced in 1997 in RFC 2131. When using DHCP, network administrators run one or more DHCP servers on the network. These servers are given the responsibility of managing the IP addresses available for the network. At home, your wireless router acts as the DHCP server. Figure 1 shows the DHCP server settings of a typical home wireless router. The DHCP server on this router has been configured to allocate 150 IP addresses in the range 192.168.1.1–192.168.1.150. This is more than adequate for the average home network.

By default, all PCs are configured at the factory to look for a DHCP server out of the box and obtain an IP address from the server. PCs do this as part of the booting up process. Figure 2 shows the dialog of Windows Vista that shows this setting (accessed from Control Panel → Network and sharing center → View Status → Properties → IPv4 → Properties). As the figure shows, you can also assign an IP

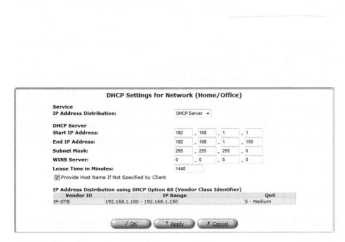

**FIGURE 1**   DHCP server allocating IP addresses in the range 192.168.1.1–192.168.1.150

**FIGURE 2**   Windows PCs use DHCP by default

address manually if you prefer, but for convenience of end users, the default settings on all PCs is to look for a DHCP server for an IP address.

## DHCP operation

The basic DHCP operation is very simple. Every network that uses DHCP has at least one DHCP server listening for DHCP client requests on the network. During startup, DHCP clients broadcast requests asking for network parameters from DHCP servers listening on the network. Since the client DHCP request is broadcast, clients need not know the IP address of the DHCP server to locate it. When the broadcast reaches the DHCP server, the server responds by providing the client with an IP address and other essential network parameters for a fixed duration. *The duration for which an IP address is provided is called the DHCP lease-time.* Before the lease-time expires, clients can request an extension of the lease.

DHCP servers try to be courteous toward clients. If the DHCP server had provided an IP address to the client before (say the previous day) and if the address is still available, the server provides the same IP address to the client. For this reason, you may notice that the IP address provided to you by your ISP can stay the same for many days, even though the ISP uses DHCP to allocate IP addresses.

The sequence of messages exchanged between DHCP clients and servers is shown in Figure 3. At a high level, a client requests an IP address and DHCP servers provide one. When the client accepts an IP address, the server marks this address in its records as allocated.

At a greater level of detail, at boot time, clients broadcast DHCP DISCOVER messages asking for network parameters. DHCP servers intercept these messages and search their configuration files to determine the IP address and network configuration to be allocated to the client. Servers send the IP address to clients in a DHCP OFFER message. If the client receives more than one DHCP OFFER, it selects one of the offers and broadcasts a DHCP REQUEST message informing all DHCP servers of its selection. The server whose offer was selected records this selection in its own configuration files so that the offer is not repeated to other clients. The DHCP server then sends a DHCP ACK to the client to confirm that the client may now use the OFFERed IP address. All these messages are shown in Figure 3 and are exchanged while the computer is booting up (before you get the login prompt).

When the computer is shut down, clients send a DHCP RELEASE message to the server. Upon receipt of the DHCP release message, the server discards the lease and adds the IP address into its pool of available addresses so that the address can be reused if necessary. If no DHCP RELEASE message is received, the lease automatically terminates at the end of the lease-time. This usually happens when the computer is abruptly shut down.

## DHCP allocation schemes

To allow maximum flexibility for network administrators, DHCP can allocate IP addresses in three different ways.

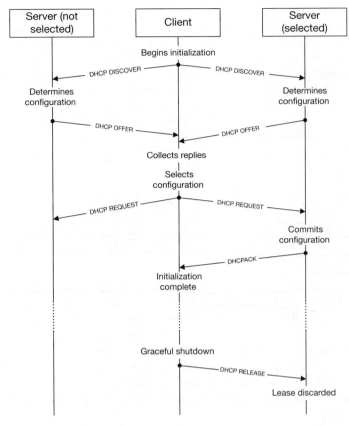

**FIGURE 3**   DHCP operation timeline

*Automatic allocation:* In automatic allocation, DHCP allocates IP addresses to hosts on the network on a first-come, first-serve basis. Once allocated, this IP address remains assigned to the host forever. This can be very convenient in networks where devices are referred directly by IP address. For example, if a networked printer is assigned an IP address by automatic allocation, client PCs only need to be set up once to use the specified IP address. The network administrator can be assured that each time the printer is switched on, it will be assigned the same IP address by the DHCP server, and the software on client PCs will have no difficulty in locating the printer on the network. For this reason, some home routers use automatic allocation to distribute IP addresses.

*Manual allocation:* In manual allocation, the network administrator manually specifies the IP addresses to be allocated to individual devices on the network. Each time a device with a manually allocated IP address is switched on; it is given the IP address manually specified by the network administrator. Thus, both automatic allocation and manual allocation permanently assign IP addresses to clients.

If both automatic and manual allocation assign IP addresses permanently, are there any cases where you would prefer manual allocation over automatic allocation? Manual allocation is useful when the network administrator wishes to use some preferred address-allocation scheme for specific devices. Automatic allocation would simply assign the first available IP address to each device when it is switched on for the first time. Manual allocation is therefore most commonly used for printers and other non-server devices. Usually this is done for security reasons to simplify the configurations of firewalls. Firewalls are discussed in the chapter on network security.

*Dynamic allocation:* In dynamic allocation, IP addresses are leased out for short durations by the DHCP server. Before the lease expires, clients can ask the DHCP server to extend its lease. If the DHCP server does not hear from the client before the lease expires, the DHCP server reclaims the IP address and the address becomes available for another client.

Dynamic allocation is very useful for computers such as client PCs that are only intermittently connected to the network. Since most residential customers need Internet connectivity only in the mornings and evenings, they fall into this category. Dynamic allocation is therefore popular among ISPs to allocate IP addresses to subscribers. Dynamic allocation is also popular in enterprise networks to provide IP addresses to client PCs, since these are usually connected to the Internet only during office hours. It is easy to see that of the three allocation mechanisms, dynamic allocation enables address reuse and helps administrators use IP addresses efficiently when their availability is limited.

Each DHCP server can mix and match allocations methods for different devices on the network. For example, the DHCP server may use manual allocation for printers, automatic allocation for a few selected clients, and dynamic allocation for all other devices. You may note that DHCP is typically not used to configure servers. Servers are almost always assigned static IP addresses. This ensures that DHCP errors will not interrupt server operations.

## DHCP configuration

For reference, Figure 4 shows a sample DHCP server configuration file for one of the most popular DHCP servers—the DHCP server maintained by the Internet Systems Consortium, ISC. (You may remember ISC from the domain survey in Chapter 4.) The configuration creates a dynamic pool of 18 IP addresses in the range 10.1.1.236–10.1.1.253 in the subnet with base address 10.1.1.128. The lease time is 6 hours (21,600 seconds). The configuration also specifies a manual allocation of 10.1.1.2 for the web server. As seen from the manual allocation entry, DHCP identifies hosts by their Ethernet MAC addresses. The other information in the configuration file allows DHCP to provide additional information to clients, including the addresses of DNS servers, the subnet mask, and default gateway. (DNS is covered later in this chapter.)

```
option domain-name              "datacomm.example.com";
option domain-name-servers      10.1.1.1, 10.2.1.1, 10.3.1.1;
option routers                  10.1.1.254;
option subnet-mask              255.255.255.128;

default-lease-time              21600;

subnet     10.1.1.128 netmask       255.255.255.128        {
           range     10.1.1.236     10.1.1.253;
}

host www {
     hardware          ethernet    00:06:5B:CE:39:05;
     fixed-address     10.1.1.2;
     host-name   "www.datacomm.example.com";
}
```

**FIGURE 4**   Sample DHCP server-configuration file

# Non-routable (RFC 1918) addresses

DHCP was the first component of the three-part short-term solution to address the problems arising from the shortage of IP addresses. Address reuse is the second important piece of the solution.

When reusing IP addresses, more than one computer on the Internet can be assigned the same IP address. If this can be made to work, a small pool of IP addresses can be used to network a large number of computers. The main problem with reusing IP addresses is that if IP addresses are no longer globally unique, routers will not know how to route packets addressed to computers sharing an IP address. Say two computers, one in California and one in New York, have the same IP address, 192.168.2.8. If a packet with a destination address of 192.168.2.8 reaches a router located in Chicago, the router will have no way of deciding whether to send the packet east to New York, or west to California. For this reason, reused IP addresses have to be handled very carefully. Most importantly, the challenge is to ensure that the destination address of every packet reaching every router on the Internet is unique, even if IP addresses are reused in different parts of the Internet.

RFC 1918, defined in 1996, provides a very interesting solution to this challenge. RFC 1918 defines three pools of IP addresses for IP address reuse. These address pools are:

10.0.0.0/8       :   10.0.0.0–10.255.255.255 (Class A address pool)          *Non-routable*

172.16.0.0/ 16   :   172.16.0.0–172.16.255.255 (Class B address pool)

192.168.0.0/16   :   192.168.0.0–192.168.255.255 (Class B address pool)

IP addresses within these three address pools may be used by anybody within any network without permission from the Internet registries. Thus, these IP addresses may be reused as often as necessary. One IP address can only be used once within a network, but other networks can reuse the same IP address for addressing within their own networks.

RFC 1918 addresses are a lot like common names such as "John" or "Jane." If you were to go to the visitors' reception center at your university and ask to see John, the staff at the reception desk would find it almost impossible to locate "John" among the many people on campus named John. However, if you reached the department where John worked, chances are high that there would be only one person named John within the department, making it likelier for you to locate him. Similarly, RFC 1918 addresses are locally unique but globally common.

To preserve the uniqueness of IP addresses on the global Internet, routers and firewalls at the edge of the enterprise limit the packets using RFC 1918 addresses to the LANs in which they originate. Packets do not leave any router with an RFC 1918 address in either the source IP address or destination IP address field. If a packet were to leave a router with an RFC 1918 address in the destination address field, other Internet routers would have no way of uniquely identifying which of the many computers on the Internet with that IP address to deliver the packet to. Similarly, if a packet left a router with an RFC 1918 address in the source address field, replies to this packet would have an RFC 1918 address in the destination address field. Again, it would be impossible to deliver the reply because many computers on the network would have the same IP address.

Routers also do not advertise routes that include RFC 1918 IP addresses to other routers outside the enterprise. All routers are aware that since these addresses can be reused, they may not be unique on the Internet and are not useful for routing. Since packets cannot be routed to IP addresses defined in the RFC 1918 address pool, these addresses are also called non-routable addresses or private addresses.

Figure 5 shows an example of how RFC 1918 IP addresses are used in practice. In the example, the home has a wireless router, a laptop, and a PC. The laptop has IP address 192.168.2.2, the PC has IP address 192.168.2.3, and the wireless router has the IP address 192.168.2.1 on its interface facing inside the home. Computers within a home can connect to each other using these IP addresses.

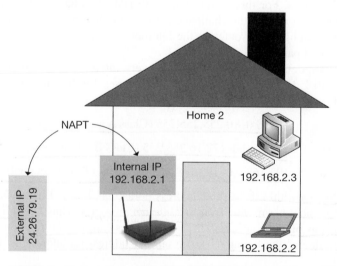

**FIGURE 5**   Using non-routable RFC 1918 IP addresses

# Network Address Port Translation (NAPT) NAT

So, what is the point in getting an RFC 1918 IP address if it cannot be used for routing? After all, isn't routing pretty much the only thing IP addresses are used for? The answer to this question lies in NAPT (Network- Address Port Translation)—the third component of the three-part solution to address the problem of shortage of IP addresses. RFC 1918 addresses are meant to be used in conjunction with NAPT. In this section, we will see how the combination of RFC 1918 and NAPT allows routing even while using RFC 1918 addresses.

*NAPT, often abbreviated as NAT or PAT, is the method by which IP addresses are mapped from one address block to another, providing transparent routing to end hosts*. The details of NAPT have been specified in RFC 3022. Network address translation (NAT) refers to changing IP addresses from one IP-address block to another. Port-address translation (PAT) refers to changing port addresses during network-address translation if necessary. NAPT is typically used to connect networks using RFC 1918 non-routable IP addresses to networks using globally unique addresses. As shown in Figure 5, home networks are almost always set up as RFC 1918 networks. ISPs use NAPT to serve computers within customer homes. NAPT is often also used to connect desktops in large enterprises.

In conjunction with RFC 1918 non-routable IP addresses, NAPT vastly expands the availability of IP addresses. An important design feature of NAPT is that all the complexity of address translation is located at the edge router, and no change is required in end clients inside the network. This greatly simplifies the deployment of NAPT into a network. If all clients on a network use DHCP, a simple change in the DHCP address pool will ensure that when the current IP-address lease expires, clients will be allocated addresses from the new internal IP-address pool. Clients will not even be aware of the change.

The sequence of operations when using NAT is shown in Figure 6. Say, a student using his home PC wishes to browse his university's website. His home wireless router has been allocated an IP address of 65.32.26.70 by his ISP, most likely using dynamic allocation by a DHCP server running within the ISP network. His home PC has the IP address 192.168.2.3, most likely assigned using automatic allocation by the DHCP server running at the wireless router. The IP address of the university's website in the example is 131.247.80.88 (USF). In the first step, the PC sends out an HTTP request with source IP address 192.168.2.3 and destination address 131.247.80.88. As the packet leaves the home, it is intercepted by the home router, which also acts as the NAPT translator. In step 2, when the packet leaves the wireless router, the source IP address of the packet is translated from 192.168.2.3 to 65.32.26.70.

This packet reaches the university web server. In step 3, the web server sends a response to the source IP address, i.e., to the home router at 65.32.26.70. Finally, in step 4, the home wireless router translates the destination address of the incoming packet from 65.32.26.70 to 192.168.2.3 using NAPT. This packet is sent to the PC over the home network. To correctly translate incoming packets, NAT routers maintain a record of outgoing requests in a NAT forwarding table or translation table.

RFC 1918 and NAPT are designed to support outbound connections from computers inside networks. If an incoming packet does not match an existing entry in the NAT forwarding table, the NAT translator will not know which computer in the

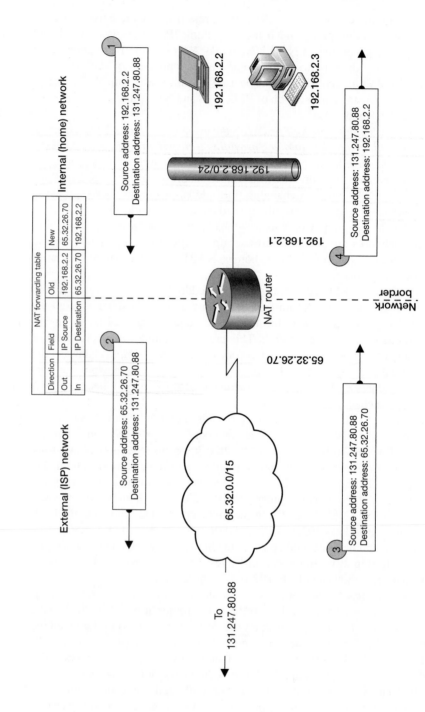

**FIGURE 6** Basic NAT operation

internal network to send the packet to. For this reason, in many organizations, clients use RFC 1918 addresses, while web servers, e-mail servers and a small number of other devices that need to accept connection requests from external hosts are given unique addresses.

The combination of the source and destination IP address and port address makes each translation unique. Since there can be 65,536 ports associated with each IP address, and each port can support one communication channel, each globally unique IP address can support 65,536 separate connections with one specific host using NAPT. If you talk to a second host, you can have another set of 65,536 unique connections to the second destination from the same source.

The example of Figure 5 may be extended using NAPT as shown in Figure 7. The homes in the example are served by an ISP with address pool (24.24.0.0/14). Two IP addresses from this pool, 24.26.79.18 and 24.26.79.19, are used to serve the two homes. The outward-facing ports of the routers in Home 1 and Home 2 are assigned these IP addresses. Since these IP addresses are not in the RFC 1918 pool, they are globally unique. These addresses can be used to route packets to the two customer homes. When packets leave Home 1, they leave with source IP address 24.26.79.18 and packets leaving Home 2 have source IP address 24.26.79.19. When replies are received at Home 1, the router uses NAPT to translate from the ISP's IP address 24.26.79.18 to the internal RFC 1918 IP address 192.168.2.1 used inside the home.

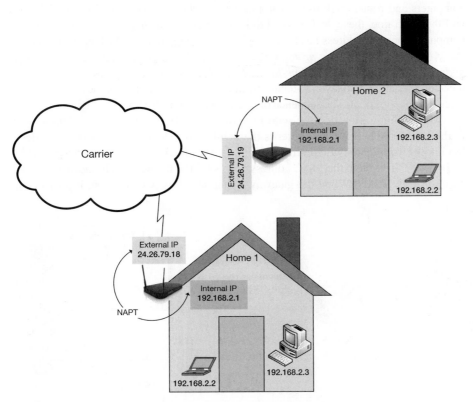

**FIGURE 7**    Using NAPT and non-routable RFC 1918 IP addresses in ISPs

Since NAPT is so useful and is so easy to use, NAPT has become a huge commercial success. All wireless routers sold in retail stores implement NAPT by default. Many experts involved in the development of networking technologies dislike NAPT because IP addresses are expected to be preserved from end-to-end, and NAPT disrupts this model. Many applications do not work behind NAT. Some experts also believe that the success of NAPT has delayed the deployment of IPv6.

## Address Resolution Protocol (ARP)

After discussing the three-part solution used to increase the availability of IP addresses, we turn our attention to two other support services used to facilitate network operation. ARP, discussed in this section, is used by devices within networks to obtain MAC addresses corresponding to known IP addresses. DNS, discussed in the next section, is used by devices to translate hostnames to IP addresses.

From Chapter 3 and Chapter 4, we know that each computer connected to the network has at least one MAC address and at least one IP address. As packets traverse networks, computers and routers use the IP addresses to forward packets. Within the LAN, computers typically obtain the IP address of their immediate neighboring device—the gateway router—from DHCP. To send the packet to the gateway router or the next hop, computers and routers will use a data-link-layer technology such as Ethernet. To form an Ethernet frame, these devices need to know the MAC address of the gateway or the computer whose IP address has been supplied by the application. ARP is used to obtain the MAC address. *ARP is a protocol that dynamically determines the network-layer IP address associated with a data-link-layer physical hardware address.* ARP therefore links the addresses at the two layers—data-link and network—within the same device. ARP is a very simple protocol. The sequence of operations in ARP is shown in Figure 8.

In the figure, the desktop with IP address 192.168.2.11 has some data to send to the Internet. The gateway router is the neighboring device in the route. The desktop knows from its network configuration that the IP address of its gateway router is 192.168.2.1. To obtain the MAC address of this router, the desktop broadcasts an ARP request on the LAN. When the gateway router sees this ARP request, it provides its

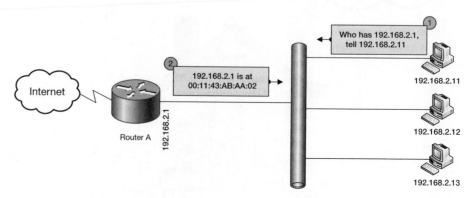

**FIGURE 8** ARP sequence of operations

ARP request

```
Sender MAC Address    : 00:11:50:3a:da:22
Sender IP address     : 192.168.2.11
Target MAC Address    : 00:00:00:00:00:00
Target IP address     : 192.168.2.1
```

ARP response

```
Sender MAC Address    : 00:18:8b:c9:24:6b
Sender IP address     : 192.168.2.1
Target MAC Address    : 00:11:50:3a:da:22
Target IP address     : 192.168.2.11
```

**FIGURE 9**   ARP packets exchanged in Figure 8

**FIGURE 10**   ARP cache displayed using arp −a

MAC address in its reply. The PC can now use this MAC address to format the Ethernet frame for transmission on the LAN.

Figure 9 shows the contents of the fields in the ARP request and ARP response frames exchanged in Figure 8. Observe the destination MAC address of 00: 00: 00: 00: 00: 00 in the ARP request. This is a placeholder that is to be populated by the receiver. The ARP request is encapsulated in an Ethernet frames with destination address ff:ff: ff:ff:ff:ff, which is the broadcast address on the LAN.

Hosts typically cache the MAC addresses obtained from ARP for short durations, say 2–10 minutes. The cached arp information can be retrieved in Windows using the `arp −a` command at the DOS prompt as shown in Figure 10.

ARP works in the background and completely hides data-link-layer addresses from end users.

## Domain Name System (DNS)

Let us now look at the last important support service that simplifies the use of computer networks on a day-to-day basis. This service is called the Domain Name System, DNS for short. *The Domain Name System is the set of databases that performs the correspondence between the domain name and its IP address*. DNS translates domain names such as www.slu.edu to IP addresses, wherever in the world the domain name may be located. DNS is such an important service that it is probably the very first networked service used by every computer user. However, like all support services, DNS runs in the background and users are largely unaware of its existence.

We know from Chapter 4 that computers are uniquely identified on the network using IP addresses. We also know from personal experience that we rarely ever type IP addresses into the address bar of a browser or e-mail address field. We almost always refer to sites by user-friendly names such as www.osu.edu. DNS allows us to refer to computers by these names, instead of IP addresses. Only after DNS completes the translation from domain name to IP address does the application create a packet to send to the destination over the Internet.

From an end-user perspective, using DNS is very simple. Clients typically obtain the IP address of a designated DNS server from DHCP during bootup. Whenever a

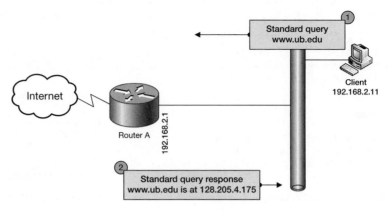

**FIGURE 11** DNS use

user types in a hostname in any network application, the client sends a DNS request for the host name to the designated DNS server. The designated DNS server looks up the host name in the domain name system to retrieve the IP address, which it forwards to the client. This is shown in Figure 11 for a client resolving the IP address corresponding to UB's website. In the example, the DNS server is at 192.68.2.1 (the local wireless router). This is common in home networks.

> An important thing to note is that all DNS requests are sent to the local DNS server. This server will take care of all the complexity of translating the host name, wherever in the world it might be located.

Though the use of DNS by clients is easy, creating the DNS databases is more involved. In the early days of the Internet, long before the advent of the web, the domain name to IP address mapping was done using a simple text file called hosts. This file had entries such as the following, one line per networked host:

```
127.0.0.1              localhost

131.247.222.249        www.usf.edu

161.116.100.2          www.ub.edu
```

Every user maintained a local copy of the hosts file. Users could use the hostname www.ub.edu in any application and the computer would resolve the host name to the IP address 161.116.100.2. As users became aware of more computers on the network, they manually added entries to their hosts[2] file.

Gradually however, the Internet became too large for end users to be able to maintain their hosts files. This motivated the need for a name → IP address mapping system that was (1) accurate in mapping hostnames to IP addresses; (2) easy to maintain; and (3) easy to use.

---

[2]The hosts file is still present in Windows at C:\Windows\System32\drivers\etc\hosts. It typically contains one entry: 127.0.0.1 localhost, to map the hostname localhost to the IP address 127.0.01.

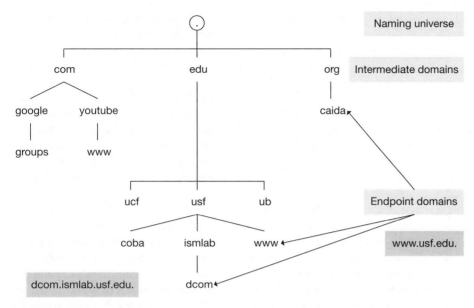

**FIGURE 12**   View of a section of the domain name hierarchy

DNS, defined in 1987 in RFC 1034 and RFC 1035, emerged as the solution to this need. DNS created the concept of domains. Domains are arranged hierarchically, originating from a common root. The key feature of DNS is that the responsibility for maintaining the name → IP address mappings within each domain is delegated to administrators within the domain.

Figure 12 shows a section of the domain name hierarchy.

The top level of the naming universe is written as ".". At the highest level within the naming universe are the top-level domains such as ".com."; ".edu."; and ".org." These top-level domains generally delegate mapping responsibilities to organizations and networks. These organizations get domain names such as fau.edu. or youtube.com. Domains can further delegate to sub-domains. Organizations usually delegate further until endpoint domains such as www.fau.edu. are reached. Endpoint domains are the host names that users typically access on the Internet.

With this method of decentralized domains, the root of the domain name system is written as ".". Domain names are read from right to left. The domain name www.slu.edu. (Observe the "." at the end of the domain name.) is interpreted as the domain "www," located within domain "slu," which is located within the "edu" domain. "Edu." is a top-level domain and originates from the root of the domain name system. Though every domain name ends in a ".", it is customary for end users to write domain names without the "." representing the naming universe. DNS completes this detail for you in the background.

A number of top-level domains (TLDs) have been defined.[3] TLDs are maintained by the Internet Assigned Numbers Authority (IANA). You may recall from Chapter 4 that this is the same organization that also maintains the entire pool of IP

---

[3] The list of TLDs is available at http://www.iana.org/domains/root/db/.

addresses. The IANA delegates the responsibility of maintaining the name servers at each TLD to a sponsoring organization. End users can sign up with any accredited registrar such as GoDaddy to obtain a sub-domain within any open TLD. Registrars inform the sponsoring organization of the TLD about the new sub-domain registration and the sub-domain is added to the DNS system.

There are various kinds of TLDs. The most familiar TLDs are open domains such as .com, .org, and .info. Anybody can register a domain as a sub-domain of any of these open TLDs. There are also limited domains such as .gov, .edu, and .mil. The administrators of these domains require that organizations must satisfy certain conditions before they can register themselves as sub-domains of these domains. For example, only U.S. federal, state, and local governments can register themselves as sub-domains of the .gov domain.

Some industries have been given their own top-level domains. These include the .aero and .travel TLDs. However, these industry-specific TLDs do not seem to have become very popular. (Even www.aaa.travel is redirected to www.aaa.com.) Finally, there are country domains such as .us and .af, one for each country. You might think that only residents of the country are allowed to register a country domain name. However, contrary to what you might think, sponsoring organizations of most country domains keep their domains open. A resident in the U.S. can just as easily register a sub-domain of .us as a sub-domain of .vg.

The complete name of any domain is obtained by including the path to the domain from the top level. Paths are written from right to left as we go down the naming hierarchy. In Figure 12 for example, google.com, ub.edu, and caida.org are domains. Child domain names must be unique within the immediate parent domain. Thus, there can only be one www subdomain in google.com, but we can have www.google.com, www.yahoo.com, www.netcraft.com, etc.

Until this point we have described how domain names are interpreted. We can now examine why it is useful to organize domain names in a hierarchical manner. Recall that the Domain Name System was created to make it convenient to maintain an up-to-date mapping between computer names and IP addresses. To accomplish this, each domain maintains jurisdiction over its immediate sub-domains and only over its immediate subdomains. For example, the .edu domain maintains the mapping between the domain name usf.edu and the IP address belonging to usf.edu. The usf.edu domain in turn maintains the mapping between names within usf.edu, such as coba.usf.edu, and the corresponding IP addresses. The administrator of the .edu domain has no idea about the IP address of coba.usf.edu. It has to defer to the administrator of the usf.edu domain to retrieve the IP address of coba.usf.edu. Similarly, the administrator of usf .edu has to defer to the administrator of coba.usf.edu to resolve www.coba.usf.edu.

In short, if anyone asked the .edu domain for the IP address of <u>coba</u>.usf.edu, the .edu domain would reply by saying, "I do not know what the IP address of <u>coba</u>.usf.edu is. But I do know that .usf.edu knows the IP address of <u>coba</u>.usf.edu. I also know that the IP address of .usf.edu is 131.247.100.1. Please contact .usf.edu at 131.247.100.1 to obtain the IP address of <u>coba</u>.usf.edu." The user would then contact .usf.edu to obtain the IP address of <u>coba</u>.usf.edu, which is 131.247.92.201.

The delegation of host-naming responsibilities to child domains ensures that each domain administrator only has a relatively small set of domain names to maintain.

No single administrator is responsible for maintaining the name $\rightarrow$ IP address mappings for the entire Internet. As a result, name-IP-address mappings are usually always current.

The use of a hierarchical system for managing domain names follows the examples of using a hierarchical system for naming in other large networks. We saw in Chapter 4 how the telephone number system, zip codes, and credit cards also use a hierarchical system for managing their address space. Most large networks find it convenient to use a hierarchical system to manage names.

Say a user enters the hostname www.yahoo.com on their browser. How does the browser get the IP address corresponding to the host name?

The DNS server is a piece of software that is used to resolve host names. The domain name server maintains the name $\rightarrow$ IP address for a domain. For clients it serves, the DNS server also retrieves IP addresses for host names maintained by other DNS servers. To use DNS, a computer needs to know the IP address of a domain name server it can use. It typically gets this at boot time from DHCP. You can see the DNS server information on your PC using the command `ipconfig /all` at the DOS prompt. All operating systems also have a DNS resolver or a DNS client. When a user enters a URL in a browser, the browser passes the host name in the URL to the DNS resolver on the PC. The resolver contacts its DNS server to obtain the required IP address. The DNS server performs all necessary lookups in the DNS system to obtain the IP address. When the IP address is obtained, the DNS server passes it to the DNS client, which passes the IP address to the browser. Now, the browser can populate the header fields in all layers and send out the request packets to the Yahoo web server.

It is easy to see how DNS works on a Linux/UNIX terminal. The DNS client is accessible using the `dig` command. Figure 13 shows the results of a DNS query to obtain the IP address of www.buffalo.edu. The answer section of the response provides

```
# dig www.buffalo.edu

;; Got answer:

;; QUESTION SECTION:
;www.buffalo.edu.       IN          A

;; ANSWER SECTION:
www.buffalo.edu.        86400       IN      A       128.205.4.175

;; AUTHORITY SECTION:
buffalo.edu.            71951       IN      NS      ns.buffalo.edu.
buffalo.edu.            71951       IN      NS      sybil.cs.buffalo.edu.
buffalo.edu.            71951       IN      NS      accuvax.northwestern.edu.

;; ADDITIONAL SECTION:
ns.buffalo.edu.             71951       IN      A       128.205.1.2
sybil.cs.buffalo.edu.       53404       IN      A       128.205.32.8
accuvax.northwestern.edu    11624       IN      A       129.105.49.1

;; Query time: 3 msec
;; SERVER: 131.247.100.1#53(mother.usf.edu)
```

**FIGURE 13**  Typical DNS query (to obtain the IP address of www.ub.edu)

the desired information—that the IP address is 128.205.4.175. In the example, the authority section lists the name servers that have authoritative information about the domain. These are the name servers that maintain the name → IP address mappings for buffalo.edu. It is interesting to see that not only is the university maintaining a backup name server on its own premises, it is also maintaining a third backup name server at northwesten.edu. The additional section provides the IP addresses of the authoritative name servers.

DNS domains are sometimes also called zones. Thus buffalo.edu is a zone. As described earlier, each name server is responsible for its zone and only for its zone. Zones may have sub-zones, and each sub-zone is responsible for its own zone.

To reduce the number of DNS queries, name servers and clients cache resolved domain names. The administrators of each zone specify the time-to-live (TTL) for their zone. They may even specify TTLs for each record in their zone. Domain names within the zone can be cached till the TTL expires. In Figure 13, the IP address for www.buffalo.edu can be cached for 86,400 seconds (1 day) while the IP address for buffalo.edu can be cached for another 71,951 seconds. If another user requests this name server within 86,400 seconds for the IP address of www.buffalo.edu, the name server will not perform a DNS query; instead it will provide the requested IP address from its cache.

What happens if your domain name server does not have a cached entry for a TLD for a domain it is asked to search? For example, say a user types in the URL www.gm.com.cn. Let us also assume that no one using this DNS server has visited a site in China in the last few days. The DNS server therefore has no cached entry for the .cn TLD.

In this case, the name server starts the search from the naming universe. There are 13 name servers distributed around the world that maintain information about the top-level domains.[4] These are called root name servers. Information about these root name servers is hardwired in all name servers. When a DNS query is made, the DNS server can start with one of the root name servers and search down the domain-name hierarchy till it finds the authoritative name server for the domain being searched. This process is shown in Figure 14 for a client asking its local name server for the IP address of the URL www.usf.edu; this is step 1. In step 2, the local DNS server queries a root name server, which refers the local DNS server to the "edu" name server. The process continues until, in step 7, the usf.edu name server authoritatively provides the IP address for www.usf.edu. Finally, in step 8, the local DNS server sends this IP address to the client. The client sees only the information exchanged in steps 1 and 8, as shown in Figure 14. The complete trace using dig +trace is shown in Figure 15.

The `dig` command also has a `+trace` option. Using the trace option shows the information retrieved as the DNS server traverses the domain name hierarchy. The trace results from a query for www.usf.edu are shown in Figure 15. The DNS server first locates the root name server, then the .edu name server and finally, the usf.edu name server, which provides the IP address for www.usf.edu. This re-creates the query of Figure 14.

---

[4] http://www.root-servers.org/ has an image of the locations of all the root-name servers.

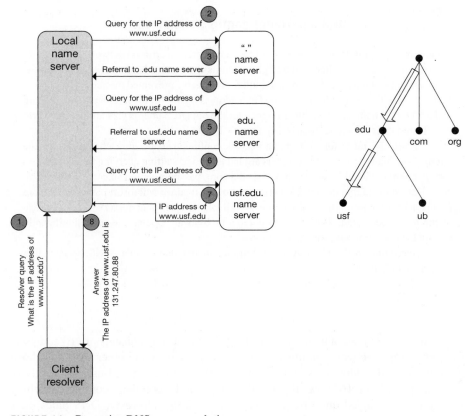

**FIGURE 14**   Recursive DNS query resolution

```
pns:~# dig +trace www.usf.edu
; <<>>DiG 9.2.4 <<>>+trace www.usf.edu

.            77639     IN    NS    E.ROOT-SERVERS.NET.
(and other root name servers

edu.         172800    IN    NS    E.GTLD-SERVERS.NET.
(and other .edu name servers)

usf.edu.     172800    IN    NS    justincase.usf.edu.
usf.edu.     172800    IN    NS    mother.usf.edu.
(and other usf.edu name servers)

www.usf.edu.    600    IN    A     131.247.80.88
```
**FIGURE 15**   Tracing the DNS query for www.usf.edu

## DNS and router configuration error[5]

An interesting example of the impact of DNS configuration error on network connectivity is reported by CAIDA. Microsoft had placed all its externally visible name servers on the same subnet. In January 2001, a router configuration error prevented the subnet from communicating with the outside world. The DNS address record for the microsoft.com domain had a TTL of 2 hours. As a result, 2 hours after the outage, name servers around the world had cleared their cached records of Microsoft's IP address.

When the microsoft.com name servers continued to be unreachable due to the wrongly configured router, name servers around the world starting querying the root servers for microsoft.com and related names (expedia.com, passport.com, msn.com, msnbc.com, etc.). Data showed that during this period, the query load for Microsoft names went from normal rates of approximately 0% of the overall load at the root name servers to over 25% of the total query load. Thus, local problems in DNS at popular sites can significantly disrupt the operations at root name servers.

According to the CAIDA article, Microsoft outsourced their DNS provisioning after the incident.

An important advantage of using DNS is that it hides changes in IP addresses from end users. Network administrators can relocate web and other servers to hosts with different IP addresses when required, without affecting end-user connectivity. For example, Figure 16 shows that the IP address of the popular e-commerce website Amazon.com changed quite frequently in March 2010. However, DNS hides these changes from end users. As long as Amazon can ensure that DNS resolves its IP address correctly, it does not have to worry about informing end users about its current IP address.

One of the most popular DNS servers is BIND, maintained by the ISC (which also maintains the most popular DHCP server). Figure 17 shows a sample configuration file for the BIND DNS server for a domain example.com. The configuration specifies a TTL of 1 day (86,400 seconds). The e-mail address of the administrator is hostmaster@example.com (any problems with the DNS server can be automatically e-mailed to the administrator). The name server (NS) for the domain is pns.example.com, which is located at IP address 192.168.16.129. The e-mail server (mail exchange, or MX) is at mail.example.com, with IP address 192.168.16.130. The web server, www.example.com, is at 192.168.16.129. In other words, the same host (192.168.16.129) acts as both the web server and name server in this domain. A subdomain, test.example.com, is also defined. The name server for the test.example.com domain is located at 192.168.16.143. The administrator of test.example.com can define subdomains of test.example.com.

---

[5] Brownlee, N., K.C. Claffy, and E. Nemeth. *"DNS Measurements at a Root Server." Cooperative Association for Internet Data Analysis. San Diego.* (2001) Available at http://www.caida.org/outreach/papers/2001/DNSMeasRoot/.

| Site report for www.amazon.com | | | |
|---|---|---|---|
| **Site** | http://www.amazon.com | **Last reboot** | unknown    Uptime graph |
| **Domain** | amazon.com | **Netblock owner** | Amazon.com, Inc. |
| **IP address** | 72.21.210.250 | **Site rank** | 102 |
| **Country** | US | **Nameserver** | dns-external-master.amazon.com |
| **Date first seen** | October 1995 | **DNS admin** | root@amazon.com |
| **Domain Registrar** | networksolutions.com | **Reverse DNS** | 210-250.amazon.com |
| **Organisation** | Amazon.com, Inc, Legal Dept, P.O. Box 81226, Seattle, 98108-1226, United States | **Nameserver Organisation** | Amazon.com, Inc, Legal Dept, P.O. Box 81226, Seattle, 98108-1226, United States |
| **Check another site:** | | **Netcraft Site Report Gadget** | +  Google  [More Netcraft Gadgets] |

**Hosting History**

| Netblock Owner | IP address | OS | Web Server | Last changed |
|---|---|---|---|---|
| Amazon.com, Inc. 605 5th Ave S SEATTLE WA US 98104 | 72.21.207.65 | Linux | Server | 21-Mar-2010 |
| Amazon.com, Inc. 605 5th Ave S SEATTLE WA US 98104 | 207.171.166.252 | Linux | Server | 20-Mar-2010 |
| Amazon.com, Inc. 605 5th Ave S SEATTLE WA US 98104 | 72.21.207.65 | Linux | Server | 19-Mar-2010 |
| Amazon.com, Inc. 605 5th Ave S SEATTLE WA US 98104 | 72.21.207.65 | Linux | Server | 18-Mar-2010 |
| Amazon.com, Inc. 605 5th Ave S SEATTLE WA US 98104 | 207.171.166.252 | Linux | Server | 17-Mar-2010 |
| Amazon.com, Inc. 605 5th Ave S SEATTLE WA US 98104 | 72.21.207.65 | Linux | Server | 16-Mar-2010 |
| Amazon.com, Inc. 605 5th Ave S SEATTLE WA US 98104 | 72.21.210.250 | Linux | Server | 15-Mar-2010 |
| Amazon.com, Inc. 605 5th Ave S SEATTLE WA US 98104 | 72.21.210.250 | Linux | Server | 14-Mar-2010 |
| Amazon.com, Inc. 605 5th Ave S SEATTLE WA US 98104 | 72.21.210.250 | Linux | Server | 13-Mar-2010 |
| Amazon.com, Inc. 605 5th Ave S SEATTLE WA US 98104 | 207.171.166.252 | Linux | Server | 12-Mar-2010 |

**FIGURE 16**    Changes in IP address of www.amazon.com over 10 days

```
$TTL     86400
     @    IN   SOA  pns.example.com.   hostmaster.example.com. (
               serial    2008072701
)
             IN           NS    pns.example.com.
             IN           MX    10    mail.example.com.

pns      A    192.168.16.129
www      A    192.168.16.129
mail     A    192.168.16.130

test     NS   demo
demo     A    192.168.16.143
```

**FIGURE 17**    Sample BIND DNS server configuration file

The caching of domain names can lead to websites becoming unreachable if their IP addresses are changed. DNS servers will pass obsolete IP addresses from their cache to clients. Eventually, as the DNS entries are timed out in the caches of name servers around the world, the new IP address is retrieved and the site becomes reachable again. Therefore, if you plan to change IP addresses of any of your Internet servers, it is a good idea to reduce the TTL of your name server to say 15 minutes. This should be done sufficiently in advance so that records with the old TTL expire before the change. This way, when you do change IP addresses, it will only be 15 minutes before the old IP address expires within the cache of all DNS servers on the Internet.

In most home networks, the wireless router also acts as the DNS server to perform DNS lookups.

## Home networking

Starting from Chapter 2 and ending in the previous section of this chapter, we have covered all the components that work together to bring Internet connectivity to your home. In this section, we will see how all the different components are put together in your home network.

The focal point of your home network is your wireless router. This router may have been provided by your ISP, or you may have purchased it the shelf from a retail store such as Best Buy. This router typically acts as your DHCP server, your DNS server, and your NAPT router.

To understand your network, perform the following three steps. In step 1, type `ipconfig/all` at your DOS prompt. This will show you the network configuration of your PC as shown in Figure 18. You will generally see an RFC 1918 address ending in .1 as your default gateway, DHCP server, and the DNS server. This is the internal IP address of your wireless router. In step 2, check your wireless router's network configuration. Most routers allow you to see and modify the router configuration by pointing your browser to this IP address from a computer in the home. Manufacturers have different interfaces, but if you type in your router's RFC 1918 IP address in your browser, you should see a page similar to that in Figure 19. Most routers let you see information such as the different computers that have been assigned IP addresses by the DHCP server on the router.

Finally, in step 3, you can visit the website `http://www.whatismyip.com`. This website will show you the IP address assigned to the external port of your router by your ISP. This IP address is generally a globally unique IP address from the IP address pool assigned to your ISP by the network registry.[6]

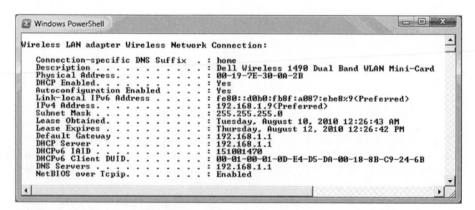

**FIGURE 18**   Home PC IP configuration

---

[6] If you are adventurous, you can type in your external IP address into the "whois" search box at www.arin.net to confirm that your IP address indeed belongs to your ISP.

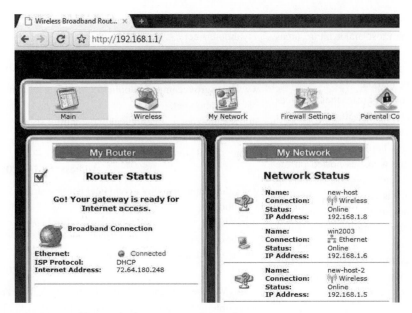

**FIGURE 19**    Home wireless router web interface

Putting these pieces together, how does your home network work? All PCs in your home get an RFC 1918 IP address from your wireless router at boot time. The DHCP server in your router also informs the computers in your home that the wireless router is the next hop (default gateway) as well as the DNS server on the local network (though some ISPs use one of their own DNS servers for end users). When a packet leaves your home network, your home router translates the source IP address field in the packets from the internal RFC 1918 address to the external IP address assigned by the ISP. When reply packets reach the wireless router, the router translates IP addresses back from the ISP's address to the correct internal IP Address.

| CASE STUDY | DNS SIMPLIFYING E-COMMERCE BEHIND THE SCENES: YAHOO STORES |
| --- | --- |

*Electronic commerce has reduced the barriers faced by entrepreneurs in trying to sell their products and services to a global audience. Leading technology firms and IT entrepreneurs have developed technology solutions so that anybody can create and operate e-commerce websites at reasonable costs. In this case, we see how DNS and another technology, virtual hosting, help in improving the utilization of computer hardware powering these websites. By improving hardware utilization,*

*DNS and associated technologies significantly lower e-commerce costs.*

It is quite likely that you have set up a simple HTML website in some class or have tried using one of the many free website builders to create a website. Building a simple HTML website is quite easy. However, e-commerce websites need many additional functions, such as the ability for the seller to add products, be notified about orders, print shipping labels, and notify customers when orders are shipped. Since there is a reasonably large customer base interested in these services, most major metro areas have many competing providers offering web hosting and related services to enable e-commerce websites. Yahoo is one of the national players in the market.

How do these service providers offer their services at such reasonable prices, often less than $50 per month? It turns out that service providers can host multiple websites at a single server, thus amortizing hardware and software costs for each server over all the websites hosted on the server. DNS plays an important enabling role in making this happen. The other technology is virtual hosts, the ability of a single web server to host multiple websites. Let us see these technologies in action using the Yahoo small business website as an example.

Figure 20 shows some example websites hosted by Yahoo. Let us find out the ip addresses of these websites. The utility to do that is `nslookup`. What do we see?

```
# nslookup www.green-tooth.com
Non-authoritative answer:
www.green-tooth.com    canonical name = stores
  .yahoo.net.
stores.yahoo.net       canonical name = html.store
  .yahoodns.net.             Address: 68.142.205.137

www.invitationshack.com canonical name = stores
  .yahoo.net.
```

**FIGURE 20** Example websites hosted by Yahoo!

```
stores.yahoo.net       canonical name = html.store
  .yahoodns.net.
Name:  html.store.yahoodns.net
                           Address: 68.142.205.137

www.mangrovecampingsupplies.com canonical name =
  stores.yahoo.net.
stores.yahoo.net       canonical name = html.store
  .yahoodns.net.
Name:  html.store.yahoodns.net
                           Address: 68.142.205.137

www.duematernity.com   canonical name = stores
  .yahoo.net.
stores.yahoo.net       canonical name = html.store
  .yahoodns.net.
Name:  html.store.yahoodns.net
                           Address: 68.142.205.137
```

We see that the websites hosted by Yahoo are all accessible at the same IP address, 68.142.205.137. These e-commerce websites hosted on Yahoo also use the Yahoo! favicon on their websites, indicating their affiliation with Yahoo.

How is it beneficial for businesses if many websites can be hosted at the same computer? Think what it would cost businesses if each website had to be hosted on a different computer. Web hosting companies would need to find space to locate all of these computers. Each computer would draw power. More hardware would lead to more repair needs and more personnel for maintenance and updates. Each of these would raise costs.

Hosting multiple websites on a single computer saves costs. However, if there are many websites hosted at one website, how is the web server to know which site a user is requesting? Here, DNS and virtual hosts come into play. When a user types in a URL, DNS directs the user to the computer with the IP address at which the site is hosted. The user request contains the name of the target website in the URL.

The web server uses the name of the target website in the URL to determine which site the client is requesting and sends the request to the site for handling, as shown in Figure 21. The requested resource is served from the site's folder on the web server.

The following example shows how the popular Apache Web Server can be configured to serve three web sites—www.example.com; www.example.net; and www .example.org.

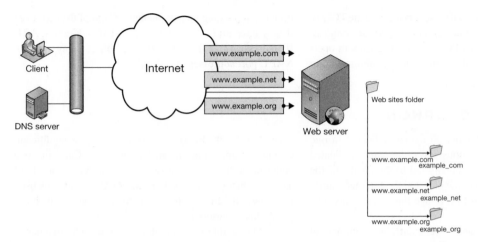

**FIGURE 21**  Virtual hosts architecture

```
<VirtualHost *:80>
    DocumentRoot "/export/home/websites/example_
                 com"
    ServerName www.example.com
    DirectoryIndex index.php index.html
    ErrorLog "/export/logs/example_com/example_
             com-error_log"
    CustomLog /export/logs/example_
              com/example_com-access_log
  combined
  </VirtualHost>

<VirtualHost *:80>
    DocumentRoot "/export/home/websites/
                 example_net"
    ServerName www.example.net
    DirectoryIndex index.php index.html
    …
  </VirtualHost>
```

```
<VirtualHost *:80>
  DocumentRoot "/export/home/websites/
               example_org"
  ServerName www.example.org
  DirectoryIndex index.php index.html
  …
</VirtualHost>
```

Each virtual host section specifies one website and maps a folder on the computer to the website. For each client request, the web server uses the information in the virtual host definitions to determine which folder on the computer to serve pages from. Client requests for all websites hosted on a server arrive at the server. Based on the URL, the web server responds with data in the corresponding folder.

## REFERENCES

Yahoo merchant solutions, http://smallbusiness.yahoo.com/ecommerce/customerstores.php (accessed 1/13/10)

## SUMMARY

In this chapter we looked at a number of support services that make IP addresses easy to use even by novices who know nothing about how the Internet works. DHCP allocates IP addresses to computers during booting up and before users see a login prompt on their PCs. Most organizations allocate reusable RFC 1918 addresses to client PCs within their networks so that they can use a small number of IP addresses to provide connectivity to a large number of computers in the organization. This conserves IP addresses. ARP finds the MAC addresses corresponding to known IP addresses and is used to populate the destination MAC address-field of frames.

DNS allows end users to address computers using friendly names such as www.yahoo.com instead of the more cumbersome IP addresses like 69.147.76.15.

Finally, we saw how all these services and the TCP/IP stack help end users seamlessly obtain network connectivity when they start up a PC at home. The smooth operation of these services allows users to get online within minutes of opening up a brand new PC out of the box, even if they have no idea about signals, MAC addresses, ARP, IP addresses, DHCP, RFC 1918, default gateway, routing, NAPT, port addresses, or DNS.

## ABOUT THE COLOPHON

What's a name worth? What do names indicate? In one of Shakespeare's most famous plays, the names indicated family affiliations and eventually led to the deaths of the two principal characters in the play. On the Internet, names are a way for companies to leverage the investments they make in their brands.

Can names influence personal and commercial outcomes? In Shakespeare's play, changing names would probably not have changed consequences for the doomed characters. On the Internet, however, names are significant. Changing names may mean lost business. Cars.com is a better name for a site that sells cars than A123.com. Ford.com is a better name for Ford Motor Company's website than www.48126.com. (48126 is the zip code of the company's headquarters.)

On the Internet, as in drama, there's a lot in a name. Fortunately, there is DNS.

## REVIEW QUESTIONS

1. What is *DHCP*? Why is it useful?

2. What are some of the reasons for the inefficiencies in allocating the available IP addresses?

3. What are the three types of address allocation schemes in DHCP? Under what conditions is each of these categories of address allocation preferred?

4. What is *address leasing* in DHCP?

5. Use ipconfig /all at the command prompt of a Windows computer. What is the lease duration of the IP address?

6. Briefly describe the sequence of operations that allow a freshly booted DHCP client to obtain an IP address from a DHCP server on the network.

7. What are *non-routable IP addresses*?

8. IP addresses are used for routing. Why are non-routable IP addresses useful?

9. Why can't a computer with an RFC 1918 IP address be used as a public-facing web server?

10. What is *network address translation*? Why is it useful?

11. How do DHCP, non-routable addresses, and NAT help improve the efficiency of utilizing IP addresses and reduce the shortage of IP addresses?

12. What is *NAPT*? How can it improve the efficiency of utilizing IP addresses, compared to NAT, without port translation?

13. Describe the NAPT operation, i.e., describe how the IP addresses in a packet change as a request packet travels from a source with an RFC 1918 address to a destination and the reply comes back to the source.

14. What is *ARP*? What is it used for?

15. Briefly describe the operation of ARP.

16. List the entries in the ASP cache of your computer using the arp –a command.

17. What is *DNS*? What is it used for?

18. Describe the hierarchical organization of domains on the Internet.

19. Why is it useful to organize domain names such as www.usf.edu hierarchically as they are done in DNS?

20. What are the different kinds of top-level domains?

21. Describe the process used by a name server to resolve the IP address of a URL typed by a user.

22. What is a zone in the context of DNS?

23. What is a recursive query in DNS? When does it become necessary?

**24.** What are the different network services provided by the typical home wireless router provided by ISPs?

**25.** Use the nslookup command to obtain the IP address of www.google.com. (You may have to type in "." after com.) Which name server performed the name resolution for you—your local name server or the Google name server?

## HANDS-ON EXERCISE—NSLOOKUP

nslookup is a utility included with almost every operating system to resolve domain names to IP addresses. In this exercise you will use nslookup to resolve a few URLs. Figure 22 shows an example of using nslookup to obtain the IP address of www.ucf.edu. The IP address of the website is 132.170.240.131. To convince ourselves that this is indeed the case, we can use the IP address in the browser to bring up the web page as shown in Figure 23.

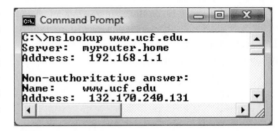

**FIGURE 22**   Using nslookup to resolve a URL

**FIGURE 23**   Using IP address to navigate to a website

Answer the following: (Note: you may find that you need to end the URL with a "." to resolve the names correctly, as shown in Figure 23.)

**1.** Use nslookup to obtain the IP address of your university's website. Show the output.

**2.** Use nslookup to obtain the IP address of the home page of one of the major employers in your area. Show the output.

**3.** Use nslookup to obtain the IP address of the home page of one of the companies included in the S&P 500 index. The list of these companies can be found from many sources by searching online for the term "s&p 500 companies." Show the output from nslookup.

## CRITICAL THINKING QUESTIONS

**1.** Read about the lawsuit filed by Nissan Motors Corporation against Nissan Computer Corporation. A timeline of the lawsuit is at http://www.nissan.com/Lawsuit/The_Story.php. Which of the two parties do you think is rightfully entitled to own the Nissan.com domain name? What are your principal arguments in favor of the party?

## NETWORK DESIGN EXERCISE

Coolco eventually decided not to obtain an address block from ARIN. Instead, it chose to obtain a few static externally-addressable (non-RFC 1918) IP addresses from its ISP for its Internet-facing applications such as web servers. The company also decided to obtain a few more IP addresses from its ISP to share internally using NAPT. It will use a /10 address block to assign IP addresses to all the other computers in the company. It also decided to have a single connection to the Internet from Tampa.

Answer the following questions:

1. What services in Coolco's network will require externally addressable IP addresses?

2. Update your network diagram by adding an Internet connection from the Tampa office. The Internet is typically drawn as a cloud. You may find it convenient to use the *Network design exercise icons and template* document available with the readings for Chapter 1 on the companion website.

3. Further update the diagram to include a NAPT device that translates between the internal /10 network and the external IP addresses obtained from the ISP.

## CASE QUESTIONS

1. What are some of the essential features needed in an e-commerce website? A good starting point for your answer would be Yahoo's small business site (http://smallbusiness.yahoo.com/ecommerce/features.php).

2. What is an important agricultural or other natural product that your state is known for? Find a business that sells this product online. Describe some important e-commerce capabilities of the company's website. If there is no such product, select one from a nearby state.

3. Find a hosting service provider in your city or the nearest metropolitan area. Visit the company's website and describe some of the services offered by the company. (Select up to three services if the company offers many services.) What are the monthly fees for each of these services? For each of these services, think of a business or non-profit that might find the service useful.

4. From the ISP's website, what are some of the job openings at the hosting service provider you selected? What are the required skills for these openings? If the selected provider has no openings at this time, pick another provider whose website lists at least one job opening.

5. Instead of using the full suite of e-commerce services from a hosting provider, you could limit yourself to hosting services and use free software such as Zen Cart to create your online store. What are some of the capabilities of Zen Cart (www.zen-cart.com)?

6. What is a favicon? What is your university's favicon?

# Subnetting

*Nothing is particularly hard if you divide it into small jobs.*

—HENRY FORD

## Overview

Subnetting is the method by which network administrators divide the large number of IP addresses allocated to an organization into smaller address blocks called subnets. Each department within the organization can be assigned one or more of these smaller address blocks. Each department's network administrator can use these smaller address blocks to manage their networks. Subnetting is one of the core skills for all network administrators. At the end of the chapter, you should know:

- what subnets are and why they are useful
- what factors determine the size of subnets
- what subnet masks are
- what the relationship is between subnet masks and subnet size
- how to compute subnet masks

Subnets were discussed briefly in Chapter 4. However, given the importance of the topic, subnetting has been placed in its own chapter.

## Why subnetting

Subnetting helps organize IP addresses. *Subnetting is a way of breaking down large blocks of IP addresses into smaller address blocks.* We know from Chapter 4 that Internet registries prefer to allocate large blocks of IP addresses. For example, a large ISP may be allocated a /12 address block, giving the ISP about 1 million IP addresses ($2^{(32-12)} = 2^{20}$ 1,048,576 IP addresses).

This is a very large number of IP addresses to manage. DHCP servers managing so many IP addresses are likely to become a bottleneck for the ISP. Instead, if the ISP serves 20 markets nationwide, wouldn't it be convenient to divide the pool of 1 million IP addresses into 20 smaller blocks of about 50,000 IP addresses each (50,000 * 20 = 1 million)? Each block of 50,000 addresses could be used to serve one market and the network administrators in each market could be given the responsibility of managing their own pool of 50,000 IP addresses.

Subnetting is very flexible and allows organizations to delegate IP addresses as appropriate for the organization. As another example, say an organization has a /16 IP address block ($2^{(32-16)}$ = 65,536 IP addresses). Using subnetting, the organization may distribute these addresses as 256 subnets with 256 addresses/subnet (256 * 256 = 65,536). Alternately, the organization may choose to have 128 subnets with 512 hosts/subnet (128 * 512 = 65,536). Note that in each case, the total number of available IP addresses in the organizations is 65,536 (256 * 256 or 128 * 512). The difference is in the number of smaller address blocks that the available addresses are divided into.

## Business motivation for subnetting*

As an example, consider a typical state university. It is likely to have a /16 IP address pool such as 131.247.0.0/ 16. This means that it has $2^{(32-16)}$ = 65,536 IP addresses available. How can the network administrator at this university go about allocating IP addresses to individual computers from this large pool of available IP addresses?

A simple mechanism would be to use a first-come, first-serve scheme. If the university network uses DHCP, the first computer to come online on a given day could get the IP address 131.247.0.1. Say, this is a student in the business school using a wireless laptop while working on a project past midnight.

The second computer that comes online could get the IP address 131.247.0.2. Say, this is a computer being used by a student browsing on a kiosk in the library. Allocating a few more IP addresses on a given day, the university network might appear as in Figure 1. This IP address-allocation scheme is functional as far as network

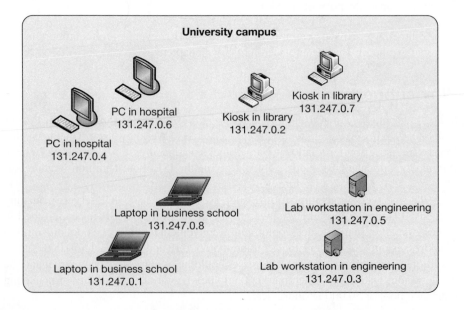

**FIGURE 1** IP address allocation without subnetting

* We will illustrate our discussion of subnetting with an example set in a university campus. Technically, this setting is very similar to a large business campus, and has the advantage of being familiar to students who have limited real-world networking experience.

connectivity is concerned. Every host on the network will get an IP address and will be able to communicate with all other hosts within the university network and outside.

But think about the implications of the addressing scheme from the perspective of the network administrator. He will not have any idea where a host with a given IP address is located on campus. Therefore, if a user with a network connectivity problem calls the network administrator for help, the network administrator would have a very difficult time trying to troubleshoot the problem.

Also, most organizations break up large networks into smaller departmental networks with administrators responsible for the departmental networks. It is very convenient if these departmental IT managers can be given address blocks of their own to manage their departmental networks.

Now consider an alternate method to allocate IP addresses. In this method, each college is allocated a contiguous set of IP addresses. For example, the library is given IP addresses in the range 131.247.1.0−131.247.1.255; the college of business is given IP addresses in the range 131.247.2.0−131.247.4.255; the hospital is given IP addresses in the range 131.247.5.0−131.247.5.255; and the college of engineering is given IP addresses in the range 131.247.6.0−131.247.7.255. Figure 1 may be updated to reflect this departmental addressing scheme as shown in Figure 2.

Observe the pattern of IP addresses allocated to laptops in the college of business in Figure 2. Not only do they share the network part of the IP address (131.247), even the third octet in the IP addresses, 2, is common to all the laptops in the college of business. Similarly, the IP addresses of all the PCs in the hospital have three octets in common—131.247.5. The same pattern is followed in the college of engineering (131.247.6) and the library (131.247.1).

It is clear that a network administrator would much prefer the neatly organized allocation of IP addresses shown in Figure 2 over the chaos seen in Figure 1. If a user calls the administrator with a connectivity problem, the administrator can ask the user to provide their IP address (Start → Cmd → ipconfig/ all) and the administrator can immediately locate the computer on the network. If a network component such as a switch fails, all hosts within a department are likely to experience connectivity problems. Identifying patterns in the IP addresses of the disconnected hosts is likely to suggest the cause of the problem.

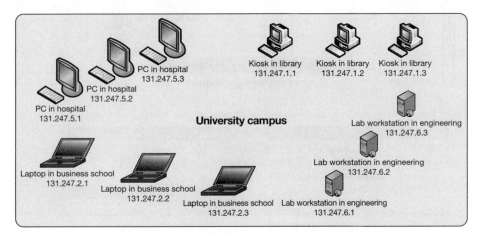

**FIGURE 2** IP address allocation with subnetting

Therefore, subnetting is useful because it helps organize IP addresses within a network or organization. As the name suggests, a subnet is a subnetwork of a network.

## Subnets–the technical motivation for subnetting

So, the primary motivation for subnetting is to organize IP addresses within large organizations. This motivation is facilitated by the technical organization of large networks. We know from Chapter 3 and Chapter 4 that large networks such as campus-wide networks are composed of smaller local area networks, usually Ethernets. We have also seen in Chapter 3 that since Ethernet is a broadcast network, it has a practical limit on the number of computers per network. A university with more than 10,000 computers, clearly needs many Ethernets. The network of Figure 1 is likely to be composed of many Ethernets, as shown in Figure 3.

When a large network is built up of smaller networks, as shown in Figure 3, each smaller network is called a subnet. Subnets are described in RFC 950. As defined in RFC 950, *subnets are logically visible subsections of a single Internet network*. In Figure 3, the university network may be said to be composed of the library subnet, the engineering subnet, the business school subnet and the hospital subnet. Each subnet generally has all the support services such as DNS and DHCP required for network operation.

Subnetting allows network administrators to carve out small blocks of IP addresses from the organization's large address pool and assign these small blocks of IP addresses to the different subnets. Mapping the IP addressing scheme of Figure 2 to the network architecture of Figure 3 gives the subnet addressing scheme shown in Figure 4.

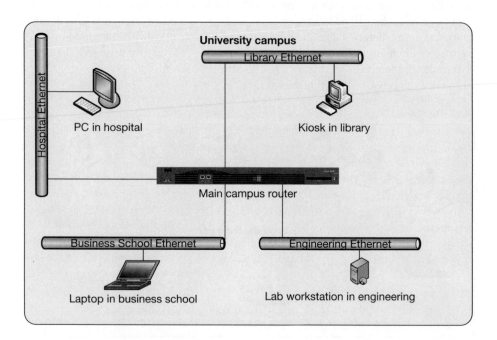

**FIGURE 3** Internal structure of large campus-wide network

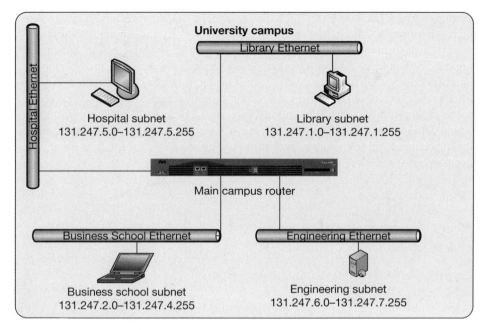

FIGURE 4  Subnet structure of a large network

## Three-part IP addresses with subnetting

We saw in Chapter 4 that IP addresses have two parts: the network part and the host part. The network part identifies the network to which the IP address belongs and the host part identifies the host within the network. This is shown in Figure 5. In this example, the first 16 bits of the IP address identify the network and the remaining 16 bits identify the host within the network.

With subnetting, the IP address shown in Figure 5 may be interpreted as shown in Figure 6. This time, instead of treating the host part of the IP address as one unit, we interpret it as being made up of two IDs—a subnet ID and a host ID. The first few bits of the host part identify the subnet to which the host belongs (e.g. library, business, hospital, etc.), and the remaining bits of the host part identify the computer within the

FIGURE 5  Two-part interpretation of IP address

subnet. Since IP addresses in subnetted networks are interpreted as having three parts—network ID, subnet ID, and host ID, they are called three-part IP addresses.

Recall from the discussion of multi-part addressing in Chapter 4 that subnetting organizes IP addresses a lot like telephone numbers. As seen in Figure 7, telephone numbers have three parts. The first part denotes the metro area, the second part identifies the exchange within the metro area, and the last four digits identify the phone receiver within the exchange. Similarly, as seen in Figure 6 and Figure 7, in an IP address, the network ID identifies the organization or ISP, the subnet ID identifies the department within the organization and the host ID identifies the host within the department.

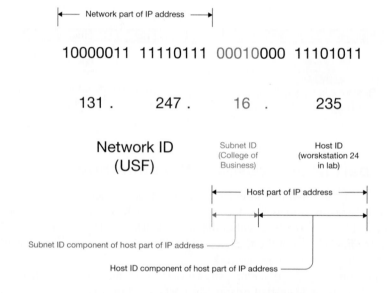

**FIGURE 6** Three-part interpretation of IP address

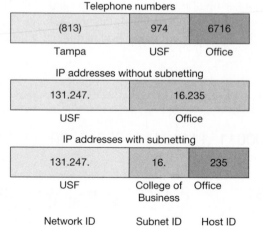

**FIGURE 7** Similarities between subnetting and phone numbers

There is one major difference between phone numbers and subnetting. The difference is the varying lengths of the three IDs in subnetting. The phone system has fixed lengths for each part—the area code always has three digits, the exchange code is always three digits long, and the number is always four digits. But IP addresses can be broken at any bit boundary. Organizations can have /12, /13, or /16 network IDs. Subnet IDs can have 5 bits, 8 bits, 9 bits, or 10 bits. These numbers are only illustrative. The 32-bit IP addresses can be partitioned as required between network ID, subnet ID, and host ID.

## Subnetting the network address block

Now that we know why subnetting is useful, we can take on the challenge of subnetting a network's address block. This is the part that appears mathematically challenging to students when they deal with it for the first time. We will proceed one step at a time. While the math can seem intimidating, subnetting essentially boils down to calculating the number of bits required to create the desired number of subnets.

An analysis of the business determines the number of subnets the organization needs. You then calculate how many bits are needed to label each of these subnets. The rest of this section describes the details of this process using the example of a university network.

In the standard subnetting scenario, the network administrator examines the technical and network structure of the organization to determine how many subnets the network should have. The network of a typical university is composed of subnetworks for each college. There are also some additional subnetworks such as the dorm network, a subnet for the administration, subnets for branch campuses and a subnet for campus IT. Add these up, and our example university may have, say, 16 subnets.

How many bits do we need to be able to assign a unique subnet ID to each of these subnets? We know from Chapter 4 that with 4 bits, we can have 16 ($2^4$) subnets. While this may meet the immediate needs of the university, what happens if a few new units are created on campus? If we provide for 16 subnets when our current needs are for 16 subnets, we limit our room for growth in the future. Therefore, in this situation, most network administrators will prefer to plan for 32, or even 64 subnets. Thus, using 5-bit ($2^5 = 32$) or 6-bit ($2^6 = 64$) subnet IDs seems like a good choice for this university.

Say we choose 5-bit subnet IDs. If we use 5-bit subnet IDs, one possible numbering scheme for the 32 subnets of the university is shown in Table 1. Subnet IDs are shown as 5-bit binary numbers. The numbers in parentheses are the decimal representations of the subnet IDs.

Since we have 32 possible subnets with 5-bit subnet IDs but only 16 usable subnets at this time, some subnets are yet unused. These are highlighted in Table 1. The unused subnet IDs are available for future units that may get added to the university. These unused subnet IDs may also be used to accommodate growth within existing units on the campus. For example, if the college of business experiences

**Table 1**   Possible subnet ID assignment using 5-bit subnet IDs in an example university

| Subnet ID | Campus unit | Subnet ID | Campus unit | Subnet ID | Campus unit |
|---|---|---|---|---|---|
| 00001 (1) | College 1 | 00010 (2) | College 2 | 00011 (3) | College 3 |
| 00100 (4) | College 4 | 00101 (5) | College 5 | 00110 (6) | College 6 |
| 00111 (7) | College 7 | 01000 (8) | College 8 | 01001 (9) | College 9 |
| 01010 (10) | College 10 | 01011 (11) | <future college> | 01100 (12) | <future college> |
| 01101 (13) | Dorm 1 | 01110 (14) | Dorm 2 | 01111 (15) | <future dorm> |
| 10000 (16) | <future dorm> | 10001 (17) | Branch campus 1 | 10010 (18) | Branch campus 2 |
| 10011 (19) | <future branch campus> | 10100 (20) | Administration | 10101 (21) | Campus IT |
| 10110 (22) | <future expansion> | 10111 (23) | <future expansion> | 11000 (24) | <future expansion> |
| 11001 (25) | <future expansion> | 11010 (26) | <future expansion> | 11011 (27) | <future expansion> |
| 11100 (28) | <future expansion> | 11101 (29) | <future expansion> | 11110 (30) | <future expansion> |

growth and a new building is added to the college, one of the available subnet IDs may be allocated to the college of business to accommodate the new computers that would get added to the new building. Similarly, if the university decides to deploy wireless networks across the campus, the wireless network could be assigned one of the unutilized subnet IDs.

You may have observed that subnet ID 00000 (0) and 11111 (31) have not been shown in Table 1. This is because according to RFC 943 on assigned numbers, all zeros and all ones have a special meaning in IP addressing. All zeros within any part of the IP address is interpreted to mean "this," and all ones are interpreted to mean "all." Therefore, all zeros and all ones are not used in any of the three parts of an IP address. As a result, though a 5-bit subnet ID allows 32 subnets, only 30 subnets are actually possible.

Once we know the subnet IDs for the different subnets, we know the first two parts of the IP address of any host on any subnet on campus. For example, if the network ID of the organization is 131.247.210.0.0/16, the first 16 bits of the IP address of any host in the university will be 10000011.11110111 ($10000011_2 = 131_{10}$) and ($11110111_2 = 247_{10}$). We can now use the information about subnet IDs in Table 1 to get the second part of the IP addresses of hosts within each of the 10 colleges. These are shown in Table 2. Subnet IDs have been highlighted.

Consider College 1 in Table 2. We know that the network part of the IP address of all hosts within the university is 131.247. So, the first 16 bits of the IP address of every host in the college will be 10000011.11110111. We also know from Table 1 that the 5-bit subnet ID assigned to the college by the university's network administrator is 00001. Therefore, we know that the IP address bits in positions 17–21 for all hosts in College 1 will be 00001. Therefore, the first 21 bits of all IP addresses in the college are

**Table 2**   Network ID and subnet ID for hosts within each of the 10 colleges in our example university

| Campus unit | Subnet ID (from Table 1) | First two parts of IP addresses by college Network ID    Subnet ID |
|---|---|---|
| College 1 | 00001 | 10000011.11110111.00001_ _ _ . _ _ _ _ _ _ _ _ |
| College 2 | 00010 | 10000011.11110111.00010 _ _ _ . _ _ _ _ _ _ _ _ |
| College 3 | 00011 | 10000011.11110111.00011 _ _ _ . _ _ _ _ _ _ _ _ |
| College 4 | 00100 | 10000011.11110111.00100 _ _ _ . _ _ _ _ _ _ _ _ |
| College 5 | 00101 | 10000011.11110111.00101 _ _ _ . _ _ _ _ _ _ _ _ |
| College 6 | 00110 | 10000011.11110111.00110 _ _ _ . _ _ _ _ _ _ _ _ |
| College 7 | 00111 | 10000011.11110111.00111 _ _ _ . _ _ _ _ _ _ _ _ |
| College 8 | 01000 | 10000011.11110111.01000 _ _ _ . _ _ _ _ _ _ _ _ |
| College 9 | 01001 | 10000011.11110111.01001 _ _ _ . _ _ _ _ _ _ _ _ |
| College 10 | 01010 | 10000011.11110111.01010 _ _ _ . _ _ _ _ _ _ _ _ |

10000011.11110111.00001. Now, the remaining 11 bits $(32 - 16 - 5)$ are available to assign to individual hosts within College 1. These 11 bits are shown as "_" in Table 2.

With 11 bits available for the host ID, College 1 can accommodate $2^{11} = 2,048$ hosts. The network administrator of College 1 may run a DHCP server within the college to dynamically assign these 2,048 IP addresses to hosts within the college.

Let us quickly recapitulate what we have learned in this section:

1.  Given the required number of subnets, we can calculate the length of the subnet ID part.

2.  Given the length of the network ID part, we can calculate the length of the host part. Length of host part $= 32 -$ length of network ID part $-$ length of subnet ID part.

3.  Given the length of the host ID part, we can calculate the number of hosts/subnet.

## Addressing a subnet

Once the subnets shown in Table 1 have been created and assigned to the individual campus subnetworks, individual subnets can be addressed by setting the host ID field to all zeros following RFC 943. For example, the subnet address of College 1 is 10 000011.11110111.00001000.00000000, which is 131.247.8.0. The subnet address of College 2 is 10000011.11110111.00010000.00000000, which is 131.247.16.0. Similarly, we can get the subnet addresses of all other colleges in the university. Each of these subnets uses 21 bits for the network ID and subnet ID parts of the IP address. In CIDR notation, therefore, each of these college subnets is said to have a /21 address. This leaves 11 bits for the host ID part, which allows each subnet to have up to $2^{11} = 2,048$ hosts. We can write these subnet addresses as shown in Table 3. Subnet IDs are underlined.

With the subnet addressing scheme shown in Table 3, a possible configuration for the university network is shown in Figure 8. In the example, the university has three internal routers that serve the different colleges. Colleges 1, 2, and 3 are served by the router on the west side of the campus; Colleges 4, 5, and 6 by the router on the south side of the campus; and Colleges 7, 8, 9, and 10 by the router on the east side of the campus. The other units (branch campuses, etc.) are also connected to these routers, but have not been shown for simplicity.

Once we have the arrangement of Figure 8, how does the main campus router handle incoming packets from the Internet? If the destination address of a packet

**Table 3** Subnet addresses of colleges in our example university shown in Table 1

| Campus unit | Subnet addresses (binary) | Subnet addresses (decimal) |
|---|---|---|
| College 1 | 10000011.11110111.**00001**000.00000000 | 131.247.**8**.0/ 21 |
| College 2 | 10000011.11110111.**00010**000.00000000 | 131.247.**16**.0/ 21 |
| College 3 | 10000011.11110111.**00011**000.00000000 | 131.247.**24**.0/ 21 |
| College 4 | 10000011.11110111.**00100**000.00000000 | 131.247.**32**.0/ 21 |
| College 5 | 10000011.11110111.**00101**000.00000000 | 131.247.**40**.0/ 21 |
| College 6 | 10000011.11110111.**00110**000.00000000 | 131.247.**48**.0/ 21 |
| College 7 | 10000011.11110111.**00111**000.00000000 | 131.247.**56**.0/ 21 |
| College 8 | 10000011.11110111.**01000**000.00000000 | 131.247.**64**.0/ 21 |
| College 9 | 10000011.11110111.**01001**000.00000000 | 131.247.**72**.0/ 21 |
| College 10 | 10000011.11110111.**01010**000.00000000 | 131.247.**80**.0/ 21 |

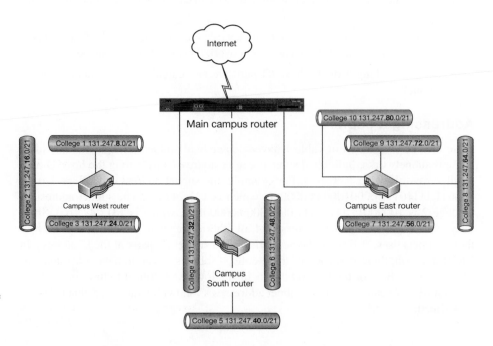

**FIGURE 8** Example university college subnets

belongs to a host in College 1, the router needs to send the packet to the Campus West router. If the destination is in College 10, the packet needs to be sent to the Campus East router. Note that the main campus router is not responsible for sending the packets to the destination hosts. The main campus router is only responsible for sending the incoming packet to the correct router on campus. This means that in our example university, the main campus router only needs to figure out which of the three internal routers to direct a packet to.

How can we tell the main campus router which college a specific destination address belongs to? One possibility is to give the router an exhaustive list of all IP address on campus and their affiliations. For our university with a /16 address, this means that the router's lookup table will have $2^{(32-16)} = 2^{16} = 65,536$ entries. Given this list, when a packet comes into the university, the router can look up the 32-bit destination address against this list, identify the college that the address belongs to, and direct the packet to the appropriate router serving that college.

This process will work, but it is easy to see that it is rather inefficient. If the main campus router only needs to know which of the 16 campus units (or 30 units when the campus is fully built out) the incoming packet needs to go to, the router only needs to look at the subnet part of the destination address of incoming packets. For every incoming packet, we just need a way to tell the main campus router which of the 5 bits of the destination IP address identifies the subnet to which the address belongs. If we can do this, the router's lookup table can be reduced to just $2^5 = 32$ entries, instead of 65,536 entries—a huge improvement. This speeds up router performance and reduces the hardware requirements for routers, thereby lowering costs.

The standard technique used to help network devices identify the subnet ID of an IP address is the use of a subnet mask. This topic is covered in the next section.

## Subnet masks

We are now left with the last challenge of making subnetting work—how do hosts and routers on the network know which bits of an IP address constitute the subnet part of an IP address? For example, in our example university, how can we convey to routers and hosts that bits 17–21 identify the subnets on campus?

We start by making an observation. We really do not need to know where the subnet ID begins in an IP address. We only need to know where it ends. For example, in our university, we only need to know that the subnet ID ends at the 21$^{st}$ bit.

Why is this? Recall that all hosts in our university have the same network ID. If we ignore where the subnet ID begins, we add the same network ID bits to every subnet ID. In other words, instead of defining the subnet ID of college 1 as 00001 (Table 1), we can define its subnet ID as 10000011.11110111.00001 (Table 3). Similarly, the subnet ID of college 3 becomes 10000011.11110111.00011 instead of 00011. The number of subnet IDs does not change. Our example university will still have 32 subnets.

What is the advantage of doing this? After all, isn't it easier to work with smaller numbers? Isn't it easier for routers to deal with 5-bit subnet IDs than 21-bit subnet IDs?

The big advantage of adding the network ID to define the subnet ID is that all subnet IDs begin at the first bit. We then have a uniform representation of subnet IDs for all organizations. Consider two organizations, one with a Class A address block, and another with a Class B address block. If both organizations decide that they need about 2,000 IP addresses per subnet, they will both have /21 subnets. In the Class A organization, bits 9–21 will define the subnet ID, and in the Class B organization, bits 17–21 will define the subnet ID. In both cases, the subnet ID will end at bit position 21. The only difference is that the Class A organization will have $2^{13} = 8,000$ (approximately) subnets and the Class B organization will have $2^5 = 32$ subnets.

If we try to specify where the subnet ID part begins, we will need to come up with one subnet mask procedure for Class A networks, another for /9 networks, and so on. Not only will subnetting become more complex to implement, the extra complexity will serve no useful purpose.

Instead, if we add the network ID to the subnet ID, we are assured that within any organization, we are prepending all subnet IDs with the organization's network ID. A Class A organization will prepend its 8-bit network ID to all its subnets. A Class B organization will prepend its 16-bit network ID to all its subnets. There will be no change to the number of subnets within the organization. At the cost of a slightly larger subnet ID field, we have gained a uniform representation for subnet IDs across all networks. We therefore identify subnets by the network ID + subnet ID bits within the organization.

With this simplification, we only need a mechanism to convey where the subnet ID ends. Observe that this is equal to the length of the network ID + length of subnet ID. The standard method to convey the length of the network ID and subnet ID parts of IP addresses in a network is to use a subnet mask. *A subnet mask is a number that tells the host what bits in an IP address constitute the network ID and subnet ID of the network.* Every network interface on every host on the network is assigned a subnet mask. The interface gets the subnet mask information at the same time that it gets an IP address either from an administrator or from DHCP. You can see your subnet mask using the command ipconfig (Windows)/ ifconfig (MAC/ Linux). Figure 9 shows an example.

Subnet masks look like IP addresses, but have a very special structure. Written as 32-bit binary numbers, subnet masks are a sequence of 1s followed by a sequence of 0s. The 1s indicate the bits in IP addresses that constitute the network ID + subnet ID of the subnet. For example, since the subnets in our example university have a total of 21 bits in its network ID and subnet ID, the subnet mask used in the university will have a sequence of 21 ones, followed by 11 zeros. This gives us the subnet mask for the university:

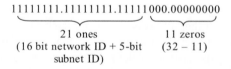

$$11111111.11111111.11111\underbrace{000.00000000}$$

21 ones       11 zeros
(16 bit network ID + 5-bit    (32 − 11)
subnet ID)

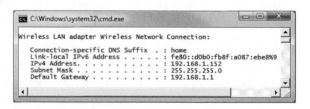

**FIGURE 9** Using ipconfig to find subnet mask

We can express this subnet mask in the familiar dotted-decimal notation as 255.255.248.0. You may note that this mask has some similarity to the subnet mask shown in Figure 9. Both start with 255.255.

How do subnet masks help hosts and routers? It is easier to show this by example. Let us start with two hosts in two different colleges in our university. For our example, let us consider one host in College 1 and another host in College 3. Say the host in College 1 is 131.247.8.45 and the host in College 3 is 131.247.27.231. In binary notation, these IP addresses are:

Host 1: 10000011.11110111.00001000.00101101

Host 2: 10000011.11110111.00011011.11100111

What happens when we apply the subnet mask to these addresses? Recall that the 1s in the subnet mask indicate the network part + subnet ID and 0s indicate the host ID. To implement this, when we apply the subnet mask to an IP address, the bits in the IP address corresponding to the 1s in the subnet mask are passed through. The 0s in the subnet mask block the bits in the corresponding positions in the IP address.[1] The result for our example is shown in Table 4.

In the example of Table 4, consider host 1. Its IP address is 10000011.11110111 .00001000.00101101. When we mask this IP address with the subnet mask 11111111 .11111111.11111000.00000000, since this mask has 21 ones, the first 21 bits of the IP address pass through unchanged. The remaining 11 bits are masked and replaced with 0. We see the result as the masked host IP address.

What is interesting about the masking process is that the masked IP addresses will match the subnet IDs of the corresponding hosts. The mask essentially removes the host ID part from the destination IP address, leaving behind just the network ID + subnet ID parts of the IP address.

Put another way, the masked IP address of any host is the subnet ID + network ID of the host.

Once the router has extracted the subnet ID using the subnet mask, it can look up the subnet ID in its routing tables and forward the packet to the appropriate router within the campus. This process is shown for a few representative packets in Figure 10. To keep things simple, the network ID is shown in decimal.

In Figure 10, five packets are shown arriving at the router. The router views the destination IP address of each packet through the subnet mask. The 0s in the mask

**Table 4** Example of masking using a subnet mask

|  | Host 1 | Host 2 |
|---|---|---|
| Host IP address | 10000011.11110111.00001000.00101101 | 10000011.11110111.00011011.11100111 |
| Subnet mask | 11111111.11111111.11111000.00000000 | 11111111.11111111.11111000.00000000 |
| Masked host IP address | 10000011.11110111.00001000.00000000 | 10000011.11110111.00011000.00000000 |
| College matching masked IP address | College 1 | College 3 |

---

[1] You may observe that this is a bit-wise logical AND operation.

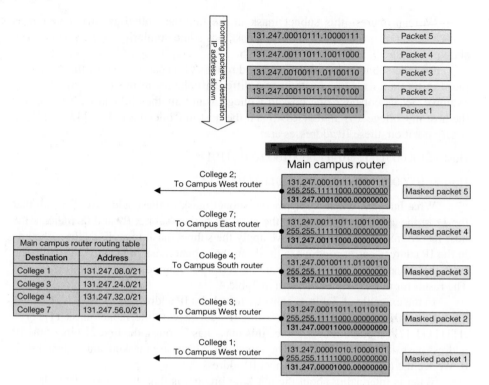

**FIGURE 10** Subnet masking of packets at router to determine subnet ID

remove the host ID part of the destination address. The remaining bits in the destination address give the router the subnet ID of the destination address of each packet. The router can look up this subnet ID in its routing table to identify the router to which the packet should be forwarded. For example, packet 2 is addressed to a host in College 3, and is sent to the Campus West router.

When creating subnets, the longer the subnet ID, the shorter the host ID part, leading to fewer hosts/ subnet. Further, within each subnet, we lose at least three IP addresses. One IP address is used for the gateway router, one IP address is used for the broadcast address (all 1s in the host part) and one IP address is used for the subnet ID (all 0s in the host part). Therefore, it is not advisable to create very small subnets except when specifically necessary or for point-to-point links.

## Benefits of subnetting within subnets

The previous section describes how subnetting is useful for routers to direct incoming packets. However, Figure 9 shows that hosts on subnetted networks also have the subnet mask information. These hosts do not perform routing functions. What is the benefit of providing the subnet mask information to hosts that do not perform routing?

It turns out that letting hosts know the subnet mask of the network can reduce the amount of work that routers need to do in processing outgoing packets. Recall from Chapter 7 that if the destination is outside the local network, hosts send outgoing packets to their gateway router for onward transmission to the destination. However, what if the destination is in the host's own subnet?

If the destination is in the host's own subnet, the router is going to send the packet back into the same subnet from which the packet originated. But, if hosts can detect that the destination of a packet is in its own subnet, the packet does not need to be routed. The sender can simply broadcast the packet over the local Ethernet. This can improve network efficiency by reducing the workload of routers.

Subnet masks help hosts detect when a destination host lies in their own subnet. Before sending packets out, hosts apply their subnet mask to the destination address. This gives the subnet ID of the destination as seen by the host. If the subnet ID of the destination matches the sender's own subnet ID, the sender sends out an ARP request to obtain the MAC address of the destination and broadcasts the packet directly into the subnet. Ethernet ensures that this packet reaches the destination.

If on the other hand, the host detects that the subnet ID of the destination of a packet is not the same as its own subnet ID, it knows that the destination is not in its own subnet. The host then sends the packet to the gateway router. The gateway router then routes the packet to its destination.

Subnetting can therefore help in limiting network traffic at routers. If network administrators can identify hosts within networks that exchange a lot of data with each other, they should place these hosts within the same subnet. This can reduce networking costs by reducing the packet processing requirements at routers. An example is an application server and the linked database server.

We can see this mechanism in place in the simple packet-capture shown in Figure 11. The IP address of the source host is 192.168.1.3 and its subnet mask is 255.255.255.0. The capture shows two transactions. The first transaction is a ping to host 192.168.1.153 (same subnet as sender) and the second transaction is a ping to 131.247.100.1 (different subnet from sender). The IP address of the gateway router is 192.168.1.1. Observe the difference in the two ARP queries.

In the first transaction, a user on the host pings host 192.168.1.153. The subnet ID of both hosts is 192.168.1.0. The host recognizes that the destination is on its own subnet and therefore makes an ARP request for IP address 192.168.1.153 (packet 1 in Figure 11). It receives the reply in packet 2. Packets 3–6 are two ping requests and replies

| No. . | Time | Source | Destination | Protocol | Info |
|---|---|---|---|---|---|
| 1 | 0.000000 | 00:21:70:bf:ff:40 | Broadcast | ARP | who has 192.168.1.153? Tell 192.168.1.3 |
| 2 | 0.000227 | LacieGro_84:8d:4e | 00:21:70:bf:ff:40 | ARP | 192.168.1.153 is at 00:d0:4b:84:8d:4e |
| 3 | 0.000242 | 192.168.1.3 | 192.168.1.153 | ICMP | Echo (ping) request |
| 4 | 0.000444 | 192.168.1.153 | 192.168.1.3 | ICMP | Echo (ping) reply |
| 5 | 1.009324 | 192.168.1.3 | 192.168.1.153 | ICMP | Echo (ping) request |
| 6 | 1.009612 | 192.168.1.153 | 192.168.1.3 | ICMP | Echo (ping) reply |
| 7 | 10.852764 | 00:21:70:bf:ff:40 | WestellT_c0:9a:43 | ARP | who has 192.168.1.1? Tell 192.168.1.3 |
| 8 | 10.853030 | WestellT_c0:9a:43 | 00:21:70:bf:ff:40 | ARP | 192.168.1.1 is at 00:18:3a:c0:9a:43 |
| 9 | 11.444676 | 192.168.1.3 | 131.247.100.1 | ICMP | Echo (ping) request |
| 10 | 11.472657 | 131.247.100.1 | 192.168.1.3 | ICMP | Echo (ping) reply |
| 11 | 12.444083 | 192.168.1.3 | 131.247.100.1 | ICMP | Echo (ping) request |
| 12 | 12.471847 | 131.247.100.1 | 192.168.1.3 | ICMP | Echo (ping) reply |

**FIGURE 11** Packet transmission to hosts within and outside subnets

between the two hosts. The critical thing to note about packet 1 is that the ARP request is for the actual destination (192.168.1.153) and not the gateway router (192.168.1.1).

In the second transaction, the same host pings 131.247.100.1. The host sees that the subnet ID of the destination (131.247.100.0) is not the same as its own subnet ID (192.168.1.0). Therefore, packet 7 in the capture shown in Figure 11 is an ARP request for the gateway (192.168.1.1) and not the final destination (131.247.100.1). When the host gets the ARP response, it sends the ping request to the gateway for onward transmission to the destination. This is accomplished by setting the destination IP address of the ping requests to the IP address of the destination and the MAC address to the MAC address of the gateway.

Subnetting therefore improves network efficiency by limiting the volume of traffic that needs to be routed. If the destination is on the same subnet as the source, subnetting helps the source determine this fact and bypass routing so that it can reach the host directly over Ethernet.

## Representative subnetting computations

Now that we have seen how subnetting is done and why subnetting is useful, we can wrap up the chapter by looking at representative subnetting computations to determine the subnet mask. Typically, the business requirement is to create subnets that accommodate a certain number of hosts per subnet. For example, you may need to create subnets with about 500 hosts per subnet.

To accomplish this, we calculate the number of bits necessary in the host ID part of the network address. To accommodate 500 addresses, we know that we need 9 bits ($2^9 = 512$). Now, the bits that remain after taking away the network ID and the host ID parts in IP addresses can be used for subnet IDs.

For example, if the organization has a /15 network address, the first 15 bits in IP addresses will be used for the network ID, the last 9 bits will be used for the host ID and the remaining 8 bits ($32 - 15 - 9 = 8$) will be used for subnet IDs. This will give us $2^8 = 256$ subnets in the organization. This is shown in Figure 12.

The organization will express this information in the subnet mask assigned to routers and hosts. How do we express the subnet mask for the organization in dotted decimal notation? Since the subnet mask has 1s in the positions of network ID and subnet ID, the subnet mask in the organization will have 23 ones (15 for the network ID and 8 for the subnet ID). This leaves $32 - 23 = 9$ zeros in the mask. This gives a subnet mask of 11111111.11111111.11111110.00000000. In the dotted decimal notation, this mask is written as 255.255.254.0.

Alternately, if the organization requires a certain number of subnets, we can calculate the number of bits required to label all the subnets. For example, if the

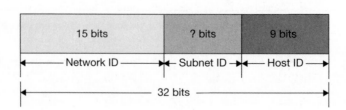

**FIGURE 12** Calculating the length of the subnet ID

organization requires 20 subnets, we will need 5 bits to label all 20 subnets. 4 bits will be inadequate because we can only label $2^4 = 16$ subnets with 4 bits. Given the organization's network ID, we can calculate the number of hosts that can be accommodated in each subnet. If the organization has a /17 network address, the first 17 bits will be taken up for the network ID, the next 5 bits will be used for subnet IDs and the remaining 10 bits ($32 - 17 - 5 = 10$) will be available for the host ID part within each subnet. This will allow each subnet to have 1,024 hosts ($2^{10} = 1,024$). The subnet mask will have 22 ones (17 for the network ID and 5 for the subnet ID). The remaining 10 positions will be zeros. The subnet mask is therefore 11111111.11111111.11111100.00 000000. In the dotted decimal notation, this is 255.255.252.0.

We can summarize the above in the following algorithm to determine the subnet mask for an organization.

Step 1: If the required number of subnets is known, calculate the number of bits needed to uniquely label each subnet. This is the length of the subnet ID part of network addresses. Alternately, if the required number of hosts is known, calculate the number of bits needed to uniquely label each host. This is the length of the host ID part of network addresses.

Step 2: Find the number of bits in the network part of the IP address. This is the length of the network ID part of network addresses.

Step 3: Using the information from step 1 and step 2, calculate the lengths of each of the three parts of IP addresses within the organization (network ID, subnet ID, and host ID). The total length of all three parts is 32 bits.

Step 4: Write the subnet mask in binary notation. The subnet mask is 32 bits long. It has (length of network ID + length of subnet ID) 1s followed by (length of host ID) 0s.

Step 5: Write the subnet mask in dotted decimal notation.

As an example of the algorithm, consider a /18 organization requiring 200 hosts per subnet. What is the subnet mask?

Step 1: We know the number of hosts. So we start by calculating the length of the host ID part. We need 8 bits for the host ID part because $2^8 = 256$. Thus, the length of the host ID part is 8 bits.

Step 2: The length of the network ID part is given as 18 bits.

Step 3: The missing information is the length of the subnet ID. Since network ID + subnet ID + host ID = 32 bits, we can calculate the length of the subnet ID as $32 - 18 - 8 = 6$ bits.

Step 4: The subnet mask has 18 (length of network ID) + 6 (length of subnet ID) = 24 ones. The remaining 8 bits ($32 - 24$) are zeros. In binary notation, the subnet mask is 11111111.11111111.11111111.00000000.

Step 5: The subnet mask in dotted decimal notation is 255.255.255.0.

## CASE STUDY | AN ISP IN TEXAS

*Internet service providers (ISPs) provide Internet service to homes and businesses. In this case, we see an example of how one such ISP, Texlink Communications, which provided Internet and phone services to customers in four major metros in Texas—San Antonio, Austin, Dallas, and Houston—subnetted its IP addresses.*

Texlink Communications was an ISP that served customers in four metros in Texas—San Antonio, Austin, Dallas, and Houston—as shown in Figure 13. As can be verified from ARIN, the ISP obtained a /18 address block, 66.118.0.0/18, which gave it $2^{(32-18)} = 2^{14} = 16,384$ IP addresses. How did it organize these IP addresses?

Over half the ISP's customers were in Houston. The fewest customers were in Austin and Dallas, where the ISP estimated it needed about 2,000 IP addresses each. The ISP therefore decided to subnet its 16,384 IP addresses into 8 subnets with about 2,000 IP addresses per subnet (16,384/ 8). Since $2^{11} = 2,048$, the ISP needed 11 bits in the host ID part, leaving 21 bits (32 − 11) in the network and subnet ID parts. Since 18 of these 21 bits were already taken by the network ID part, three bits were available for the subnet IDs part in this network.

If we label the address bits as N if they represent the network ID, S if they represent the subnet ID, and 0 if they represent the host ID, the IP addresses in the organization will have the following structure:

NNNNNNNN.NNNNNNNN.NNSSS000.00000000

We see that all the subnets are identified by the three bits labeled SSS in the third octet, giving us $2^3 = 8$ octets. Writing out these 8 subnets, we get the following:

**Table 5** Subnets in Texlink communications

| SSS | Subnet | Aggregate | City |
|-----|--------|-----------|------|
| 000 | 66.118.0.0 /21 | | San Antonio |
| 001 | 66.118.8.0 /21 | | Austin |
| 010 | 66.118.16.0/21 | | Dallas |
| 011 | 66.118.24.0/21 | | Houston |
| 100 | 66.118.32.0/21 | 66.118.32.0/20 | Houston |
| 101 | 66.118.40.0/21 | | Houston |
| 110 | 66.118.48.0/21 | 66.118.48.0/20 | Houston |
| 111 | 66.118.56.0/21 | | Houston |

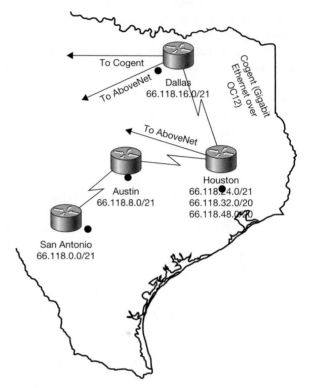

**FIGURE 13** Coverage map of Texlink Communications

To see how the SSS bits lead to the corresponding subnets, let us look at the last Houston subnet, 66.118.56.0/21, and see how we arrive at the subnet address. The first two octets, 66 and 118, come from the network address. Since the third octet in the network address block (66.118.0.0) is 0, the 2 NN bits in the third octet are 0. The three SSS subnet ID bits are 111 from the first column in Table 5 above. Finally, the host ID bits for any network address are 00. Combining this information, the third octet in the subnet address is 00111000, which translates to $56_{10}$. Finally, the fourth octet is 0. Combining all four, the subnet address is 66.118.56.0, of which 21 bits identify the subnet part of the address. We therefore write the subnet address as 66.118.56.0/21.

The third column shows how some subnets have been merged. To understand how this is done, let us look at the subnets 66.118.32.0/21 and 66.118.40.0/21 and see how they aggregate to 66.118.32.0/20. To keep things simple, let us focus only on the third octet in both subnets. These two octets are written below, with the subnet IDs in bold:

00**100**000 (third octet in 66.118.32.0/21)

00**101**000 (third octet in 66.118.40.0/21)

If both subnet IDs are used for the same subnetwork (a subnet in Houston), the last bit in the subnet ID (the underlined bit above), does not play any role in identifying a subnet. The subnet is then identified by just the first 2 bits of the subnet ID—**10**. If that is the case, we can include this bit in the host ID part and use it to identify hosts within the subnet. To complete the subnet address, we include the 18 bits of the network ID to the 2-bit subnet ID, giving us a subnet ID that is 20 bits long. The result is therefore the /20 subnet, 66.118.32.0/20.

The ISP obtains upstream connectivity to the Internet through two national service providers—Cogent and AboveNet. Texlink peers with both these ISPs at Dallas. AboveNet also connects at Houston. A dedicated OC-12 line brings Cogent to Houston. Austin and San Antonio are connected to the rest of the network as shown in the figure.

### Acknowledgments

Special thanks to Pete Templin of Texlink Communications (now Pac-West Telecomm) for providing the information used in this case.

## SUMMARY

Subnetting allows network administrators to divide an organization's IP addresses into smaller address blocks. This simplifies delegation of network responsibilities within the organization. In cases where a lot of network traffic is generated by a small group of computers exchanging data with each other, subnetting can be used to limit network traffic by isolating these computers within a subnet.

Subnetting is implemented using subnet masks. Subnet masks look like IP addresses and are composed of a sequence of 1s followed by a sequence of 0s. The 1s in the subnet mask indicate the positions of the network ID and subnet ID bits in IP addresses.

The chapter implicitly assumes that organizations use the same subnet mask everywhere within the network. This has been done for simplicity because this is the first exposure to subnetting for most students. In reality, subnet sizes are allocated based on the actual needs of each subnet.

## ABOUT THE COLOPHON

Henry Ford founded the Ford Motor Company and was one of the first entrepreneurs to use assembly-line manufacturing to mass-produce affordable automobiles. His success with the technique revolutionized industrial production in the United States and the world. In a quote in the *Reader's Digest* in 1936, he suggested that even extraordinary challenges such as setting up the assembly line are manageable if broken down into simple tasks.

Subnetting brings the idea of breaking complex tasks into small jobs to computer networks. The structure and traffic patterns on the global Internet are extremely complex. However, the Internet is organized as a network of networks. It is simpler to first identify closely interacting computers and use appropriate data-link-layer technologies to organize these computers into subnets. These smaller networks, taken together, result in ever larger networks and eventually create the global Internet. Also, once the Internet is broken down into subnets, even relative novices can manage some of the individual subnets. As an example, most homes are now subnets, but are managed relatively easily by end users.

## REVIEW QUESTIONS

1. What is *subnetting*?

2. What is the organizational motivation for subnetting?

3. In large organizations, what are some disadvantages with allocating IP addresses on a first-come, first-served basis?

4. How does the typical campus network structure facilitate subnetting?

5. How do you determine the number of subnets needed in an organization?

6. Using an example, describe the three-part interpretation of IP addresses when subnetting is used.

7. Describe how subnetting is similar to the three-part organization of telephone numbers.

8. Describe how subnetting is similar to the multi-part organization of zip codes.

9. How does the three-part numbering system used in telephones facilitate the switching of long distance calls?

10. How does the multi-part numbering scheme used in zip codes simplify the mail handling tasks at a typical post office?

11. What are the three IP addresses on any network that are not available for allocation to hosts?

12. What factors determine the subnet structure of an organization? For example, if you have a Class B address, how will you determine if you should have 512 subnets, 256 subnets, 128 subnets, 64 subnets, or some other number of subnets?

13. What is a subnet mask?

14. Why are subnet masks needed?

15. What do the 1s and 0s in a subnet mask represent?

16. Can 255.255.253.0 be a subnet mask? Why or why not?

17. What information about a network can be gathered by looking at its subnet mask?

18. Say you have a /14 network address. You are asked to create subnets with at least 1,000 hosts/ subnet. What subnet mask should you use?

19. How many subnets can you have on the network in the question above?

20. The broadcast address on a subnet is obtained by replacing the bits in the host part with 1s instead of 0s. What is the broadcast address of the subnet 192.168.1.192/28?

21. How many hosts can a /18 network support?

22. Say you have a /15 network address. You are asked to create subnets with at least 1,000 hosts/ subnet. What is the maximum number of such subnets you can create?

23. What is the subnet mask you will use for the question above?

24. Consider two IP addresses: 192.168.35.56 and 192.168.36.135. If the subnet mask used is 255.255.252.0, what are the masked IP addresses (subnet IDs) for the two IP addresses?

25. How can subnetting help limit network traffic at routers?

## CRITICAL THINKING QUESTIONS

Say you are using the 192.168.0.0/16 address block to create subnets for a typical medium-sized business with about 2,000 employees.

1. You have been told to provide a subnet for each major department in the business. Assuming that the business has a typical organization structure for a business of this size, list the different subnets you would like to set up for the business.

2. How many bits would you need in the subnet ID to provide the required number of subnets?

3. How many hosts IDs would be available in each subnet in your design?

4. Present your results in the form of a table like Table 3 in the chapter.

## HANDS-ON EXERCISES

For this exercise, we will revisit the utility we have used in many prior exercises—ipconfig. On my computer, the output of ipconfig /all | more appears as shown in Figure 14. We see that the subnet mask on the network is 255.255.255.252.

```
C:\WINDOWS\system32\cmd.exe                               _ □ ✕
C:\>ipconfig /all | more                                        ▲
Windows IP Configuration

        Host Name . . . . . . . . . . : u246310
        Primary Dns Suffix  . . . . . . . : forest.usf.edu
        Node Type . . . . . . . . . . : Peer-Peer
        IP Routing Enabled. . . . . . . : No
        WINS Proxy Enabled. . . . . . . : No
        DNS Suffix Search List. . . . . : forest.usf.edu
                                        usf.edu

Ethernet adapter Wireless Network Connection:

        Connection-specific DNS Suffix  . : laptops.usf.edu.
        Description . . . . . . . . . . : Dell Wireless 1370 WLAN Mini-PCI Car
d
        Physical Address. . . . . . . . : 00-0E-9B-C3-E0-95
        Dhcp Enabled. . . . . . . . . . : Yes
        Autoconfiguration Enabled . . . . : Yes
        IP Address. . . . . . . . . . : 10.247.197.61
        Subnet Mask . . . . . . . . . . : 255.255.252.0
        Default Gateway . . . . . . . . : 10.247.199.254
        DHCP Server . . . . . . . . . . : 1.1.1.1
        DNS Servers . . . . . . . . . . : 131.247.254.3
-- More --                                                      ▼
```

**FIGURE 14**   ipconfig /all | more showing subnet mask information

Answer the following questions:

1. Write the subnet mask in Figure 14 in 32-bit binary notation.

2. How many bits in IP addresses on the network are used for the *host part* of the IP address?

3. How many hosts can the subnet of Figure 14 accommodate?

4. How many bits in IP addresses on the network are used for the *network part* of the IP address?

5. The IP address of the computer is 10.247.197.61 (Figure 14). Write this IP address as a 32-bit binary IP address.

6. What is the masked address of the host in binary notation? (This is the network ID + subnet ID part of the IP address.)

7. Express this masked address in dotted decimal notation. Express the masked address in CIDR notation.

8. Show the `ipconfig /all` output on your computer. What is the subnet mask on the network?

9. Based on the subnet mask, how many computers can be addressed on the subnet on which your computer is located?

## NETWORK DESIGN EXERCISE

In this exercise, you will design the subnets for Coolco, based on the information about Coolco provided in Chapter 1. In Chapter 7, we saw that the company has decided to use a /10 address block to provide addresses to hosts within the company. For quick response, the company has decided to use a DHCP server at each of its four locations—Tampa, Amsterdam, Mumbai, and Singapore. Using this information, answer the following questions:

1. What subnets would be suitable for use in the company's four locations?

2. Update the network diagram from Chapter 7 to show the subnets you created in the previous question.

3. Further update the network diagram to show the four DHCP servers, one server at each location.

## CASE QUESTIONS

1. How many customers can the ISP serve in San Antonio?

2. How many customers can the ISP serve in Houston, combining the capacity of all the subnets?

3. If the two /20 Houston subnets are merged together, what is the subnet address of the resulting network?

After deploying the network as shown in the case, the ISP experienced slow customer growth in Dallas and Austin, but high customer growth in San Antonio and Houston. To accommodate these growth patterns, the ISP pulled some /24 subnets from Dallas and Austin and allocated them to San Antonio and Houston. The ISP had to do this to demonstrate IP address utilization before it could apply to ARIN for more IP address blocks.

4. What are the /24 subnets that comprise the Dallas /21 subnet? (Hint: there are $2^{24-21} = 2^3 = 8$ such subnets.)

5. What are the /24 subnets that comprise the Austin /21 subnet?

6. Use BGPlay to show the network connectivity diagram for the 66.118.0.0/18 network.

7. What is the data rate of an OC-12 connection?

   (Optional) Now, assume that the last /24 subnet in each case (Dallas and Austin) is pulled out and allocated to San Antonio and Houston.

8. What are the remaining subnets in Dallas and Austin? Aggregate the subnets where possible.

# Routing

*I think that I shall never see*
*A graph more lovely than a tree.*
*A tree whose crucial property*
*Is loop-free connectivity.*
*A tree which must be sure to span*
*So packets can reach every LAN.*
*First the root must be selected*
*By ID it is elected.*
*Least-cost paths from root are traced.*
*In the tree these paths are placed.*
*A mesh is made by folks like me,*
*Then bridges find a spanning tree.*
—*Algorhyme,* by RADIA PERLMAN

## Overview

Routing is the process of moving information from the source network to the destination network through intervening LANs and WANs. Routing is used every time a computer sends packets to another computer that is not a member of its own local network. This chapter describes how routing works and describes the components, such as routing tables, that make routing work. At the end of the chapter, you should know:

- how routing is different from switching
- what autonomous systems are
- what routing tables are
- how to view routes to a network
- the two categories of routing protocols
- what route aggregation is and why it is useful

# Introduction

In Chapter 3, we saw how broadcasting is used to transfer data between computers on the same local network. Unfortunately, broadcasting is generally very inefficient to exchange data across networks. For example, your home network is directly connected to your ISP networks through your home router. Your ISP's network serves thousands of homes and handles very large amounts of data, most of which is not relevant to any computer within your home. Broadcasting the ISP data to computers within your home would create an unnecessary processing burden on the computers. There would also be privacy concerns if you could read data from other subscribers to the ISP's service.

Therefore, when networks are connected together to form larger networks, some suitable non-broadcast mechanism is necessary to transfer data that needs to go from one network to another. For example, a request from a PC in the home network to a web server on a remote site will need to be transferred from the home network to the ISP's network. The reply from the remote web server will need to be transferred from the ISP's network to the home network. These non-broadcast data transfers between networks are performed by routing.

Therefore, when data traffic reaches a network boundary, instead of broadcasting the data to all connected networks, it is efficient to direct the data along a suitable path toward its destination. *Routing is the process of selecting paths to move information across networks from the source network to the destination network.* Within LANs, the simple technique of broadcasting is preferred to directed transmission for its simplicity. But in large networks, routing improves efficiency by limiting broadcasts.

Routing is performed in networks by devices that are called routers. Routers are one of the most important components of data networks. They are made by companies like Cisco, Juniper, and Force 10. Routers can be expensive, costing tens of thousands of dollars, and need to be operated by trained administrators. The commercial importance of routers may be gauged from the fact that these are some of the largest companies in the IT industry.[1] You may not have heard of some of these firms because routers are located deep inside computer networks where end users are generally not aware of their existence. Routers are sold directly to corporate IT, and not through traditional retail channels. End users see only the home routers made by companies such as Linksys and Belkin, which are sold at many retail outlets.

## Switching vs. routing

Before we look at the details of routing, it is useful to contrast it with switching. Switching was covered in Chapter 3 and, at first glance, seems to perform the same functions as routing. When frames arrive at a switch, the switch examines the MAC header and directs the frame to the device with the destination MAC address. This improves network efficiency by curtailing broadcasts. Routers seem to perform the same task. They look at the destination IP address and send packets to the network closest to the destination.

Thus, both switches and routers look at destination addresses and direct packets toward the destination. Then, are there any differences between routing and switching?

---

[1] At one time during the dot-com boom, Cisco was the largest company in the world by market cap.

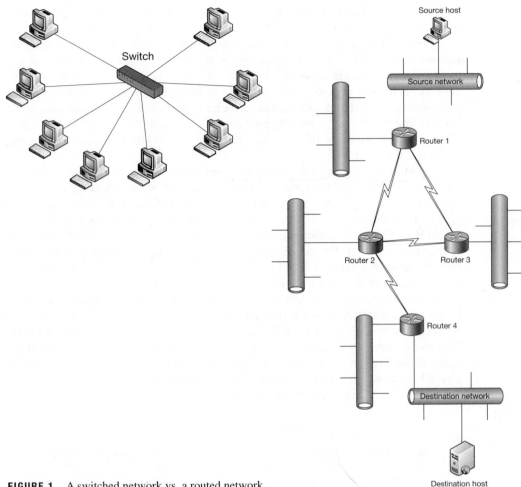

**FIGURE 1**   A switched network vs. a routed network

Indeed, there are. Figure 1 shows a prototype switched network and a prototype routed network. As seen in the figure, switches are found within LANs and there is only one path from source to destination in a switched network.[2] Routers connect LANs and there can be multiple paths from source to destination in routed networks. Hence switches have a relatively simple job—to select the correct path within a LAN. Routers on the other hand, need to be capable of choosing the best possible path among multiple possible paths through networks across the globe.

## Routers in networks

Routing protocols help routers gather the required information to select a route. Routers save the gathered information in routing tables. In the rest of this chapter, we will

---

[2] Switches have evolved to the point where switches can also select from multiple available paths. But for this book, we limit our treatment to the basic capabilities of switches.

see the contents of routing tables and other elements of routers. Let us begin by looking at the typical placement of a router in computer networks.

Routers are the glue that holds the Internet together. Without routers, each individual LAN and WAN would function very well internally, but we would have no way to guide packets across networks. Routers are placed at the interface between two networks and guide packets across networks in the right direction to their respective destinations. For example, ISPs place a router at the interface between your home network and the ISP's network. Figure 2 shows an example of one such router, which is located at the interface of two networks—USF and Bright House, an ISP serving the Tampa Bay area.

Routers have at least two interfaces (connection points). In the example above, one of the interfaces of the router connects to the USF network and the other interface connects to the Bright House network. Each interface of the router gets an IP address from the network to which it is connected. Thus, the interface connected to Bright House has an IP address from the Bright House address pool and the interface connected to the USF network has an IP address from the USF address pool. When packets arrive at a network interface, the router looks at the destination address of the packet and sends it out through the appropriate interface.

The router provided to you by your ISP also operates essentially the same way. It acts as the interface between two networks—your home network and your ISP's network. One of the ports of the ISP router acts as the interface with the ISP's network. This port is generally labeled "WAN" on most ISP routers. The other interface of the router connects to the home network. Generally, this port is internally connected to a switch as shown in Figure 3. The switch usually provides a wireless port and two–four ports to connect computers and printers in the home.

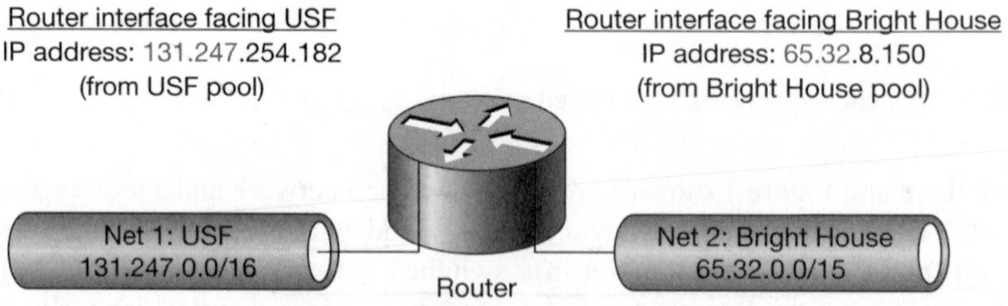

Router interface facing USF
IP address: 131.247.254.182
(from USF pool)

Router interface facing Bright House
IP address: 65.32.8.150
(from Bright House pool)

Net 1: USF
131.247.0.0/16

Net 2: Bright House
65.32.0.0/15

Router

**FIGURE 2** Router at the interface between USF and Bright House networks

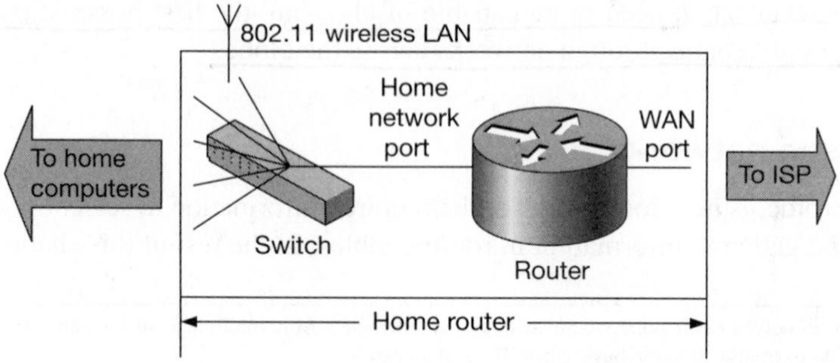

802.11 wireless LAN

To home computers

Home network port

WAN port

To ISP

Switch

Router

Home router

**FIGURE 3** Home router

# Autonomous systems

Before we look at routing tables, there is one more concept to introduce—autonomous systems (AS). *An autonomous system is a collection of routers that fall under one administrative entity.* RFC 1930 defines an AS as a connected group of one or more IP prefixes (network IDs) which has a single and clearly defined routing policy. What this means is that once a data packet reaches an AS, the administrator of the AS guarantees the delivery of data to destination computers within the AS. Routers on the Internet only have to worry about getting data packets to the destination AS. The details of packet delivery within the AS are left to the administrator of the AS.

To use an analogy, post offices are a lot like autonomous systems. Each post office announces the zip code(s) for which it takes responsibility to deliver mail. We may treat the zip code served by the post office as its AS number. The USPS system knows that all it has to do to get a piece of mail delivered to a home address within a zip code is to pass the mail item to the post office announcing responsibility for the zip code. The USPS system in the rest of the country does not have to worry about how the post office internally manages its mailmen, mail routes, new addresses, staff shortages, and the like. The post office will take care of the details of timely delivery within its area.[3]

Autonomous systems are the basic units of Internet routing. Having introduced the idea of autonomous systems, we can redefine routing as sending data from the source AS to the destination AS. In our example of Figure 2 both USF and Bright House are autonomous systems. Each AS has a globally unique AS number assigned by the IANA in a manner similar to the assignment of IP address blocks. IANA allocates AS numbers to the Internet registries, which in turn allocate AS numbers to organizations within their jurisdiction. For example, the AS number for USF is AS 5661.[4] As of August 2009, there are over 30,000 autonomous systems in the global Internet.

How are ASes relevant to routing? As we will see shortly, routes on the Internet are written as a chain of ASes. For example, the path from AT&T (AS 7018) to USF (AS 5661) through Cogent (AS 174) is written as 7018 174 5661.

The key elements of routing have been introduced. Let us now take a peek inside the Internet to see some routes between networks. The simplest way to do this is to use BGPlay, a tool developed at the University of Oregon to display changes in network connectivity around a specified network.[5] The network neighborhood around USF (prefix 131.247.0.0/16) looks as shown in Figure 4. You may note in Figure 4 that networks are identified by their AS numbers. Each link (dotted line) in the figure

---

[3] The analogy of AS with post offices is not perfect though. All Internet traffic moves through ASes. However, once the source post office (PO) collects all the mail to be delivered to other post offices, the USPS has a distribution system that bypasses post offices and uses aircraft, subcontractors and other mechanisms to directly deliver the mail to the destination PO, where it gets delivered. If the analogy between post offices and ASes were perfect, mail would be handed from PO to PO until it reached the destination PO.

[4] AS numbers can be found from www.cidr-report.org/as2.0/autnums.html.

[5] BGPlay is accessed from the "Start BGPlay" button at http://bgplay.routeviews.org/bgplay/. You can use BGPlay to view the network neighborhood around any AS. The critical information required is the IP network address of the AS you are interested in. This can be obtained from the network registry at www.arin.net. Entering an IP address in the WHOIS search field at the registry's home page returns the CIDR address block assigned to the organization. This CIDR address can be entered in the prefix field of the BGPlay utility to produce a map around the network as shown in Figure 4.

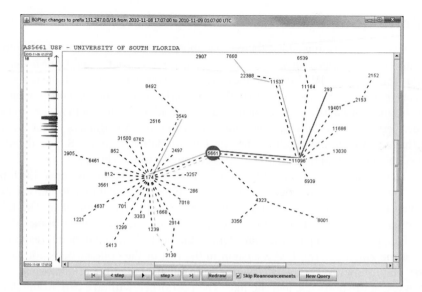

**FIGURE 4** Network routes in the neighborhood of 131.247.0.0/16 (USF)

represents a connection between two ASes through a router. Packets use these connections to traverse from any AS to any AS. Routers enable this transfer by maintaining connectivity information between ASes on the Internet in a routing table.

## Routing tables

Routers help data packets navigate through networks. Routers do this by maintaining the network connectivity information available to them in the form of a routing table. As each packet reaches a router, the router looks at the destination IP address of the packet, and searches its routing table to find a suitable route to the destination. The router then forwards the packet to the next router on the selected path to the destination. The process is repeated at every router until the packet reaches the destination AS. Inside the destination AS, the local network delivers the packet to the destination computer.

The discussion above shows that each router is only responsible for passing the packet on to a suitable neighboring router. As long as the neighbors are correctly chosen, the packet will reach the destination. This process is very similar to the process of following a route map as discussed in Chapter 4. You follow the route map hop-by-hop until the destination is reached. As long as you get each hop right, you are assured of reaching your destination.

To enable routers to select the correct neighbor, each entry in the routing table lists a network that can be reached, the neighboring router to forward the packet to in order to reach this network, and details about the path to the destination through this neighbor. Since a router is only responsible for passing the packet to the correct neighboring router, this information is adequate for the router to make its forwarding decision. Consider the following route in the routing table (from the Route Views project):

```
131.247.0.0/16        64.71.255.61        0        812 174 5661 5661 i
```

| Network | Next hop | Routing metric | Path |
|---|---|---|---|
| 131.247.0.0/16 | 64.71.255.61 | 0 | 812 174 5661 5661 i |
| 131.247.0.0/16 | 66.185.128.1 | 563 | 1668 174 5661 5661 i |
| 131.247.0.0/16 | 217.75.96.60 | 0 | 16150 3549 174 5661 5661 i |
| 131.247.0.0/16 | 208.51.134.246 | 13186 | 3549 174 5661 5661 i |
| 131.247.0.0/16 | 12.0.1.63 | 0 | 7018 174 5661 5661 i |
| 131.247.0.0/16 | 67.17.82.114 | 2503 | 3549 174 5661 5661 i |
| 131.247.0.0/16 | 192.203.116.253 | 0 | 22388 11537 11096 11096 5661 i |
| 131.247.0.0/16 | 203.181.248.168 | 0 | 7660 22388 11537 11096 11096 5661 i |
| 131.247.0.0/16 | 64.57.28.241 | 1045 | 11537 11096 11096 5661 i |
| 131.247.0.0/16 | 216.18.31.102 | 0 | 6539 11164 11096 5661 i |
| 131.247.0.0/16 | 216.218.252.164 | 0 | 6939 11096 5661 i |

**FIGURE 5**  Part of routing table from Route Views project

This route shows that the network 131.247.0.0/16 (USF) can be reached from the Route Views network by sending the packet to the router at 64.71.255.61. The third column in the route indicates that a measure of the cost of sending the packet to the destination through this router is 0. This number is called the routing metric. Finally, the last column in the route is the actual path, which in this case is Rogers Cable (AS 812) → Cogent (AS 174) → USF (AS 5661).

Example routes to USF (131.247.0.0/16) from the Route Views project are shown in Figure 5 for reference.[6]

One common feature of all the paths in Figure 5 may be noted—they reach USF (AS 5661) either through Cogent (AS 174), or through FloridaNet (AS 11096). You can relate this to the network neighborhood around USF shown in Figure 4, which shows that USF is connected to the rest of the Internet through Cogent and FloridaNet. Hence, packets from the outside world can get to USF only through Cogent or FloridaNet. This is reflected in the routes in the routing table maintained at the route-view project in Oregon.

As seen from the example paths to USF in Figure 5, there generally are multiple paths available to get to any network on the Internet. Routers maintain records of all these available routes to networks. The routing metric in each route is a measure of the cost of sending packets through the route. Paths with smaller routing metrics are considered cheaper and are preferred to paths with higher routing metrics. Administrators can assign routing metrics to enforce any suitable policy on their network. The metric for a path is the sum of the metrics for the components of the path. An example routing metric could be hop count, since the total hop count will be the sum of the component hop counts.

---

[6] If you have access to a UNIX/ Linux system, it is easy to view the paths to any network from the Route Views router using the following steps:

a) $ `wget http://archive.routeviews.org/oix-route-views/2009.08/oix-full-snapshot-latest.dat.bz2` (replace 2009.08 with the current year and month). This downloads the compressed routing table.

b) $ `bunzip2 oix-full-snapshot-latest.dat.bz2`. This uncompresses the table.

c) $ `ggrep --after-context=10 oix*` (for example ggrep --after-context=10 131.247 oix*). This prints out the routes to the selected network.

```
Windows PowerShell                                                    _ □ ×
PS C:\> tracert www.wsj.com

Tracing route to uslb.wsj.akadns.net [205.203.132.1]
over a maximum of 30 hops:

  1   <1 ms   <1 ms   <1 ms  vlan95.edu-msfc.net.usf.edu [131.247.95.254]
  2   <1 ms   <1 ms   <1 ms  vlan254.campus-backbone2.net.usf.edu [131.247.254.46]
  3   <1 ms   <1 ms   <1 ms  vlan256.wan-msfc.net.usf.edu [131.247.254.81]
  4    1 ms    1 ms    1 ms  gil-5.ccr01.tpa01.atlas.cogentco.com [38.104.150.41]
  5   10 ms   10 ms   10 ms  te4-4.ccr01.mia01.atlas.cogentco.com [154.54.29.197]
  6    7 ms    7 ms    7 ms  te3-1.ccr01.mia03.atlas.cogentco.com [154.54.24.234]
  7   10 ms   10 ms   10 ms  sl-crs1-mia-.sprintlink.net [144.232.24.213]
  8   54 ms   38 ms   38 ms  sl-crs1-atl-0-0-0-0.sprintlink.net [144.232.18.216]
  9   42 ms   42 ms   41 ms  sl-crs1-nyc-0-5-3-0.sprintlink.net [144.232.20.49]
 10   40 ms   40 ms   40 ms  sl-gw35-nyc-14-0-0.sprintlink.net [144.232.13.37]
 11   44 ms   42 ms   42 ms  sl-dowjo-129545-0.sprintlink.net [144.232.234.142]
 12   42 ms   42 ms   42 ms  online.wsj.com [205.203.132.1]

Trace complete.
PS C:\> _
```

**FIGURE 6** Example tracert output

# Viewing routes

All operating systems have utilities to help you see Internet routes from your computer to a specified destination. In windows, this utility is called `tracert`. An example of the use of `tracert` is shown in Figure 6. The example shows a trace of the route from a PC at USF to the website of the *Wall Street Journal* (www.wsj.com). The trace shows that the path from USF to WSJ passes through Cogent and Sprint. The presence of Cogent on the path should not be surprising, given the information in Figure 4. The presence of Sprint Networks on the path (hops 7–11) indicates that the WSJ is connected to the Internet through Sprint. Hence Cogent has to pass on the packets from USF to Sprint for onward transmission to the WSJ.

# Routing protocols

At the heart of understanding routing is to understand how routers generate their routing tables. We have already seen how routing tables are used. Given the size of the Internet, it is clearly inefficient to expect network administrators to manually enter routes into their routing tables. Automated procedures are necessary to help routers exchange connectivity information with each other so that all routers on the Internet are informed about the connectivity of all other routers on the Internet. This information should change in a timely manner so that, as new routes are added and old routes are dropped, the changes are automatically propagated to all routers on the Internet. All these activities involved in maintaining routing tables are done using routing protocols.

*Routing protocols are the mechanisms used by routers on the Internet to maintain routing tables.* Details of routing protocols are beyond the scope of this book. However, it is useful to be aware of the broad outlines of how routing protocols work. That will be done in this section.

All routers are configured by their administrators with information about their immediate network neighborhood. The challenge for routing protocols is to propagate this local information about network connectivity to routers in other parts of the Internet. To consider a simple case, take the routed network shown in Figure 1. Here, router 4 is connected to the destination network, but is not directly connected to router 1 or to router 3. The challenge then is—how can router 4 inform all other routers in the network that it is connected to the destination network and can deliver packets to the destination network?

Broadly speaking, there are two kinds of routing protocols to accomplish this task—exterior and interior.

In exterior routing protocols, each router informs its immediate neighbors about the networks it can connect to. Routers collect this information from all their neighbors and pass this information on to their other neighbors. For example, in Figure 1, once router 2 is informed by router 4 about a path to the destination network, router 2 can then pass this information on to router 1 and router 3. In routing parlance, informing neighbors about paths is called advertising. Thus, router 4 advertises a path to the destination network to router 2. Router 2 then advertises this path to router 1 and router 3. Eventually, all routers on the network become aware of all routes on the network. The most popular implementation of an exterior routing protocol is BGP, or the Border Gateway Protocol.

In interior routing protocols, routers periodically broadcast information about their immediate neighborhood to all other routers on the network. Continuing with our example of Figure 1, if an interior routing protocol is used, router 4 will broadcast its connectivity to the destination network to all routers on the network. Once broadcasts from all routers are received, each router independently uses the information in all the broadcasts to compute the layout of the entire network. Thus router 1 will receive information from router 4 about a connection to the destination network. It will also receive information from router 2 about a connection to router 4. Router 1 already knows that it is directly connected to router 2. From these pieces of information, router 1 will infer that a path to the destination network exists through router 2 and router 4. The most popular implementation of an interior routing protocol is OSPF, or the Open Shortest Path First protocol.

Both interior and exterior routing protocols lead to the same routing table. The trade-offs are in speed of propagation and computational complexity. Exterior routing protocols can take time to propagate path information because the information has to be passed from neighboring router to neighboring router. Interior routing protocols propagate information quickly because connectivity information is broadcast to all routers. However, the trade-off is that interior routing protocols can require more computation to process the information received from all the broadcasts.

As the names suggest, interior routing protocols are generally used within autonomous systems and exterior routing protocols are used by ASes to exchange routes with other ASes.

## Simplifying routing tables—route aggregation

As the Internet has grown in popularity, more and more organizations have come online, resulting in an increasing number of IP address blocks being advertised. Clearly, if not managed properly, routing tables can get quite large when all address blocks are added to routing tables. For example, the routing table downloaded from the Route Views project is over 900 MB in size. For each packet that arrives at a router, the router has to search through this vast 900-MB database to select the most suitable route to forward the packet. The tables keep growing in size as new organizations join the Internet. As routing tables get larger, searching the routing tables for a path can take longer and

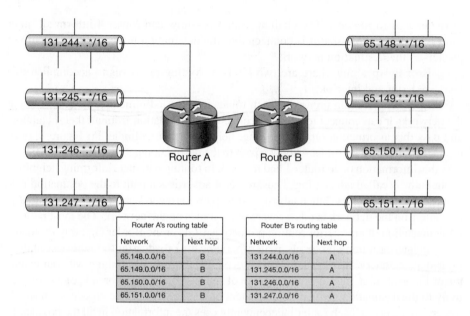

**FIGURE 7** Routes without route aggregation

longer. Alternately, to keep the search time low, routers can get more and more expensive as they add hardware to speed up the search.

There is, therefore, an effort in the Internet community to reduce the size of routing tables. This is done through route aggregation, which is specified in RFC 1338 and RFC 1518. You may recall from Chapter 4 that RFC 1518 also specified CIDR addressing. The goal of route aggregation is to reduce the number of routes advertised by networks.

*Route aggregation is the combination of two or more IP address blocks to one larger address block.* The idea behind route aggregation is to stop assigning IP address blocks to small organizations and, instead, assign larger blocks of IP addresses to large network service providers. Small organizations would be asked to obtain address blocks from network service providers. The key idea is that network service providers would take care of routing details to smaller organizations within their own networks. Routes to organizations within the network service provider would not be advertised to the outside world. If successful, routing tables would only record routes between large ISPs. Let us see this by an example, shown in Figure 7 and Figure 8.

Consider the interface between two networks shown in Figure 7. Both networks have four constituent /16 networks. Without route aggregation, the routing tables at each of the two routers will record four routes as shown in Figure 7, one for each constituent /16 network on the other side. For example, the routing table of router A has four routes, one to each /16 network connected to router B. Observe that since all the constituent networks are connected to the other network through the same router, the next hop information in all the four routes in each router is the same. For example, all the four routes in router A point to router B as the next hop. Clearly, there is redundancy in the information and some optimization is possible. Can we condense the four routes to just one entry in the routing table?

Indeed, it is possible. The routes in the same network with route aggregation are shown in Figure 8. This time, the four routes on each side are compressed to one /14 route. Therefore, the routing tables now only have one route each.

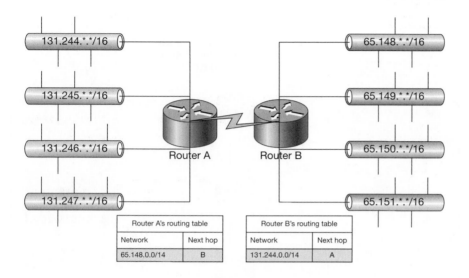

**FIGURE 8** Routes with route aggregation

How can one aggregated route consolidate four unaggregated routes? It may be noted that each route in the aggregated routing table points to a /14 network, whereas the routes in the table without aggregation pointed to /16 networks. Recall from our discussion of CIDR in Chapter 4 that in a /14 network, the network part of IP addresses is 14 bits long. The remaining 18 bits $(32 - 14)$ are used to identify hosts within the network. This allows a /14 network to have $2^{18}$ computers within the network. By comparison, a /16 network can accommodate $2^{16}$ computers. Thus, the 2 extra bits in the host part of the /14 network allow the /14 network to be four times as large as the /16 networks $(2^{18}/2^{16} = 2^2 = 4)$. Since the routes in Figure 8 point to networks that are four times as large as the networks in Figure 7, one entry in Figure 8 is equivalent to the four entries in Figure 8. In general, the routes in the aggregated routing tables point to larger networks. Since the total number of IP addresses is fixed $(2^{32})$, if we distribute these addresses among larger networks, we will have fewer networks. This will reduce the size of routing tables because routing tables keep track of networks, not individual IP addresses.

Figure 9 shows another example of how a network service provider may hide the details of its internal structure and only advertise its entire address block to the outside world. In the example, the 38.0.0.0/8 network has many smaller networks within it. However, the network hides the details about its interior structure and only advertises one route to the outside world. This spares the rest of the world from having to record paths to each network within the 38.0.0.0/8 network. These internal paths are irrelevant to routers outside the 38.0.0.0/8 AS if the 38.0.0.0/ 8 network acts as an AS and takes care of routing within its boundaries.[7]

---

[7] The site www.cidr-report.org provides a wealth of information relating to route aggregation and is worth a look. Specifically, the page www.cidr-report.org/as2.0/#General_Status provides such statistics as the number of ASes advertised and the biggest ASes that could meaningfully reduce the size of the global routing tables if they aggregated their routes. As of Aug 2009, BellSouth had the potential to make the greatest impact in reducing the size of the routing table by aggregating routes.

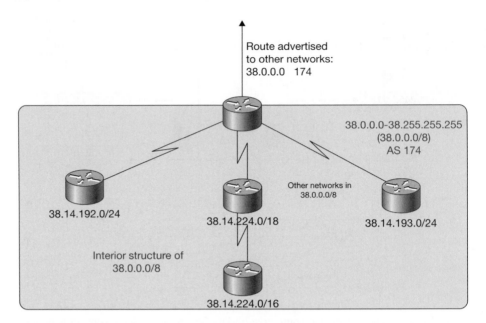

Route advertised
to other networks:
38.0.0.0   174

38.0.0.0-38.255.255.255
(38.0.0.0/8)
AS 174

38.14.192.0/24

Other networks in
38.0.0.0/8

38.14.224.0/18

38.14.193.0/24

Interior structure of
38.0.0.0/8

38.14.224.0/16

**FIGURE 9** Example of advertisement of aggregated route

## Multiprotocol Label Switching (MPLS)

Route aggregation, discussed in the previous section, is one of the methods by which attempts are being made to simplify routing. In recent years, a second method to simplify routing has become increasingly popular among carriers. This is called Multiprotocol Label Switching, or MPLS. *MPLS is a packet-forwarding mechanism that uses predefined labels to determine how to deliver packets.* The technology eliminates the need to examine IP header information and has been specified in RFC 3031, which was published in 2001.

The development of MPLS is motivated by the observation that whereas routers have only one job, selecting the next hop to forward the packet, the packet header that is processed by routers contains a lot more information than is needed to do the job. For reference, the IP header introduced in Chapter 4 is shown in Figure 10. Of all the fields in the header, the only information field that is required to make the routing decision is the destination address field. Processing other header fields such as TTL puts an unnecessary processing load on routers. What if we could find a way so that only the destination address field was presented to routers for processing? This would simplify the processing required at each router, potentially simplifying routers.

Also, in traditional routing, as a packet makes its way to the destination, each router along the path will independently make a routing decision to forward the packet. A lot of this processing can be redundant. For example, consider two students at Michigan State University, browsing the websites of two schools in the Golden State—University of San Diego (sandiego.edu) and San Diego State University (sdsu.edu). The schools are located within 10 miles of each other. Looking up the network neighborhood of the University of San Diego (CIDR 192.55.87.0/24) at BGPlay, we see that sandiego.edu is actually connected to the Internet through the California State University network (AS 2152), which also includes sdsu.edu (Figure 11).

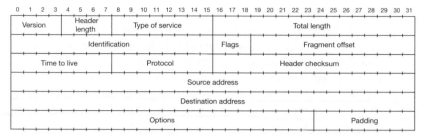

Note: Each tick mark represents a bit position

**FIGURE 10**   IP header

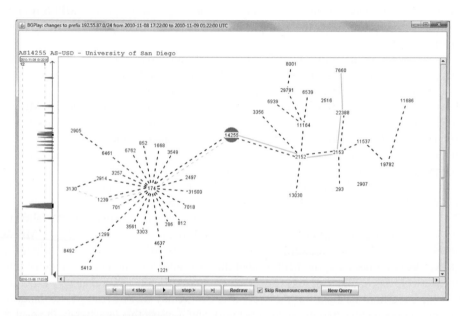

**FIGURE 11**   Network neighborhood around sandiego.edu (AS 2152 is the California State University network and includes sdsu.edu).

Given this network arrangement, consider how the two packets flowing from MSU to the two schools will be processed by routers along the path. Both packets will essentially follow the same path almost to the very end. The path to SDSU is (MSU → Internet 2 → California State University Network → SDSU) and the path to USD is (MSU → Internet 2 → California State University Network → USD). In traditional routing, each router on the path will independently make a routing decision on each packet. If one packet is sent to each of the two networks, assuming three routers handle the packet within each AS, a total of 24 routing decisions have to be made to deliver the 2 packets (3 routers/ network * 4 networks * 2 packets).

This process appears inefficient and seems to require too much processing by routers. What if we could find a way to tell all the routers in each network on the path that the two packets are going to take the same route? Even better, what if we could make the routing decision just once near the entry of the packet into the network and give all the routers in the network an instruction such as "send these packets by route 5"? The routers in the rest of the network would not have to make any routing decisions at all. The 24 routing decisions in the previous paragraph could be replaced by 8 routing decisions (1 decision per network * 4 networks * 2 packets).

MPLS addresses these two problems—too much header information to process by routers, and too much processing by each router on the paths. To address the second problem, MPLS defines the concept of forwarding-equivalence classes. *A forwarding-equivalence class is a group of IP packets which are forwarded in the same manner, for example over the same path.* In MPLS, the forwarding-equivalence class is called a label. All packets with the same label are handled identically. To address the first problem of too much packet overhead to process, MPLS adds the label to the packet. Routers in the network only look at the label to determine the next hop for the packet. MPLS routers maintain a forwarding table to determine the next hop for packets from the MPLS label of the packet.

If routers in the MPLS network still have to look up a table to forward packets, how is packet forwarding in MPLS simpler than traditional IP routing? The key difference is that in traditional routing, routers gather information from all routes advertised by all networks on the global Internet. This can lead to large routing tables. In MPLS, the labels are local to each network. Routers only know how to forward packets with a small set of labels. There are no global route advertisements, and administrators configure the forwarding table in each MPLS router. The forwarding table in the MPLS router shows the next hop for packets that arrive with allowed labels.

Thus, in MPLS, the routing decision takes the form of a labeling decision. The labeling decision is only done once on a packet, when the packet enters the network. The label is added to the packet at the point of entry into the network after the labeling decision is made. Throughout the packet's path through the network, only the MPLS label is used for packet forwarding. MPLS labels are local to a network; when the packet leaves a network, the MPLS label that was added to the packet on entry into the network is removed. If the packet now enters a second MPLS network before reaching the final destination, the second network may add a fresh MPLS label to the packet upon entry into the second network and remove this label when the packet leaves the second network.

---

**CASE STUDY** | ROUTING AROUND DISASTERS: IN THE WAKE OF KATRINA AND 9/11

---

*In this book, we have focused almost exclusively on the efficiency of modern data networks. We have been studying how breaking data down into small packets and interleaving data streams from multiple users allows a given network infrastructure to serve more customers. In this case we see how the redundancy provided by routing can offer another benefit. Properly designed Internet-based networks can be more resilient to disasters than traditional circuit-switched phone networks.*

Hurricane Katrina attained Category 5 status on the morning of August 28, 2005 and reached its peak strength at 1:00 p.m. CDT that day. The maximum sustained winds from the hurricane reached 175 mph. The hurricane had a devastating impact on communications networks in the

Gulf Coast region. More than three million customer telephone lines lost service. More than a thousand cell sites lost functionality. Thirty-eight 911 call centers went down. Approximately 100 television broadcast stations were unable to transmit. Hundreds of thousands of cable TV customers were affected.

Immediately after Hurricane Katrina struck land, the city government of New Orleans was operating out of the Hyatt hotel. Fifteen of the top officers of city government, including the mayor and the chief of police, had camped in a conference room at the hotel since it appeared to be the safest refuge from the storm.

Amidst the carnage, these people found that the Internet was the only communication service still working. The phones were dead. Cell phones were not working. The group did have satellite phones for emergencies such as this, but the phone batteries rapidly lost charge and could not be recharged. Fortunately, one of the members of the technology team, Scott Domke, had recently set up a phone account with Vonage, a nationwide voice-over-IP service provider. Just past noon on August 31, the mayor's team used this VoIP service to make its first call to the outside world in two days. A few hours later, President George Bush contacted the mayor at the same VoIP number from Air Force One.

The Katrina panel established by the FCC also noted the fragility of traditional (circuit-switched) voice networks and lauded the robustness of Internet technologies such as VoIP and text messaging.

## 9/11

The reliability of the Internet was tested in another recent major disaster, 9/11. Due to the importance of the Internet, the Association for Computing Machinery (ACM) and the Computer Science and Telecommunication Board (CSTB) established an expert committee to report on the performance of the Internet on 9/11. Overall, the committee found that though 9/11 had only a marginal impact on the Internet, there were also some surprising effects around the world. Due to the unique structure of the Internet, the Nimda virus (released one week later, on September 18, 2001) caused more damage to the Internet than 9/11 (Figure 12). South Africa suffered more damage in Internet connectivity than New Jersey. The most significant issues arose from power outage in Manhattan.

The events of September 11, 2001, damaged the physical infrastructure of the Internet in one of the network's most important hubs—New York City. Verizon had a central office at 140 West Street, very near the World Trade Center complex. This office was destroyed. Electrical power in Lower Manhattan was disrupted, and backup power systems to telecommunications facilities in the area quickly ran out of fuel. At least 74 U.S. and multinational telecommunications carriers have equipment in New York.

Reachable Prefixes, September 2001

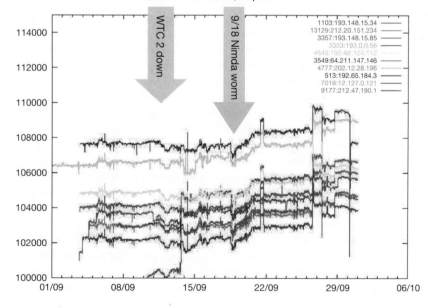

**FIGURE 12**
Reachable prefixes around 9/11 (Source: Renesys)

The city is served by more than 100 international Internet carriers, and it has direct links with 71 countries. Many of these connections take place over the network of the local exchange carrier, Verizon, and the long-haul fiber networks pass through Verizon's central offices. Less than half a mile from ground zero, Telehouse operates an Internet exchange point on 25 Broadway, serving about 40 Internet providers from NYC area, Europe, South America, and South Africa. About 70% of Internet traffic from Europe to the U.S. passed through 25 Broadway.

In spite of this, serious effects on communications networks were confined to New York City and some other regions that were highly dependent on NYC for their Internet connectivity. In some cases, automatic rerouting allowed Internet traffic to bypass many of the damaged areas. This was very different from the experience of other communications media such as the cellular phone services in greater New York, which suffered due to the infrastructure damage and congestion around NYC.

Internet routing, which dynamically adjusts the routes that packets follow in response to changes in the network (such as failures of communications links), can easily leverage redundancy. The redundant design of the Internet assisted quick healing of the network on 9/11. When the New York Academy of Medicine lost its connection to the Internet, it found it relatively easy to restore Internet connectivity using a jury-rigged wireless link outside a window to a nearby ISP. Some network operators used instant messaging and voice-over-Internet Protocol (IP) to coordinate activities when telephone service was impaired through local damage to telephone circuits.

Interestingly, while the Internet effects of September 11 were largely limited to the immediate neighborhood of the WTC, some parties far from the physical disaster sites were affected. ISPs in parts of Europe lost connectivity because they interconnected with the rest of the Internet in New York City. Some Internet customers in Western New England could not dial in to their ISP because the ISPs had located their modems in Manhattan. South Africa was largely cut off from the Internet because of its dependence on Domain Name System (DNS) resolution from servers in New York City. Users in South Africa had difficulty resolving domain names ending in .za, the top-level domain for South Africa, in the days following September 11. As a result, they could not access Internet services (such as web servers) within the country, even though there were no physical network disruptions in South Africa itself at that time.

In fact, of all Internet users, those in South Africa were the most seriously affected by the incidents of 9/11.

The Internet did not suffer the kinds of overloads that are often associated with the telephone system in a time of crisis. The events of 9/11 do not indicate how the Internet may perform in the face of a direct attack on the Internet itself because many ISPs had not concentrated their facilities on 140 West Street. However, the performance of the Internet on 9/11 demonstrated the benefits of the Internet's inherently flexible and robust design and its overall resilience in the face of significant infrastructural damage.

## Internet traffic patterns on 9/11

While not directly related to routing, the National Academy report on 9/11 also reported on how Internet traffic patterns were affected on 9/11. A very interesting part of the report details the steps taken by content providers to respond to the event.

Internet traffic volumes were somewhat lower on September 11 than on a typical business day. Many people who would normally have been using the Internet turned to the television for news and to phone calls for reaching loved ones. Traffic did increase in two areas—the quest for news and the use of Internet communications as a substitute for telephone calls. Low bandwidth e-mail and instant messaging were used as substitutes for telephone service, especially where conventional-telephone and cellular network congestion was high.

Internet-based communications alternatives such as text messaging and e-mail make more efficient use of limited communications capacity than do services such as telephones. By midday on September 11, the cellular-phone networks in Manhattan were severely congested. Yet, there were reports that people who used their cell phones or wireless-equipped PDAs to send instant messages were able to communicate effectively.

People used the Internet very differently in the aftermath of the September 11 attacks. Less e-mail was sent overall. News sites and instant messaging were used more heavily. The overall conclusion was that individuals used the Internet to supplement the information received from television (which was the preferred source of news). Those unable to view television often substituted Internet news. The telephone, meanwhile, remained the preferred means of communicating with friends and loved ones, but chat rooms and e-mail were also used, especially where the telephone infrastructure was damaged or overloaded. Other activities on the Internet, such as e-commerce, declined.

One consequence of this decrease was that in spite of larger numbers of person-to-person communications, total load on the Internet decreased rather than increased, so that the network was not at risk of congestion.

As a result of the unprecedented demand, news websites took a number of steps to enhance their ability to handle the traffic. Since the Internet technologies group at CNN was represented at the committee, CNN's experience, in particular, and the strategies it employed are documented in the report. On September 11, CNN's overall demand surged greatly, with page views increasing on September 11 to 132 million—nearly 10 times the more typical load of 14 million on September 10. The number of page hits (pages or images requested) doubled every 7 minutes, resulting in an order-of-magnitude increase in less than 30 minutes. The demand for news continued to increase following the attack, reaching 304 million page views on September 12—more than twice that measured on September 11. CNN responded with a combination of several techniques to deal with the load:

- Reduced web page complexity: CNN had a strategy in place for dealing with high-demand periods that called for reducing web page complexity. Accordingly, on 9/11, the CNN.com main web page was significantly reduced in size by eliminating elements such as headline pictures and graphical menu bars. In fact, the main page was stripped down to the bare bones—even further than the usual minimum—to increase its ability to serve pages. At its minimum complexity, the CNN.com home page could fit into a single IP packet.

- Adding more servers: CNN's other servers normally used for other CNN and Turner Broadcasting content were experiencing significantly reduced volume that day. A number of them were reconfigured and added to the CNN.com server pool. Interestingly, CNN did retain server capacity for the Cartoon Network, which saw an increase in volume—likely reflecting parents' desire to provide children with an alternative to the disturbing news.

- Temporarily employing a third-party content-distribution network: CNN increased its use of the Akamai content-delivery network to reduce the load on the CNN servers themselves.

## REFERENCES

Federal Communications Commission. *"Independent Panel Reviewing the Impact of Hurricane Katrina on Communications Networks: Report and Recommendations to the Federal Communications Commission."* June 12, 2006.

National Research Council. *"The Internet Under Crisis Conditions: Learning from September 11."* Washington, D.C.: National Academies Press, 2003.

Ogielski, A. and J. Cowie. *"Internet Routing Behavior on 9/11."* Renesys Corp., 03/5-6/2002.

Rhoads, C. "Cut Off: At Center of Crisis, City Officials Faced Struggle to Keep In Touch." *Wall Street Journal* (September 9, 2005): A.1.

Von.org. *"VoIP and Homeland Security."*

## SUMMARY

In this chapter we introduced routing and saw how routing is different from switching. We saw how the global Internet is organized as a mesh of autonomous systems. Routers are responsible for transferring packets from the source autonomous system to the destination autonomous system through intermediate ASes. Routers advertise known routes to all other routers using routing protocols. Routers save these advertised routes as routing tables. When a packet reaches a router, the router selects the best route from its routing table and forwards the packet to the neighboring router specified in the route. Passed from router to neighboring router, packets eventually reach their destination networks. At the destination network, Ethernet and other data-link-layer technologies are used to deliver packets to the destination host.

As network traffic has grown, procedures and technologies have been developed to simplify routing. Route aggregation attempts to reduce the number of routes advertised on the Internet to reduce the size of routing tables. MPLS is a technology that attempts to reduce the number of routing decisions that have to be taken to deliver packets to their destinations. MPLS also reduces the amount of processing that has to be done at each router.

## ABOUT THE COLOPHON

Radia Perlman, the inventor of the spanning tree algorithm to find the shortest paths between nodes on a network, wrote this poem to describe the algorithm. In her book,[8] Dr. Perlman states that it took her more effort to compose the poem than to create the spanning tree algorithm.

## REVIEW QUESTIONS

1. What is *routing*?

2. LANs use broadcasting to ensure that data reaches its destination. Why is it not advisable to use broadcasting between LANs?

3. What are *routers*? Find three carrier-grade router models made by the major vendors. What is the range of list prices on these routers?

4. What are the important similarities between switching and routing?

5. What are the important differences between routing and switching?

6. Consider a router at the interface of two networks; say your university and its ISP. Draw a figure showing the IP addresses of the two interfaces of the router and the CIDR address blocks of the two networks. (You may need to use `tracert` to obtain the IP addresses at the two interfaces and arin.net to obtain the address blocks of the two networks.)

7. What is an autonomous system?

8. How are post offices like autonomous systems?

9. Briefly describe how routing works.

10. What is a routing table? What information is stored in a routing table?

11. One route from the routing table at the Route Views project is shown below. What does each term in the route indicate?

    128.210.0.0/16        194.85.4.55
    0    3277 3267 9002 11537 19782 17 i

12. Use the AS numbers website (www.cidr-report .org/as2.0/autnums.html) to find the names of all the autonomous systems referred to in Question 11.

13. What is a routing metric? How is the routing metric used to select the path when multiple paths are available?

14. Use the `tracert` utility to record the route from your home computer to your university's home page.

15. What are *routing protocols*?

16. What are the two kinds of routing protocols? Give an example of each of the two kinds of routing protocols.

17. Provide an overview of how exterior routing protocols work.

18. Provide an overview of how interior routing protocols work.

19. What is *route aggregation*?

20. Why is route aggregation useful?

21. Give an example of routes before and after route aggregation.

22. What is *MPLS*?

23. What is the motivation for the development of MPLS?

24. What is a label in MPLS? Where is the label attached to a packet? Where is it removed?

25. What is a forwarding equivalence class (FEC) in MPLS? Give an example of two packets that may be assigned the same FEC even though they are addressed to two destinations.

---

[8] Perlman, R. *Interconnections: Bridges, Routers, Switches, and Internetworking Protocols*. 2nd ed. Boston: Addison-Wesley Professional, 1999.

# HANDS-ON EXERCISE

In this exercise, you will view the autonomous systems in the vicinity of your university using a Java applet called BGPlay. The Route Views project at the University of Oregon has direct connections to many major ISPs and collects routing information from around the world. This information is archived daily. When a CIDR network address is provided as input to the BGPlay applet, the applet searches through this database of routes to provide a graphical view of the network connections. BGPlay can also search back through the archives for up to a month and display route changes around the network during the month. Upon completing the exercise, you will get a visual picture of network routes and their volatility.

The exercise is to be completed in three steps. In the first step, you use `ping` or `tracert` to find your university's IP address. In the second step, you use ARIN's WHOIS database to obtain the CIDR address of your university. In the third step, you use this CIDR address as input to the BGPlay applet to see an animation of the route changes around your university.

We have used `ping` and `tracert` before, so we know how to use these utilities to obtain the IP address of

a URL as shown in Figure 13. In Chapter 4, we have seen how to use ARIN's search interface as shown in Figure 14 to obtain the CIDR address block for the IP address as shown in Figure 15.

Once we have the CIDR address of the network we are interested in, we can use BGPlay. The BGPlay applet is available at bgplay.routeviews.org/bgplay/→ "Start BGPlay" button. This brings up the BGPlay query form, shown in Figure 16. The CIDR address goes into the prefix textbox. The ending date is typically chosen to be the current date or a day or two earlier. For example, the screenshot of Figure 16 was captured on August 12 and the ending date was chosen to be August 11. The beginning date is a day earlier than the ending date but no more than 30 days in the past. In Figure 16, this date is chosen to be July 13. When you click OK, BGPlay uses this information to search through its database and extract all routes to the selected network and displays its results, as shown in Figure 17. You can click on the "play" button to see an animated view of path changes between the selected dates. You can also click on any AS icon to see the name of the network at the top left of the window.

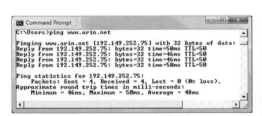

**FIGURE 13**   Using ping to obtain the IP address

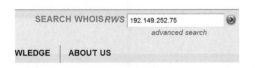

**FIGURE 14**   Using ARIN's WHOIS search to obtain CIDR address

**FIGURE 15**   CIDR address block from ARIN

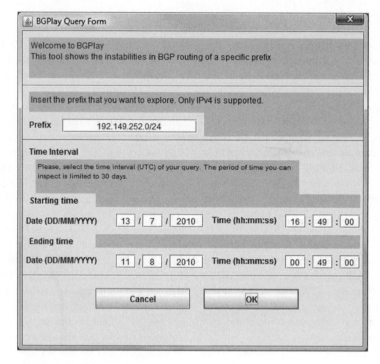

**FIGURE 16** BGPlay query form

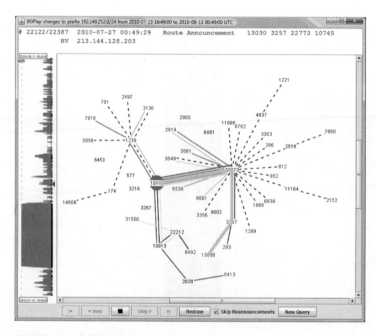

**FIGURE 17** BGPlay query results

Answer the following:

1. Write a brief summary of the goals of the Route Views project from the project home page at www.routeviews.org.

2. What is the network ID of the network to which your university belongs? (In some states, university networks are part of larger state networks).

3. Show a screenshot (similar to Figure 17) of the BGPlay query results for your university's network.

4. Pick a route originating from your university that passes through at least three autonomous systems.

Write the route as a sequence of ASes (e.g. 2905 701 1239 19151 3851 in Figure 17).

5. What are the network names of the ASes selected above?

6. Pause BGPlay during a route announcement. Show a screenshot as shown in Figure 17. What is the new route added?

7. Pause BGPlay during a route withdrawal. Show a screenshot as shown in Figure 17. What is the route withdrawn?

## NETWORK DESIGN EXERCISE

Although Coolco is not an AS, since it has chosen to maintain only one connection to the Internet, Coolco does use OSPF internally. It does this so that its routers can respond to network connectivity issues and direct traffic through the slower ISDN links in case the primary WAN links fail. This process is called failover. Answer the following question:

1. Write a brief report (two–three paragraphs) on how OSPF can be helpful in dynamically adjusting network traffic between ISDN and the primary WAN. You may find it useful to search for terms such as "ospf failover."

## CASE QUESTIONS

1. Describe some of the damage caused to communications networks due to Hurricane Katrina.

2. Describe some of the damage caused to communications networks on 9/11.

3. Why is text messaging and VoIP more reliable than circuit-switched voice networks?

4. Name some leading Voice-over-IP service providers in the country. Compare their services—pricing, equipment required, etc.

5. What are content delivery networks? How are they useful during disasters?

6. View the statistics on the nyiix website. What is the busiest time of day for Internet traffic? Why do you think traffic peaks at this time?

7. What were some changes in Internet traffic patterns on 9/11?

8. Why is it useful to reduce the size of a web page so it fits into one IP packet?

9. What is a possible extreme disaster that is likely to strike your city? Create a disaster continuity plan for communication that will allow you to maintain communication with the two most important people in your life in case this disaster strikes your town. If you wish to maintain the privacy of these individuals, just call them A and B, or use other such anonymous names.

## CHAPTER 10

# Wide Area Networks

*It's a small world.*
—*L.A. Times*, December 27, 1896

## Overview

Wide area networks (WANs) are networks that span large areas, such as states, countries, and even continents. All ISP networks are WANs. WANs serve as the backbone for the global Internet. You use WANs almost every time you connect to a computer that is located outside your immediate neighborhood. LANs (Chapter 3) connect to WANs to get connectivity to other networks. This chapter describes WANs and highlights the primary differences between LANs and WANs. It also introduces the most popular wide area networking technologies. At the end of the chapter, you should know:

- the need for wide area networking technologies as distinct from local area networking technologies
- the three standard approaches to creating WANs—SDM, TDM, FDM
- common WAN technologies, including dial-up, T links, SONET, DWDM
- virtual circuits
- location of WANs on the TCP/IP stack

## Introduction

*WANs are networks that provide data communications to a large number of independent users. These users are usually spread over a larger geographic area than a LAN.* As the definition suggests, WANs are distinguished from LANs in their ability to scale up to networks serving hundreds of millions of users located anywhere around the world.

As we will see in this chapter, WAN technologies are more complex than the simple broadcast technology used in LANs. Before we look at specific WAN technologies, it is useful to first understand why CSMA/CD will not work in WANs and why other, more complex approaches are required for WANs. With this understanding in place, the specific WAN solutions will be seen as specific approaches to address the challenges specific to WANs.

LANs typically connect computers in the immediate neighborhood. Computers within a classroom lab are a very good example. In such networks, the cables that connect computers to the central switch are short, usually less than 100 meters long. Since the cost of each link is much less than the cost of the computer it connects, it is not very important to optimize the utilization of these links. Thus, in Ethernet LANs, link utilization is very low, as the links are active only when network traffic is specifically directed to the connected computers. This inefficiency in link utilization is acceptable in LANs because it results in low costs for the technology, which can be built using low-cost network cards and switches.

Cables that connect computers across cities, states, or even countries are extremely expensive to install and maintain. For example, the submarine cables that connect continents can cost billions of dollars to install and hundreds of millions of dollars in annual maintenance costs. We cannot afford low rates of utilization for these expensive assets. It therefore becomes absolutely necessary to ensure that long-distance data-links are utilized to the greatest extent possible.

Another issue to address is that though broadcasting is very effective for communication in small networks, it becomes very slow as the number of users on the network increases. To avoid interfering with other users, each station in a broadcast network has to wait for the network to go silent before it can transmit. It is easy to see that as more computers join the network, the wait times for transmission will get longer and longer.

WANs overcome these two challenges—the need to increase link utilization and the need to reduce wait times. WANs do this by sharing each link among multiple users and merging the traffic from all these users onto the same link.

## The road network as an analogue for LANs and WANs

It may be easier to visualize the distinction between LANs and WANs by relating them to the road network. There are many similarities between the architecture of the Internet and the architecture of the road network. Seen this way, LANs are the Internet analogue for neighborhood roads and WANs are the Internet analogue for interstate highways.

To see the analogy, observe how LAN links are short like neighborhood roads. Also, just as traffic entering the neighborhood road waits for the road to clear before entering it, LAN traffic also waits for the link to be clear before inserting traffic into the network. Collisions are prevented by drivers looking out for other traffic on the road. By contrast, WAN links are long just like Interstate highways. Also, just as traffic entering the interstate merges seamlessly into existing traffic, WAN traffic also merges with existing data traffic on the WAN without waiting for silence on the WAN network. Just as merge ramps facilitate integration of local traffic with preexisting traffic on the interstate, routers merge multiple streams of traffic on WANs.

Figure 1 and Figure 2 show these features of the two kinds of roads. In the neighborhood road (Figure 1), the STOP sign encourages carrier-sense behavior by asking vehicles to stop and look before joining the road. For example, in Figure 1, the white car will wait for the black car to pass the intersection before entering the road. In Figure 2, there are no stop signs on the ramp or the interstate to slow down the traffic

**FIGURE 1**   Neighborhood intersection as CSMA example

**FIGURE 2**   Traffic merging onto interstate

merging onto the interstate. Both streams of traffic (existing traffic and entering traffic) continue at their regular speeds, and the merging traffic finds gaps between vehicles and blends into the existing traffic. WANs operate in a similar manner and allow multiple streams of traffic to blend together into one seamless stream.

What are the advantages in the road network of creating two different kinds of roads—one for the neighborhood and one for interstates? Why can't all roads be built like the interstate? The problem is that while interstates can handle large traffic volumes moving at very high speeds, they are very expensive to build. Entry and exit ramps and dedicated lanes have to be created to facilitate entry and exit from the interstate. They can also be very inconvenient in the neighborhood since traffic can only enter and exit the highway at designated exits. By contrast, neighborhood roads are less expensive to build. They are adequate to carry lower volumes of traffic at relatively slow speeds around the neighborhood. They are also convenient since homes can be built anywhere along the road and traffic can enter the road from anywhere. They are safe as long as all drivers watch out for each other and avoid collisions.

Therefore, there are good reasons to have two different kinds of roads. For pretty much the same reasons, it is good to have two different kinds of networking technologies—LANs and WANs.

## Categories of WANs

To summarize the above, the key capabilities of WANs are: (1) their ability to transport data over long distances and (2) merge traffic from multiple sources into one seamless stream. We will examine some of the popular WAN technologies in this chapter. Approximately in chronological order of development, these are:

1. Point-to-point technologies: These include dial-up, T/ DS and ISDN links

2. Statistical multiplexing: X.25, Frame Relay, and ATM

3. TDM: SONET optical carriers

4. FDM/WDM/DWDM (dense wavelength division multiplexing)

# Point-to-point WANs

## Dial-up networking

Each phone line is capable of providing a data rate of 56 Kbps. The earliest WANs used the phone network to create wide area links. A phone connection could act as a point-to-point line connecting any two networking nodes located anywhere in the country. For example, the first Internet, shown in Figure 3, used phone lines to connect the four Internet nodes. (You have seen this figure before, in the data-communication timeline in Chapter 1). Each node was connected to a phone modem that was connected to a modem attached to another node on the network. These early networks were simple and did not perform any traffic aggregation or routing. Routing was performed by the nodes themselves. Thus, if node #1 (UCLA) wanted to send data to node #4 (Utah), it would send the data to node #2 (SRI), which would, in turn, route the data to node #4.

Though dial-up networks were very rudimentary, and responsibility for traffic aggregation fell to the nodes themselves, these networks were important because they proved the viability of wide area networking.

## T-carriers/DS-signals

*telecom   digital singaling*

As wide area networking became popular in corporations, the speed limitations of dial-up networking immediately became apparent. Simultaneously, telecom firms saw the business opportunity in providing higher speed point-to-point connections by aggregating the data-carrying capabilities of multiple phone lines. This led to the development of T-carriers. T-carriers, or telecom carriers, combine the data-carrying capacity of multiple phone lines to provide higher data rates. The simplest T-carrier is

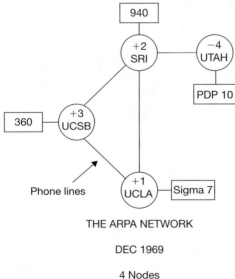

THE ARPA NETWORK

DEC 1969

4 Nodes

**FIGURE 3**   Early Internet-used phone lines

called T-1 and it combines the data-carrying capacity of 24 phone lines. This number was presumably chosen because it resulted in a data rate of slightly over 1.5 Mbps, which is suitable for most small–medium businesses.[1]

The data-carrying signals transmitted over the T-carriers are called digital signals, or DS for short. Formally therefore, the T-carrier is the physical line carrying signals and the DS-signal is the signal or data transported over the T-carrier. In practice, the two terms are used interchangeably in the industry.

Higher data rates than 1.5 Mbps are possible by aggregating T-carriers. Table 1 shows the most common T-carriers/DS-signals popular in the industry and the number of phone lines aggregated to provide the data rates.

T-carriers have been extremely useful in helping organizations connect offices spread across the world. An organization with one headquarters and four branch offices can create a WAN as shown in Figure 4. Each branch office connects to the headquarters using a T-1 line. Traffic between branches is routed through the headquarters.

**Table 1**   T-carrier/DS-signal hierarchy

| No. of phone lines aggregated | T-carrier name | DS-signal name | Data rate |
|---|---|---|---|
| 1 | | DS-0 | 64 Kbps |
| 24 | T-1 | DS-1 | 1.544 Mbps |
| 96 | T-2 | DS-2 | 6.312 Mbps |
| 672 | T-3 | DS-3 | 44.736 Mbps |

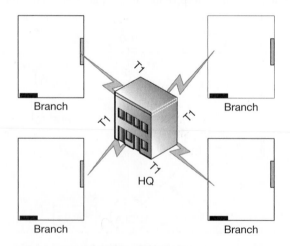

**FIGURE 4**   WAN built using T-1 lines

---

[1] 56 Kbps * 24 = 1.344 Mbps, which is less than the T-1 data rate of 1.544 Mbps. The higher data rate is achieved because the T-1 carrier attains a slightly higher data rate than the 56 Kbps available to end users on each phone line. Phone carriers achieve 64 Kbps per phone line.

### Integrated services digital network (ISDN)

Another data service developed by the phone companies was ISDN. The coaxial cable used by cable companies was capable of serving much higher data rates than the twisted pair used by phone companies. To meet the growing data needs of its customers, phone companies developed ISDN as a defensive measure to retain customers who were likely to defect to cable service providers when cable providers became capable of offering data services.

ISDN is a service offered by telecom companies with the goal of delivering voice, video, and data services over the standard telephone line. The keyword "integrated" in ISDN refers to the ability of the service to integrate multiple services (voice, video, and data) simultaneously over the same wire. ISDN data rates are offered in multiples of 64 Kbps, with 128 Kbps being quite common. A 64-Kbps connection is called a basic rate interface (BRI). Higher data rates are obtained by combining the data capacities of multiple BRI channels.

With the increasing deployment of optical fiber to customer premises, ISDN is now primarily used as a backup data service for use in case the primary wide area network service fails.

However, point-to-point networks have a major limitation—there is very limited traffic aggregation on point-to-point networks. A separate link must be set up for each pair of nodes that need connectivity. While this is not a major issue in small networks, as more nodes get added to the network, the number of required links grows very fast.[2] Also, since each link only connects a pair of nodes, link utilization can be low on point-to-point networks.

To address these issues, low-link utilization and rapid growth in the required number of links, more recent WANs use techniques to aggregate (multiplex) traffic on WAN links. We now look at some of the popular multiplexing techniques used in WANs and the technologies that use these techniques.

## Statistically multiplexed WANs

In statistically multiplexed networks, switches collect data packets from multiple input sources and send them out over a shared long-distance link to the next node. *Statistically multiplexed WANs allocate network resources according to need*. An example is shown in Figure 5 which compares how two organizations with offices across the country would be served using point-to-point T-1 links and with statistically multiplexed links. Statistical multiplexing is closest to the principles used in aggregating traffic on the interstate highway system.

The upper figure in Figure 5 shows connectivity using point-to-point links. In the figure, organizations A and B each have their own dedicated T-1 links to connect the offices on the two coasts. It may be noted that, in this configuration, there is no sharing of resources among organizations A and B. The lower figure shows statistical multiplexing for WAN connectivity. When using statistical multiplexing in the WAN, offices

---

[2] In general, full connectivity in a network with n nodes requires n(n-1)/2 links. A network with 4 nodes requires 6 links, and a network with 8 nodes requires 28 links.

Point-to-point WAN

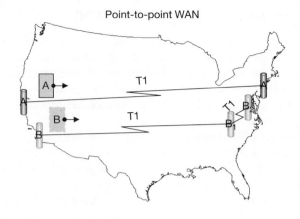

Statistically multiplexed WAN

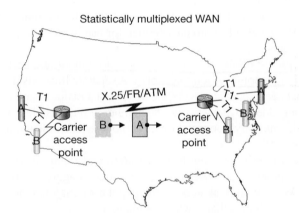

**FIGURE 5** Comparing point-to-point and statistically multiplexed WANs to connect offices in two organizations

from both organizations use dedicated short-distance T-1 links to connect to a carrier access point in their city. A switch at the access point in each city aggregates traffic from both organizations and sends it over the multiplexed link to the other city. The access point also demultiplexes (separates) incoming traffic and directs incoming traffic from the WAN link to the appropriate office, e.g. $B_1$ or $B_2$. Note that the long-distance link in this configuration is shared between organizations A and B.

Comparing the two configurations in Figure 5, it is easy to see that statistical multi-plexing is likely to give higher link utilization, albeit at the cost of slightly higher system complexity. The multiplexed system requires the carrier to create access points in each city. It also requires equipment at each access point to aggregate outgoing traffic from A and B for transmission on the WAN link. Access points must also be capable of disaggregating incoming traffic on the WAN link, to the different offices—$B_1$, $B_2$, and A. The advantage from this complexity is that the data- carrying capacity of the long- distance link, the most expensive part of the network, can now be shared among organizations A and B. This greatly improves the utilization of the capacity of the WAN link.

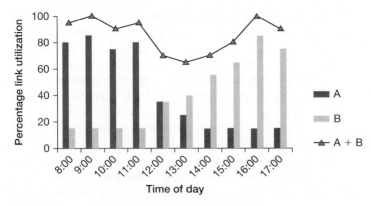

**FIGURE 6**   Reduced burstiness of aggregate traffic

Depending upon the traffic patterns of customers, aggregating traffic can improve link utilization by reducing the burstiness of the traffic on the link. As an example, consider Figure 6 where most of the traffic from organization A originates in the morning and most of the traffic from organization B originates in the evening. When the traffic from the two organizations is aggregated, the overall traffic is smoother than the traffic from either organization A or B. As a result, the investment in setting up the aggregate link will be utilized at high levels throughout the day. If each of the two organizations had dedicated point-to-point links (upper figure in Figure 5), the link serving organization A would mainly be used during the day and the link serving organization B would only be used in the evening. In general, the higher link utilization of the statistically multiplexed WANs throughout the day allows the fixed costs of operating the WAN to be shared by A and B, leading to lower communication costs for both A and B.

We now look at some specific statistically multiplexed WAN technologies.

## Virtual circuits

Before looking at the specific technologies, it is necessary to introduce one concept associated with statistically multiplexed WANs—virtual circuits. In the previous section, we saw that it was necessary for the access point at the receiving end to disaggregate and direct traffic to organizations A and B as appropriate. The question is, if all the data arrives over one link, how does the receiving access point know which data belongs to organization A and which data to organization B?

Statistically multiplexed WANs accomplish this using the concept of virtual circuits. *A virtual circuit is a communications arrangement in which data from a source user may be passed to a destination user over various real circuits.* Though the definition sounds complex, in practice it is quite simple. Virtual circuits are implemented by assigning a unique virtual-circuit ID for each source-destination pair that is sending data through the network. Packets entering the network from the specified source and directed to the specified destination are labeled with the virtual-circuit ID associated with the pair. The network uses the virtual-circuit ID to direct the packet to the correct access point. At the access point, the virtual-circuit ID helps the access point pass the data to the correct customer. You may notice that the virtual-circuit ID (VCID) shares many of the properties of MPLS labels.

To see this by example, let us assign virtual-circuit IDs to the connections in our example as shown in Table 2. Considering data flowing from the west coast to the east coast, we have three virtual circuits as shown in the table. As data from the sources reaches the west coast access point of the carrier, the data packets are labeled with the appropriate virtual-circuit IDs. For example, data from B going to $B_1$ gets virtual-circuit ID 2. Figure 7 shows some packets with virtual-circuit labels flowing through the shared network link. Switches within the network use these virtual-circuit IDs to deliver the packets to the access point on the east coast. At the east coast, the access point reads the virtual-circuit ID and passes the packets on to the correct target. For example, the virtual-circuit ID 2 tells the access point that the data should be sent to $B_1$.

You might be wondering, why do we need yet another address? Don't we have MAC addresses and IP addresses? Are they not adequate? Why can't IP addresses indicate the source and destination? What benefit do virtual-circuit IDs provide that IP addresses do not? The primary advantage of virtual-circuit IDs is that, whereas IP addresses are global, virtual- circuit IDs are local to the telecom carrier. Virtual-circuit IDs are data-link-layer addresses. This makes virtual- circuit IDs much easier to use than IP addresses. Since IP addresses are global, to make IP addressing work, routers need to advertise the accessibility of every IP network to all other networks around the Internet.[3] However, since virtual circuits are local to a carrier, virtual-circuit IDs are local to the carrier and only need to be communicated to other devices within the carrier's own network.

**Table 2**  Virtual-circuit IDs for our example

| Connection | Virtual-circuit ID |
| --- | --- |
| A-A | 1 |
| B-$B_1$ | 2 |
| B-$B_2$ | 3 |

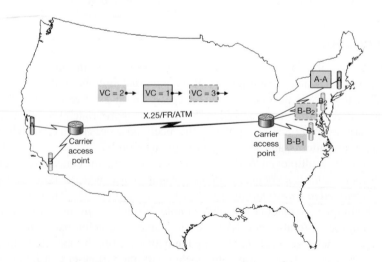

**FIGURE 7**  Virtual circuits

---

[3] There's also the issue of private addressing. If organizations "A" and "B" used the RFC1918 address space, using IP addressing on the shared link would be impossible because of possible duplication of addresses.

Whereas IP addresses and MAC addresses are assigned to the device, virtual-circuit IDs are assigned to the source-destination pair. A retailer with one head office and 50 branches would pay for 100 virtual circuits—one virtual circuit from each store to the headquarters and one virtual circuit from the headquarters to each store.

## X.25/Frame Relay/ATM → deal with frame (layer 2)

Three popular, statistically multiplexed WAN technologies, in the order in which they were developed, are X.25, Frame Relay, and ATM. Each technology defines a frame format suitable for the technology. As shown in Figure 7, customers use short-distance, dedicated links such as T-1 to connect to the most convenient access point from the carrier. Between access points, the carrier uses statistical multiplexing techniques to aggregate and switch traffic from multiple virtual circuits to the respective destinations.

X.25 is the oldest of the three technologies. It was standardized in 1976 and is capable of data transfer rates from 56 Kbps–2 Mbps. It is therefore a relatively slow technology. However, the unique feature of X.25 is that it is capable of transferring data over extremely unreliable links. X.25 accomplishes this by using link-by-link acknowledgments as the data is transferred. This is done because data networks in the 1970s were extremely unreliable and the acknowledgments enabled X.25 to repeat as many attempts as necessary to account for link failures and ensure reliable data transfer.

As telecom networks became more reliable, the link-by-link acknowledgments of X.25 became unnecessary. The additional processing required to handle the acknowledgments made the technology relatively complex. When the underlying networks became highly reliable, the additional complexity to ensure reliability served no useful purpose. Frame Relay was developed to streamline the protocol by eliminating link-by-link acknowledgments. It was standardized in 1992 and specified data transfer speeds in the range 56 Kbps–45 Mbps.

The third statistically multiplexed technology is ATM (Asynchronous Transfer Mode). It was standardized in 1992 and, like Frame Relay, eliminates link-by-link acknowledgments. ATM is an improvement over Frame Relay in two respects. First, it can support higher data rates than Frame Relay. ATM data rates are in the range 1.544 Mbps–622.08 Mbps. Second, ATM is designed to meet the needs of networks that carry different kinds of traffic. Frame Relay networks treat all data packets with the same priority. But ATM networks can transfer different kinds of data with different levels of priority. For example, voice packets can be delivered at the highest priority to ensure jitter-free voice reception, and e-mail packets can be delivered at the lowest priority because users have no expectation of instant delivery of e-mail. With this capability, ATM networks have the opportunity to charge higher prices for superior classes of service.

## TDM WANs

The third category of WANs are time-division multiplexed WANs. In this technology, the available data rate on the physical medium is divided into multiple time slots and each customer is allotted some specified time slots. The most popular implementation of TDM WAN technology is called SONET, for Synchronous Optical NETwork. Commercially, the data service on SONET is called OC, for optical carrier.

Unlike X.25, Frame Relay, and ATM, which are considered data-link-layer technologies, SONET is generally considered a physical-layer technology because SONET does not define any packet or frame formats. It is simply a method of efficiently using the datacarrying capacity of the physical medium. Each slot on a SONET network can carry bits from any technology. It is common for X.25/FR/ATM frames to be transported over SONET links. SONET data rates were first standardized in 1988 and higher data rates have been added over time as technology has evolved. The current SONET data rates are shown in Table 3. As seen from the table, SONET defines extremely high data rates. The slowest OC carrier can transport a T-3 link.

## FDM WANs

With the improvements in data-transfer capabilities of optical fibers, it is now possible to send extremely high data rates on each strand of fiber. With current technologies, each fiber can support data rates of up to 40,000 Gbps or 40 Tbps (terabits per second). No user needs such high data rates, and current electronic technology capable of handling such high data rates can be very expensive. It is therefore, much more efficient to split up the data-handling capacity of an optical fiber into multiple channels, where each channel supports a SONET channel at data rates such as OC-192 or OC-768.

To accomplish this, the data-carrying capacity of a strand of optical fiber is separated into multiple smaller channels by transmitting the signals from each channel at a different frequency. Hence, the approach is called frequency-division multiplexing (FDM).[4] The available bandwidth of optical fiber is split into three bands—L, C, and S. Each band has 50 channels and each channel can support data rates up to 10 Gbps. Comparing these rates with Table 3, we see that each FDM channel can support one OC-192 channel. The set of specified frequencies on optical fiber are called the ITU grid and were defined in 2001.

DWDM is a lot like dividing a wide interstate highway into multiple, narrower lanes. Each such lane is suitable for vehicles that typically use the highway. There is no point in making the entire highway available to a single vehicle because no vehicle is capable of utilizing the entire width of the road.

**Table 3** Optical carrier hierarchy

| SONET service name | Data rate | Data + overhead |
|---|---|---|
| OC-1 | 50.112 Mbps | 51.84 Mbps |
| OC-3 | 150.336 Mbps | 155.52 Mbps |
| OC-12 | 601.344 Mbps | 622.08 Mbps |
| OC-48 | 2.405,376 Gbps | 2.488,320 Gbps |
| OC-192 | 9.621,504 Gbps | 9.953,280 Gbps |
| OC-768 | 38.486,016 Gbps | 39.813,120 Gbps |

[4] In a wave, frequency * wavelength = constant. Therefore, there is a unique wavelength associated with each unique frequency. For this reason, FDM in optical fiber is also called wavelength division multiplexing. Modern fibers pack the multiplexed wavelengths very tightly. Hence the technology is also called dense wavelength division multiplexing (DWDM).

# WANs and the TCP/IP stack

Before closing this chapter, let us take a moment to see how WANs are related to other technologies in the TCP/IP stack. In modern networks, WANs are typically treated as long-distance equivalents of Ethernet. In general, packets traverse multiple Ethernets and WAN links on their way to the destination. As an example, a `traceroute` from USF to google.com is shown in Figure 8. We see that the first three hops in the path are within the USF LAN, and the remaining hops are WAN hops that take the packet to the destination. This `traceroute` example is intended to demonstrate that LAN links and WAN links are treated similarly within the network architecture. Since we have already discussed in detail in Chapter 3 that Ethernets are placed in the data-link layer of the TCP/IP stack, the example shows that WANs are also treated as a data-link-layer technology in networks.

Figure 9 shows what happens at a router that interfaces between a LAN and a WAN. When a data frame arrives at the LAN interface of the router, the LAN header is stripped away to retrieve the IP header. The IP destination address is then used by the network layer to determine the appropriate WAN interface to forward the packet to. The packet is passed to this interface, which formats the packet into the appropriate frame format, adding suitable virtual-circuit IDs for correct delivery.

```
# traceroute www.google.com
traceroute to www.google.com (74.125.159.103), 30 hops max
1  vlan272.edu-msfc.net.usf.edu (131.247.16.254)  0.997 ms
2  vlan254.campus-backbone2.net.usf.edu (131.247.254.46)  0.567 ms
3  vlan256.wan-msfc.net.usf.edu (131.247.254.81)  4.856 ms
4  tpa-flrcore-7609-1-te31-v1602-1.net.flrnet.org (198.32.166.177)  1.086 ms
5  mia-flrcore-7609-1-te24-1.net.flrnet.org (198.32.173.125)  31.991 ms
6  peer-google-flrnetcp-nota-1.net.flrnet.org (198.32.173.126)  6.269 ms
7  72.14.236.178 (72.14.236.178)  6.281 ms
8  209.85.254.14 (209.85.254.14)  20.159 ms
9  yi-in-f106.google.com (74.125.159.106)  20.255 ms
```

**FIGURE 8**   Traceroute showing LAN and WAN links in path

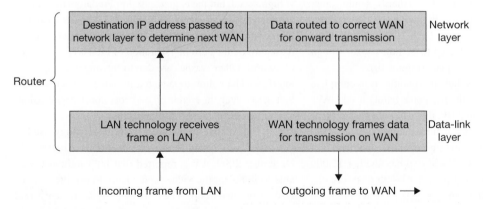

**FIGURE 9**   WANs in relation to IP and LANs

## CASE STUDY | HIGH WIRE ACT: UNMANNED AERIAL VEHICLES

*During 2000–2010, the U.S. Air Force went through one of its most radical transformations ever. In 2001, all fighter aircraft deployed by the Air Force were conventional piloted aircraft. Fast forward to 2009, and the Air Force trained more "pilots" for unmanned aerial vehicles (UAVs) than for manned fighters. The Air Force believes that UAVs have been the most effective weapon systems in Iraq and Afghanistan for saving the lives of American soldiers. UAVs are operated entirely using global satellite-based WAN data networks.*

**FIGURE 10**   The Reaper UAV (Drone)

In the war of 1973, Israeli fighter jets took a heavy beating from enemy missiles. In response, Israel developed the world's first UAV. When these UAVs were deployed in the next Arab war in 1981, the real-time images provided by the UAVs helped Israel destroy enemy air defenses, without losing a single pilot. This proof-of-concept convinced many militaries in the world of the viability of UAVs.

The U.S. Air Force has experimented with UAVs since the 1980s. In the 1990s, UAVs, also called drones, were used mainly as remote video cameras, sending pictures of enemy movements over satellite-based data networks to intelligence analysts. Each UAV is capable of sending a live video feed for up to 22 hours with enough resolution to detect a license plate (Figure 10).

In the 2000s, UAVs shot up in popularity as complete weapons systems. Where the Air Force barely used UAVs in the Iraq war of 2003, in 2010, the Air Force has approximately 7,000 UAVs. This includes approximately 200 Predators and 30 Reapers, the improved, weaponized versions of Predators. The Air Force also has another 12,000 unmanned vehicles on the ground for bomb disposal, etc. These unmanned ground vehicles help the forces remove an advantage held by enemy guerillas—their willingness

to give up their lives as human bombs in order to inflict casualties upon American forces. The Air Force is now so committed to the use of UAVs that UAVs account for 36% of the aircraft the Air Force intends to acquire in 2010.

UAVs would not be possible without global satellite-based WAN data networks. UAVs in war zones anywhere in the world are piloted from Air Force bases in the United States. UAVs use satellite-based WAN data networks to send detailed real-time video footage of enemies to intelligence analysts to determine the identity of enemy targets. On confirmation from intelligence analysts, sensor operators use data networks to launch and guide on-board missiles from the UAVs to targets.

The Predator UAV includes a satellite link which uses a 20-foot satellite dish. The satellite link is used to operate the aircraft when it is beyond the line of sight. The satellite link is also used to transmit video feeds. In 2009, the UAVs were transmitting 16,000 hours of video in war zones each month. The military's networks allow this video to even be transmitted directly to troops on the ground.

Adoption of UAVs has forced the Air Force to rethink its training and operational strategies. While it is currently transferring combat pilots to fly UAVs, the Air Force has decided to create a separate career track for UAV pilots. The training effort required to learn to fly a UAV is comparable to the effort required to earn a master's degree. Due to lack of proper training and device malfunctions, over 70 Predators have crashed so far. Some crashes are from old habits. Combat aircraft are capable of executing sharp turns at high speed, but the engines used in Predators have about as much power as a snowmobile engine, and are incapable of executing these maneuvers. When former pilots execute these moves, the current generation of Predators can go out of control. Other crashes are due to the imperfect operator interface. The button to launch a missile is adjacent to the button to switch the engine off and operators have occasionally turned the vehicles off in mid-flight.

The relative immaturity of the technology used in UAVs has caused some embarrassment to the Air Force. In December 2009, it was reported that Iraqi militants were able to intercept the video feeds being transmitted by the UAVs to ground troops. The software, `SkyGrabber`, used to intercept the videos was quite inexpensive, costing only

$26. `SkyGrabber` was effective because the transmission from the UAVs was not encrypted until April 2009. Earlier, the leadership of the Air Force had dismissed the possibility that insurgents in Iraq and Afghanistan might possess the technical competence to intercept unencrypted video. Encryption is covered in Chapter 13.

The improved capabilities of UAVs are enabling the Air Force to deploy new counterinsurgency techniques. As a result, in 2009, the UAVs were flying 34 surveillance patrols each day in Iraq and Afghanistan, almost three times the 12 daily patrols in 2006. UAVs may also be lowering the cost of war. Where each F-22 Raptor combat aircraft costs approximately $150 million, the current generation of Predators costs $4.5 million each and Reapers will each cost about $12 million. While combat aircraft are used to fire heavy weapons, in 2007 and 2008, UAVs shot missiles on 244 of the 10,949 missions in Iraq and Afghanistan. Some of these missiles killed "high-value" targets, considerably reducing the security threats facing the country.

Interface improvements may further improve efficiency. Currently, it can take up to 17 steps to fire a missile. If this can be simplified, one pilot could operate a fleet of UAVs.

For all its advantages, the use of UAVs is not without controversies. Human rights advocates argue that UAVs kill innocent civilians. Militaries argue that the detailed video footage from UAVs improves the likelihood that targets are correctly identified and the lighter bombs used by UAVs reduce collateral damage compared to the heavy artillery used by combat aircraft.

The use of UAVs also creates work-life balance issues. Combat pilots at war are close to enemy territory, away from family, and are engaged in the action round the clock. Piloting a UAV is almost a desk job. Pilots return home at the end of their shifts, where they may attend a birthday party just hours after destroying an enemy building or killing members of an enemy patrol.

UAVs may make war safer for the world's militaries. However, one of the biggest constraints on the willingness of political leaders to wage war is the public outcry that follows the death of soldiers in enemy territory. If UAVs eliminate that fear, will powerful countries be more willing to use force to resolve disputes?

## REFERENCES

Editorial. "Predators and Civilians." *Wall Street Journal,* July 14, 2009.

Dreazen, Y. J., S. Gorman, and A. Cole, "Officers Warned of Flaw in US Drones in 2004." *Wall Street Journal,* December 18, 2009.

Drew, C. "Drones Are Weapons of Choice in Fighting Qaeda." *New York Times,* March 16, 2009.

Hagerman, E. "Point. Click. Kill: Inside the Air Force's Frantic Unmanned Reinvention." *Popular Science,* August 18, 2009.

Levinson, C. "Israeli Robots Remake Battlefield." *Wall Street Journal,* January 13, 2010, A10. "MQ-1 Predator." Wikipedia.

Siobhan G., Y. J. Dreazen, and A. Cole. "Insurgents Hack US drones." *Wall Street Journal,* December 17, 2009.

Wikipedia article on MQ-1 Predator.

## SUMMARY

This chapter introduced wide area networks (WANs). WANs are used to transfer data in networks with a large number of users, usually over a large area. We started by showing why simpler broadcast technologies as used in Ethernet are unsuitable for long-range transmission in networks with a large number of nodes. The road network was used to help visualize the differences between LANs and WANs. We saw how WAN technologies help lower costs by improving link utilization even though WANs are more complex than LANs. We then saw the four major approaches to creating WANs—point-to-point, SDM, TDM, and FDM. Virtual circuits, which are used by SDM networks, were also introduced.

## ABOUT THE COLOPHON

The first known reference to human ability to reduce barriers arising solely from geographic distance appeared in the 19th century (1896) in an article in the *Los Angeles Times*. Since then, there have been vast improvements in air transport and commercial shipping, which have further reduced geographical barriers. It is now a routine matter for customers to buy goods at the neighborhood grocery store that have been manufactured around the world. Executives also routinely fly to meetings on other continents and return to their offices within the week.

Wide area networking is another recent technology that is bridging distances even further. People socialize with friends using websites like Facebook; collaborate on projects with partners worldwide using instant messaging; and use video conferencing to replace travel except when face-to-face communication is absolutely necessary. All of this is made possible by the extremely reliable WANs deployed today.

## REVIEW QUESTIONS

1. What are *WANs*?

2. Why can't we use broadcast on WANs as is done on LANs?

3. Why is Ethernet unsuitable as a WAN technology?

4. What are some similarities between the interstate system and WANs?

5. What are some similarities between neighborhood roads and LANs?

6. What are the main categories of WANs?

7. How is the phone network used as a wide-area computer-networking technology?

8. What are *T-carriers*?

9. What are the common data rates of T-carriers?

10. What are *DS signals*?

11. T-carriers are used to create a full mesh network with five nodes. How many links will be required?

12. What are the limitations of point-to-point WANs such as T-carriers?

13. What is *statistical multiplexing*?

14. How is statistical multiplexing useful in WANs?

15. How does statistical multiplexing reduce burstiness of traffic in the physical medium?

16. What are *virtual circuits*?

17. What is a circuit? How is a virtual circuit like a circuit? How is a virtual circuit different from a circuit?

18. Why are IP addresses not used for addressing within virtual circuits?

19. What is *X.25*? What are some salient features of the technology?

20. What is *Frame Relay*? What are some salient features of the technology?

21. What is *ATM*? What are some salient features of the technology?

22. What is *time-division multiplexing*? How is TDM useful in WANs?

23. What are some standard data rates of SONET, the popular TDM WAN technology?

24. What is *frequency-division multiplexing* (FDM)? How is FDM used in WANs?

25. Describe how WANs may be considered a data-link- layer technology.

## HANDS-ON EXERCISE (ESTIMATED TIME 90 MINUTES)

WAN technologies are a little difficult to experiment with. End-user computers are connected to LANs, and not WANs. Therefore, utilities on your computer do not get visibility into WAN information the way utilities such as `ipconfig` could access configuration information about the computer and the LAN.

The primary concerns of WAN network administrators are data throughput, response times, and network connectivity. *Throughput* refers to the data rates on the network; *response times* refer to the average time it takes to fulfill a user request; and *network connectivity* refers to the ability to reach all parts of the network. In this exercise, we will examine how throughput and response times change as the load on the network changes.

Since direct access to WAN is not available to students, we will use a very popular network simulation utility called OPNET. OPNET makes many simulation products, of which OPNET IT Guru is the most useful for our requirements. Fortunately, OPNET makes a version of IT Guru easily available for academic use. In this exercise, we will download and install IT Guru and use the example WAN simulation that accompanies the software to examine the impact of application loads on end-user experience. There is one FTP server in the example and we look at the end- user response times when the FTP traffic volume is low, medium, and high.

### Installing OPNET IT Guru

Google for "OPNET IT Guru academic edition". One of the first links will take you to the download site for the software (Figure 11 and Figure 12).[5]

**FIGURE 11**   OPNET's registration and download page

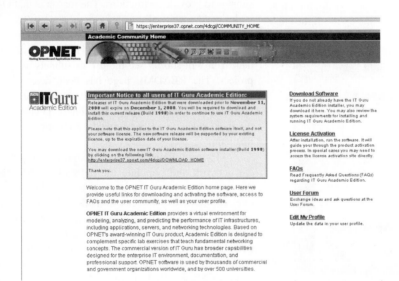

**FIGURE 12**   IT GURU download page

5 www.opnet.com/university_program/itguru_academic_edition/.

Register and download the file after accepting the license agreement. The download is about 47 MB. The downloaded file is a compressed file. Unzip or extract the file and you will get the installer file within the folder. The installer is approx 190 MB, so the compression really speeds up download times. Double-click the installer to start the install process. On my computer, it took time for the splash screen to appear, so please be patient as the installer sets up the install.

Start OPNET IT Guru. On first run, OPNET asks you to perform a three-way handshake with the OPNET registration server to authenticate your copy of OPNET. Follow the instructions to copy and paste the registration code from OPNET to the OPNET website and the license code from the OPNET website to OPNET. The process is straightforward, but if necessary, instructions for the three-way registration handshake are at www.opnet.com/itguru-academic/instructions.html. When you restart OPNET after completing the three-way handshake, it will start with a validated license.

To work with the WAN example, start OPNET IT Guru Academic Edition and go to File → Open → WAN as shown in Figure 13. Clicking OK will bring up the README scenario as shown in Figure 14. Double-clicking the icons brings up descriptions of objectives, scenarios, configuration tips, and simulation analysis. To return to the README page, right-click anywhere on the page and select "goto parent subnet". For example, Figure 15 shows what you see when you double-click the scenarios icon. The figure also shows the right-click

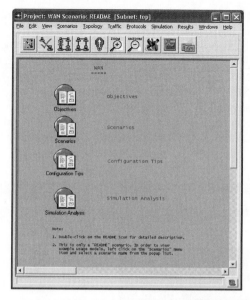

**FIGURE 14** OPNET WAN project README

menu. Selecting the first item in this menu will take you to the README scenario of Figure 14. Follow all the links in the README page to familiarize yourself with the simulation context.

You might be wondering why OPNET is using subnets to provide instructions. The reason is that OPNET is designed specifically to help simulate networks. Large networks in OPNET can be broken down into subnets and users can click into the subnets to view details of subnets. You will shortly see the use of subnets in the WAN project. The README page has been designed in the project as the WAN network and the instructions for each heading have been designed as subnets. Double-clicking the icons takes you down into the subnet represented by that icon.

To use OPNET, we first design the overall physical network and populate the network with users. We then populate the traffic loads generated by these users over the network. We can consider different scenarios of network usage. Finally we simulate the use of this network for a certain period of time (say one hour) and examine the results. If the results indicate that network performance is unsatisfactory, we upgrade network elements (e.g. speed up links or servers) and rerun the simulation. The process continues until network performance is satisfactory.

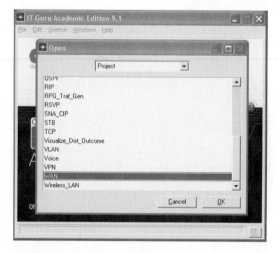

**FIGURE 13** Opening OPNET WAN sample project

**FIGURE 15**    Scenarios description

The WAN sample project includes various simulation scenarios and results for these scenarios. To access the different scenarios, use Scenarios → Switch to Scenario → <select one of the scenarios> as shown in Figure 16. For this exercise, you will run the campus_LowLoad and campus_HighLoad scenarios. Selecting the campus_LowLoad scenario brings up the scenario as shown in Figure 17. You can run the simulation with default parameters by clicking the configuration/ run simulation button (third from right in Figure 17). You will see that by default, the simulation is run for 30 minutes of network usage (1,800 seconds). Keep all the defaults and click the run button. You will see that the simulation takes approx 10 seconds to run. Now, switch to the campus_HighLoad scenario and run the simulation again.

When the simulations have been run, you can view the results. The most informative view for this exercise is available from Results → View Results (Advanced). The results are shown in Figure 18.

Answer the following questions:

1. Why is it useful to simulate network performance before investing in upgrading network equipment?

2. Run the campus_LowLoad scenario.

3. Run the campus_HighLoad scenario.

4. Show the advanced results (as in Figure 18).

5. Discuss the results in the three windows. In the discussion, describe why e-mail throughput is the same in all scenarios, but FTP throughput is higher in the high traffic scenario. Also describe why the FTP download response time is so high in the high traffic scenario.

6. (Optional) If you would like to learn how to use OPNET to set up a WAN and simulate it, please visit the companion website and follow the instructions for the OPNET WAN lab. These are included in the readings for this chapter.

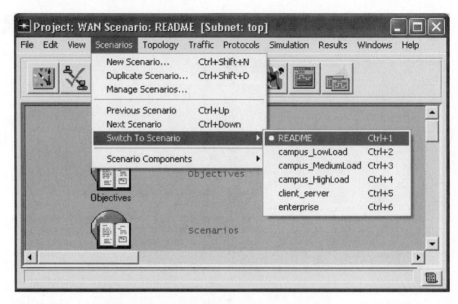

**FIGURE 16** Selecting OPNET WAN project scenarios

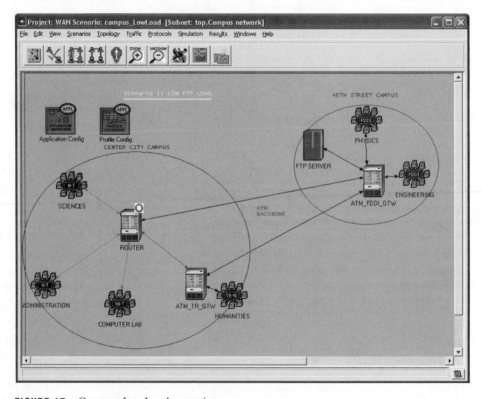

**FIGURE 17** Campus_LowLoad scenario

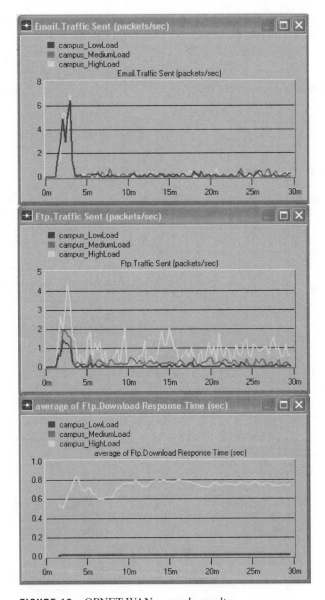

**FIGURE 18**   OPNET WAN example results

## NETWORK DESIGN EXERCISE

In this chapter, we will select an appropriate WAN technology to connect all the four locations. Assuming that Coolco will use the same WAN technology for all long-haul links, answer the following questions:

1. WAN links are typically shown using straight lines connecting the two endpoints. Different thicknesses or colors are used to show different data rates. Assume

that the company uses the following three WAN links to connect the four locations—U.S.–Singapore, U.S.–Amsterdam, and Amsterdam–Mumbai. The data rate on the U.S.–Amsterdam link is 100 Mbps to accommodate the data backup traffic. All other links are 10-Mbps links. Update the network diagram from Chapter 9 to include these WAN links.

2. Of the WAN technologies covered in this chapter—dial-up, T-carriers, X.25, Frame Relay, ATM, and SONET, which technology is best suited to meet Coolco's WAN needs?

3. After the network outage following the Middle-East cable ruptures, Coolco has decided to also maintain a backup WAN capability using ISDN. Include this backup capability in your network diagram.

4. Update your network diagram to include OSPF routers at each network location. The WAN links terminating at each location are connected to the OSPF routers so that network traffic load can be dynamically adjusted between ISDN and the primary WAN.

## CASE QUESTIONS

1. Identify three advantages and three disadvantages of UAVs compared to combat aircraft.

2. Read the Wikipedia article on the MQ-1 Predator and write a one-paragraph description of the evolution of the aircraft.

3. View the YouTube video on Predators at www.youtube.com/watch?v=O4I13Cnlpkk[6] (about 11 minutes). Identify as many satellite-based data-communication applications as possible that are used by Predators and their operators.

4. How did the military come to know that Predator feeds were being captured by militants? (Use online sources if necessary.)

5. Information about SkyGrabber is available at www.skygrabber.com/en/skygrabber.php. Briefly, in one paragraph, describe how SkyGrabber works. What is the intended use of SkyGrabber?

6. Technology developments can have unintended consequences. Some analysts have speculated that UAVs and satellite-based global data networks could make war more likely because the risks to soldiers' lives are reduced. What is your opinion about this assessment?

---

[6] If the link does not work, the video was titled, "Skygrabber Intercepts Predator Drone Intelligence." You should be able to find it online.

## CHAPTER 11

# Wireless Networks

*What is essential is invisible to the eye.*
—French novelist, Antoine de Saint-Exupéry,
*Le petit prince*, Ch. 21 (1943)

## Overview

Wireless networking has gained rapid popularity since its introduction in the late 1990s. Virtually every laptop computer sold since the early 2000s is capable of wireless networking. There are various kinds of wireless networks available today, each serving a specific user need. This chapter introduces the enabling legal provisions that make free wireless networking possible and the different kinds of wireless networks. At the end of this chapter you should know:

- the business impact of wireless networking
- the special features of frequency bands that are used for wireless networking
- how wireless local area networks work
- the types of wireless local area networks
- how wireless personal area networks work
- how wireless metropolitan area networks work

## Introduction

Wireless networks have become enormously popular among both computer users and businesses since the early years of the 21ˢᵗ century. Many cities have experimented with city-wide wireless networks to provide free or inexpensive Internet access to citizens. Reasons for the popularity of wireless networks include their convenience and ease of deployment. On battery-powered laptops, wireless networking allows users to compute and communicate without any power or network cords. Businesses like wireless networking because setting up a basic wireless network in a small office requires nothing more than an inexpensive wireless router. By comparison, wired networking requires cables to be drawn through ceilings, floors, and walls. Wireless networking is becoming so popular that many organizations are finding that more than half the Ethernet ports in the organization are unused because users prefer wireless networks over wired networks.[1] Wireless networking may be one of those rare services loved by both businesses and employees.

Wireless networking introduces some important concerns and limitations that users and businesses should be aware of. The most visible concern is information security. Wired networks have wall outlets in specific locations that can only be reached by users with access to the building. By contrast, wireless signals spread out in all directions and can easily bleed outside the organization's boundaries. Without adequate security, malicious users can easily access the organization's computer network through an improperly secured wireless access point.

In a well-publicized example, in 2006, the retail chain T. J. Maxx became the target of a hack when attackers were able to drive to the parking lot of a Marshalls' store in Minnesota and sniff the passwords of store managers as they logged into the network. Because of other weaknesses in T. J. Maxx' network, these hackers were able to retrieve most of the credit-card information stored on T. J. Maxx' computers. Over 45 million credit-card records were stolen. T. J. Maxx has provisioned $480 million to settle lawsuits resulting from the breach. All this began with just an improperly secured wireless LAN at one of its stores.

Another potentially important issue is related to health. As we will see in our discussion of the frequency bands at which wireless networks operate, the 2.4 GHz frequency used by most wireless LANs is absorbed very efficiently by water. Water is one of the biggest components of human bodies. Though the signals generated by wireless access points have very low energy and there is no evidence yet of health hazards from these signals, our knowledge of the health hazards of exposure to wireless signals is limited. Wireless LANs have only been around for about a decade. It is possible that exposure to wireless signals over longer durations could have adverse health effects.

One final introductory point is a limitation of wireless networks. Wireless networks are generally slower and less reliable than wired networks. Most wireless networks share bandwidth with other applications, such as cordless telephones, and are affected by environmental conditions. Connection drop-offs are common with wireless networks. This is not a major concern for browsing, e-mail, and other light applications. However, when continuity or speed of the connection is essential, wired networks are still greatly preferable to wireless networks.

## ISM frequency bands

Free or inexpensive wireless networking is possible because of the existence of a very special category of wireless frequencies. Before we look at wireless technologies, it is useful to become aware of these enabling frequencies.

---

[1] Cox, J. "Is It Time to Cut Back on Now-Idle Ethernet?" *Network World*. (2009) 26: 1.

The special signal frequencies that enable wireless networking are called ISM frequencies because these frequencies are available for free use for Industrial, Scientific, and Medical applications. The terms *industrial* and *scientific* are interpreted very broadly, and ISM frequencies may be put to almost any use by anybody without permission from anyone or payments of license fees to anyone. These frequencies are therefore also called unregulated frequencies. Cordless phones, remote controlled cars, microwave ovens, wireless keyboards, and mice are other applications that use ISM frequencies.

Wireless frequencies have become big business for government. We know from Chapter 2 that for distinct separation at the receiving end, there must be only one sine wave at a specific frequency in any given location. Since there are many users who would like to use sine waves for wireless transmissions, but only one user can transmit at any given frequency, some coordination and allocation is necessary to determine who can transmit at a specific frequency. In the U.S., this coordination is done by the Federal Communications Commission (FCC). In the early days, the FCC did not charge fees for the privilege of using specific frequencies for transmission. Instead, frequency bands were allocated based on technological requirements. However, beginning in 1994, the FCC realized that operators of cell phones and other services would be willing to pay for access to specific frequencies. Accordingly, the FCC began to auction off frequency bands for specific services to the highest bidders offering these services. The single largest revenue-generating auction was for cell-phone services in the 700 MHz band and was completed in March 2008. The auction generated over $18 billion. Since 1994, the FCC has earned over $75 billion from wireless auctions.[2]

Why are ISM frequencies available for free use when cell-phone operators pay billions of dollars to use other frequencies? One reason is that regulators recognize the need for wireless frequencies for experimentation and amateur use. The specific frequencies that have been selected for ISM use are generally not very useful for commercial use. ISM frequencies generally have poor transmission properties and are unlikely to fetch meaningful prices at auctions. For example, signals at the 2.45 GHz band are strongly absorbed by water. Microwave ovens operate at this frequency since almost 75% of food mass is made of water. By quickly transferring energy to the water in food, microwave ovens are able to heat and cook quickly and with very high efficiency. Similarly, water vapor in the atmosphere absorbs signals in the 2.45 GHz band, resulting in a very short range for these signals. ISM frequencies are also absorbed by walls and foliage. Commercial operators are unlikely to pay for signals that have poor transmission properties. The frequencies defined for ISM use in the U.S. are shown in Table 1.

Fortunately, ISM applications make excellent use of these otherwise useless frequencies. You may recognize some of these frequencies. Remote controls for radio-controlled cars often use the 40.68 MHz band. Older cordless phones used the 915 MHz band, while most current cordless phones use the 2.45 GHz band. Most of the popular wireless LANs also uses the 2.45 GHz band. The highest frequency ISM bands will become useful when electronic devices operating at these extremely high frequencies can be built at more affordable prices.

---

[2] Federal Communications Commission. "FCC Auctions Home Page." http://wireless.fcc.gov/auctions. (2009).

**Table 1** ISM frequency bands in the U.S.

| ISM frequency | Bandwidth |
|---|---|
| 6.78 MHz | ± 15.0 kHz |
| 13.56 MHz | ± 7.0 kHz |
| 27.12 MHz | ± 163.0 kHz |
| 40.68 MHz | ± 20.0 kHz |
| 915 MHz | ± 13.0 MHz |
| 2.45 GHz | ± 50.0 MHz |
| 5.8 GHz | ± 75.0 MHz |
| 24.125 GHz | ± 125.0 MHz |
| 61.25 GHz | ± 250.0 MHz |
| 122.5 GHz | ± 500.0 MHz |
| 245 GHz | ± 1.0 GHz |

## Wireless network categories

There are three primary categories of wireless computer networks. All these categories of wireless networks use ISM frequencies. The most familiar are wireless LANs which go by names such as 802.11 b and 802.11 g. These networks have a range of about 100 feet, which is enough to cover an average suburban home or small office. The second category of wireless networks is Bluetooth, which is called a personal area network. This technology is used for connectivity within about 10 feet, which is ideal for connecting peripheral devices such as wireless keyboards and cameras in the immediate vicinity of a computer. Finally, we have an emerging category of wireless networks called metropolitan area networks which can provide coverage over a range of about 20 miles, which is enough to cover many metropolitan towns. In the rest of this chapter, we will look at the technologies and features of each of these categories of wireless networks.

## Wireless local area networks (the 802.11 series)

Wireless local area networks are the most familiar of the three categories of wireless networks. Most college campuses now have blanket wireless LAN coverage and many college students use laptops with built-in wireless LAN capability to access the Internet using wireless LANs. The technologies used in wireless LANs are specified in the 802.11 series of IEEE standards such as 802.11 b, 802.11 g, 802.11 a, and 802.11 n. Wireless LANs are often known as Wi-Fi.

Technologically, wireless LANs share many similarities with Ethernet, which is a wired network and was discussed in detail in Chapter 3. For example, the frame structure of wireless LANs is almost identical to the frame structure of Ethernet. Also, wireless LANs use the 48-bit MAC addresses discussed in Chapter 3.

There are however, some important differences between Ethernet and wireless LANs. The most important difference is that wireless LANs have no defined boundaries. Wall jacks define the end-points for Ethernet. An Ethernet wall jack is hardwired to a specific port on a specific switch. As a result, a network administrator can control every aspect of the network traffic that flows through the wall jack and to the computer connected to the jack. When you connect to the network through a wall jack, you become part of a well-defined network. Typically one area of an office is served by one switch and most users have no choice but to become a member of the Ethernet network that is closest to them.

On the other hand, wireless networks can overlap and they often do. At home, if you open up your "connect to network" dialog (right-click on the wireless icon in your system tray → Connect to a network), you are likely to see wireless networks from many of your neighbors as shown in Figure 1. If any of these wireless networks is not security enabled, you can use it to connect to the Internet. At the airport, you are likely to see overlapping wireless networks from the airport operator, Starbucks, mobile-phone companies, etc. Again, if any of these is not security-enabled, you can use it to get Internet access.

Therefore, whereas geographical location uniquely defines network membership in Ethernet, it does not define network membership in wireless LANs. The technical implication is that, whereas the signal strength of a wired connection always meets Ethernet standards, the signal strength, and hence the network experience of a wireless connection, cannot be specified. The network performance of a wireless connection depends upon the distance of the host from the access point. A user who is very far from an access point will get very weak signals. To best serve users at different distances, wireless LAN standards specify different signal-modulation schemes for users at different distances from access points. Users who are close to an access point are served by faster-changing signals that can carry higher data rates but need strong signal strength for reliable detection. Users who are farther away from access points are served by signals that can only provide lower data rates but are easier to detect in the presence of noise. (You may be able to relate this to the discussion on signaling in Chapter 2.)

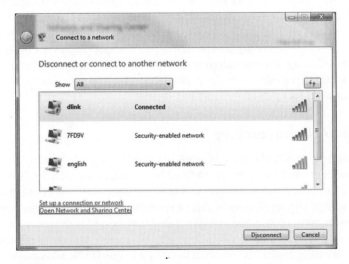

**FIGURE 1**   Wireless networks can overlap

Another difference between wireless LANs and wired LANs is that, whereas wired networks are extremely reliable, wireless is an inherently unreliable medium. Wireless networks are hurt by adverse weather, humidity, temperature, and other environmental conditions. As a result, the boundaries of a wireless network are not stable and keep shifting as environmental conditions change. Also, wireless networks are unprotected from competing signals from other devices such as cordless phones, walkie-talkies, fluorescent lamps, car ignitions, etc. By contrast, Ethernet cables do not carry any signals besides data, providing excellent signal transmission properties.

Yet another difference concerns multiplexing. Ethernet does not use multiplexing because it uses all the available bandwidth in the medium to transmit signals. This is possible because Ethernet cables are not used for other applications. But wireless LANs share the bandwidth in the air with other users and have to send signals in specified signal bands. Therefore, wireless LANs use multiplexing. To use the available bandwidth efficiently, multiple channels have been defined within the 2.4 and 5.8 GHz bands. Since stations may be transmitting on any of these channels; wireless stations have to scan all the available channels to locate transmissions.

One last factor that makes wireless networks different from Ethernet is that, whereas all stations on an Ethernet can hear every transmission, stations at two opposite ends of a wireless LAN may not be able to hear each other. As a result, collision detection may be unsuccessful in wireless LANs. Wireless LANs therefore do not use CSMA/CD for medium access control. Instead, wireless LANs use collision avoidance, and the medium access control (MAC) mechanism used in wireless networks is called carrier sense multiple access with collision avoidance (CSMA/CA). What this means is that a waiting wireless station does not start transmitting immediately after a previous transmission ends. This is because the station knows that this is the time when other waiting stations are also likely to try to transmit and therefore the chances of a collision are highest at this time. Therefore, wireless stations wait for a certain time after a transmission ends, before attempting to transmit data.

The primary implication of all these differences between wireless LANs and Ethernet is that wireless LANs require far greater error-detection capabilities than Ethernet. We will see that this is manifested in the physical layer of wireless LANs which adds error protection over and above the CRC error detection introduced in Ethernet. This relates to the discussion in Chapter 2 about the impact of the transmission medium on data-communication technologies. The primary challenge in wireless networks is the increased noise level. The technology response is to increase error protection in wireless LANs compared to Ethernet.

## Wireless LAN architecture

Like Ethernet, wireless LANs are a data-link-layer technology. Technology standards for both Ethernet and wireless LANs are defined by the 802 group at IEEE. The IEEE 802 group defines standards for local area networks. As a result of this common origin, the frame structure of wireless LANs is almost identical to the frame structure of Ethernet. The differences between wireless and wired media discussed in the previous section are handled by differences in the physical layer. To account for the greater need for error detection in wireless media, the physical layer in wireless LANs adds header fields that help the receiver in error detection. We will see these fields later in this section.

To facilitate mobility, the designers of wireless LAN technologies planned wireless LANs in such a way that larger wireless LANs can be built from smaller wireless LANs. The smallest component unit of a wireless LAN is the area covered by a single access point. This area is called a basic service area (BSA). The basic service area and the access point covering that area together are called a basic service set (BSS).

To create a larger network, such as a campus-wide wireless LAN, basic service sets can be connected to each other using any suitable networking technology. This connecting technology is called a distribution system. Thus, a campus-wide wireless LAN consists of many basic service sets connected to each other through a distribution system. The entire wireless LAN is connected to the rest of the wired Internet at a connection point called a portal. This structure is shown in Figure 2. The larger campus-wide wireless LAN is called an extended service set. The 802.11 standard does not consider the distribution system to be a part of the extended service set because end users cannot directly connect to the distribution system for wireless access. End users have to use a basic service set for wireless access.

In Figure 2, when the first laptop (station 1) wants to send a message to the second laptop (station 4), it creates a MAC frame with the MAC address of the second laptop 2 as the destination MAC address and sends the message to its access point (station 2). Station 2 will forward the message to station 3 over the distribution system and finally station 3 will send the message to the laptop at station 4.

The advantage of composing large wireless LANs from multiple basic service areas is that it facilitates mobility. The extended service set appears to end users as one large LAN. Users can move anywhere within an extended service set and still retain the same IP address and subnet membership. If wireless LANs were not designed as

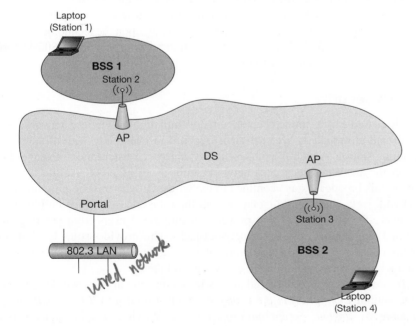

**FIGURE 2**   Structure of a campus-wide wireless LAN

an extended service set, and each access point served as a router, each BSS would become an independent subnet. Each time a user moved from one access point to the next, he would connect to a different subnet. This would potentially give him a different IP address and gateway router address. This address reallocation would stop any ongoing transfers and could also potentially disturb the network connectivity of some applications. With the concept of an extended service set, when users move from one access point to another, there is no change to any network setting, and ongoing network transfers can continue without interruption.

Within an organization, basic service sets may be placed as appropriate to deliver the required coverage and reliability. For example, in high traffic areas, basic service sets may overlap to provide redundancy and to share traffic. If areas requiring network coverage are far from each other, basic service sets may be organized as in Figure 2 where they are separated from each other.

On one extended service set, a host needs to get associated with one access point through which it will send and receive messages. The distribution system uses this association information to deliver messages for a host to the correct access point.

The 802.11 standard does not specify how the distribution system should send messages between access points. Any local area network technology can be used for the purpose. It is common for network administrators to use Ethernet for the distribution system.

The portal acts as the gateway between the extended service set and the rest of the Internet. When a message is sent to a host that is not in the extended service set, the distribution system sends the message to the portal. The portal performs all necessary packet format changes required for the message to be transported on the neighboring network. For example, in Figure 2, the portal transforms the outgoing message from the wireless 802.11 frame format to the 802.3 Ethernet frame format.

Most likely, your home network is built using one wireless router. This router acts as the access point as well as the portal. Depending upon the technologies used by your Internet service provider, this router may transform packets from 802.11 format to 802.3 format, or from 802.11 to the WAN frame format used by the ISP.

## Wireless security

As we discussed earlier in the chapter, a major limitation of wireless networks is that the information broadcast over the air is exposed to everybody within range of the transmitting station. Anybody with a wireless laptop can listen in on messages being sent over the air. Wired local area networks built using Ethernet also use broadcast. However, this broadcast stays confined to the wires. Only users who plug into one of the network jacks in the building can access these broadcasts. Office buildings have some level of access control that prevents unauthorized users from entering office spaces and plugging into one of the network jacks. This provides some level of confidentiality in a wired network. However, wireless signals can bleed outside to parking lots and lobbies where unauthorized users can read them.

To prevent such unauthorized access to organizational data, wireless networks use encryption. *Encryption is the transformation of data into a form that makes it unreadable by anyone except authorized users.* Wireless LAN standards define three encryption techniques to securely transmit information over the air—WEP

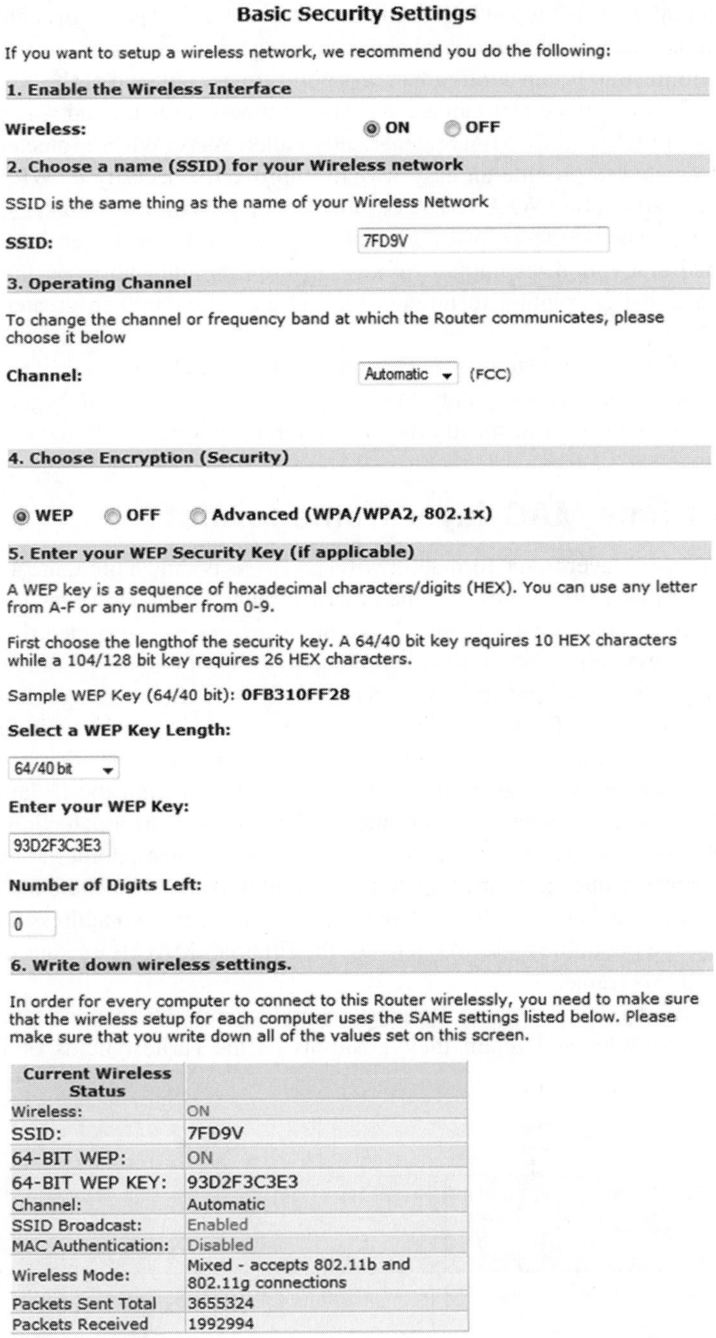

## Basic Security Settings

If you want to setup a wireless network, we recommend you do the following:

**1. Enable the Wireless Interface**

**Wireless:**                    ◉ ON      ○ OFF

**2. Choose a name (SSID) for your Wireless network**

SSID is the same thing as the name of your Wireless Network

**SSID:**                        7FD9V

**3. Operating Channel**

To change the channel or frequency band at which the Router communicates, please choose it below

**Channel:**                     Automatic ▾  (FCC)

**4. Choose Encryption (Security)**

◉ **WEP**    ○ **OFF**    ○ **Advanced (WPA/WPA2, 802.1x)**

**5. Enter your WEP Security Key (if applicable)**

A WEP key is a sequence of hexadecimal characters/digits (HEX). You can use any letter from A-F or any number from 0-9.

First choose the lengthof the security key. A 64/40 bit key requires 10 HEX characters while a 104/128 bit key requires 26 HEX characters.

Sample WEP Key (64/40 bit): **0FB310FF28**

**Select a WEP Key Length:**

64/40 bit  ▾

**Enter your WEP Key:**

93D2F3C3E3

**Number of Digits Left:**

0

**6. Write down wireless settings.**

In order for every computer to connect to this Router wirelessly, you need to make sure that the wireless setup for each computer uses the SAME settings listed below. Please make sure that you write down all of the values set on this screen.

| Current Wireless Status | |
|---|---|
| Wireless: | ON |
| SSID: | 7FD9V |
| 64-BIT WEP: | ON |
| 64-BIT WEP KEY: | 93D2F3C3E3 |
| Channel: | Automatic |
| SSID Broadcast: | Enabled |
| MAC Authentication: | Disabled |
| Wireless Mode: | Mixed - accepts 802.11b and 802.11g connections |
| Packets Sent Total | 3655324 |
| Packets Received | 1992994 |

**FIGURE 3**   Home router security settings

(wired equivalent privacy), TKIP (temporal key integrity protocol), and CCMP (Counter-mode with Cipher-block chaining message authentication code protocol). Network administrators can configure access points to use any one of these encryption techniques. Of these three techniques, WEP is extremely insecure and is now considered obsolete. TKIP and CCMP are generically called WPA (Wi-Fi protected access). TKIP was created to provide an easy way to improve the security of WEP devices. TKIP is popularly called WPA 1. The current recommendation is to use CCMP, also called WPA 2. The access point informs all stations on the basic service set to use the specified encryption technique. As a result, all communication on the network uses the specified encryption technique. We discuss encryption in greater detail in Chapter 13.

It is highly advisable to use encryption on wireless networks. For end-user convenience though, most access points do not use encryption by default. Figure 3 shows a dialog allowing the user to specify the encryption technique on a home router.

## 802.11 frame MAC-layer frame format

The general MAC-layer frame format for wireless LANs is shown in Figure 4. You may note that it has many similarities with the Ethernet frame format. However, the wireless frame is more complex than Ethernet. Extra fields are necessary to identify the basic service set, access points and to provide reliable transmission in the presence of noise. Also, most wireless LAN packets do not have all the fields in the general frame structure shown in Figure 4. The header fields in a captured packet are shown in Figure 5.

As in Ethernet, the wireless LAN frame format includes the source and destination MAC addresses, a frame check sequence, and data from the IP layer. These fields perform the same functions as in Ethernet – addressing, error detection, and data transfer. However, we see that wireless LANs also have some additional fields such as frame control, sequence control, QoS control and duration/ ID. There are also four possible address fields (recall that Ethernet frames only have two address fields). We also see that the preamble and SFD fields of the Ethernet MAC frame are missing in the wireless LAN frame.

The missing fields are the simplest to understand. These are moved to the physical-layer header and retain their positions as the earliest fields of incoming

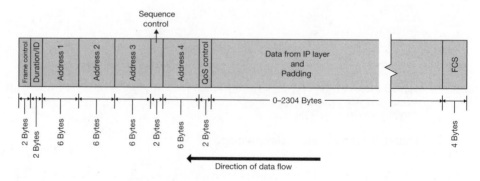

**FIGURE 4**   802.11 frame format

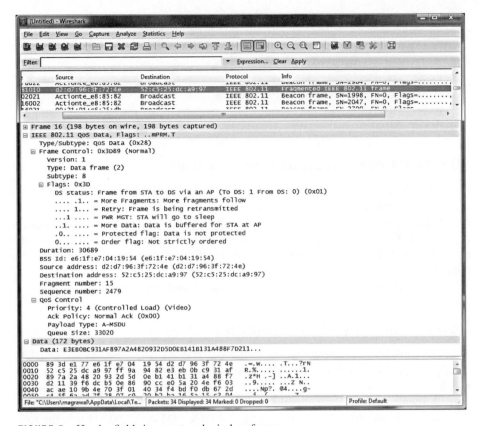

**FIGURE 5**    Header fields in a captured wireless frame

frames. It is the additional MAC-header fields that are more complex to describe and to understand. These additional fields help in identifying the access points and in improving reliability. Their functions are described below:

Frame control: This field describes attributes of the frame. For example, does the frame carry data, or does it report the status of the network? Is the frame going toward an AP? Is it being sent by an AP?

Duration/ID: This field announces the expected amount of time required to transmit this frame. All listening stations will wait for this duration before attempting to send data.

Sending/receiving access-point addresses (address 1–address 4): Since wireless LAN packets need to pass through access points, the MAC addresses of the sending or receiving access points are added to the frame as required. Packets leaving an access point have the sending AP address, and packets sent to an AP have the receiving access point address.

QoS control: This field specifies the desired type of service. The available types of service include best effort, voice, and video.

Since 802.11 frames have different values in the address fields depending upon the type of packet, you might wonder how a receiver knows that a packet is addressed to it. To deal with this issue, the address to be used for address matching is always placed in the address 1 field. If a station finds that the value in the address 1 field is the same as its own MAC address, it knows that the packet is addressed to it.

## 802.11 frame physical-layer format

Recall from Chapter 3 that the physical layer in Ethernet added no header fields to the frame. It simply converted the frame to a signal. However, the wireless LAN physical layer does add fields to the frame header. The wireless LAN physical-layer header is shown in Figure 6. The primary function of the physical-layer header is to add error protection to the frame header. It also specifies the data rate being used in the transmission.

Figure 5 shows the header fields in a captured wireless packet.

## Popular 802.11 technologies

Three technologies are currently specified for wireless LANs—802.11 a, 802.11 b, and 802.11 g. 802.11 a and 802.11 b were specified in 1999, and 802.11 g was specified in 2003. A fourth technology, 802.11 n was recently specified to increase the speed and range of wireless networks.

802.11 b and 802.11 g operate in the 2.4 GHz ISM band. 802.11 b is the simpler technology and can support a data rate of up to 11 Mbps. The signal modulation techniques used in 802.11 b are defined in Chapters 14, 15, and 18 of the 802.11 standard.[3] 802.11 b uses the direct sequence spread spectrum (DSSS) modulation technique. 802.11 g adds the orthogonal frequency division multiplexing (OFDM) modulation technique to get higher data rates than 802.11 b. 802.11 g can support data rates up to 54.11 Mbps.

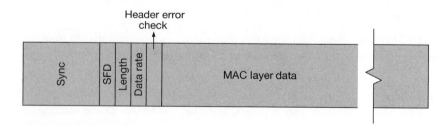

**FIGURE 6** Wireless LAN physical-layer header

---

[3] The 802.11 standard is accessible from the companion website.

802.11 a operates in the 5.5 GHz ISM band. It was the first 802.11 technology to use OFDM to achieve data rates of up to 54 Mbps. OFDM is defined in Chapter 17 of the 802.11 standard. 802.11 a has many features such as a greater number of channels that should make it the wireless technology of choice. Unfortunately, the signals in the 5.5 GHz band do not travel as far as signals at the same power in the 2.4 GHz band. As a result, each 802.11 a access point covers a slightly smaller area than a 802.11 b/g access point. 802.11 b/g are, therefore, economically more efficient than 802.11 a for wireless coverage. Hence 802.11 b/g technologies are more popular than 802.11 a.

## 802.11 n

The latest wireless LAN technology to be introduced is 802.11 n. The standard was finalized in September 2009. The primary goal of 802.11 n is to provide a higher data rate, up to 600 Mbps. 802.11 n also aims to provide wider coverage than 802.11 b/g, so that a single access point can cover over twice the area covered by a 802.11 b/g access point.

The primary innovation of 802.11 n is multiple input, multiple output signal transmission. 802.11 n access points and receivers use multiple antennas. Each antenna pair creates an independent data channel. Each 802.11 n transmission may therefore be seen as multiple 802.11 a/b/g transmissions.

Apart from the technical innovations introduced in 802.11 n, the technology is also very interesting because it allows us to peek into the process by which new data communication technologies are developed and standardized. The IEEE website maintains a log of the standardization process for 802.11 n.[4] According to the logs, four candidate technologies were proposed for 802.11 n in November 2004. The TGn technology that will be used in 802.11 n obtained the required level of support from the standards committee in March 2007. In late 2008–early 2009, the technical and editorial issues in the standard were being fixed. Since technology vendors already knew most details of the 802.11 n technology, and only editorial changes were expected in the standards document, draft 802.11 n products became available in the market in 2008, even before the final standards document had been published.

Most data communication technologies go through this process of standardization. The standardization process begins with the recognition of a need. In the case of 802.11 n, it was the need for a high-speed, long-range wireless technology. A neutral standards-making body takes the lead in organizing an expert group to identify technical solutions that meet the need. In the case of 802.11 n, this body was the IEEE, which has led the standardization of all local area network standards. Any interested persons from universities, technical companies, and even members of the public can become members of the group. The group develops proposals and votes on them till one technology solution receives overwhelming support. Finally, the technology is described in adequate detail in a standards document so that any interested vendor can use the standards document to create an implementation of the standard. The standardization process assures users that equipment they buy from one vendor will always be compatible

---

[4] http://grouper.ieee.org/groups/802/11/Reports/tgn_update.htm.

with equipment sold by other vendors. In the case of 802.11 n, for example, you can buy a network interface card from Broadcom and be assured that it will work with access points sold by Linksys.

It is also hoped that the formal standardization process will lead to the adoption of the best possible technical solution to meet requirements.

## Personal area networks (the 802.15 series)

The previous section described wireless local area networks. These networks use an access point and provide high-speed connectivity to any hosts within a radius of about 100 feet. Hosts typically use wireless LANs for Internet access.

While wireless LANs are extremely useful, there are many connectivity applications where wireless access would be very useful, but where Internet access is not necessary. An important example is replacing on desktops the short wires that are used for data transfer at low speeds, for example, to connect keyboards and mice to the desktop. This is where personal area networks (PANs) come in. PANs, specified by the IEEE 802.15 standard are designed to remove these wires that clutter desktops and make many devices cumbersome to use.

Personal area networks like Bluetooth have been developed to provide communication over short distances, usually within 30 feet. This distance is sometimes called the personal operating space because people and devices within this range are usually in visual range. By limiting itself to this range, Bluetooth is designed to serve a small group of participating devices, usually carried by one person. Apart from keyboards and mice, other devices that use Bluetooth include cell-phone headsets and digital cameras, to transfer pictures to computers.

The focus of Bluetooth is to develop extremely small, inexpensive, and low-power connectivity solutions. This makes it easy for electronics manufacturers to add Bluetooth capabilities to virtually any electronic device, even devices such as headsets and telephones, which are not traditionally considered computers. Since many of these devices are very small, and can carry only a limited amount of battery power, power efficiency is an extremely important requirement for Bluetooth. Since signal transmission requires power, and more power is needed to send signals to greater distances, power efficiency concerns are the reason why Bluetooth devices have very short communication ranges.

Bluetooth operates in the 2.4 GHz ISM band, the same as 802.11 b/g wireless LANs. Bluetooth is designed to offer data rates of up to 1 Mbps. This is much slower than the 11/ 54 Mbps offered by 802.11 LANs. But 1 Mbps is adequate for applications such as keyboards and headsets that use Bluetooth. Bluetooth uses frequency hopping spread spectrum (FHSS) modulation for signal transmission.

Though Bluetooth has some similarities with wireless LANs, there are some important distinctions between the two, such as:

1. Wireless LANs are largely used by computing devices such as laptops. Bluetooth is designed to be used by any electronic device to communicate with any other Bluetooth-capable electronic device.

2. Wireless LANs are typically used to obtain Internet connectivity. Bluetooth is typically used to connect to other nearby devices, for example a keyboard to a

desktop, or a headset to a cell phone. As a result, while high data rate is a very important requirement for wireless LANs, it is less important for Bluetooth.

3. Wireless LANs require an infrastructure of access points. Bluetooth requires no such infrastructure. In fact, each Bluetooth device is capable of acting as a Bluetooth access point. Bluetooth devices automatically locate other Bluetooth devices in their vicinity.

4. Devices using wireless LANs are typically connected to power outlets and there are no special power-efficiency concerns in wireless LANs. Bluetooth devices are almost always driven by battery power and long battery life is an important concern for Bluetooth.

5. Finally, since Bluetooth is often used by devices that are relatively inexpensive, it is important for Bluetooth solutions to be extremely inexpensive, generally costing less than $10.

## Bluetooth architecture

The basic unit of a Bluetooth network is the piconet. A Bluetooth piconet serves a function similar to the basic service set (BSS) in 802.11 LANs. However, whereas an 802.11 BSS has a dedicated device called an access point that performs various management functions in the BSS, any device in a Bluetooth piconet can perform the management functions of a piconet. The device that performs this function is called the master. All other devices in the piconet are called slaves. The master provides a synchronization clock that helps all other devices in the piconet remain in sync with each other. Whereas a device may be a slave on multiple piconets at the same time, it can only be a master on one piconet at a time.

Many piconets may coexist in the same location. All the co-located piconets are called a scatternet. Think of a gathering of tech-savvy students in a classroom, with many students carrying Bluetooth-capable cell phones and music players. Each such student forms a piconet and the entire classroom becomes a scatternet. Devices connected to two different piconets in a scatternet do not have to route packets between the piconets.

To enable interference-free communication within co-located piconets, Bluetooth has mechanisms that enable each piconet to operate on a different physical channel. Recall from Chapter 2 that only one signal may be transmitted at a given frequency at a given location. Since all Bluetooth transmissions are in the 2.4 GHz ISM band, Bluetooth needs to create mechanisms whereby multiple transmissions can occur at the same frequency.

Bluetooth creates multiple communication channels at the same frequency by enabling devices to transmit at different time slots. Though only one device may transmit at a given time in a given location at a specified frequency, different devices may transmit at different time slots on the same frequency. Stations keep hopping from frequency to frequency in a systematic manner within the 2.4 GHz ISM band. This is called frequency hopping. Devices in each piconet use a different hopping sequence, thereby reducing chances of collisions. Finally, to maintain confidentiality, devices in each piconet use a different access code and header encoding to ensure that even if their signals are received by devices in other piconets, the data is unreadable.

*[handwritten margin note: eg: all students have bluetooth on phones in the same classroom]*

*[handwritten margin note: same as Wi-Fi]*

| Channel access code | **Packet header**<br>Includes flow control,<br>seq number, header<br>error check (HEC) | **Payload header**<br>Includes data length,<br>transport link ID | **Payload**<br>User data such as IP packet, possibly<br>segmented by Bluetooth | CRC |
|---|---|---|---|---|

**FIGURE 7**  Bluetooth frame structure

## Bluetooth frame structure

The structure of Bluetooth frames is shown in Figure 7. The payload header is similar to the MAC header of 802.11 wireless LANs. The packet header is analogous to the 802.11 physical-layer header. The channel access code is unique to Bluetooth.

You may note that the Bluetooth frame has some fields such as flow control, sequence number, and channel access code that are absent in wireless LANs. These fields help Bluetooth devices operate within a scatternet without interfering with each other. These fields also help Bluetooth provide reliable signal transmission for voice applications.

## Bluetooth device discovery

A very special capability of Bluetooth is device discovery. Two Bluetooth devices in close proximity to each other will automatically discover each other. If you have used a Bluetooth-enabled keyboard, you may have noticed this behavior when bringing the keyboard near your desktop. Your computer becomes aware of the presence of the keyboard and instantly pairs up with it.

To enable device discovery, Bluetooth defines a special channel for inquiry requests and responses. Devices that are looking for nearby devices are called inquiring devices. Inquiring devices send out inquiry requests on the special inquiry channel. Devices willing to be found are called discoverable devices. Discoverable devices listen on the inquiry channel for inquiry requests and respond to these requests. Once the two devices become aware of each other, the inquiry procedure ends and the connection procedure begins.

In the connection procedure, one of the devices must be willing to receive a connection request from the other device. This device is called the connectable device. The connecting device sends a connection request to the connectable device on a connection channel specified by the connectable device. According to the Bluetooth standard, the device initiating the connection becomes the master for the connection.

If you think about it, you may notice that the Bluetooth device discovery and connection procedure is almost identical to the connection procedures used on social networks such as LinkedIn or Facebook. The websites act as the inquiry channel. Without websites such as Facebook or LinkedIn, you would not know where to search for your old friends. People willing to be found create profiles. People with profiles become discoverable. People searching for friends inquire of (search) the social-network site to see if their friend has a profile on the site. If the profile is found, the inquiry procedure is over.

For the connection procedure, you need to send a special connection-request message (friend request or invitation) to your friend. If the friend is connectable (responds favorably) and accepts your invitation, the two of you become connected.

# WLAN and WPAN coexistence

Wireless LANs and Bluetooth operate at the same ISM band (2.45 GHz). Therefore, there is a high possibility that the signals from the two technologies may interfere with each other. Since Bluetooth is the more recent of the two technologies, it is only natural that the designers of Bluetooth had the responsibility of ensuring that Bluetooth minimized interference with the existing wireless LAN technology. Therefore, the Bluetooth standard defines two mechanisms to minimize interference between 802.11 and 802.15.

The first of these two mechanisms is collaborative and occurs where Bluetooth and 802.11 communicate with each other. This is possible when both 802.11 and 802.15 are present on one device, such as a laptop with both 802.11 and 802.15 capability. In the collaborative mechanism, Bluetooth avoids transmission during an ongoing 802.11 transmission. Alternately, Bluetooth transmits signals on a different channel from the channel on which the ongoing 802.11 communication is taking place.

The second mechanism is non-collaborative. The non-collaborative method is used when communication between 802.11 and 802.15 systems is not possible. For example, Bluetooth keyboards do not have 802.11 capability and the Bluetooth system on the keyboard has no way to collaborate with 802.11. In the non-collaborative method, the 802.15 system senses the medium before transmitting. It tries to find a channel in the 2.45 GHz ISM band that is not very busy and transmits signals on that channel.

# Bluetooth categories

The early Bluetooth specification supported data rates of up to 1 Mbps. However, as Bluetooth grew in popularity, newer applications for the technology were identified, each with slightly different requirements. As a result, two additional categories of Bluetooth have been defined as subcategories of Bluetooth. The traditional Bluetooth specification is now called 802.15.1.

The first additional Bluetooth category supports picture transfers. It is useful to be able to transfer pictures from digital cameras to computers without the need to take out the picture card or connect the camera to the computer using a wire. Since digital images can get very large (a compressed picture from a 4-MP camera is about 1.5 MB), high data rates are very useful for image transfers. Accordingly, the high-data-rate Bluetooth specification, 802.15.3, supports data transfer rates of up to 20 Mbps. This is accomplished by improving the efficiency at which the physical layer encodes data into signals, so that more data can be sent using the same bandwidth.

The second additional category of Bluetooth is for remote-control devices such as the remote controls for TVs, door openers, fans, lights, etc. These devices need very low data rates because, after all, the only data these remotes send is "ON", or "OFF", or "CHANNEL = 2". However, we expect the batteries in remote controls to work for at least a couple of years. A unique feature of remote controls is that they are idle most of the time, used only for a few seconds in a day to operate remote devices. In almost every case, it is also true that the remote control does not need to be a connectable device. Only the controlled device, which usually is connected to a power outlet, needs to be connectable. To meet the requirements of remote controls, the 802.15.4 standard supports very low data rates, up to 250 Kbps. But to achieve long battery life, 802.15.4 devices are not in a connectable state (i.e., are switched off) when they are not being used. As a result, they do not lose power by scanning the medium, listening for other devices that may be interested in connecting to them.

## 802.16—Wireless Metropolitan Area Networks

The final category of wireless networks operating in the ISM band is wireless metropolitan area networks (MANs). Though these networks aren't well-known yet, wireless MANs are being pushed by leading computer manufacturers. The professional organization of the wireless MAN industry is called the Worldwide Interoperability for Microwave Access (WiMAX). Accordingly, wireless MANs are often known as WiMAX networks.

Wireless MANs have been standardized by the IEEE 802.16 group and, accordingly, these networks are also called IEEE 802.16 networks. 802.16 was initially designed to serve as an alternative to data connections by ISPs over cable and DSL. Since ISPs connect to homes from a central office to a fixed, wired router in the home, 802.16 was designed to provide connectivity between a fixed-base station (similar to cell-phone towers) and stationary subscriber stations (similar to TV antennas at some homes). The technology was designed to support data rates exceeding 20 Mbps to a range of up to 10 miles. With the evolution of technology, in 2005, support for mobile stations was added to WiMAX as 802.16e. This is a very promising development, because 802.16 networks can now be used to create wireless "metro zones" to cover large cities and provide metro-wide mobile Internet access. Broadband wireless access could be made available to mobile users anywhere within the "metro zone", just as 802.11 enables wireless access in a BSS.

Most efforts to create city-wide LANs using 802.11 technologies have failed due to the high costs of maintaining the large number of 802.11 access points required to provide city-wide coverage. 802.16 will enable wireless coverage over the same area using just one base station. Perhaps 802.16 may enable the vision of city-wide LANs after all.

In some developing countries, WiMAX has been used successfully to provide phone connectivity to far-flung rural areas. Pulling a wire from a phone company central office to a remote rural switch is extremely expensive. Instead, WiMAX can be used to wirelessly connect a small rural phone switch to the central office. Homes can be connected to the switch using the traditional twisted pair. These links are affordable because they are short.

In a typical data-communication application, 802.16 provides data rates up to 40 Mbps per channel to stations as far as six miles away from a base station. A very popular data rate for small businesses is 1.5 Mbps. 802.16 data rates are sufficient to support hundreds of such small businesses from a single base station. Alternately, each 802.16 base station can be used to support thousands of homes with high-speed Internet access.

### 802.16 data rates

Figure 8 shows the theoretical data rates supported by 802.16 as a function of distance. It also shows the modulation techniques used to achieve the data rates. As expected, stations close to the base station can receive the highest data rates (up to 134 Mbps). As the station gets farther away, the data rates fall to 90 Mbps. The farthest stations can expect data rates up to 45 Mbps. These are theoretical data rates; actual data rates may be lower. Stations closer to the base station use quadrature amplitude modulation

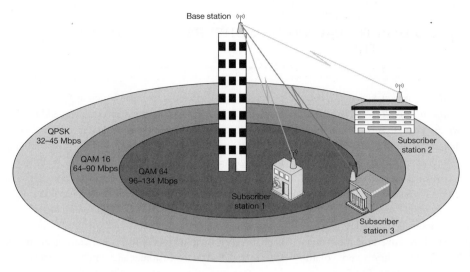

**FIGURE 8**   WiMAX
data rates

(QAM) and farther stations use quadrature phase shift keying. You may recall from Chapter 2 that amplitude modulation generally supports high data rates, but is very susceptible to noise. It is therefore suitable near the base station where signals are strong. Phase modulation offers high immunity to noise, but at the expense of slower data rates using the same bandwidth. It is useful at longer distances.

## 802.16 vs. 802.11

802.16 networks are likely to be used in a similar manner as 802.11 networks—to obtain Internet connectivity on mobile laptops. The two technologies also share other similarities. Both are standardized by the IEEE. Both use ISM frequency bands. 802.11 uses the 2.4 GHz and 5.5 GHz bands; 802.16 networks can use either of these bands.

In spite of these similarities, there are some significant differences between 802.11 and 802.16. The primary difference is that, whereas 802.11 access points cover only a radius of about 300 feet, a single 802.16 base station can cover large parts of a metro area. Another difference is that all communication in 802.16 networks is required to pass through the base station. Though most 802.11 networks also send all communication through the access point, 802.11 allows ad hoc networking where stations can directly communicate with each other.

In a very significant difference with 802.11 and 802.15, 802.16 allows operators to use licensed frequencies if desired. This is to facilitate commercial adoption and to improve signal quality. We saw earlier in this chapter that licensed frequencies generally have superior signal-transmission properties compared to ISM frequencies. Their use is also strictly controlled by the licensee. As a result, 802.16 devices operating on licensed bands are likely to see better network performance. The trade-off is that the use of licensed bands costs money to compensate the carriers for the costs incurred in acquiring the spectrum. Current 802.16 hardware is designed to support signals at 2.5–3.5 GHz. 802.16 access over licensed frequencies is likely to cost a subscription fee.

# CASE STUDY | DIGGING BLACK GOLD: CHEVRON AND THE OIL INDUSTRY

*When gas prices rose rapidly in recent years, oil companies earned record profits during 2007–2008. When the economy slowed down in late 2008, oil companies experienced slumping demand for the first time in years. Improved supply-chain management using computer networks is helping oil companies deal with these boom-and-bust cycles and also to lower oil prices.*

Integrated petroleum firms are some of the largest companies in the world. The industry had sales of $1.99 trillion in 2008, comparable to U.S. government tax revenues of $2.54 trillion in 2008. The industry is very volatile however, with estimated net sales in 2009 of $1.28 trillion; a drop of over 35% compared to 2008, due to falling prices and reduced demand due to weaknesses in the economy. It also has very low profit margins, with net profit margins of 8.1% in 2008. With political sensitivities and customer behavior limiting price increases, the way to improve profitability in the industry is to lower costs.

We saw in the case on Walmart that utilizing point-of-sale data to optimize distribution and manufacturing can eliminate inventory accumulation, reduce wastage, and lower costs. In most industries, this requires information sharing between many companies that complete the supply chain. But the petroleum industry has a unique advantage. It is probably the only industry still dominated by vertically integrated firms. Vertical integration refers to a single firm controlling all aspects of a product's manufacture from raw materials to distribution. The major oil companies such as Exxon-Mobil, British Petroleum, Shell, and Chevron own or control all factors of production starting from the oil fields where oil is drilled from the ground to the gas stations where drivers fill their cars.

Whereas retailers such as Walmart have to work out legal and technical barriers to protect their intellectual property from being stolen by business partners with whom they share information, vertically integrated oil companies have a unique advantage. With the right systems, they can share point-of-sale data from company-owned gas stations all the way up the supply chain to company-owned or controlled oil rigs and refineries, optimizing distribution and storage to lower costs. Publicly available information indicates that Chevron is a leader in this field in the industry.

A large distribution company such as Chevron has a number of places where unnecessary costs can add up. For safety reasons containers such as oil tankers and trucks do not deliver unless they can be emptied fully. Ships waiting for storage space to accept their crude can pay port charges as high as $30,000 per day. Delivery charges for a truckload of gas can be as high as $150. If a truck returns because the gas station is not empty enough to receive the entire load of fuel, the company incurs an unnecessary expense. On the other hand, if the gas station is out of fuel when a customer arrives, Chevron could lose the customer and earn a bad reputation.

Chevron uses wireless and satellite networks in many parts of the company to manage its supply chain. Many of its gas stations are linked by a satellite network to a central dispatch center. These stations have electronic level monitors in the underground gas tanks to monitor fuel levels in real time. A wired network in the gas station transports the data to the satellite dish on top of the station from where the data is sent to the dispatch station. Using this real-time data, the dispatch station is able to optimally schedule fuel deliveries from terminals located on the outskirts of major metros, minimizing unsuccessful deliveries (retains) and stock outs (run outs). Chevron can also use the computer network to monitor fuel levels in the terminal tanks to schedule oil tanker deliveries so that oil tankers do not have to wait at ports to make deliveries.

The popular satellite communication technology for retail data-communication applications is called VSAT, or very small aperture terminals. This technology uses small-sized dish transmitter-receivers communicating with a central hub with a large dish transmitter-receiver through a geostationary satellite. The high performance antenna at the hub improves the data-transmission capabilities of the overall network. The low performance requirements from antennas at each retail outlet such as gas stations reduce the costs of the overall system. The data-transfer mechanism in a VSAT system is shown in Figure 9. All data exchange occurs through the hub. The geostationary satellite acts as a broadcast medium for the network. If a station wants to send data to another station in a VSAT system, the transmission has to be routed through the hub to get adequate signal strength, making two hops through the satellite.

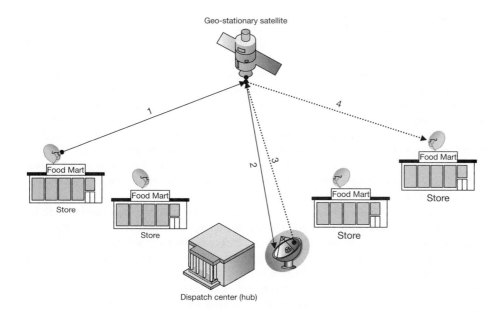

**FIGURE 9**  VSAT system operation

The satellite network has helped Chevron move toward being a demand-driven company where upstream activities are performed only in response to observed demand. The company has been moving in this direction since 1997. In 2000, demand-driven operations were improving profits by almost 15% in parts of the company where they were being applied.

Chevron and other oil companies also use computer networks in other parts of their businesses. By linking equipment to Internet-based networks, these companies are able to centralize all operational information to a central monitoring location. Improved monitoring helps companies respond quickly to problems, preventing fires and other hazards, and improving the uptime of pipelines and storage tanks. Industry experts believe that the benefit from these efforts is equivalent to adding 2% to 5% refining capacity.

Wireless networks are particularly useful to Chevron in its drilling operations. As new oilfields are becoming difficult to find, oil companies are focused on improving the productivity of existing oilfields. Installing wireless sensors on pumps and other equipment allows operators to access maintenance data on all equipment in a location directly from their trucks, significantly improving their productivity. Equipment defects that may have gone undetected for months can now be attended to in days.

At remote oil fields, Chevron has used a type of wireless network called a "mesh" network to monitor its oil wells. Unlike traditional 802.11 networks where dedicated devices act as base stations and routers, in mesh networks, each field device acts as both a sensor and as a wireless router. By placing devices suitably close to each other, each device in a mesh network requires very little power because the radio signal from the device has to travel only a short distance to the nearby node. The devices can also be designed to transmit only when needed further reducing power requirements and allowing sensor batteries to last for up to seven years. For many sensor-deployment projects, wiring costs can be up to 75% of the cost of the project. Wireless technologies can eliminate this huge cost.

## REFERENCES

Davis, A. "Job Losses Cut into U.S. Driving." *Wall Street Journal,* January 2, 2010, A3.

Malik, N. S. "Refiners Keep Tab with Real-Time Monitoring." *Wall Street Journal,* December 23, 2009, B2.

Mir, R. M. "Satellite Data Networks." www.cis.ohio-state.edu/~jain/cis788-97/satellite_data (accessed January 18, 2010).

Pister, K., and G. LaFramboise. *"Wired Warriors."* www.isa.org (accessed January 18, 2010).

Value Line, Industry Report. *"Integrated Petroleum Firms,"* December 11, 2009.

Worthen, B. "Drilling for Every Drop of Value." *CIO,* June 1, 2002.

## SUMMARY

Wireless networks enable mobility and have become extremely popular in homes and businesses. Wireless networks enable inexpensive Internet access in many homes and offices. Most wireless networking technologies use ISM frequency bands. Frequencies in these bands can be used without cost or licensing restrictions. To meet the requirements of different applications that benefit from wireless access, three different categories of wireless technologies have been defined.

The best-known wireless technology is the 802.11 wireless LAN technology, sometimes also called Wi-Fi. Wireless LANs use access points to provide high-speed Internet access within a range of about 300 feet from the access point. Multiple access points can be connected using a distribution system to provide wireless LAN coverage over an arbitrarily large area. There are three wireless LAN standards popular today—802.11 a, 802.11 b, and 802.11 g. 802.11 technologies can provide network connection speeds of up to 54 Mbps. The newest wireless LAN technology, 802.11 n, is expected to provide data rates of up to 600 Mbps.

The second category of wireless networks is personal area networks, better known as Bluetooth. These are standardized by the IEEE as 802.15 networks. Bluetooth provides data rates of up to 1 Mbps within a radius of about 30 feet. Bluetooth helps eliminate wire clutter created by peripheral devices such as keyboards and mice. The primary design goal of Bluetooth is to provide adequate data connectivity while maximizing battery life and minimizing costs.

The last category of wireless networks is IEEE 802.16 wireless metropolitan area networks, also known as WiMAX. These networks can substitute for cable and DSL connections and provide high-speed connectivity to fixed receivers at large distances. Mobile functionality has recently been added to WiMAX. WiMAX is likely to be offered as a paid service in many metro areas in the coming years.

## ABOUT THE COLOPHON

The line in the colophon was uttered by the fox to the little prince in French aviator Antoine de Saint-Exupéry's most famous novella, *The Little Prince*. The novella is believed to have been inspired by the aviator's real-life experiences in the Sahara desert. It is one of the bestselling books ever, translated into more than 180 languages and selling more than 80 million copies.

Though written and illustrated for children, the book makes many thoughtful observations about life. One of the best known of these is *"On ne voit bien qu'avec le cœur. L'essentiel est invisible pour les yeux,"* which translates as, *"It is only with the heart that one can see rightly. What is essential is invisible to the eye."*

Computers and networks have no heart. At the heart of their operations though, are properties of the universe that are invisible to the eye. Computer networks do not need a visible medium to transport data. The properties required from nature to support signal transmission are invisible to the naked eye. The invisible outer space can transport data just as effectively as visible wired networks. In an earlier age, this ability of the universe to carry electronic signals was given a name—Ether.

## REVIEW QUESTIONS

1. What are *wireless networks*? Why are they useful?

2. Some cities took up projects to setup wireless LANs all over the city. Read about the project taken up by one such city. Was the project a success? Why, or why not?

3. What are some of the concerns with using wireless networks?

4. What are *ISM frequency bands*? Why are they useful?

5. What are some differences between wired and wireless LANs? How do they impact the design of the wireless LAN header?

6. What is a basic service set? A basic service area?

7. What is an access point? What are some reasons why you would prefer access points to wireless routers to create a wireless network in your organization?

8. What is a distribution system in wireless LANs?

9. What is an extended service set?

10. What is a portal in a wireless LAN?

11. What are some differences between the physical layers in wireless and wired LANs?

12. What are the common wireless LAN categories? What are the important differences between them?

13. What is *802.11 n*? What are some likely advantages of 802.11 n over the traditional wireless LANs? How does 802.11 n obtain these advantages?

14. What are *personal area networks*? How are they different from LANs?

15. What are some important characteristics of Bluetooth?

16. What is a piconet? What are some differences between a piconet and a basic service set?

17. What are master and slave devices in a piconet?

18. What is a scatternet?

19. What are some advantages of having distinct physical channels in Bluetooth?

20. Why is device discovery useful in Bluetooth? How is device discovery accomplished? Why is device discovery not needed in wireless LANs?

21. Describe the mechanisms that have been defined for WLANs and WPANs to coexist at the same frequency bands without interfering with each other.

22. What are the different categories of Bluetooth? What are they used for?

23. What are wireless MANs? What are their primary uses?

24. What data rates and ranges are likely to be available on wireless MANs?

25. What are the differences between wireless LANs and wireless MANs?

## HANDS-ON EXERCISE—AIRPCAP WIRESHARK CAPTURES

In the hands-on exercise in Chapter 6, you have used Wireshark to capture packets on your local computer. In this exercise, you will use two Wireshark captures on the wireless interface to visualize the operation of IEEE 802.11 networks. Both captures capture the download of an early version of the companion website over a wireless LAN. The network topology of the setup for the capture is shown in Figure 10.

The two captures are included in the readings for this chapter on the companion website—Wireshark

HTML capture – 802.11-header only (called "802.11 only" in this exercise) and Wireshark HTML capture – 802.11 header and radio header (called "radio header" in this exercise). These captures have been made using AirPCap, which includes the hardware and software required to capture information specific to the IEEE 802.11 protocol. You may need to look at online resources to answer some of these questions. Answer the following questions from the 802.11-only capture:

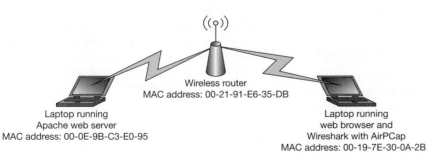

FIGURE 10   AirPCap capture topology

1. Look at the first frame. What is the role of a Beacon frame in IEEE 802.11? Why is this frame not necessary in IEEE 802.3 Ethernet?

2. Which device on the wireless LAN sends out the beacon frame? Based on this information, what is the MAC address of the wireless router?

3. Based on the above question and the information in the beacon frame header fields, what information serves as the basic service set (BSS) identifier?

4. The second packet in the capture is a probe request. What is the role of a probe-request frame in IEEE 802.11? Why is this frame not necessary in IEEE 802.3 Ethernet?

5. Which device(s) send(s) out probe requests?

6. What is the BSS ID of the destination in the probe request? What does this number signify?

7. How are frames identified as beacon frames or probe-request frames or data frames? (Hint: look at the type/subtype field.)

8. Examine the MAC address fields in a few frames. What are the three MAC addresses included in all frames?

9. Recalling the Wireshark captures in Chapter 6, there were only two MAC addresses in the Ethernet header—source and destination. Why is it necessary to include a third MAC address, the BSS ID, in 802.11 frames?

Now, answer the following questions from the radio-header capture:

1. Select any frame in the capture and expand all the sub-headers of the radiotap header (e.g. present flags and flags). What is the channel frequency at which the frame was transmitted?

2. Briefly describe the channels used by 802.11 b/g.

3. Why is channel 6 one of the recommended channels for transmitting 802.11 wireless LAN data?

4. Was the frame transmitted using FHSS (Frequency Hopping Spread Spectrum) or OFDM (Orthogonal Frequency Division Multiplexing)?

## NETWORK DESIGN EXERCISE

The employees at the Amsterdam service center use laptops for work and need wireless coverage throughout the two floors of the building. The company has therefore decided to install a wireless LAN at this location. It will also create an additional subnet for this wireless network. Answer the following questions:

1. What wireless technology would you recommend to create the wireless LAN—IEEE802.11 a, IEEE802.11 b, IEEE803.11 g, or IEEE802.11 n? Justify your choice.

2. Assume that both floors of the building have the same dimensions. Making typical assumptions about the needed work space for each employee, what is the total area in the building that needs wireless coverage?

3. Given your technology choice and the area calculated above, how many access points would you need to provide satisfactory coverage everywhere on both floors?

4. Update your network diagram from Chapter 8 to include the wireless subnet at Amsterdam.

## CASE QUESTIONS

1. What are the different kinds of wireless data communication technologies used in the case?

2. What is a retain in the context of supply chains?

3. What is a runout in the context of supply chains?

4. What is a mesh network in the context of wireless sensor networks? What are its advantages and disadvantages? (Wikipedia is a good resource).

5. Why do companies with a nationwide footprint use satellite-based data networks for data transmission instead of wired networks such as DSL?

6. A leading provider of satellite-based data-communication services is DirecPC. Visit the company's website and write a short (one-paragraph) report on the services offered by the company based on information provided at the website. Include information such as data rates, plan prices, and other information relevant to new subscribers.

# Phone Networks

> *Mr. Watson—come here—I want to see you.*
> —ALEXANDER GRAHAM BELL

## Overview

The earlier chapters have focused on the technologies that enable the Internet. However, a large volume of information exchange occurs over a more humble technology—the telephone. As we saw in Chapter 10, toward the end of the 20th century, phone networks also served as the precursors of modern WAN networks. In recent years, the telephone has evolved with the introduction of cell phones, which add mobility to phone technology. Given the importance of the technology for modern businesses, it is useful to know about the technologies that underlie land and cellular phone networks. At the end of this chapter you should know about:

- the architecture and components of landline phone networks
- the signals used in phone networks
- DSL—an early technology developed by phone companies to offer high-speed Internet access
- the architecture and components of cellular networks
- the evolution of cell-phone networks
- code division multiple access—the signaling scheme used in modern cell-phone networks

## Introduction

Phone networks served as the early access mechanism for the Internet. In the 1990s, as Internet service providers such as AOL were perfecting their business models and technologies (recall the reference to AOL's growth in Chapter 6), the phone network served as the medium over which most residents obtained their Internet connections. Only in the early years of the 21st century have carriers installed dedicated networks for Internet service. It is therefore useful to have a high-level understanding of the architecture of phone networks.

The phone network is best seen as an analog information- transmission system. Signals are not digitized or packetized by landline phones. Instead, signals are simply allowed to flow over the wires in the same form in which they are generated at the source. In this chapter, we will look at the components of the phone system, and some significant events that helped the phone system evolve to its current form.

Figure 1 is the data communications timeline from Chapter 1. The timeline shows that for over 100 years (1840–1969), the only technologies available for long-distance information exchange were the telegraph and the telephone. Of the two, the telephone continues to be widely used globally. The basic technology underlying the phone system is quite simple. When a user dials a phone number, the switches in the phone network establish a dedicated circuit from the sender to the receiver so that signals can flow uninterrupted between the sender and the receiver. As long as the call is in progress, the network resources allocated to the call are unavailable to other callers. This mechanism of connecting users is called circuit switching. *Circuit switching is a process that, on demand, connects two or more communicating devices and permits the exclusive use of a data circuit between them until the connection is released.*

Once the circuit is established, a microphone in the handset converts the talker's voice to electronic signals. These signals are carried over the phone network from the sender to the receiver. A speaker in the receiver handset converts these signals to voice that is heard by the receiver.

Since the phone technology is so simple, particularly compared to the more complex packet-switched technologies used on the Internet, the phone network is sometime also called plain old telephone service (POTS), with the term "plain old" implying that the phone is a plain vanilla kind of service. However, such descriptions should not lead us to underestimate the importance of phone service. Though the phone technology is quite simple, it is one of the most important technologies for businesses. Figure 2 shows the levels of adoption of landline phones in different parts of the world.[1] As seen in the figure, over the last decade, landline adoption has been relatively steady around the world. Assuming 3 inhabitants per family, there would be approximately 35 families for every 100 inhabitants (100/3) and with about 50 phones for every 35 families, the figure shows that on average, there is more than 1 phone line per family in the developed world.[2]

## Phone network components

The phone network is called the public-switched telephone network (PSTN). For basic understanding, the components of the network are shown in Figure 3. The PSTN terminates on the walls of end-user homes and offices. Customers maintain the phone networks within their own premises. Between the customer premises and the central office is a very visible and critical component of the phone network—the local loop. *The local loop is a circuit from the customer premises to the last switch of the phone company's network.* The local loop ends at the end office or central office of

---

[1] www.itu.int/ITU-D/ict/statistics/ict/.

[2] Since the statistics also include business phones, it is fair to say that most homes in the developed world have a landline phone connection.

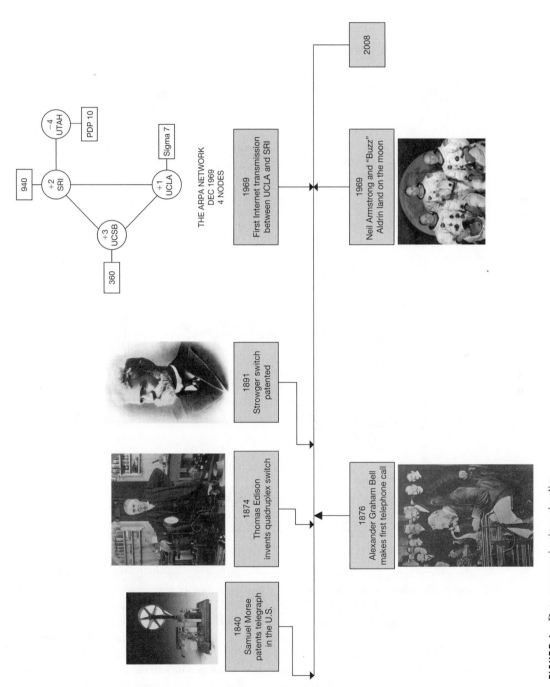

**FIGURE 1** Data communications timeline

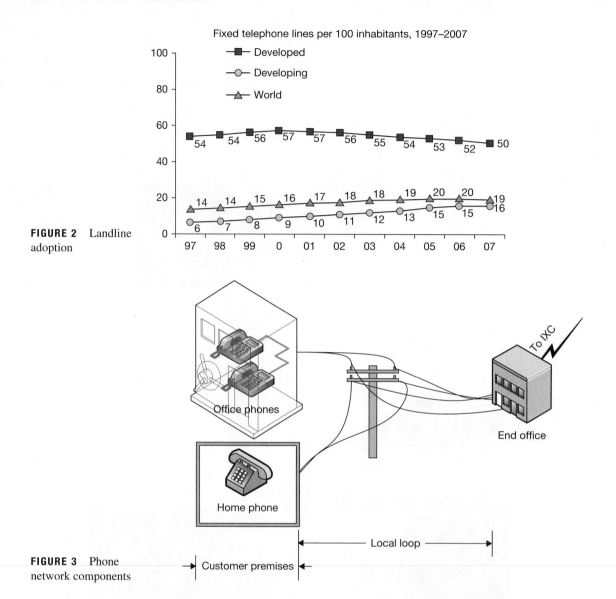

Fixed telephone lines per 100 inhabitants, 1997–2007

**FIGURE 2** Landline adoption

**FIGURE 3** Phone network components

the phone company. *The end office, also called the central office, is the location where the phone company operates equipment that is responsible for providing the customer's dial tone.* The last switch of the PSTN is in the end office.

If a call is made to a user connected to the same end office, it is connected to the user by the end office. The user then hears the phone ring. If the call is being made to a user who is connected to a different end office, the call is forwarded to the appropriate end office for completion. Figure 3 shows this as a link to the interexchange carrier (IXC). *IXCs are networks that carry traffic between end offices.* When the remote end office connects the call, there is a completed circuit between the sender and receiver over which signals can flow.

The IXC link in Figure 3 has some special properties. This link is where phone networks get integrated with WAN technologies that were introduced in Chapter 10. It may be noted that whereas the local loop is dedicated to a single user, the IXC link is shared among all users of the end office. Since the end user can only make one phone call at a time, there can only be one signal at any given time on a local loop. However, at any given time, multiple customers of an end office may need connections to the IXC to get connected to users in other end offices. Hence, the phone network needs a multiplexing technology in the IXC link to enable multiple users to simultaneously share the common IXC link. As we saw in Chapter 10, this can be accomplished using WAN technologies. Hence, the IXC link shown in Figure 3 is where WAN technologies such as ATM were first deployed for widespread use.

## Phone signals

Voice is carried over the phone wires as signals. In this section, we will take a high-level look at the properties of phone signals. We have avoided getting into the details of signals in this book because the information can get very technical. However, some aspects of phone signals are useful to know because they define the capabilities of phone modems.

The phone system tries to reproduce the speaker's voice at the receiving end. This can be accomplished if all the tones in the speaker's voice can be captured and transmitted to the receiver. Tones are determined by signal frequencies. Frequencies are measured in hertz. *Hertz is a unit of frequency which is equivalent to one cycle per second.* Observations suggest that the human voice lies in the frequency range 80 Hz–about 1,100 Hz. Male voices typically lie at the lower end of this range and female voices are at the higher end of this range. A system that can capture, transmit, and reproduce all the signals in the range 80 Hz–1,100 Hz should therefore be able to reproduce voice with high fidelity.

The phone system has been designed to transmit signals in the 300 Hz–3,400 Hz range. Since 3,400 is greater than 1,100, the high end of the range captures all human voice at high frequencies. However, the cutoff at the low end, at 300 Hz, causes some loss of information. So, why does the phone system not capture the signals in the frequency range 80 Hz–300 Hz? Why are we willing to lose the information in these frequencies? The reason to eliminate lower-frequency signals is that the power line transmits power at 60 Hz. Filtering away signals below 300 Hz eliminates the strong hum that is likely to be created in the phone receiver by the power line and its harmonics. Transmitting signals within the frequency band of 300 Hz–3,400 Hz has been found to be adequate to convey the human voice over the telephone. While this does not create a high fidelity (hi-fi) reproduction of the sender's voice, the sender's voice is clearly recognizable over the phone network.

The phone system only needs to transmit a signal within a relatively narrow bandwidth of about 3 kHz (3,400 Hz–300 Hz = 3,100 Hz). The transmission of phone signals does not require a very high quality of wire in the local loop. As a result, the phone network was built using relatively inexpensive copper cables (inferior in quality even to Cat 3 cables) in the local loop. This kept costs low and served the phone network well throughout the 20th century. By comparison, Ethernet signals require thousands of times the bandwidth for signal transmission. When customers began to demand broadband connections in the last decade of the 20th century, the poor signal-carrying properties of Cat3 phone cables in the local loop became a stumbling block for phone companies. Serving high data rates requires transmission of high-bandwidth signals, something the local loop could not do. To overcome this limitation, phone companies developed DSL, a technology that allowed high data-rate signals to be carried over phone lines for short distances.

# Legal developments

The evolution of the phone network in the United States has been influenced not just by competitive forces, but also by legal action taken by the government. Alexander Graham Bell had created AT&T to commercialize his invention of the telephone. Over the years, AT&T invested in creating a nationwide telephone network. Many residents were located in remote areas. Even though it was very expensive to connect these users to the telephone network, AT&T provided these customers with phone service at the same rates as urban customers. To facilitate these investments, in the early years of the 20th century, the U.S. government allowed AT&T to operate as a regulated monopoly. The monopoly status guaranteed the company suitable returns on its investments in developing a national network which provided phone service to all residents in the United States. This was a lot like the way most states allow gas and electric utilities to operate as regulated monopolies. The utilities agree to invest in providing services to all residents, however inaccessible they might be. In return, the state protects them from competition (monopoly) and allows them to earn reasonable (regulated) profits.

### 1984—Competition in long-distance phone service and the modified final judgment

By the mid-1970s, technological innovations had led to the emergence of a number of competitors to provide long-distance phone service. There was no longer any need to provide monopoly protection to AT&T in long-distance phone service. To level the playing field for competitors in the long-distance phone business, the U.S. government filed an anti-trust lawsuit against AT&T in 1974. The lawsuit ended in 1982 when AT&T and the U.S. government agreed on the terms of a solution to enable competition in long-distance phone service. As part of the agreement, seven regional phone companies that offered local phone service were divested (separated) out of the old AT&T. AT&T continued in business as a long-distance phone company, competing with other firms such as MCI in providing long-distance phone service. The seven local phone companies were called Regional Bell Operating Companies (RBOCs). These RBOCs were granted regulated monopoly status in providing local phone service, as the government believed that this was necessary to ensure continued investments in operating the local loop. The RBOCs were prohibited from providing long-distance service. This new structure was put in place effective January 1, 1984. Figure 4 shows a map of the operating areas of the seven RBOCs in the United States after the breakup of AT&T on January 1, 1984.

The judgment that led to the divestiture of the seven RBOCs in 1984 is sometimes called the modified final judgment. This is so because there had been a judgment

**FIGURE 4** Map showing operating areas of the seven RBOCs in 1984

in 1956 from an earlier anti-trust lawsuit filed against AT&T. As a result of the 1956 judgment, AT&T agreed to restrict its activities to running the national telephone system and perform other government work. The 1956 judgment is referred to in the industry as the final judgment. The decision in 1984 modified the final judgment from 1956, and is therefore called the "modified final judgment" in the telecom industry.

## 1996—Competition in local and long-distance phone service: Telecommunications Act

There were rapid developments in the telecom industry following the modified final judgment. To respond to the changes in the industry from these developments, in 1996, the U.S. Congress passed the Telecommunications Act. The website of the Federal Communications Commission states that "the Telecommunications Act of 1996 was the first major overhaul of telecommunications law in almost 62 years. The goal of this new law was to let anyone enter any communications business—to let any communications business compete in any market against any other." Specifically, for our purposes, the major provision of the act was that it introduced competition in both local and long-distance phone service. Thus, whereas a judicial decision introduced competition in long-distance phone service in 1984, the legislative process introduced competition in both local and long-distance phone service in 1996 through a new law, the Telecommunications Act of 1996.

The Telecommunications Act of 1996 had other features that affected the phone industry. In a very novel provision, to create competition in local phone service, the act required RBOCs or other local phone companies to provide access to their networks at reasonable rates to competitors who wanted to provide local phone service. This provision created two classes of local phone companies—the incumbents and the competitors. The incumbents (the RBOCs) were called the incumbents local exchange carriers (ILECs). The competitors were called the competitive local exchange carriers (CLECs). You may remember regularly receiving solicitations from startup phone companies offering phone services at very competitive rates in the late 1990s and early 2000s. These startups were the CLECs. The law also allowed the RBOCs to offer long-distance phone service.

## Digital subscriber line (DSL)

We saw earlier that when customers began to demand broadband Internet access, the limitations of the phone network immediately became apparent. The local loop in the phone network was designed to carry narrow band signals in the range 300 Hz–3,400 Hz. Broadband signals need cables capable of carrying much higher bandwidths than what the local loop was designed for.

So, when users began to demand broadband connections, the phone companies were at a disadvantage compared to cable companies. The coaxial cable used by cable TV companies is capable of carrying signals over a very high bandwidth. Cable companies were therefore capable of offering broadband Internet access to customers using their existing network infrastructure. Cable companies began to offer service packages that bundled cable TV, phone, and broadband Internet access. If replacing the cables in the local loop is extremely expensive, how were phone companies going to compete with cable companies once broadband Internet access became important to customers?

To respond to this business need, phone companies developed the digital subscriber line (DSL) technology. *DSL is technology that provides full-duplex service on a single twisted metallic pair of phone wires at a rate sufficient to support basic high-speed data service.* Phone companies realized that though Cat3 cables could not carry high bandwidth signals over long distances, they could carry these signals over short distances, say up to 3–5 miles. From a business perspective, this was very useful. In densely populated areas (e.g. places with many apartment complexes), phone companies could create end offices in a central location and offer DSL services to as many nearby customers as possible. By suitably locating end offices, DSL could allow phone companies to offer broadband Internet access to a large number of customers.

When the phone line carries DSL signals, the signals are transmitted in the frequency ranges shown in Figure 5. The phone signals are carried as before in the 300 Hz–3,400 Hz range. The upstream (upload) DSL signals are carried in the frequency band 25.875 kHz–138 kHz. The downstream (download) signals are carried in the frequency band 138 kHz–1,104 kHz. For reference, Figure 5 also shows the frequencies used by the phone channel (the narrow column at the extreme left, identified as "phone channel" in the figure).

We see from Figure 5 that the upstream bandwidth is about 112 kHz (138–25.875), while the downstream bandwidth is about 966 kHz (1,104–138). Thus, the downstream bandwidth is more than eight times the upstream bandwidth. Why this asymmetry? Is there something special about the downstream signal that it requires such a high bandwidth compared to the upstream bandwidth?

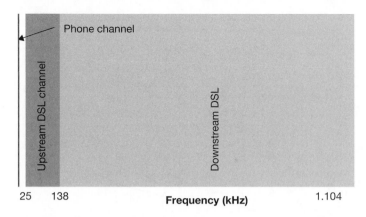

**FIGURE 5**   Phone and DSL signal frequencies

The large downstream bandwidth has to do with typical customer behavior. Most end users download huge quantities of data, but upload very little data. Downloads include video, web pages and other Internet content. The most common data uploaded by end users is e-mail. The total bandwidth of the upstream and downstream channels is fixed ($1,104-25 = 1,079$ kHz). Since most end users care most for high-speed downloads and not so much for high-speed uploads, most Internet service providers engineer their systems to provide acceptable upload speeds and the highest download speeds possible.

You may note a slight gap in Figure 5 between the phone channel and upstream DSL channel. This gap is deliberate. End users of DSL service install a DSL splitter that separates out the phone and DSL signals on the cable. The gap between phone and DSL channels helps the DSL splitter separate out the phone and DSL signals.

As an analogy for how Cat3 cables can carry high bandwidth signals over a short distance, but not long distances, imagine driving a Corvette over a dirt road. You will be able to reach high speeds over short distances. But if you try to maintain the high speed over long distances, you will end up with a sprained back, a damaged vehicle, or both. A Cat3 cable is like a rough road for signals. You can carry low speed signals for long distances, but high speed signals can only be carried for short distances.

## Cell phones

*Cellular telephony is a mobile communications system. It uses a combination of radio transmission and conventional telephone switching to permit mobile users within a specified area to access full-duplex telephone service.*

The rapid adoption of cellular telephony is one of the most important developments in telecommunication technology in the first decade of the 21ˢᵗ century. Figure 6 shows how cell phones have rapidly become popular in most regions of the world. There is almost one cell phone for every individual in the developed world. In developing countries, cell-phone adoption seems to be rising at an even faster rate than in developed countries, and there is now approximately one cell phone per family in the developing world (approximately 45 cell phones for every 35 families).

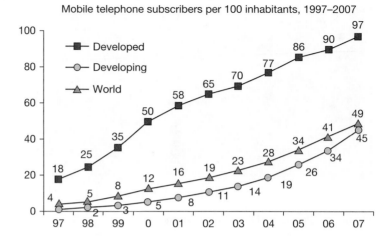

Mobile telephone subscribers per 100 inhabitants, 1997–2007

**FIGURE 6** Cell-phone adoption

To enable cellular telephony, large geographical areas are segmented into many smaller areas. Each small area is called a cell. Each cell has its own radio transmitters and receivers and a single controller interconnected with the public-switched telephone network.

Since one cell-phone tower can provide phone coverage to a wide area, and laying landlines to each home can get very expensive, building a cell-phone infrastructure can sometimes actually be cheaper than building a landline infrastructure. Thus cellular telephony can help developing countries build nationwide phone networks at lower costs than is possible with conventional landline telephony.

## Cell-phone technology evolution

Commercial cell-phone networks have been available in different parts of the world from the early 1980s. Since then, there has been steady evolutionary improvement in the technology. There have also been two clearly identifiable revolutionary improvements in cell-phone technologies. Each revolutionary improvement in cell-phone technology is labeled as a generation in the telecommunications industry. Figure 7 shows the key features of each generation of cell phones.[3]

The earliest cell-phone networks were built starting around 1980 and are now called first-generation cell-phone networks. These phones used analog signals, using frequency modulation to transmit the speaker's voice over the allocated carrier frequency. This is a very simple technology which had been used for over 50 years for wireless communication in applications such as car radios. Though the phones using this technology were heavy and unwieldy, did not support data transmission, and used wireless frequencies very inefficiently, the first generation set the stage for

---

[3] Exerpted from Agrawal, M., K. Chari, and R. Sankar "Demystifying Wireless Technologies: Navigating Through the Wireless Technology Maze. " *Communications of the AIS* 12 (2003): 166–182. Used with permission from the Association for information systems, Atlanta, GA 404-413-7444. All rights reserved.

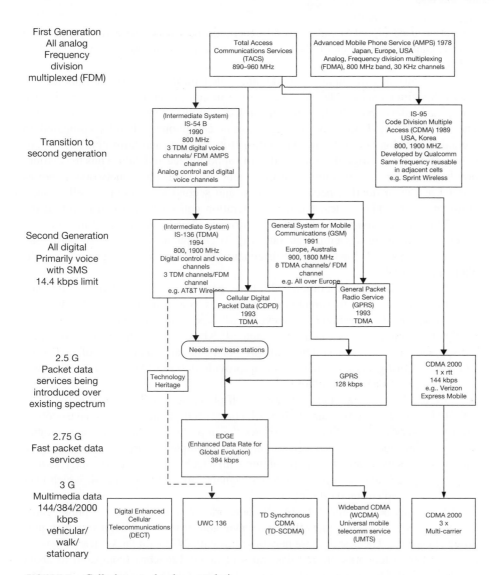

First Generation
All analog
Frequency
division
multiplexed (FDM)

Transition to
second generation

Second Generation
All digital
Primarily voice
with SMS
14.4 kbps limit

2.5 G
Packet data
services being
introduced over
existing spectrum

2.75 G
Fast packet data
services

3 G
Multimedia data
144/384/2000
kbps
vehicular/
walk/
stationary

**FIGURE 7**   Cell-phone technology evolution

future development of the technologies and markets. First-generation cellular-phone networks were popular throughout the 1980s.

In the first revolutionary change, digital signals replaced analog signals to carry voice. Networks and equipment using this technology are called second-generation cell-phone networks. The primary advantage of using digital signals is that, using data-compression techniques, it is possible to send multiple digital signals using the same bandwidth used by one analog signal. Thus, second generation networks made more efficient utilization of bandwidth compared to the first-generation cell-phone networks. Second-generation networks began to be deployed just after 1990. Since the second generation used digital signals, second-generation networks also added packet data service, enabling cell phones to be used as data modems at data rates of approximately 15 Kbps.

The current cell-phone networks are called third-generation cell-phone networks. Specifications for the third generation of cell-phone networks were defined under the leadership of the International Telecommunications Union (ITU) in 2000. The revolutionary feature of third-generation cell-phone networks compared to second-generation networks are data rates. Both second- and third-generation cell-phone networks use digital signals and both support voice and data. Thus the distinction between second-generation and third-generation cell-phone networks is not as distinct as the distinction between the first and second generation of cell phones. However, as the ITU states, the third-generation cell-phone networks "raised the bar." Third-generation networks offer performance levels significantly in excess of those obtainable from second-generation (2G) cell-phone networks. In particular, minimum data speeds for various environments are defined for third-generation cell-phone networks.[4]

In general, third generation cell-phone networks are designed to offer data rates that are sufficient to simultaneously support voice and high-speed data communication. Third-generation (3G) networks are expected to offer minimum speeds of 2 Mbps for stationary or walking users, and 348 Kbps in a moving vehicle. By comparison, second-generation systems only provided data rates in the range of 9.6 Kbps – 28.8 Kbps. Third-generation networks help provide desktop-like network experience on smart phones such as the iPhone.

Figure 7 summarizes the evolution of cell-phone networks. There were two early cell-phone services—TACS and AMPS. All current cell-phone networks have evolved from these services. The figure also shows the important evolutionary technologies that were introduced between generations. For example, before 2G was deployed, some operators were already experimenting with a technology called the intermediate system. This technology introduced digital signals and TDM over FDM, which later became the accepted standard for 2G.

Similarly, before high data-rate 3G networks were deployed, cell-phone carriers introduced higher data rates than were available from 2G, though less than proposed 3G speeds. The first of these networks was called General Packet Radio Service (GPRS). These networks offered data rates of about 128 Kbps (compared to about 14 Kbps in 2G). One hundred and twenty-eight-Kbps GPRS is popularly called 2.5G. GPRS evolved to EDGE (Enhanced Data rates for Global Evolution), offering data rates of 384 Kbps. EDGE is popularly called 2.75G.

One interesting technological feature of 3G cell-phone networks is that all 3G networks are built using a form of multiplexing that we have not seen before. This is called code division multiple access, or CDMA. To support a large number of wireless users, with each user transmitting at very high data rates as required by the 3G standard, while using the limited wireless bandwidth that is available, requires multiplexing technology that uses bandwidth very efficiently. Fortunately, CDMA is such a technology. CDMA is discussed later in this chapter.

---

[4] www.itu.int/ITU-D/imt-2000/DocumentsIMT2000/What_really_3G.pdf.

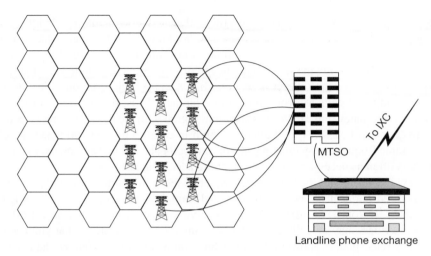

**FIGURE 8**   Cell-phone system architecture

## Cell-phone system architecture

The architecture of the cell-phone system appears as shown in Figure 8. The service area of the mobile-phone network is divided into small areas called cells. Cells can be of different sizes but it is quite common for cells to be approximately 2–4 miles in diameter. Each cell is served by a base station which houses antennas and other electronic equipment to send and receive signals from end-user devices (cell phones) within the cell. Base stations in an area are connected to a mobile-telephone switching office (MTSO). The MTSO connects the cell-phone network in its area to the PSTN, or the landline phone system, through a connection to a nearby phone exchange. This way, phone calls can be seamlessly connected between landline and cellular phones.

## Frequency reuse

Why do we divide the service area into cells? Why can't we just have one tower to serve all customers in an entire metro area? Such a system would cost far less than the current system that uses multiple towers to cover a single metro area. At first glance, it might appear that multiple cells are created to provide strong signals. We saw the case of 802.11 networks in Chapter 11, where signals from a base station only reach about 100 meters away. Similarly, is it that signals from a cell-phone base station can only reach about 1–2 miles in each direction from the base station, for a cell diameter of 2–4 miles?

This is not true. The frequencies used for cell-phone communication have excellent propagation properties. Signals from the base station can reach as far as 40 miles away. Therefore, a single cell tower can indeed serve an entire metro area. In fact, base stations are designed to limit the signal range within the boundaries of the cell served by the base station. Then why do we create cells and deliberately raise the costs of the cell-phone system?

The cellular design of the cell-phone system is primarily motivated by the need to serve a large number of users using the limited amount of wireless bandwidth that is allocated for cell-phone service. To efficiently use the available bandwidth, cell-phone networks reuse frequencies across cells. We know from Chapter 2 that a single frequency can serve one customer at a time in any single area covered by one cell-phone tower. By reusing the same frequency in different nonadjacent towers, the same frequency can serve multiple customers within a metro region. Frequencies are not reused in adjacent cells to avoid mutual interference. Thus, the network in Figure 8 may use a frequency reuse pattern as shown in Figure 9. In the figure, the network uses four frequencies $f_1$, $f_2$, $f_3$, $f_4$ and allocates them in cells so that no two adjacent cells use the same frequency. By creating appropriate cell patterns, these frequencies can be reused as often as necessary to cover the entire service area.

Let us understand the benefits of frequency reuse by a simple example. Say you operate a cell-phone network and are allocated enough bandwidth to serve about 1,000 subscribers. If you have just one tower to serve your entire territory, only 1,000 of your subscribers may be calling at any given time. Suppose, instead, that you use the frequency reuse pattern shown in Figure 9, and you would divide your available bandwidth into four frequency sub-bands. Each sub-band would be capable of serving 250 (1,000/4) subscribers. Thus, each cell would be capable of supporting 250 simultaneous conversations. But since the network now reuses frequencies, the same sub-band can support another 250 conversations in another cell. Thus, by dividing the service area into cells as necessary, cell-phone operators can support as many subscribers as they can sign up. For example, if Figure 9 represents the layout of cells in your network, you will have 39 cells. With each cell supporting 250 simultaneous conversations, you will be able to support 39 * 250 = 9,750 simultaneous cell-phone calls. It is expensive and complicated to divide a service area into cells, but by organizing the service area into cells, there is no limit to the number of subscribers who may be supported using a limited amount of bandwidth. If a particular cell becomes too busy, you can simply subdivide it into more cells. Figure 10 shows an example.

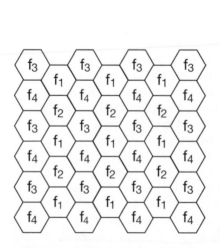

**FIGURE 9** Cell-phone frequency reuse pattern example

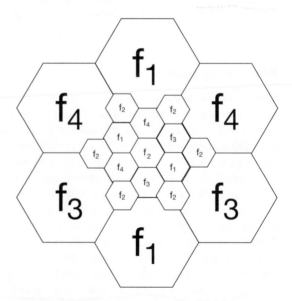

**FIGURE 10** Resizing cells to accommodate subscribers

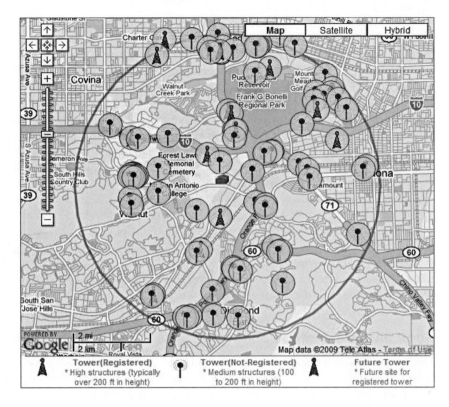

**FIGURE 11**
Cell-phone towers in
Pomona, CA

An example of this is shown in Figure 11. Though cells are most frequently shown as regular hexagons, in practice, cell shapes and sizes are influenced by population, terrain, buildings, hills etc. For example, Figure 11 shows the actual locations of cell towers in Pomona, CA.[5] We see that the arrangement of cells is not very regular. Areas with a high density of users have more towers, with each tower covering a smaller cell. The figure shows that the regular hexagonal pattern commonly used to represent cell-phone coverage areas of cell-phone towers is only a convenient representation of the actual pattern of cells.

## Roaming and the role of the MTSO

The mobile telephone switching office (MTSO) is the nerve center of cell-phone service, as shown in Figure 8. *The MTSO is the switching office that connects all of the individual cell towers to the Central Office (CO). The MTSO is responsible for monitoring the relative signal strength of cell phones as reported by each of the cell towers, and switching conversations to the cell towers with the best possible reception.*

Every cell phone has a home MTSO. When a cell phone is switched on, it periodically broadcasts its presence. These broadcasts are received by all the towers in its coverage area, and all the towers send the signal strength and other information about

---

[5] Retrieved from www.antennasearch.com.

the phone to the MTSO. The MTSO identifies the tower receiving the best signal from the phone and instructs the tower to handle calls from the phone. The selected MTSO also informs the home MTSO of the mobile phone user that the phone is located within its service area. For example the home MTSO for a cell-phone number with area code 407 will be in Orlando, Florida. If the cell phone is currently located in Kingston, Rhode Island, the local MTSO in Kingston, Rhode Island, will inform the home MTSO of the cell phone in Orlando that the cell phone is located in Kingston. When someone dials the 407 number, the call is first connected to the user's home MTSO in Orlando. The home MTSO will then direct the call to the MTSO in Kingston, Rhode Island, where the user is located. This MTSO will forward the call to the tower that is responsible for the phone.

If the user moves away from a cell, its signals to its current cell tower weaken. Simultaneously, the signals get stronger at a tower in a neighboring cell. The MTSO uses these differences in signal strengths to transfer responsibility of handling the call to the appropriate neighboring tower. This process is called handoff. *Handoff is the process of transferring a phone call in progress from one cell transmitter and frequency pair to another cell transmitter and receiver, using a different frequency pair without interruption of the call.*

## Code division multiple access (CDMA)

Third-generation cell phones use a kind of multiplexing method that we have not seen before. It is called CDMA, which stands for code division multiple access. *CDMA is a coding scheme, used as a modulation technique, in which multiple channels are independently coded for transmission over a single wideband channel. Several transmissions can occur simultaneously within the same bandwidth, with the mutual interference reduced by the use of unique codes in each transmission.*

In Chapter 2 we saw frequency-division multiplexing (FDM), where different signals are sent at different frequencies. By tuning into one frequency, the receiver can obtain the signal at the frequency, eliminating the signals being transmitted at all other frequencies. Another common multiplexing technique is time division multiplexing (TDM). In this scheme, each station is allowed to transmit in an allocated time slot. The receiver only listens to transmissions at the specified time slots and ignores transmissions made at other times. In Chapter 10, we saw SONET as an example of TDM.

Whereas multiplexing schemes such as FDM and TDM are useful, they have a major limitation. Each channel is only allowed to use a fraction of the transmitting capacity of the medium. Thus, if an FDM scheme has 10 frequency slots, it can serve at most 10 users. The 11th user will have to wait till one of the earlier users hangs up.

CDMA eliminates this limitation. CDMA allows an almost unlimited number of users to transmit signals at any time using the entire bandwidth of the medium. Each communication is allocated a unique chipping code. Before transmission, signals are processed using the assigned chipping code. Analogous to the FDM example of Chapter 2, the receiver processes the incoming signal using the same chipping code as used by the sender. This extracts the communication of interest and eliminates most of the information in all other signals. Any number of chipping codes may be generated and therefore any number of users may be added to a cell. The only limitation is that

CDMA does not eliminate all information from other signals. As a result, the background noise level in CDMA increases when the number of users increases. Eventually this can make the sound quality in the cell unacceptable. When this happens, the operator divides a large cell into smaller cells and adds new towers to serve the new cells. This is why, as shown in Figure 10, densely populated areas have many towers in close proximity. The companion website has a spreadsheet that uses an example to demonstrate how four users can use CDMA to send and receive 5 bits each.

---

**CASE STUDY** | GRAMEENPHONE: THE CELL PHONE THAT CHANGED (PART OF) THE WORLD

---

*What the telegraph did to America in the middle of the 19th century, the cell phone is doing to many parts of the world in the 21st century—simplify commerce. Both technologies have helped local merchants and farmers solicit price quotes from distant traders without having to leave their stores or farms. In 21st century Bangladesh, the cell phone is also a device for social change. Grameenphone (rural phone) is a company that empowers rural women through small business loans to buy cell phones and offer commercial cell phone services to a village community.*

With a population of over 150 million people, Bangladesh is the 7th most populated country in the world. It also has the 6th highest population density in the world, over 2,500 people per square mile. This is over 30 times the population density of the United States (about 80 people per square mile (Figure 12)).

With a nominal per capita income of approximately $1500 per annum, Bangladesh is one of the poorest countries in the world. Fifty percent of the population of Bangladesh lives on an income of less than a dollar a day. The country suffers from political instability, poor infrastructure, corruption, insufficient power, and slow implementation of economic reforms. Nearly two-thirds of the country's population subsists on agriculture, with rice as the single most important product. Fortunately, Bangladesh's growth was resilient during the 2008–2009 global financial crisis and recession. Garment exports totaling $12.3 billion and remittances from overseas Bangladeshis totaling $9.7 billion accounted for almost 25% of the country's GDP in 2009.

Bangladesh Telecommunications Company Limited (BTCL) has been providing basic landline service in the country since the 1960s. As of 2009, there were about 1.5 million landline phones in the country. By comparison, cell-phone service began in the country in 1997 and is provided by five competing cell-phone operators. These operators now serve over 45 million cell-phone subscribers.

The largest cell-phone operator in the country is Grameenphone (which translates to "rural phone"), serving over 20 million customers. Grameenphone is a joint venture between Telenor, a cell-phone operator based in Norway and Grameen Telecom Corporation, a non-profit subsidiary of Grameen Bank, the much-admired micro-credit pioneer launched by Nobel Prize winner Muhammad Yunus.

Apart from its commercial benefits, the cell phone has also become an instrument of social change in this part of the world. The goal of the program is to put every villager in the country within 2 kilometers (1.25 miles) of a cell phone.

Grameen Telecom operates a village phone program. Bangladeshi women can obtain a cell-phone kit through a micro-credit "in kind" loan from the program, and begin operating a phone service for the rest of their village and its surroundings areas. After they are trained by Grameen Telecom on the operation of the cell phone, they offer mobile-phone service as a retail offering. Their service is available wherever they are—in the farm or home or family business. The service never closes, and customers even wake them up past midnight to make calls to relatives in places such as New York City (Figure 13).

There is a reason why Grameen Phone only offers its loan program to women. Women in rural Bangladesh are

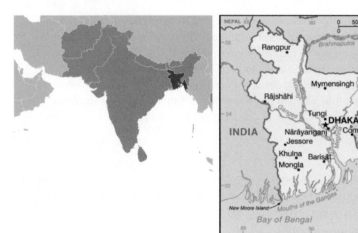

**FIGURE 12**    Maps of Bangladesh

**FIGURE 13**    The cell phone as an all-in-one socially uplifting device—helping women and farmers

at a great disadvantage compared to men, lagging behind men in health, literacy, and income. Only 13% of women get skilled attendants during delivery. Women do not own land, are commonly married early, and depend upon male family members to accompany them while traveling outside their village. "Phone ladies," as they are called, believe that operating a cell-phone service immediately improves the respect they receive from their husbands and family.

An article in *The Wall Street Journal* in 1999 reported on the economics of the Grameenphone. The phone costs the phone ladies $375 each. The average local cell-phone call costs approximately 10 cents per minute on which the phone ladies add an approximately 20% mark-up. In a typical month, the phone charges come to around $215, leading to a profit of $40. This is almost twice the average gross monthly income in Bangladesh. For approximately the first two years

of phone ownership, a phone lady pays weekly installments of less than $5 toward the cost of the handset. The remainder of the profit is invested in other family businesses such as farms, chicken co-ops, and buffaloes. Most months, the ladies deposit about $5 in their savings accounts at Grameen Bank. They are also able to afford the occasional splurge on jewelry and furniture.

Grameenphone also serves rural farmers. The company believes that when a rural farmer purchases a SIM card, he opens up a gateway of hope and possibilities, not just a means of communication. While tending to their fields, farmers can gather market information over the cell phones to make informed decisions about what crops to grow and where to sell the crops.

Further, in Bangladesh, the isolated and uninformed farmers have little bargaining power with exploitative middlemen. Connectivity reduces the dependency of these farmers on middlemen. Grameenphone operates a service similar to Craigslist where buyers and sellers are able to trade goods (e.g. rice, motorcycle, electronics, etc.) through their mobile phones. Trade information is exchanged using technologies such as SMS, or browsing with WAP (Wireless Application Protocol). On average, the service attracts 600 new postings and 90,000 hits per day. Over a million subscribers have accessed the service since its inception.

This idea is being replicated and pushed further in other parts of the world. Moca, a nonprofit company associated with MIT Media Lab's NextLab program, is developing cell-phone applications to help patients in remote locations transmit their health information, including pictures, to a doctor or nurse in a clinic. A preliminary diagnosis determines whether the condition warrants a trip to the clinic. Zaca is a mobile-phone-based application to aggregate produce information and query current and historical market price of produce. Celedu aims to help improve living standards through education and literacy.

## REFERENCES

CIA. *"The World Factbook—Bangladesh."* https://www.cia.gov/library/publications/the-world-factbook/geos/bg.html.

Contact Information for mobile phone operators in Bangladesh. www.btrc.gov.bd/licensing/operators/mobile_operators.php (accessed 1/30/010).

Grameenphone, www.grameenphone.com.

Jordan, M. "It Takes a Cell Phone: A New Nokia Transforms a Village in Bangladesh." *Wall Street Journal,* June 25, 1999, B1.

MIT NextLAB. http://nextlab.mit.edu (accessed 1/30/10).

WorldAtlas.com. *"Countries of the World."* www.worldatlas.com/aatlas/populations/ctydensityh.htm (accessed 1/30/10).

## SUMMARY

This chapter provided a high level overview of landline and cell-phone networks. Though many functions of the phone system are moving over to computerized communication technologies, such as e-mail, IM, and VoIP, the phone continues to be an important medium for business and personal communication. The phone system transmits signals in the frequency range 300 Hz–3,400 Hz. Each end user is connected to the nearest end office of the phone company using a dedicated pair of copper wires called the local loop. The phone system is used in many parts of the world to offer high-speed Internet service using a technology called Digital Subscriber Line (DSL).

The phone system in the United States was initially operated by one company, AT&T. In 1984, the company agreed in a court settlement to focus exclusively on providing long-distance phone service. AT&T's local phone service networks were divested as seven local phone companies. Later, in 1996, Congress passed the Telecommunications Act, which opened up all sectors of telephony to competition. The Telecommunications Act also required incumbent local phone companies with established phone networks to allow competitors to use the incumbent phone company's networks at reasonable prices to compete with the incumbent.

Of late, cellular telephony is becoming increasingly popular, even in developing countries. In many cases, developing countries actually find it cheaper to set up a cell-phone network than to set up a landline phone network. Cell-phone networks divide the coverage area into small cells. Users in each cell are served by a cell-phone tower located in the cell. As users move from cell to cell, their calls are handed off to the most appropriate cell-phone tower in the area. The division of the coverage area into cells allows frequency reuse, which allows a small set of frequencies to be used to serve as many subscribers as necessary.

Cell-phone technologies have evolved in three distinct phases. Each phase is called a generation. We are currently using the third generation of cell-phone technologies, creatively called 3G. The third generation uses a multiplexing technology called CDMA, which is very efficient in using bandwidth. CDMA enables cell-phone networks to offer high data-rate network connections to a large number of end users using the very limited bandwidth available for 3G networks.

## ABOUT THE COLOPHON

First impressions are lasting impressions. It is therefore not surprising that the first phrase spoken on the telephone by the inventor of the technology is also one of the most memorable phrases ever communicated using the technology.

Alexander Graham Bell maintained meticulous diaries of his experiments to create the telephone. In his diary entry of March 10, 1876[6] (Figure 14), Alexander Graham Bell has described his first successful communication using the telephone. When he

---

[6] www.loc.gov/exhibits/treasures/trr002.html.

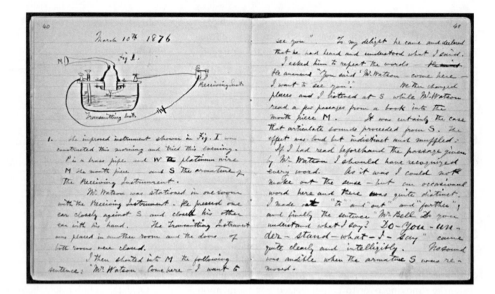

**FIGURE 14**
Alexander Graham
Bell's diary,
March 10, 1876

spoke through the instrument, his assistant, Thomas A. Watson, was in the next room. In the diary, Graham Bell has written, "*I then shouted into M the following*

*sentence: 'Mr. Watson—come here—I want to see you.' To my delight he came and declared that he had heard and understood what I said.*"

## REVIEW QUESTIONS

1. What are some of the ways in which the phone network has been important for data communications over the years?

2. What are some of the important landmarks in the development of phone service?

3. What is *circuit switching*?

4. How has the adoption of landline telephony evolved in the last decade?

5. What is the local loop in the context of phone service?

6. What is the central office or the end office?

7. What are *inter-exchange carriers* (IXC)? What are some similarities and differences between the local loop and IXC links?

8. What is *hertz*?

9. Why is the phone system designed to carry signals in the frequency range 33 Hz–3,400 Hz?

10. What is *digital subscriber line* (DSL)?

11. What was the motivation for the development of DSL technology?

12. What are the three kinds of signals on a cable providing DSL and phone service? What are the frequency ranges used by the three signals?

13. Why do most ISPs provide much higher downstream data rates than upstream data rates?

14. Why is the modified final judgment important to the development of phone service in the United States?

15. What was the outcome of the modified final judgment?

16. What were the circumstances that led to the Telecommunications Act of 1996?

17. What were some of the implications of the Telecommunications Act of 1996?

18. What is *cellular telephony*?

19. What are the three generations of cellular telephony service? Describe the important features of each generation of cell-phone service.

20. What is *frequency reuse* in the context of cellular telephony? Why is frequency reuse necessary for cellular telephony?

21. Why are service areas divided into small cells for cellular telephony?

22. What is the MTSO in cell-phone service? What are the important roles of the MTSO?

23. What is *handoff*? Why is handoff important? How does it work?

24. What is *CDMA*?

25. How is CDMA better suited that TDM or FDM for cellular telephony?

## HANDS-ON EXERCISE

Creating a hands-on exercise for telephony is not simple because end users have no access to phone carrier networks. Therefore, instead of trying to poke into phone company networks, the hands-on exercise for this chapter will give you the opportunity to learn about one of the most important recent developments in telephony—CDMA. You will create CDMA codes and use these CDMA codes to multiplex data transmission. You will also decode the data for reception at the receiver.[7]

In the discussion below, we will find it convenient to use $-1$ to represent binary 0. This makes it easier to show the computations involved.

In CDMA, transmitters use mutually orthogonal codes, called chipping codes, to process data. Orthogonality of chipping codes means that the dot product of any two chipping codes is 0. The dot product, or inner product, of two codes is calculated by multiplying the respective elements of the two codes, and taking the sum of the products. Figure 15 shows an example. The two chipping codes in the example are [1 1] and [1 −1]. Writing the codes in columns as in Figure 15, we can evaluate the dot product of the two codes and confirm that it is zero.

Techniques exist to create chipping codes of any length.[8] The chip rate is higher than the bit rate. Once a chipping code is selected, processing data for transmission involves calculating the exclusive OR of each bit of the data with every element of the chipping code. The result is transmitted into the medium.

The receivers multiply the resulting signal in the medium with the transmitter's chipping code and add

| Element | Code 1 | Code 2 | Product of elements |
|---|---|---|---|
| 1 | 1 | 1 | 1 |
| 2 | 1 | −1 | −1 |
| Dot product = sum of product of elements = | | | 0 |

**FIGURE 15**  Dot product of two codes

■ Chipped data
— Data

**FIGURE 16**  Data and chipped signal example

the result for each bit period. This recovers the transmitted data. This is the basic CDMA operation.

The spreadsheet CDMA.xlsx in the readings for this chapter at the companion website has an example of four pairs of users transmitting 5 bits each. Figure 16 shows the data and chipped signal for user D in the spreadsheet example.

---

[7] There is some level of math involved in this exercise. But every attempt has been made to keep it simple.
[8] For one such technique, please search Wikipedia or other resource for Walsh codes.

The README worksheet walks you through the spreadsheet to see the data, chipping codes, sender processing, and receiver processing. You will find it convenient to also download the CDMA.xlw workspace and open the workspace. This will show you both the README and data worksheets simultaneously.

Use the CDMA.xlsx worksheet to answer the following:

1. Use Wikipedia or other resource to write a brief summary of CDMA.

2. Use Wikipedia or other information resource to write a Walsh matrix of size 4*4.

3. Pick any two different codes in the 8*8 Walsh matrix used in the data.xlsx worksheet (cells A[28]–H[36]). Using a procedure similar to Figure 15, confirm that the dot product of the two codes is zero.

4. Repeat Question 3, but use the chipping code for B for both codes. Confirm that the dot product of a code with itself is not zero.

5. The example in the spreadsheet uses the chipping codes from the first four columns in the Walsh codes of size 8. Replace the chipping code for D with one of the unused chipping codes (any code in columns E[29-36] ... H[29-36]). Confirm that the data is recovered correctly with the new code (contents in cells A22–D26 should not change).

6. You saw in Question 4 above that the dot product of a code with itself is not zero. To see the impact of this, repeat Question 5 above, but this time, reuse the chipping code for user B for user D. Confirm that the data is not recovered correctly.

## NETWORK DESIGN EXERCISE

While the Mumbai location uses VoIP for all its voice traffic, the Singapore location is trying to decide whether to switch its users from traditional phones to VoIP phones. Answer the following questions:

1. Using the Internet or other information resource, compare the advantages and disadvantages of VoIP compared to traditional phone service (PSTN) along dimensions such as cost, performance, and reliability.

2. Based on the above, would you recommend that Coolco switch from PSTN to VoIP?

## CASE QUESTIONS

1. How have cell phones improved the lives of people in Bangladesh?

2. What do you think are some of the reasons that there are over 30 times as many cell-phone subscribers in Bangladesh as landline subscribers?

3. What do you think are some of the important difficulties in establishing landline connectivity to all villages in Bangladesh?

4. What information is available about the current status of the village-phone project in terms of number of subscribers, villages covered, etc? Use online and other resources for information.

5. Look at MIT media lab's note, "A phone is not just a phone," available at www.facebook.com/note.php?note_id=138098999263.[9] Think of a problem that afflicts over a billion people in the world and describe in about 1–2 paragraphs how cell phones may help alleviate the problem. Note: cell phones will not solve all aspects of every global problem. Try to make your answer relevant. You may find initial ideas at the MIT Nextlab website.

---

[9] URLs may change. If the link does not work, please search the web for "A phone is not just a phone."

## CHAPTER 13

# Network Security

*To err is human, but to really foul things up requires a computer.*
−"Capsules of Wisdom", *Farmer's Almanac*, 1978

## Overview

Thus far in this book, we have considered the positive aspects of computer networks, such as their ability to speed up organizational decision making and lower the costs of doing business. However, computer networks also expose the information in the organization to dangers from the network. In this chapter we will look at the common methods used to defend organizational information against dangers originating from computer networks. At the end of this chapter you should know:

- what information security is
- what network security is and how it is related to information security
- the common elements of a risk management model—vulnerabilities, threats, and controls
- what network security controls are commonly used to protect outgoing information
- what network security controls are commonly used to protect incoming information

## Introduction

Network security is a component of information security. Considerable management attention is paid to information security. We will therefore start with a high-level introduction of information security to see why information security is important and how network security fits into an organization's overall information security setup.

*Information security is the provision of confidentiality, integrity, and availability to information. Confidentiality is to preserve authorized restrictions on information to protect personal privacy and proprietary information. Integrity is to guard against improper modification or destruction of information and ensure authenticity of information. Availability is to ensure timely and reliable use of information.* Together, the three dimensions of information security provide assurance to end users that they can depend upon an information system to store data without fear of theft or loss, and also depend upon the output of an information system to take decisions, without fear of the data being tampered with.

There is general agreement in legal and technical circles about confidentiality, integrity, and availability (CIA) as being the three dimensions of information security. Title 44, Chapter 35, section 3542 of the U.S. Code defines information security in terms of the above three dimensions. RFC 2196, the site security handbook, also defines information security in terms of these three dimensions.

Why do organizations care so much about information security? Information security matters because we are increasingly dependent upon information for our livelihoods and way of life. As manufacturing moves offshore, professionals in the United States are increasingly involved in product design and software development. The IT sector constitutes almost 20% of the value of the S&P 500 index of large cap companies in the United States.[1] If we use the size of the IT sector in the S&P 500 as a proxy for the importance of IT in our economy, we might say that IT constitutes almost 20% of the U.S. economy. Accounting and financial data in most companies is now stored almost exclusively on computer systems with no paper trail available for verification. Increasingly, our own personal workflows are becoming computerized. For example, most of our life's memories are now stored on computers as image files. A single hard disk crash can cause permanent loss of this information. Information security then, is critical for the smooth functioning of our economy, our businesses, and our personal and professional lives. Imagine what would happen to your career if it were trivially easy for hackers to steal designs and computer codes you created? Or tamper with financial records such as your checking account balance?

If information security is so important, how do you go about providing information security? At a very high level, it helps to start with developing a risk-management model that shows how an organization's information security might be compromised. Risk-management models have three components—vulnerabilities, threats, and controls. This is shown in Figure 1 as a general risk-management model for information security. The figure shows the primary drivers of information risk.

Information security begins with an identification of information assets in an organization that are worth protecting. These are shown as gold bars in Figure 1. Business needs generally determine what information systems are used and what information is considered worthy of protection. At a university, these assets include student academic records, staff HR records, and intellectual property developed by university faculty and students that has the potential to be commercialized. Typically, this information is stored in an information system as files and databases. In Figure 1, these information systems are shown as the cup holding the gold bars (information assets). It is possible for the information systems to have vulnerabilities. *Vulnerabilities are weaknesses in an information system that could be exploited by interested hackers to compromise the security of the information held in the information systems.* Insecure services such as telnet, if running, are an example of vulnerabilities.

Organizations connected to networks are constantly under threat from a variety of sources that are interested in exploiting the organization's vulnerabilities. *Threats*

---

[1] www2.standardandpoors.com/spf/pdf/index/SP_500_Factsheet.pdf (retrieved September 14, 2009).

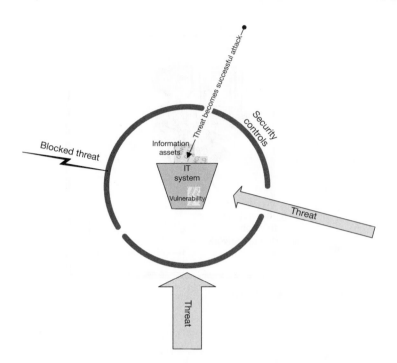

**FIGURE 1** General information risk-management model

*are capabilities, intentions, and attack methods of adversaries to cause harm to information*. In Figure 1, these threats are shown as directed arrows coming into the organization. For example, if the organization is a retailer, hackers might be interested in reading credit-card numbers as they are swiped at check-out counters. To counter these threats, professionals like you deploy information security controls in the organization. *Controls are measures taken to mitigate the dangers arising from information security threats*. Figure 1 shows these controls as a circle around the information system. Controls block threats to the greatest extent possible. However, due to limitations of the technology or due to limitations in the skills of the administrators responsible for these controls, it is possible that controls leave room for attackers to reach the information systems holding the information assets. If that happens, it is possible that some such attacks will successfully compromise information security.

Figure 1 provides a model for the responsibilities of all IT administrators and for security professionals in particular. All IT systems are constantly under threat from various sources to compromise the information security of the system. Of the three components of the risk-management model (vulnerabilities, threats, and controls), IT administrators are usually powerless to determine either the threats or the information assets that create vulnerabilities. What IT administrators can do however, is to deploy the most effective controls possible. Therefore, most discussions of information security are focused on information security controls.

IT systems face a variety of threats, and administrators use a variety of controls to secure information against these threats. To facilitate understanding of these controls, they are classified in various ways. A common classification is to classify information security controls into procedural, physical, and technical controls.

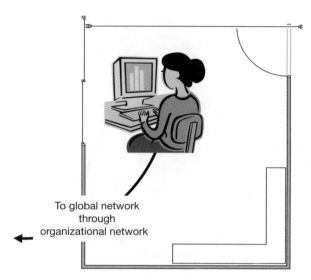

**FIGURE 2** A typical office worker

For example, consider the typical office worker shown in Figure 2. What are the information security threats faced by this worker? One category of threats comes from the user's incorrect practices. For example, she might download some tempting software that also installs malware on the system. To counter these kinds of threats, she may undergo awareness training to learn best practices. This would be an example of procedural controls. *Procedural controls are controls based on formal orders and procedures.* Another category of threats comes from the office space. For example, by mistake, the user might leave office doors open after work, which may lead to theft. To counter these threats, security guards may periodically verify that office doors are locked off-hours. This is an example of physical controls. *Physical controls are security measures used to deter or prevent unauthorized access.* Finally, skilled intruders may use the network connection to hack the computer. To prevent this, IT might install a firewall to block unauthorized network intrusions. This would be an example of a technical control. *Technical controls are controls that use technology to secure information.*

> The classification of security controls into procedural, physical, and technical controls is quite common in the industry.

An important source of threats is the network. As seen in Figure 2, the network connection gives intruders the opportunity to compromise information security from anywhere in the world. Having introduced the concept of information security and the role of network security in information security, in the rest of the chapter, we will see the important technical controls used in network security.

# Network security

*Network security is the provision of information security in the presence of dangers created by computer networks.* Thus, protecting network devices (routers, computers, and other devices connected to the network) is not the primary goal of network security. Rather, the goal of network security is to provide information security from threats originating in the network. Protecting network devices is important to the extent that it secures valuable information in the organization. At the end of the day, the information connected to the network is more valuable than the hardware connecting to the network. Viruses, phishing attacks, and intrusion attempts are all examples of information security threats of being connected to the Internet. All these threats attempt to compromise valuable information in the organization. Intruders are generally less interested in causing damage to equipment. Network security controls are our defense against these dangers arising from the network.

Why does network security matter? What makes network security a particularly interesting area of an organization's overall security plan? Network security matters because increasing parts of the nation's and the world's infrastructure are connected to the network. Financial systems, payment systems, hospital records, control systems for the nation's electricity grid, and vital installations such as NASA, are now connected to the network. Weakness in network security can allow hackers to obtain unauthorized access to vital information on these resources. This can get expensive. In a highly publicized incident, during 2006–2007, hackers gained access to the network of retailer T.J. Maxx by exploiting weaknesses in wireless network security and stole information on over 40 million credit cards. At one point, there were estimates that the retailer would have to pay as much as $480 million to settle the issue with banks and state regulators. In 2009, the leader of the group that was charged with the intrusion into T. J. Maxx was also charged with intruding into the databases of Heartland Payment Systems, a credit-card processor, and stealing information on about 130 million credit cards. The common intruder, Albert Gonzalez, was just 28 years old, and was a former government informant. There were also reports in 2009 that the U.S. electrical grid appears to have been penetrated by hostile interests.[2] Network security is therefore a persistent and significant challenge. In March 2010, Albert Gonzalez was convicted to 20 years imprisonment for the offenses.

In this chapter, we will focus on the technical controls used to provide network security. Many technical controls are used to provide network security. Since the network is used to receive and to send information, network security controls are used to protect both incoming and outgoing information. Therefore, in this chapter, we have classified network security controls according to whether they primarily defend against incoming or outgoing data. In each case, we look at the important controls to provide confidentiality, integrity, and availability. The result is shown in Table 1. Though most of these controls defend against many threats, the table tries to identify the primary goal of each control. For example, one of the primary goals of firewalls is to maintain integrity by limiting network access to friendly computers. But firewalls also help maintain availability by blocking out intruders who send large volumes of data to networks to try to keep devices busy without reason.

In the rest of this chapter, we will look at each of the six cells in Table 1 in more detail.

---

[2] Gorman, Si. "Electricity Grid in U.S. Penetrated by Spies." *Wall Street Journal*, April 8, 2009.

**Table 1** Network security controls by category

|  | Incoming information | Outgoing information |
| --- | --- | --- |
| **Confidentiality** | Patching, authentication and authorization | Encryption |
| **Integrity** | Firewalls | Digital signatures |
| **Availability** | Virus protection, end-user training | Redundancy |

# Network security controls for incoming information

What are the threats from incoming information? Most of us have encountered at least one situation where we received a virus as an e-mail attachment. We also often get e-mails trying to get our bank account credentials. Without our knowledge, intruders constantly try to send information to our computers to take control of them and install malicious software. The controls discussed in this section defend against these threats from incoming information.

## Controls for confidentiality

*Confidentiality is to preserve authorized restrictions on information to protect personal privacy and proprietary information.*

In 2006–2009, two of the most publicized incidents of information-security compromise related to the ability of a group of hackers to read credit-card data without authorization. At Heartland Systems, in 2008, the group exploited an improperly coded website to insert an application on the system that allowed the intruders to read credit-card data from Heartland's databases. At T. J. Maxx, the group was able to use passwords of store managers to read credit-card records.

## Patching

Modern software is extremely complex. In spite of the best efforts of developers, software products, including operating systems and applications, have weaknesses that can be exploited by intruders. A common example is web applications that do not check user input. Knowledgeable attackers can exploit this weakness and compromise information security. This is what happened in the case of Heartland in 2008. A web application at the company was not adequately verifying user input in a form field. The attackers were able to use this weakness to send carefully crafted SQL commands as form inputs and insert a malicious application on Heartland's systems. This application allowed the intruders to read credit-card data from the databases behind the website. This attack is called an SQL injection attack. Many other software vulnerabilities to incoming data are possible.

When such software weaknesses become known, developers quickly issue updates to fix problems. These updates are called patches, and the process of applying updates is called patching. A suitable patch at Heartland would have added input checks to block the ability to attackers to send improper form inputs and compromise the system.

Regular patching ensures that applications get updated as soon as updates become available. Most applications and operating systems are capable of automatic updates. Large organizations prefer to test patches before applying them to make sure that updates do not adversely affect other applications. However, for homes and small organizations, automatic updates are highly recommended.

As we will see shortly, patching is also an extremely important measure to reduce the organization's vulnerability to viruses and worms. Many viruses and worms exploit vulnerabilities in unpatched software. A specific example of the Slammer worm is discussed in a later section.

## Authentication and authorization

What if your computer did not ask you to provide a user name and password before allowing itself to be used? Anybody who succeeded in getting physical access to your computer would be able to read any file on your computer. The same thing can happen in networks. At T. J. Maxx, the attackers found a retail store where the attackers were able to read the user names and passwords of store managers. Due to poor authorization policies at the company, the user name and password of store managers gave the attackers access into the central databases at the organization where credit-card records were stored.

What could T. J. Maxx have done to guard its information? Later in this chapter we will see what T. J. Maxx could have done to prevent the intruders from obtaining the user names and passwords of store managers. But, even if the user names and passwords of some users at retail stores had been compromised, had T. J. Maxx limited database access to a small set of system administrators, the unfortunate incident that cost the company $480 million might have been avoided.

*Authentication is the verification of a claimed identity.* Authentication is what users do when they provide a user name and password to access a secure website. No person other than the rightful user is expected to know the correct password. Therefore, providing the correct password is used as a confirmation of identity. Authentication should be necessary before allowing users to perform sensitive operations. For example, banks ask you to prove your identity before allowing you to open an account. Various forms of proof are acceptable, for example a driver's license or a passport. The important thing is that satisfactory proof of identity is required before the bank will allow you to open an account. Similarly, computers connected to protected data should be configured to require users to provide proof of identity.

To give access to new users, IT administrators typically assign new users a username and the system immediately generates a random password which the user changes at the earliest opportunity. The new password is known only to the user. Therefore, the username and password authentication scheme is reasonably secure. When higher levels of security are required, users may be asked to provide thumbprints or other forms of identity for authentication.

Typically, authentication is performed in three ways—something you know (e.g. a password); something you have (e.g. an ATM card); and something you are (e.g. a thumbprint). Each of these ways is called a factor of authentication. Increasing the required number of factors for authentication typically improves security.

Authentication is useful, but it is only one half of the process to maintain information confidentiality from outsiders. The other half is authorization. *Authorization is the granting of rights to a user to access, read, modify, insert, or delete certain data, or to execute certain programs.* Authorization is what happens in normal security procedures. Employee ID cards allow employees access to the offices where they should have access, but not to all offices in the organization. Now, consider what happened at T. J. Maxx. The hackers were able to obtain the credentials of store managers due to a weakness in the wireless setup at a store. Now, there was no reason for store managers to have permissions to access corporate databases. Accordingly, the company should have given store managers access only to the terminals in the stores. Had this been done, the problem might not have escalated. However, since store managers had the required authorization on corporate databases, when their accounts were compromised, the attackers were able to read credit-card data stored in these databases. T. J. Maxx did perform authentication, but does not seem to have performed proper authorization. Limiting authorization on the database to a small set of IT administrators could have prevented the incident even if the passwords of store managers were compromised.

Therefore, authentication should be followed by authorization. A good initial set of permissions might be the ability to read and write files in the user's own home directory and the permissions to execute the company's default set of computer applications. This will allow employees to do their jobs, while at the same time maintaining confidentiality and integrity.

Patching and authentication and authorization are commonly used to thwart attacks on confidentiality from incoming data.

> Since passwords are so important, best practices for passwords have been developed to guide administrators. The goal of a good password policy is to prevent intruders from being able to guess passwords. To that end, recommendations from Microsoft include the following:[3] (1) good passwords should include characters other than just the alphabets; (2) actual names or words should be avoided; (3) passwords should have at least eight characters (in fact, 12–14 characters are increasingly becoming the recommended standard) and (4) passwords should be changed regularly.

## Controls for integrity

*Integrity is to guard against improper modification or destruction of information and ensure authenticity of information.*

> During the battle over South Ossetia between Russia and Georgia in August 2008, a number of Georgian government websites were defaced. These included the websites of the President of Georgia, the Ministry of Foreign Affairs, and the National Bank (the country's central bank). In most cases, the home pages of the sites were replaced with images of well-known dictators.

---

[3] www.microsoft.com/protect/fraud/passwords/create.aspx.

## Firewalls

*A firewall is a computer that lies between two networks and regulates traffic between the networks in order to protect the internal network from electronic attacks originating from the external network.* Typically, firewalls peek into incoming packets to obtain the source and destination IP addresses and destination port address of the packet. This information helps the firewall determine where the packets are coming from and what applications the packets are trying to reach. Firewalls allow administrators to specify rules that limit which packets may be allowed to enter the network. With a good set of rules, administrators can ensure that only friendly packets reach computers within the network. The typical use of a firewall is shown in Figure 3. The firewall examines every packet reaching the local network from the Internet and verifies that the packet passes the specified rules before allowing the packet into the local network.

In general, firewalls can do two things to packets—allow them, or block them. Typically, the first rule that matches the packet is applied. For example, consider a firewall which has the following set of rules:[4]

```
block in from 165.228.0.0/16 to any
pass in proto tcp from any to 131.247.95.68 port = 80
block in all
```

The first rule in this rule set blocks all incoming packets from the network 165.228.0.0/16. The network 165.228.0.0/16 has been blocked because the administrator identified it as a blacklisted network.[5] The second rule allows all remaining TCP packets to reach the web server (port 80) located at IP address 131.247.95.68. The third rule blocks all other packets. Effectively, this rule set allows packets from non-blacklisted networks to come into the network, but only if they want to access the specified web server. All other incoming packets are blocked. Administrators can build more elaborate rule sets based on experience.

As a starting point, firewalls should block any access to insecure services inside the organization. An example of an insecure service is telnet. The service allows remote

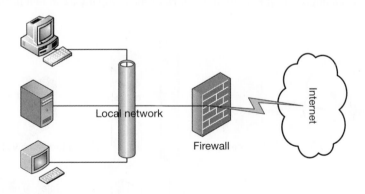

**FIGURE 3**   Typical firewall setup

---

[4] These rules use the syntax for `ipfilter`, a popular software firewall.
[5] www.yutrade.net/blacklist.php.

users to control computers. However, telnet data is unencrypted and most implementations of the telnet service have not been patched for a long time. As a result, any computer in the organization that runs telnet by mistake is a valuable target for intruders. Firewalls can protect such computers by blocking all attempts to access telnet.

Once insecure services are shielded, the firewall should only allow remote computers from trusted networks to access safe and secure services inside the network. Examples of safe or secure services include SSH, DNS, e-mail, and http.

Large organizations typically implement firewalls in two stages as shown in Figure 4. Facing the Internet is a network that hosts public services such as e-mail, web, and DNS. This network is popularly called the demilitarized zone or the DMZ. *The DMZ is a network that contains the organization's external services and connects them to the Internet.* The first firewall (public firewall in Figure 4) faces the Internet and provides basic protection to the DMZ and the organization by keeping out hostile networks.

The second firewall (internal firewall in Figure 4) connects the DMZ to the organization's internal network. This internal firewall blocks out all incoming requests from outside the organization. Sensitive organizational data is placed behind the internal firewall. Here, sensitive data is only accessible to authenticated and authorized users and services. For example, internal users may access proprietary information inside the organization. Or, a web application in the DMZ may be allowed access to a database hosted on a host in the internal network.

The two-tier firewall architecture for network security in Figure 4 parallels the physical security architecture of most businesses. Typically a business such as a store or a bank has an exterior door, which has a function analogous to the functions of the public firewall in Figure 4. This door allows all legitimate customers to enter the establishment, while offering some rudimentary protections. For example, the door prevents people from bringing large vehicles into the store. Inside, customers are free to browse products and use the check-out counters or tellers for transactions. This area may be considered the DMZ of the store. In a corner of the store, there is usually an area marked for employees only. This is the area where the store management keeps its records such as sales, salaries, etc. This area is typically out of bounds for customers. This area is analogous to the internal network of the company as shown in Figure 4.

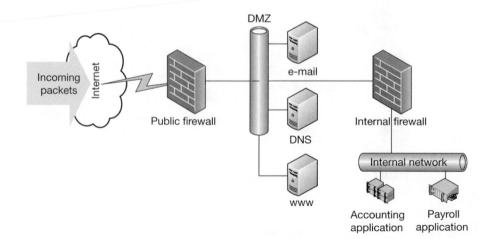

**FIGURE 4** Typical enterprise firewall configuration

Firewalls have limitations. First, if an internal computer is compromised, it can successfully attack other computers in the local network. Second, firewalls are unable to protect services that Internet users are allowed to access. For example, if you run a web application inside your organization, you probably would want the world to visit it. If the web application has any vulnerability, the firewall cannot prevent it from being exploited because the firewall rules will allow access to the web application. Finally, a firewall is only as good as the rules specified by its administrator. If the firewall rules do not block packets from attackers, the firewall will not stop the attacker.

In the case of the Georgian attacks, clearly, the fact that the contents on the sites were modified indicates that the attackers were able to overcome any authentication and authorization controls the Georgian sites may have implemented. In this case, in addition to better patching, authentication and authorization, suitable implementation of firewalls may have prevented the attackers from gaining access to the computers in the first place. Firewall rules could have been created to block suspicious traffic and all incoming packets from suspicious networks, particularly those in Russia.

## Controls for availability

*Availability is to ensure timely and reliable use of information.*

On January 25, 2003, at around 12:30 pm EST, the Slammer worm scanned the Internet for computers running an unpatched version of MS SQL server. Within 10 minutes of its release, it had infected over 50,000 hosts, over 90% of all vulnerable computers on the Internet, causing outages and consequences such as ATM failures and flight cancellations.

## Viruses and worms

Have you encountered through personal experience or heard from a friend the experience of being attacked by a computer virus or worm? Typically, when this happens, the computer appears very slow without reason. Occasionally, some data files get corrupted and have to be deleted. If a computer file is damaged or has to be deleted, it is also no longer available. Therefore, the end result of most virus attacks is a loss of availability.

According to the ATIS Telecom glossary, *a computer virus is an unwanted program which places itself into other programs, which are shared among computer systems, and replicates itself. A worm is a self-contained program that causes harm and can propagate itself through systems or networks.* You may have read in many sources that the distinction between worms and viruses is that worms replicate themselves, whereas viruses do not. However, the above definition is more formal. Both viruses and worms can replicate themselves. The major difference between the two is that worms are self-contained programs whereas viruses use e-mail clients or other software to cause damage and to replicate themselves. Viruses and worms are often designed to use up available resources such as storage or processing time, thereby compromising availability.

Most surveys of CIOs indicate that of all information-security threats, virus attacks cause the greatest financial losses to organizations.[6] Therefore, IT professionals should pay particular attention to protect computers within their jurisdiction from computer viruses and worms. A major challenge in defending against viruses and worms is that new viruses and worms are actively being developed and they are now designed to spread very fast. The Code Red virus of 2001 is considered the first global-scale worm attack. It affected 359,000 computers in less than 14 hours of being launched. The Slammer worm of 2002 reached 90% of its susceptible 75,000 targets in less than 10 minutes.[7]

How can organizations defend themselves against viruses and worms—particularly if new viruses and worms are emerging all the time and can cause extensive damage within minutes of release? Defense against viruses and worms typically involves two controls. The first is patching. Most viruses and worms are designed to exploit some vulnerability in software. Usually these vulnerabilities are known well in advance and patches for these vulnerabilities are almost always available. For example, the Slammer worm was released on January 25, 2003, and a patch to fix the vulnerability exploited by the worm had been issued by the vendor (Microsoft) six months earlier in July 2002. Computers that had applied the patch were immune to the worm.

The second control used to defend against viruses and worms is the use of antivirus programs. These programs are aware of a large number of viruses and worms. Antivirus programs constantly scan incoming network traffic (e-mails, web pages, etc.) to check whether the bytes in the traffic look like viruses or worms. When they do, the programs alert the user and delete the offending incoming viruses or worms before they can cause any damage.

Since viruses and worms are constantly being developed, and viruses can cause most of their damage within minutes of being released, much before the mainstream media becomes aware of their existence, the virus knowledge base of antivirus programs needs to be constantly updated with information about the newest viruses and worms. Hence, it is good practice to update the antivirus definitions regularly. If the antivirus program has the option to automatically apply updates, the use of the feature is highly recommended.

Patching and the use of antivirus software would have protected computers against the Slammer worm.

Not all available controls are technical. It is also important to educate users so that they are careful when they are on the network. For example, suspicious e-mail should be deleted, and suspicious links in e-mails should not be followed through. Only reliable websites should be visited. End-user awareness has many benefits and affects all aspects of organizational security, not just network security or information security.

## Denial-of-service attacks

A special kind of threat called a denial-of-service attack creates availability problems. *A denial-of-service (DOS) attack is when an attacker consumes the resources on a computer or network for things it was not intended to be doing, thus preventing*

---

[6] Lawrence A. G. M. P. Loeb, W. Lucyshyn, and R. Richardson. "CSI/FBI Computer Crime And Security Survey." *CSI/FBI Computer Crime and Security Survey,* GoCSI.com, Editor. 2006.
[7] www.caida.org/publications/papers/2003/sapphire/sapphire.html.

*normal use of the resources for legitimate purposes.* Home users are generally not much affected by DOS attacks, but occasionally, well-known websites have become unavailable because hackers or commercial rivals send a large volume of irrelevant traffic to the website. The computer becomes busy trying to process these unnecessary requests, and in doing so, is unable to respond to legitimate requests. These attacks are popularly called DOS attacks.

An excellent and highly readable analysis of a DOS attack is available at the companion website[8] in the readings for this chapter. Essentially, the site grc.com was brought down by a DOS attack initiated by a 13-year-old kid who bore a grudge against the administrator of grc.com. The analysis also shows how easy it can be to launch a DOS attack.

As described in the GRC case, a firewall is a good initial defense against a DOS attack. Once the source of the attacking packets is identified, a firewall rule can be added to block all incoming packets that match the rule. This prevents the offending packets from being able to reach their target and cause loss of availability. However, if the attack is consuming all of your incoming bandwidth, you may have to contact your upstream ISP to block it from reaching your network.

# Network security controls for outgoing information

What information security threats affect outgoing information? The major concern is that strangers may be able to read passwords and sensitive credit-card information as it passes through the network. Another important concern is that an occasional hardware or software failure may cause a website to become unavailable. The controls we will see in this section will defend against these threats.

## Controls for confidentiality

In 2006–2009, one of the most publicized incidents of information-security compromise related to the ability of a group of hackers to read credit-card data during transmission. The group exploited weak wireless security at T. J. Maxx to steal user names and passwords, ultimately using this information to steal over 40 million credit cards.

How do you prevent strangers from reading your passwords when you log into a remote website? After all, it is relatively easy to use network sniffers such as Wireshark to read packets flowing through a network. Is there anything you can do so that even if someone captures data packets leaving your computer, they could still not read the information contained in the packet? If strangers cannot read the information in the packets, how can you ensure that the target destination can read the information in the packets?

---

[8] Gibson, S. "The Strange Tale of the Denial of Service Attacks Against grc.com." 2001.

Thanks to the power of mathematics and to the efforts of researchers who have discovered the rules of mathematics that make it possible, we can indeed send information to a destination over wires in such a way that enemies cannot read the information in the wire even though the destination can easily read it. This is done through encryption. As shown in Figure 5, using encryption, Alice and Bob can carry on a private conversation even in the presence of enemies trying to snoop on the wire.

*Encryption is the process of rendering plain information unintelligible in such a manner that it may later be restored to intelligible form. The output from encryption is called ciphertext. Decryption is the process of converting ciphertext to plaintext.* Figure 5 shows the role of each of these activities in encryption. When using encryption to send data confidentially, the raw data for transmission is called plaintext. An encryption algorithm uses an encryption key to create ciphertext. The ciphertext is transmitted. The receiver uses a decryption algorithm and a decryption key to convert the ciphertext back to plaintext.

There are two general kinds of encryption techniques—symmetric key encryption and asymmetric key encryption.

## Symmetric key encryption

Recall questions on general intelligence tests that look like this—If *cat* is *dbu*, what is *dog*? This is a simple example of symmetric encryption. In this example, we observe that for each character of the plaintext (*cat*), the encrypted text (*dbu*) is created by picking the next letter of the alphabet. In semiformal terms, we may write this encryption scheme as:

Character in encrypted text = character in plaintext + 1

More generally, our encryption scheme can generate encrypted text by replacing each character in the plaintext with a character $n$ letters away in the alphabet. In our example, $n = 1$. In general, encryption involves an algorithm and a key. *An encryption algorithm is a mathematically expressed process to create ciphertext.* In our example,

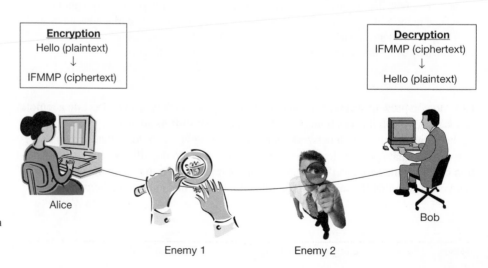

**FIGURE 5** Encryption prevents enemies from reading data

Encryption
Hello (plaintext)
↓
IFMMP (ciphertext)

Decryption
IFMMP (ciphertext)
↓
Hello (plaintext)

Alice

Bob

Enemy 1

Enemy 2

we may write the encryption algorithm as: add *n*. *An encryption key is a sequence of symbols that control the operation of the encryption algorithm.* In our example, we may write the encryption key as +1. This way, encryption algorithms use encryption keys to convert plaintext into ciphertext. Once we understand this scheme, it is easy to encrypt *dog* as *eph*.

Now, how would the receiver decrypt the encrypted text in this example? In other words, how would the receiver know that to decrypt the message, it has to subtract 1 from each character in the encrypted text? In our simple example, Bob could guess the key by simply looking at the ciphertext. In the more general case, before they begin communicating over the wire, Alice and Bob would have to agree upon both the encryption algorithm and the encryption key. This could happen in a face-to-face meeting at work. Or, Bob may send the algorithm and key through a courier or by mail. Whatever mechanism is used to exchange the encryption key, the wire cannot be used to exchange the encryption key because the enemies could read the key as it is being transmitted over the wire and successfully decrypt any information flowing through the wire.

Symmetric key encryption is so called because the same key is used for both encryption and decryption. In our example, we added 1 to encrypt and subtracted 1 to decrypt.

Symmetric key encryption has many advantages. Its biggest advantage is that it is computationally simple. However, its limitation is the key-exchange problem. Symmetric key encryption cannot be used to securely transmit the encryption key in such a way that the receiver can decrypt it but intruders cannot. Symmetric key encryption would be useful to secure network communication if a technique could be developed to solve the key-exchange problem. If we could somehow safely exchange the encryption key, no other known technique provides the same level of security for a given level of computation effort as symmetric key encryption. Fortunately, safe key exchange over an unsafe medium is possible using asymmetric key encryption.

Symmetric key encryption is very commonly used to store information. A number of symmetric encryption techniques have been developed for commercial use including the Data Encryption Standard (DES), International Data Encryption Algorithm (IDEA) and Triple DES. After evaluation, in 2001, the National Institute for Standards and Technology standardized a symmetric encryption technology called the Advanced Encryption Standard (AES) to securely store sensitive non-classified U.S. Government information. AES uses an encryption algorithm developed by two Belgian cryptographers.

## Asymmetric key encryption

We saw that the symmetric key cannot be exchanged over the network because our enemies would be able to read the key during the exchange. What if we could encrypt information in such a way that even if our enemies knew how the information was encrypted, they could still not decrypt it, even though the receiver could decrypt it easily? Miraculously, this is possible using asymmetric key encryption.

Instead of dealing with asymmetric key encryption in abstract terms, let us look at it by example.[9] Most asymmetric key encryption techniques involve the modulo

---

[9] This example is based on an example in *Network Security: Private Communication in a Public World* (2nd Ed.), by Charlie Kaufman, Radia Perlman, and Mike Speciner.

operation. Modulus is the remainder when a number is divided by another number. For example, when we divide 21 by 10, the remainder is 1. We write this as 21 mod 10 = 1. How can we use this operation for asymmetric key encryption?

An example of using the modulo operation for encryption is shown in Table 2. Asymmetric encryption uses mathematical operations and it is convenient to describe asymmetric encryption using numbers. This is not a limitation because, as we have seen in Chapter 2, text can be converted to numbers using ASCII or Unicode.

The example encrypts the 10 digits 0–9 using modulo 10. The plaintext is in the first row of Table 2 as $n$. To encrypt a digit, we multiply it by another digit $m$, and take modulo 10 of the product. Each row in Table 2 shows the result for the value of $m$ in the row. For example, in row 2, m = 0 and all cells in row 2 are 0 because n * 0 = 0, and 0 mod 10 = 0. Let us look at the highlighted row in Table 2, for m = 3. The first number, 0, is obtained as 0*3 mod 10, which is 0. To encrypt 4, we calculate 4*3 mod 10 = 12 mod 10 = 2. Similarly, we encrypt 9 using 9*3 mod 10 = 27 mod 3 = 7. The highlighted row shows the encrypted values for n using m = 3.

How do we decrypt these numbers? That is, given encrypted digit 7, how do we get back the unencrypted digit 9? Table 3 shows how the information encrypted in Table 2 can be decrypted. The first row in Table 3 is the ciphertext and is identical to the highlighted row in Table 2. To decrypt the numbers in this row, we multiply the numbers by 7 and take modulo 10 of the result. For example, to decrypt 3, we calculate 3*7 mod 10 = 21 mod 10 = 1. We can look at Table 2 and confirm that the decryption is correct, i.e., 1 was indeed encrypted as 3. As another example, to decrypt 1, we calculate 1*7 mod 10 = 7 mod 10 = 7. Table 2 shows that indeed, 7 had been encrypted as 1. Similarly, the decryption of all other numbers may be verified.

**Table 2**  Simple asymmetric key encryption example (mod 10 table)

| Number to encrypt $n$ → (plaintext) | $m$ ↓ | 0 | 1 | 2 | 3 | 4 | 5 | 6 | 7 | 8 | 9 |
|---|---|---|---|---|---|---|---|---|---|---|---|
|  | 0 | 0 | 0 | 0 | 0 | 0 | 0 | 0 | 0 | 0 | 0 |
| n * 1 mod 10 → | 1 | 0 | 1 | 2 | 3 | 4 | 5 | 6 | 7 | 8 | 9 |
| n * 2 mod 10 → | 2 | 0 | 2 | 4 | 6 | 8 | 0 | 2 | 4 | 6 | 8 |
| n*3mod10(ciphertext) → | 3 | 0 | 3 | 6 | 9 | 2 | 5 | 8 | 1 | 4 | 7 |
|  | 4 | 0 | 4 | 8 | 2 | 6 | 0 | 4 | 8 | 2 | 6 |
|  | 5 | 0 | 5 | 0 | 5 | 0 | 5 | 0 | 5 | 0 | 5 |
|  | 6 | 0 | 6 | 2 | 8 | 4 | 0 | 6 | 2 | 8 | 4 |
|  | 7 | 0 | 7 | 4 | 1 | 8 | 5 | 2 | 9 | 6 | 3 |
|  | 8 | 0 | 8 | 6 | 4 | 2 | 0 | 8 | 6 | 4 | 2 |
|  | 9 | 0 | 9 | 8 | 7 | 6 | 5 | 4 | 3 | 2 | 1 |

**Table 3**  Decryption in the example above

| Ciphertext (x) → | 0 | 3 | 6 | 9 | 2 | 5 | 8 | 1 | 4 | 7 |
|---|---|---|---|---|---|---|---|---|---|---|
| Decrypt using x * 7 mod 10 ↓ | | | | | | | | | | |
| Decrypted plaintext → | 0 | 1 | 2 | 3 | 4 | 5 | 6 | 7 | 8 | 9 |

How can Table 2 and Table 3 be used for encryption? Table 2 used mod 10 and multiplied plain-text by 3. If Alice wanted Bob to be able to send messages to her, she would send Bob the key (3, 10) over the wire where even her enemies might see the key as it was being transmitted over the wire. To encrypt messages, Bob would perform the operations in the highlighted row in Table 2. For example, Bob would send 2 as 6, 4 as 2, and so on. The result would be sent as encrypted messages over the wire. Even enemies would be free to read this encrypted message as it was transmitted over the wire. Since they would not know the decryption key (7, 10), they would not be able to decrypt the message, even though they would know the key (3, 10) that was used to encrypt the message. However, when the encrypted message reached Alice, Alice would decrypt the messages using the decryption key (7, 10).

Why do 3 and 7 work as an encryption-decryption pair when using modulo 10? It turns out that if we use modulo $n$, we can use any pair of numbers $(a, b)$ such that a*b mod n = 1. Since 3*7 mod 10 = 1, the pair can be used for encryption and decryption with modulo 10.

In our example, it would be easy for enemies to figure out the decrypting key (7, 10) from the encrypting key (3, 10) because the numbers are very small. If enemies know that Alice and Bob are using modulo 10 operations, it will not take them too long to figure out that the encryption-decryption pair is (3, 7). To prevent this, in real life, very large numbers are used. Current practice is to use modulo $n$ where $n$ is 1,024 or 2,048 bits long (300–600 decimal digits). It is believed that with current technologies, enemies would not be able to figure out how to decode such large numbers.

In our example, the encryption key (3, 10) would be publicly known and could be used by anyone who wanted to send an encrypted message to Alice. For this reason, asymmetric key encryption is popularly called public key encryption. The key used for encryption is shared publicly and is called the public key. The key used for decryption, (7, 10) in our example, is kept private and is called the private key.

The most popular implementation of asymmetric key encryption is RSA. RSA is named after its three creators—Rivest, Shamir, and Adleman.

Asymmetric key encryption can be used to encrypt data for transmission. However, as we can see from our example in Table 2, the security of asymmetric key encryption depends critically upon the use of very large numbers for security. It is extremely computation-intensive because of the use of large numbers. Therefore, the most common use of asymmetric key encryption is to exchange a symmetric key. Once the symmetric key is exchanged using asymmetric key encryption, the rest of the communication can be securely transmitted using secret key encryption. Most commercial encryption technologies, such as SSH and SSL (Secure Sockets Layer), which is used by e-commerce websites, use this procedure.

In the T. J. Maxx case, had the company used WPA, the current implementation of wireless security, it is unlikely that the intruders would have been able to read the passwords, even if they had obtained the encrypted versions of the passwords.

## Encryption in practice

Encryption is used in data communications in two common ways—virtual private networks (VPN) and Transport Layer Security (TLS). VPN was defined in RFC 2764 in 2000 and SSL was created by Netscape communications in 1995.

In VPNs, all the network traffic over a communication channel is encrypted. To implement VPN, a router at the edge of a network negotiates encryption schemes and keys with devices it communicates with. As a result, all the communication over the link is encrypted. Mobile computers in the organization can also negotiate encryption parameters with the edge router implementing VPN.

Figure 6 shows an example of using VPN. The VPN gateway at branch office 1 negotiates encryption parameters with all devices that wish to communicate with the branch office using VPN. The example shows how a laptop or another branch office would connect to branch 1 using VPN. These devices may use WAN links from different ISPs, but the data travelling across the WAN links would not be readable by anybody on the link. Connections from the outside world that do not use the VPN gateway would be treated as insecure and could be blocked by the inner firewall.

Transport Layer Security or TLS is the standardized version of SSL, which was created by Netscape communications. In TLS, a client application running on a computer negotiates encryption parameters with a server using TLS to secure the server application. TLS uses encryption in pretty much the same way as VPN, but the biggest difference is that TLS is used to encrypt traffic from specific applications. For example, TLS may be used to encrypt web-e-mail traffic and traffic for banking transactions, while traffic from other browser tabs may be sent unencrypted. All TLS encryption is done at the end devices without any need for specialized gateway devices as in VPN. Figure 7 shows an example of TLS. In the example, one tab in the browser connects to an informational website without encryption, and another tab connects to the bank's account details page using TLS encryption. If the user in Figure 7 used VPN, all the traffic leaving his laptop would be encrypted until it reached the VPN gateway.

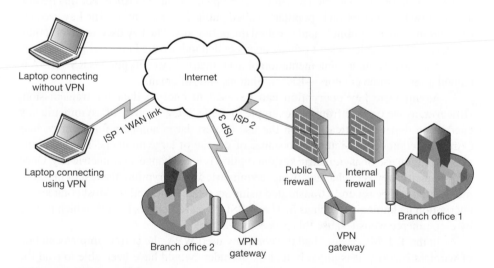

**FIGURE 6** VPN example

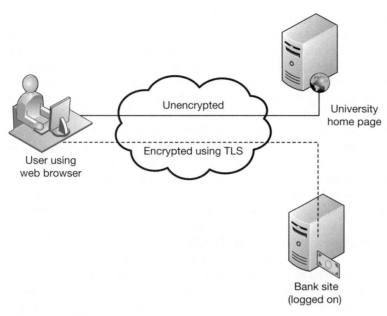

**FIGURE 7**   TLS example

## Controls for integrity

Encryption prevents an enemy from being able to read a message. Even if an enemy cannot read a message, it could cause considerable harm by simply damaging the message as it is transmitted. How is a receiver to know that the message it has received is indeed the message that the sender has sent? Error-detecting algorithms such as CRC (Chapter 3) may not work because the enemy can re-calculate any unencrypted CRC.

It turns out that asymmetric encryption can be used to also verify integrity. In our example, it may be verified from Table 2 and Table 3 that if Alice encrypts a message using her private key (7, 10) to send a message, Bob could decrypt it using Alice's public key (3, 10). If Alice wanted to assure Bob of the integrity of a message she was transmitting to him, then, in addition to the message, Alice could also send some additional information. Specifically, she could encrypt the message with her own private key and send the result as an integrity verifier. At the receiving end, Bob would use Alice's public key (which he has) to decrypt the integrity verifier. If the result is the same as the received message, Bob would be convinced that the message he has received could not have been modified along the way. This works because the enemy cannot know Alice's private key (assuming of course that Alice has kept it safely):

$$\text{Decrypt}_{\text{By Bob using Alice's public key}} (\text{Encrypt}_{\text{By Alice using Alice's private key}}(\text{Plaintext})) = \text{plaintext}$$
(done for integrity verification)

For reference, this can be contrasted with the operation used by Alice to send a secure message to Bob:

$$\text{Decrypt}_{\text{By Bob using Bob's private key}} (\text{Encrypt}_{\text{By Alice using Bob's public key}}(\text{Plaintext})) = \text{plaintext}$$
(confidential transmission)

In practice, to reduce the size of the integrity check, Alice could first create a summary of the message. The summary is called a digest and can be calculated in many ways. For example, a CRC may be used as a digest. More commonly, algorithms called MD5 or SHA are used to calculate the digest. As an integrity check, Alice can encrypt the digest with her private key and send the encrypted digest to Bob.

Upon receiving the message and the digest, Bob would decrypt the encrypted digest with Alice's public key. He can do this because he has Alice's public key. This would give him the unencrypted digest. Then, analogous to what is done in CRC verification (Chapter 3); Bob would compute the digest from the data sent by Alice and compare the results to the digest sent by Alice. If the two numbers match, Bob would be assured that the message was received without loss of integrity.

The reason this integrity check works is the same as the reason why encryption works. Even though the enemy knows the public key, it does not know the private key. Therefore, the enemy would not be able to figure out how to manipulate the digest in such a way as to successfully mislead Bob. If the enemy manipulates either the message or the digest, Bob will detect the change. Figure 8 shows how asymmetric key encryption can be used both as a control to protect outgoing data against confidentiality and also to protect against integrity threats. If Alice sends a message to Bob, for confidentiality, she uses Bob's public key, and for integrity she uses her own private key. The main thing to note about the figure is that the private key is only known to the owner of the key.

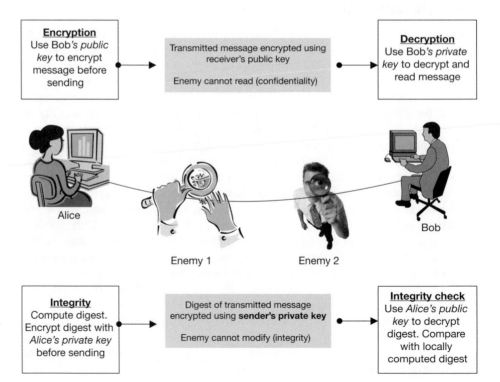

**FIGURE 8** Using asymmetric keys for confidentiality in transmission with integrity checks

## Controls for availability

On May 14, 2009, about 14% of Google's users experienced an outage that lasted about an hour beginning at 10:48 a.m. EST.[10] These users were unable to access e-mail and other Google applications such as Google analytics.

How could outgoing data become unavailable? The most common reason for outgoing data to become unavailable is a hardware or software failure that shuts some service down.

The most common control to mitigate availability threats in outgoing data is redundancy. *Redundancy is surplus capability provided to improve the availability and quality of service.* We saw an example of redundancy in Chapter 7 where we saw how most organizations maintain multiple DNS servers so that if one DNS server goes down, another DNS server can take its place. Similarly, most organizations maintain multiple web servers so that if one web server goes down, another can process user requests. Google maintains a highly redundant system. The outage of May 14, 2009, was the result of a system error.

Redundancy is also common with network connections. Most organizations maintain multiple network connections to the Internet so that if one connection goes down, another connection can be used to handle network traffic. Figure 9 shows network redundancy at MIT. The figure shows that MIT maintains six connections to the Internet. Among the networks used by MIT to maintain network redundancy are AS 174 – Cogent, AS 1239 – Sprint, AS 3356 – Level 3, and 11537 – Internet2.

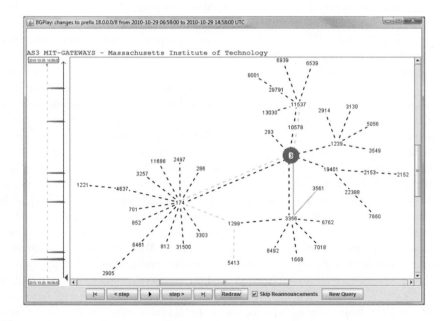

**FIGURE 9**  Network redundancy at MIT

---

[10] http://googleblog.blogspot.com/2009/05/this-is-your-pilot-speaking-now-about.html.

Most home users should consider using redundant data storage. The last few years have brought about a substantial change in the way we manage a very important part of our personal lives—photographs and videos that record our memories. Most of this information is now stored as computer files instead of photo prints. Consider using a RAID storage device to save these files. Computer hard disks can crash without warning and with it can go all the memories saved on the disk, never to be recovered again.

---

**CASE STUDY** | INTERNET VANDALS FORCE RETAILERS TO GUARD ONLINE DOORS: T. J. MAXX

---

*2007 was marked by some startling revelations of hackers getting access to credit-card databases at many of the leading retailers in the country including T. J. Maxx, Barnes and Noble, and Office Max. It was initially believed that the attacks were being led by hackers outside the country. However, the hacking spree culminated in the prosecution of 11 men in 5 countries, including the United States. The ring leader had been an informer for the U.S. Secret Service.*

On August 5, 2008, the U.S. government charged 11 individuals with wire fraud, damage to computer systems, conspiracy, criminal forfeiture, and other related charges for stealing credit-card information from prominent retailers such as T. J. Maxx, BJ's Wholesale Club, Office Max, and Barnes and Noble.

In August 2009, many members of the same gang were again charged with compromising Heartland Payment Systems, a credit-card processing company, and stealing approximately 130 million credit-card numbers. With approximately 100 million families in the United States, this translates to about 1 credit card per family being stolen.

The gang had been in operation since 2003. Between 2003 and 2007, the gang exploited weaknesses in wireless security at retail stores. This was the method the gang used in the attacks that formed the basis of the 2008 indictment. Beginning in August 2007, the gang refined its skill set and began to use SQL injection attacks to place malware on web applications and gain access to corporate databases. The gang used this method in the attacks for which it was indicted in 2009.

Albert Gonzalez, the ring leader, was a resident of Miami, Florida. Beginning around 2003, he is believed to have driven around Miami, using his laptop computer to locate insecure wireless access points at retail stores. Stores typically use these networks to transfer credit-

card information from cash registers to store servers. When an open network was located, the gang would use a custom-written "sniffer" program to collect credit-card account numbers, which were then sold in the gray market. The biggest victim was T. J. Maxx, which lost information on over 40 million credit cards. The information was stored on servers in the United States, Latvia, and Ukraine. Later, when the gang graduated to SQL injection attacks, it would visit stores to identify the transaction processing systems these companies used. The gang used this information to determine suitable attack strategies to target these companies. The gang also studied the companies' websites to identify their web applications and to develop appropriate attack strategies for these websites.

The ring-leader, Albert Gonzalez (Figure 10), earned over $1 million in profits by selling this card information. Apparently, at one time, his counting machine broke and he had to manually count $340,000 in $20 bills. In August 2009, Albert Gonzalez agreed to plead guilty to charges in the T. J. Maxx case, which had been filed in 2008.

Gonzalez became an informant for the Secret Service in 2003 after being arrested for various crimes. As an informant for the Secret Service, in October 2004, he helped the Secret Service indict 28 members of a website Shadowcrew.com. Shadowcrew stole credit-card information and sold it for profit. While in operation, Shadowcrew members stole tens of thousands of credit-card numbers. After the Shadowcrew operation was completed, however, Albert began his own exploits. Beginning with the wireless hacks into T. J. Maxx and other retailers, his attacks culminated in the SQL injection attacks against Heartland Payment Systems. In each case, he succeeded in obtaining tens of millions of credit-card numbers.

**FIGURE 10**   Albert Gonzalez, at the time of his indictment in August 2009

The direct damage from the attacks in terms of fraudulent charges on customer credit cards was limited. In March 2007, one gang in Florida was caught using cards stolen from T. J. Maxx (TJX) to buy approximately $8 million in goods at various Walmart and Sam's Club stores in Florida. However, the collateral damage from the incident has been colossal. TJX Companies, Inc. (TJX), (T. J. Maxx Stores is one of the companies owned by the group, Marshalls is another), settled with Visa for $40 million in November 2007 and with MasterCard in April 2008 for $24 million.

The impact was nationwide. Tens of millions of customers had to be reissued credit cards. Customers (including the author of this book) who had set up automated payments on these cards, received collection notices from service providers when charges did not go through because the cards had been cancelled and new ones had been issued in their place.

Surprisingly, sales at T. J. Maxx did not get significantly affected by the intrusion. Customers who noticed fraudulent charges had their accounts made good by the automatic protection programs offered by credit-card companies.

## REFERENCES

"Albert Gonzalez." Wikipedia. http://en.wikipedia.org/wiki/Albert_Gonzalez.

Gorman, S. "Arrest in Epic Cyber Swindle." *Wall Street Journal,* August 18, 2009.

Gorman, S. "Hacker Sentenced to 20 years in Massive Data Theft." *Wall Street Journal,* March 27, 2010, A1.

Pereira, J. "How Credit-Card Data Went Out Wireless Door." *Wall Street Journal,* May 4, 2007.

Pereira, J., J. Levitz, and J. Singer-Vine. "U.S. Indicts 11 in Global Credit-Card Scheme." *Wall Street Journal,* August 6, 2008), A1.

T. J. Maxx, *"10-K Report,"* March 28, 2007.

T. J. Maxx, *"8-k Filing,"* January 18, 2007; April 2, 2008; November 30, 2007.

*United States of America v. Albert Gonzalez* (the T. J. Maxx case), Criminal Indictment in U.S. District Court, Massachusetts, August 5, 2008.

*United States of America v. Albert Gonzalez* (the Heartland case), Criminal Indictment in U.S. District Court, New Jersey, August 17, 2009.

Zetter, K. "TJX Hacker Was Awash in Cash; His Penniless Coder Faces Prison." *Wired,* June 18, 2009.

## SUMMARY

This chapter described how network security is an important component of information security. Information-security controls mitigate threats to confidentiality, integrity, and availability of information. Information security and network security are becoming increasingly important as more components of our personal and professional lives revolve around computer networks and information.

In this chapter, we looked at controls that provide information security to data entering and exiting computer networks. With incoming data, we are primarily concerned that malicious attackers may be actively trying to harm our computers and information. With outgoing data, we are primarily concerned about preventing theft and manipulation of data as it flows through the network.

## ABOUT THE COLOPHON

A radical with a computer can cause more harm today than a radical with a gun. In this environment, it is difficult to put a humorous spin to computer and network insecurity.

However, the pithy remark by the *Farmer's Almanac* succeeds in doing just that.

# REVIEW QUESTIONS

1. What is *information security*? Why is it important?

2. What are *vulnerabilities*? Give some examples.

3. What are *threats*? Give some examples.

4. What are *controls*? Give some examples.

5. What is *confidentiality*? Give some examples showing a violation of confidentiality.

6. What is *integrity*? Give some examples showing a violation of integrity.

7. What is *availability*? Give some examples showing a violation of availability.

8. What is *network security*? Why is it important?

9. What controls can be used to ensure confidentiality from incoming threats?

10. How does authorization offer additional protection after authentication?

11. What controls can be used to ensure integrity in the presence of incoming threats?

12. What is a demilitarized zone? What are some of the network services offered in the demilitarized zone? What network services are not recommended to be offered in the demilitarized zone?

13. Recall your visit to a store that also includes a pharmacy. Describe how the organization of the store is similar to the two-tier firewall architecture used in network security.

14. What is a firewall? What are the capabilities of firewalls?

15. What are the limitations of firewalls?

16. What controls can be used to ensure availability in the presence of incoming threats?

17. How are viruses different from worms? Give an example of a well-known virus and a well-known worm.

18. What are *denial-of-service* attacks? What can you do to reduce the losses from denial-of-service attacks on your network?

19. What controls can be used to ensure confidentiality of outgoing information?

20. What is *encryption*? What is an encryption algorithm? What is an encryption key?

21. What are the advantages and limitations of symmetric key encryption?

22. What are the advantages and limitations of asymmetric key encryption? What is the most popular asymmetric-key-encryption technology?

23. Briefly describe how you can use asymmetric key encryption to ensure the confidentiality of outgoing information. Clearly show the sender, receiver, and how the two keys are used to provide confidentiality.

24. Briefly describe how you can use asymmetric key encryption to ensure the integrity of outgoing information. Clearly show the sender, receiver, and how the two keys are used to provide confidentiality.

25. What controls can be used to ensure availability of outgoing information?

# HANDS-ON EXERCISE

One of the most commonly used techniques to maintain network security is encryption. Encryption converts information into a form such that it cannot be read by intruders. This is very useful to prevent information leakage on the network. In this exercise, you will use Wireshark to capture and view encrypted traffic. An easy way to do this is to visit an e-commerce website, such as a bank, a retail store, or your university's student portal, and view the traffic after you authenticate yourself using your username and password. At that point, the website typically uses SSL to encrypt network data. Since you are familiar with Wireshark from Chapter 6, Wireshark will not be introduced here. Figure 11 shows a Wireshark capture after logging in to a secure site. In the figure, if you observe packet number 25 (the selected packet), you will notice that this packets starts a key exchange to switch from unencrypted transfer to encrypted data transfer. Packets following the key exchange are encrypted. Figure 12 shows the TCP stream of the encrypted packets. The most noticeable feature in Figure 12 is that the text is completely unreadable.

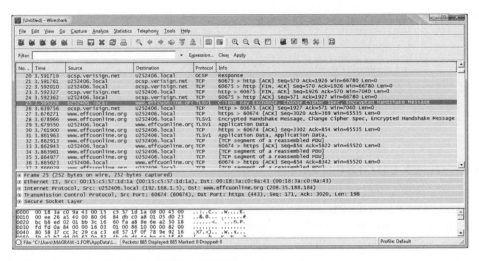

**FIGURE 11**  Transition from HTTP to HTTPS at secure website

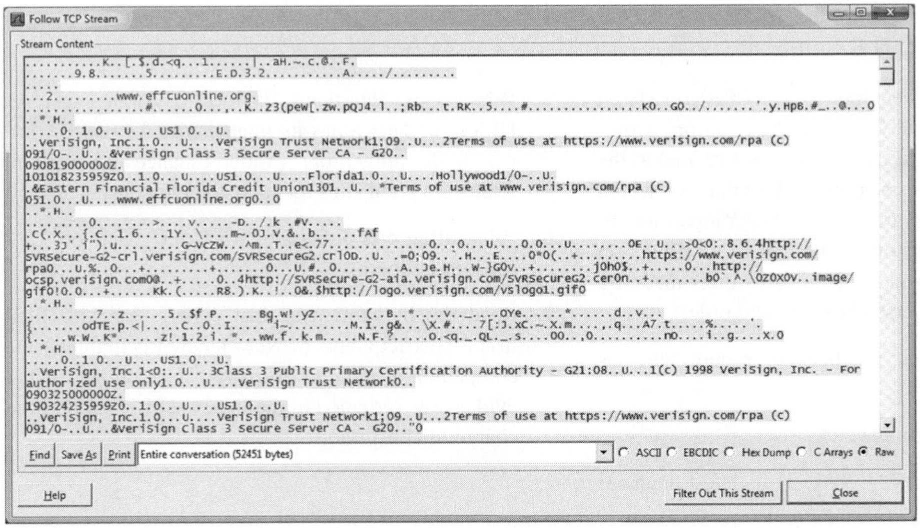

**FIGURE 12**  TCP stream showing encryption

## ANSWER THE FOLLOWING QUESTIONS:

1. Why is SSL useful?

2. Use Wikipedia or other information resources to write a brief summary of the evolution of SSL and TLS.

3. What is the port number used by the remote web server for SSL connections?

4. Right-click on a packet sent using SSL and select "Follow TCP Stream." Show the screenshot of the TCP stream.

## NETWORK DESIGN EXERCISE

Our network thus far is functional, but provides no protection for confidentiality and integrity of information transmitted over the WAN links. Therefore, Coolco has decided to invest in network security to protect its intellectual property. Answer the following questions:

1. How can a firewall help Coolco? Update your network diagram from Chapter 11 to include a firewall at Coolco's gateway to the Internet.

2. How can VPNs help Coolco in securing traffic that flows through its WAN? The routers included in the network in Chapter 9 have hardware capabilities to perform the encryption. Update your network diagram to reflect the VPN capabilities of the OSPF routers introduced in Chapter 9.

3. What encryption technology will you use to secure the wireless traffic in Amsterdam? Update your network diagram to reflect the encryption technology used in the wireless network.

## CASE QUESTIONS

1. Read the 10-K statement filed by T. J. Maxx on March 28, 2007, with the SEC. Use the section on "Computer intrusion" to list the major events related to the security breach at the company and the dates on which they occurred. (An easy way is to use Yahoo finance, search for TJX, and follow the link to all filings on EDGAR. On the resulting page, all filings made by TJX are listed in reverse chronological order).

2. What are some best practices to secure wireless networks?

3. What is a SQL injection attack?

4. Compare the sales at T. J. Maxx in its latest financial year and in 2007. Discuss any trends.

5. What does Heartland Payment Systems (NYSE: HPY) do? How does its financial performance compare to its competitors? (Yahoo Finance and Wolfram Alpha are good sites for such comparisons.)

6. What offense is defined by 18 U.S.C., Section 371? (Search online.)

7. Read the indictment against Albert Gonzalez filed in the District Court of New Jersey (available at the companion website or at many places online). What evidence is provided in the indictment to support the charge of conspiracy?

# Managerial Issues

*Let us raise a standard to which the wise and the honest can repair.*
—GEORGE WASHINGTON

## Overview

Most networks you will encounter in the professional world extensively use the technologies such as Ethernet, IP, and WANs covered in this book. In addition to the technical issues covered in earlier chapters, there are important nontechnical issues in using these technologies that are important to senior managers you will work with. Managers need to design and implement networks in ways that meet user needs and budgets. Networks need to be maintained to minimize downtime. Investment decisions for networking technologies will depend upon the maturity of technology standards to improve the interoperability of selected technologies with other technologies. Finally, many organizations, particularly the telecom carriers, are deeply affected by government policy and legal rulings. As a networking professional, you will be affected by all these issues. At the end of this chapter you should know about:

- a high-level overview of designing computer networks
- the important concerns in network management
- the process by which computer networking standards are developed
- the role of government and legal process in computer networks

## Introduction

Almost every student reading this book is likely to be the person responsible for maintaining their home computer network. These networks are small, built around a simple and inexpensive wireless router that also acts as a DNS and DHCP server for the internal home network as we saw in Chapter 7. The typical home network may have 1–10, devices including desktops, laptops, printers, etc.

Such a network is simple to maintain and generally requires no special knowledge on the part of home users to operate. As technology or user needs evolve at home, new components can be bought at big-box retail stores and added to the network in an ad hoc manner. Since these components are generally quite inexpensive, these expansions are usually done without serious consideration for costs, design, manageability, or future network expansion.

If the above is the extent of a person's involvement with computer networks, the information in the earlier chapters is enough to understand and operate computer networks. However, large networks cannot be operated in this manner. Ad hoc implementation and expansion of organizational networks will lead to very expensive and unreliable networks. Without good network design and implementation, if a user in a large network, such as a typical college or university, experienced an outage, it would become very difficult to locate the fault and fix the problem. Therefore, many managerial practices have evolved that help in cost-effective creation and maintenance of computer networks.

In earlier chapters, we have placed great emphasis on highlighting the efforts made to efficiently transfer data. Packetizing, layering, broadcasting, multiplexing, multi-part addressing, port-addressing, DNS, DHCP, and NAT are all examples of technological innovations that help in the efficient transfer of data over computer networks. It is only appropriate that we now also look at the nontechnical developments that help cost-efficient network operations. This chapter will focus on four important nontechnical innovations in computer networks that help computer networks meet user needs while keeping costs to the minimum—network design, network management, network technology standards, and legal issues.

## Network design

Thus far in this book, we have always assumed that a computer network is in operation and the focus was primarily on understanding how the network works. An example of such a network would be the computer network at a resort that was shown in the case study in Chapter 3. If you work in IT, or more specifically, in the networking group of a sizeable organization, eventually you will be involved in designing and installing a new network, or adding to an existing network. Typically, this would happen if the organization added a building or department, or merged with another organization. A formal design process improves the likelihood that the new network meets current and future user needs, is the most cost-effective solution available, uses the most appropriate technology, and addresses any organizational constraints. This section introduces the basic concepts of network design and implementation that you may find handy on such occasions.

*A design is a detailed description of a product or service.* Like any design project, the goal of network design is to meet current and foreseeable end-user needs, in a manner that minimizes costs over a specified time period. Costs include the costs of setting up the network initially and maintaining the network over the specified time period. If the network is too slow or unreliable, there are also costs associated with user downtime, when users are unable to perform their jobs because they could not access the network.

Rather than develop new design principles for networks, the basic principles of systems analysis and design have been adapted for network design. These principles are taught in the Systems Analysis and Design class you may have taken. A typical network design project will go through two stages: requirements analysis and physical design.

## Requirements analysis

Like any design and development project, the creation of a network begins with identifying the needs of end users. Most network users in professional offices and university campuses have typical network needs—web browsing, e-mail, and access to some enterprise applications. However, there usually are also pockets of users with intensive network needs—for example, graphic designers, who may need to exchange large media files or medical imaging applications which create and read very large high-resolution image files. Enterprise applications such as web servers also need high data-rate connections to the network because they are accessed by a number of users worldwide. At many universities, a good example of such an enterprise application that needs high-speed connectivity is the course portal where students access course materials, grades, etc.

During the requirements-analysis phase, the goal of network designers is to identify the different categories of users and applications. It is also necessary to determine their office locations within the organization so that the network can support high bandwidth at the required locations.

Fortunately, since most organizations already have computer networks in some form, data traffic needs are usually very well-understood. In addition to determining current needs, during the requirements-analysis phase, network designers also need to predict future network needs. Prior experience can provide baseline information on the growth rate of traffic. In addition, traffic growth comes from applications that are likely to be deployed in the future. For example, Voice over IP and desktop video conferencing are not very common right now, but are expected to soon become very popular, generating significant volumes of network traffic. The requirements-analysis phase is a good time to anticipate new networking applications that are likely to be deployed in the organization and plan for the network traffic that is likely to be generated by these new applications.

At the end of the requirements-analysis phase, it is a good idea to draw the logical network design. *The logical network design indicates the layout of the network, the subnets in the network, IP addressing and naming schemes used in the network, and management strategies used in the network.* Drawings of the logical network design provide a visual guide and facilitate group discussion. Drawings are a very effective tool to facilitate communication between end users and technical analysts. If the network does not adequately meet end-user needs, fixing the deficiencies later can be very expensive. It is therefore useful to carefully discuss and clarify current and future network needs with end users. If you don't, the end users will have to live with a suboptimal network for a long time.

To ensure that the logical design captures end-user needs, the logical diagram should show the total number of general-purpose desktops, servers, shared devices such as printers, and any devices with special network needs for every area of the network. Subnets should be indicated for each subnet, to help analysts determine the number of IP addresses available in each subnet for future expansion. The logical design also identifies network services such as DNS, DHCP, and network security and management utilities such as firewalls.

An example of a logical network design diagram for a small business specializing in video production is shown in Figure 1. In the example, the editing group needs

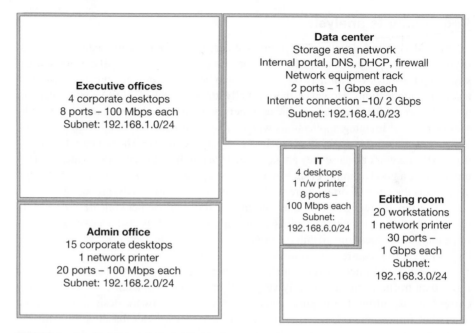

**FIGURE 1** Logical network design example

high bandwidth connectivity (1 Gbps) to its storage network, but the other groups only need plain desktop connectivity (100 Mbps). There are some extra network ports provisioned in every subnet for future expansion. The figure shows networked devices such as printers and portal servers. The connection speed to the external network is also shown. With a figure like this, all stakeholders can easily see the current and future capabilities of the proposed network. This facilitates identification of any missed requirements.

> Drawings serve another important function. They are repositories of organizational memory. It is said, "A picture speaks a thousand words." Long after the network has been implemented and the analysts and users who participated in the network design have left the organization, the drawings left behind are some of the most useful pieces of information to help future analysts and users in updating the network.

## Physical design

Once the logical design has been finalized, a physical network design is developed to deliver the functionality specified in the logical network design. *The physical network design indicates the technologies (for example, copper/fiber media for cabling; switches; routers; and data-link-layer technologies such as Ethernet) that will be used to implement the logical design.*

Since the rooms in the example of Figure 1 are adjacent to each other, all the links are likely to be shorter than 100 m long. Therefore, we can use LAN technologies

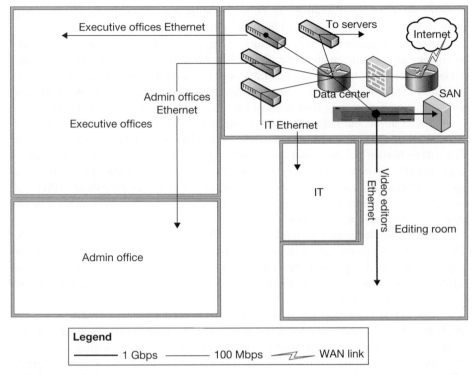

**FIGURE 2**    Physical network design example

to create the network for Figure 1. LANs were covered in Chapter 3. From Chapter 3, we know that the most popular LAN technology is Ethernet. Therefore, we could use an Ethernet in each subnet. There would be suitably placed Ethernet outlets in each room, one for each desktop or workstation. The cable from each such outlet would terminate in a port on the Ethernet switch. The storage area network and video work-stations could be located in one subnet served by a high-speed switch to isolate the high-speed traffic within the subnet. To create the subnets, we could use a router in the internal network. A firewall would provide the necessary protection for the internal network. With these choices, the physical network design for the example of Figure 1 will look as in Figure 2. Standard icons are used to denote switches, routers, firewalls, and the Internet. The legend indicates the symbols used to show the different LAN and WAN links.

## Implementation

It is commonly seen that when organizations implement computer networks, they cus-tomize the network design in each part of the network. This is driven by user needs as well as the preferences of network administrators. It is also common for networks to be built using equipment from a number of vendors. However, over time, it becomes cum-bersome and expensive to maintain expertise in using technologies from a number of vendors. Therefore, over time, organizations frequently standardize on one vendor for network hardware. Organizations also discover some common patterns and data-link-layer technologies that are used to implement the networks. Rather than try to create unique network designs for each building or department, they find it very convenient to implement networks using these standard patterns and technologies. Once a design is standardized, the network administrators can focus on developing deep expertise in the chosen technologies. This expertise helps them manage large networks with thousands, or even hundreds of thousands of routers, switches, and network devices.

For example, our network design example in Figure 2 used two different Ethernet technologies to implement the network—100 Mbps and 1 Gbps. Since the costs of Ethernet technologies have come down fairly significantly, it would also be possible to implement the entire network using 1-Gbps Ethernet. If we made this choice, the entire network would only use one switch model instead of two switch models as in Figure 2. In fact, many universities have indeed standardized on 1-Gbps outlets on all new and upgraded networks for this reason.

The network design examples shown in Figure 1 and Figure 2 are fairly simple. These simple examples have been used to introduce the components of logical and physical network designs. In general, to deal with the requirements of organizations of different sizes, network designs fall under three categories—building design, campus design, and enterprise design.

The simplest network consists of a few networked devices; all located within a single building. *A building network is a network that connects devices located within a single building.* The examples of Figure 1 and Figure 2 are examples of building networks. If the organization is successful, it grows, and expands to multiple buildings. When this happens, the data network needs to span multiple buildings. *A network that spans multiple buildings is called a campus network.* Since this market is large, the most recent updates to Ethernet have defined versions of Ethernet that can span up to 30 miles. Therefore, building and campus networks can typically be built using LAN technologies such as Ethernet these days.

Most networks begin their life as building networks. It is not unusual for the organization's earliest network to be patched together using off-the-shelf components bought from a computer retailer. However, as the network grows, it becomes important for the network to be designed to keep costs low (efficiency) and to allow future growth. A common method to accomplish that is to perfect the design for a building network and repeat the design in every building in order to create the campus network in a modular fashion. Such an approach is called a modular or building-block approach to network design.

After years of experience designing large networks, a common approach to designing campus networks has evolved. The network of a typical university is an example of a campus network. The campus network is typically organized into three layers—the core layer, the distribution layer, and the access layer. An example of a layered campus network is shown in Figure 3.

In a campus network, *the core layer is connected to all parts of the campus network and is responsible for fast and reliable transportation of data across the different parts of the network.* The core layer is also called the network backbone. All traffic between different parts of the network passes through the core. The network core is optimized for fast and efficient packet handling. *The distribution layer is the administrative layer of the network.* It organizes the network into subnets to minimize traffic that needs to be handled by the core. The distribution layer also uses policies to filter

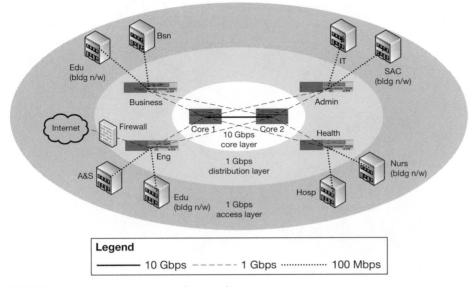

**FIGURE 3**    Layered campus network example

traffic, for example, by using firewalls and authentication to deny network access to unauthorized users. *The access layer is responsible for providing network ports to end users.* It typically comprises hubs and switches that organize the devices in a building into Ethernets. The aggregated traffic from these Ethernets is passed to the distribution layer for processing. The typical building network is at the access layer.

In the campus network example of Figure 3, the network has two high-speed routers at the core. Both the routers provide identical services and are configured to back each other up in case one of the routers fails. Each device in the distribution layer is connected to both routers so that the network is not affected from a failure in one of the core routers. The Internet connection is at one of the nodes at the distribution layer where a firewall can block unwanted connections. Buildings are also connected to the distribution layer.

Typically, there is redundancy in the core to ensure availability. But it is very expensive to create redundancy at the distribution and access layers because of the large number of devices at these layers. However, lack of redundancy at the distribution and access layers is an acceptable trade-off because a failure in one of the devices at these layers only affects network connectivity within an isolated part of the campus network.

If the organization grows even larger, and establishes offices in multiple locations around a state, country, or even the world, its network needs to expand beyond a campus network. The organization now needs WAN links to create a network that connects all the different offices. The network is now called an enterprise network. *An enterprise network is one organization's geographically scattered network.* The enterprise network connects campus networks at the organization's various locations. An ISP provides WAN connectivity between campuses. It is quite common for organizations to have offices in locations outside the service area of their ISP. In such cases, the ISP typically subcontracts with other ISPs to provide connectivity to all the campuses.

Figure 4 shows a typical enterprise network. As seen in the figure, most large organizations have a few large campuses with multi-tiered campus networks and a

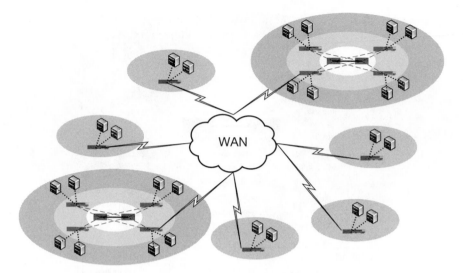

**FIGURE 4**    Enterprise network example

large number of smaller branches with smaller networks. All these sites are connected by a WAN operated by one of more telecom carriers (ISPs).

## Maintenance

After data networks are designed and implemented, they need ongoing maintenance. As can be seen from Figure 3 and Figure 4, networks are made of technical equipment. Like all machines, network equipment can fail, or degrade in performance. For example, hard drives crack after spinning at high speeds for a long time. Power supplies get overheated from power surges. Components also fail randomly. Other maintenance issues arise from the need to update software. When security vulnerabilities are identified in software, network administrators need to ensure that the updates supplied by vendors are tested and deployed to all network devices at the earliest opportunity. Finally, users often install software on their local computers and ignore applying updates to such locally installed software. If such locally installed software has security vulnerabilities, remote attackers can exploit the vulnerability and put the organization at risk. Network maintenance attends to all these ongoing issues.

*Network maintenance is the set of activities performed to keep networks in a serviceable condition or to restore them to serviceability. It includes activities such as inspection, testing, and servicing.* Broadly speaking, therefore, network maintenance requires regular monitoring and updating of both hardware and software on all the computer equipment in an organization. As organizations get large, it becomes prohibitively expensive to perform such monitoring and updating manually. For example, the network of a typical state university is likely to have more than a thousand network devices such as switches and routers and over ten thousand desktops and laptops. If all these devices were to be scanned periodically by a human administrator for maintenance, most universities would have to hire too many IT administrators, seriously hampering the universities' ability to invest in other innovative applications. Therefore, tools have been developed to perform most of these activities automatically.

Broadly speaking, these tools fall into two categories—tools to identify problems in network hardware and tools to identify software vulnerabilities.

## Maintaining network hardware

Remote monitoring is the standard procedure used to identify problems in network hardware. The technology industry has long been aware of the need to facilitate remote monitoring of computer hardware. An important development in this area was the development of network management protocols, specifically the Simple Network Management Protocol (SNMP). *SNMP is a protocol used to manage and control IP (Internet protocol) devices.* SNMP was introduced in RFC 1157 in 1990 based on the idea that "management information for a network element may be inspected or altered by remote users." Devices that can be managed store configuration information in a database called the management information base (MIB). Only information that is essential for fault management or configuration management is included in the device's MIB.

The SNMP architecture is shown in Figure 5. A managed network has one or more network management stations and a large number of managed network elements such as hosts, switches, and routers. Managed network elements include management agents. Management agents are software responsible for performing the network management functions requested by the network management stations. SNMP communicates management information from the MIB between the network management stations and the agents in the network elements. Management stations run management applications such as Openview or Spiceworks to monitor and control the managed network elements.

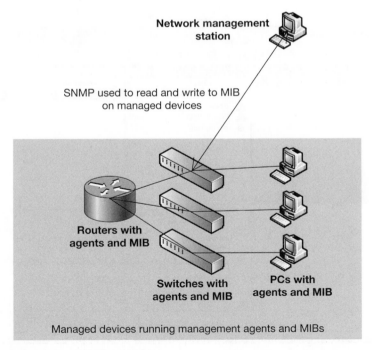

**FIGURE 5**    SNMP architecture

A network with about a thousand managed elements (a typical college), with about a hundred information items per element has about a hundred thousand items of information that need to be monitored by the network administrator. With SNMP, the management application on the network management station can poll all the managed elements, say, once per hour and observe the status of all the information items. If any discrepancy is observed, the management application can alert the administrator by e-mail, SMS, phone, page, or other mechanism. Thus, using SNMP, the network administrator can focus on his work and attend only to configuration problems and failures when they arise. The user interface of the management application on the network management station can help the administrator quickly identify issues that need attention. These identified issues can be dealt with manually.

## Maintaining software

The primary concern with maintaining network software is to ensure information security in the organization. Therefore, network administrators are interested to know the vulnerability status of all operating system and application software installed on all the devices in the network. Vulnerabilities that are thus located need to be fixed to prevent attacks on the network.

A common approach to identify vulnerabilities on the network is to use network-vulnerability scanner software to scan all devices on the network. Vulnerability scanners can scan all specified devices on a network for vulnerabilities. Like virus scanners, network vulnerability scanners use rules to identify vulnerabilities on the scanned devices. A popular vulnerability scanner is Nessus. A sample report from a Nessus scan on a host is shown in Figure 6. The report shows vulnerabilities in applications listening on

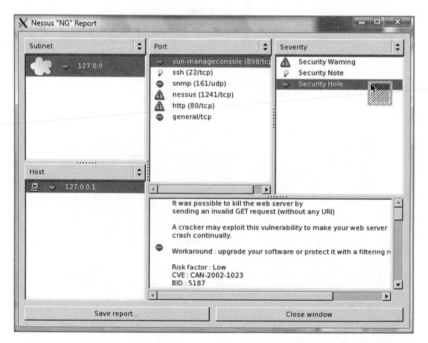

**FIGURE 6**   Sample Nessus report

ports 898 and 161. It also indicates open ports (22) and warnings on certain applications (ports 1241 and 80).

As seen in Figure 6, to help administrators, where possible, vulnerability scanners point to the common vulnerabilities and exposures (CVE) database.[1] The CVE database is a database maintained by the IT industry to centralize information on all identified software vulnerabilities. The CVE database helps users and vendors gather information about software vulnerabilities and disseminate information to fix these vulnerabilities. Here users can gather more information about the vulnerability.

## Standards

An important administrative development on the Internet is the use of technology standards. In all your experience on the Internet, most likely you have never had problems using any Internet service from anywhere in the world on any computer running any operating system. Because of the use of standardized technologies on the Internet, when you send e-mail, you are free to use any e-mail client of your choice, without concern for the operating system or brand of the e-mail server software. Similarly, when you visit websites, you are able to visit websites in any country, without concern for the operating system or brand of web server running the website. If you use wireless networks for connectivity on your laptop, you are able to move seamlessly from your home wireless network to the wireless network at school without any changes to your network hardware.

Compare this easy connectivity on the Internet to some other comparable situations you encounter. You probably have a different charger for each powered electronics device you use. Most likely, each such device also uses a different battery. In many cases, you can't even use cables from one device with another device.

> In a very well-publicized event in 2006, popular TV hostess Martha Stewart came prepared at a conference of CEOs to highlight the problems created by the lack of standards in electronics devices. In view of everybody present, she pulled out all the wires and chargers in her bag and asked Howard Stringer, the CEO of Sony, why she needed to carry so many chargers and cords for her electronic devices. The incident attracted a lot of publicity. Eventually, in February 2009, the leading mobile phone manufacturers announced their commitment to develop an industry standard for a charger usable with all new mobile phones.[2]

The lack of uniformity is pervasive. If you drive internationally, you will find that people in many countries drive on the left side of the street. Power outlets look different in each country and even supply power at different voltages, 220 volts being quite popular. If you travel abroad, you will need to carry special adapters to power electronic equipment purchased in America. In video, some countries use the PAL TV standard for conventional TV broadcast, whereas the United States uses NTSC.

---

[1] http://nvd.nist.gov/.
[2] The companion website has articles reporting on the incident.

Therefore, you cannot play DVDs purchased in many countries abroad on DVD players in the United States.

By comparison, Internet applications are remarkably well-behaved. You can use a PC, a MAC, a Linux laptop, or even a smart phone, and connect to almost any networked application hosted anywhere in the world. All this is possible because of the existence of technology standards on the Internet and the adherence of software and hardware vendors to these standards. In fact, the Internet may be the most standards-compliant global system ever created.[3]

*Standards are documents, established by consensus and approved by a recognized body, that provide, for common and repeated use, rules, guidelines, or characteristics for activities or their results, aimed at the achievement of the optimum degree of order in a given context.* More simply, standards are rules that ensure interoperability. Standards help developers, working independently of each other, to create products that are guaranteed to interoperate with other standards-based products.

Standardization on the Internet has benefited both customers and the industry. Standardization allows multiple vendors to enter the market, creating devices that are guaranteed to be compatible with devices sold by other vendors. The existence of multiple vendors creates competition in the industry, which generally lowers prices. Lower prices make technology affordable to a larger group of customers, creating an even larger market for vendors.

Many organizations have been involved in developing standards used on the Internet. Two of these are extremely important to most end users of the Internet— IEEE and IETF. The Institute for Electrical and Electronics Engineers (IEEE) develops standards used at the data-link layer in Ethernet and wireless LANs. Examples of such standards include 802.3 (Ethernet) and 802.11 (wireless). The Internet Engineering Task Force (IETF) develops standards used at the network, transport, and application layers. Examples of these standards include IP, TCP, UDP, HTTP, SMTP, POP, IMAP, SSH, and SNMP.

The development of standards usually follows a well-established procedure. Standards development begins with the identification of a user need that is not met by current technologies. There is general agreement in the IT industry about the organization that is in the best position to lead the development of a standard for the identified need. For example, the IEEE takes the lead in developing data-link-layer standards for LANs. The International Telecommunication Union (ITU) takes the lead in developing WAN standards. The IETF takes the lead in developing standards for protocols at the network, transport, and application layers. The lead organization for the standard establishes a working group to specify requirements for the proposed standard. These requirements are such that they can be implemented with current technologies at reasonable costs. Companies and expert groups next propose technical solutions to implement the proposed requirements. Members of the lead organization then vote on the various proposed solutions to identify a solution that wins an overwhelming majority of the vote. If no solution obtains an overwhelming majority, voting is conducted in multiple rounds, candidates with very few votes are eliminated, and the process

---

[3] The phone system is probably the only other system that is comparably standardized across the globe.

continues until one solution emerges as a clear winner. This solution is published as the standard for the technology. Vendors then bring products based on the standard to the market.

A very good example of the standards development process is the development of the IEEE 802.11n wireless standard.[4,5] After the IEEE approved the development of the standard, proposals were invited to implement the standard. In the first round, 4 complete and 28 incomplete proposals were received. At the working group's meeting in November 2004, all 4 complete proposals obtained the required number of votes for further consideration, and the 28 incomplete proposals were eliminated from further consideration. At the group's next meeting, only 3 of the 4 proposals were presented, and one of the three proposals was voted down, leaving two candidate proposals. In March and May 2005, one of the two proposals secured a majority, but not an overwhelming majority that is required by the IEEE for the acceptance of a proposal. As per procedure, this reinstated all three of the previously rejected proposals into the voting process. Eventually, the advocates of three proposals decided to merge their efforts. The resulting proposal secured the desired majority and work began on refining the initial draft by incorporating the changes suggested by the working group. The 802.11 n standard was finalized in September 2009.

Most communication standards have emerged through the standards development process. Therefore there is a high degree of interoperability in communication technologies. However, it is important to remember that many important computing standards have developed due to the efforts of individual companies. For example, Windows, Java, and Office are important computing standards whose development has been spearheaded by individual companies or a consortium of companies.

If a company can create a non-standardized technology that becomes extremely popular, it can be highly profitable because customers interested in using the technology have no choice but to use the products supplied by the company. This gives the company monopoly pricing power. Customers of the technology can also get locked-in with the company's products, requiring them to buy upgrades and other connected products from the same company. Therefore, standardization often creates battles between competing firms or groups of firms, with dominant firms trying to resist the standardization process and other firms promoting standardization.

## Government involvement, legal issues

Throughout the book, we have focused primarily on the role of technical institutions in the development of the Internet and related technologies. We have paid very little attention to the role of government and the judicial system in influencing the development and adoption of communication technologies.

---

[4] http://standards.ieee.org/board/nes/projects/802-11n.pdf.
[5] http://grouper.ieee.org/groups/802/11/Reports/tgn_update.htm.

In general, developments on the Internet have been led by commercial interests. The government has not played a significant role in the day-to-day evolution of Internet technologies. However, the government has played a very constructive role at critical points in the development of the technologies. This section highlights some of these developments.

## The development of packetization and TCP/IP led by the Department of Defense

It is quite possible that the Internet as we know it today would not have existed without the efforts of the U.S. Department of Defense (DoD) to develop a robust communication system that would continue to function in the event of a large-scale war. This effort led to funding for the development of packetization and related packet transfer technologies, TCP and IP. Related efforts also put in place other building blocks of the modern Internet, such as DNS.

Being a government body, and not treating TCP/IP as a classified technology, the U.S. Department of Defense made these taxpayer-funded technologies freely available for general use, without a profit motive. This allowed early UNIX implementations to use TCP and IP for networking, bringing the technologies within reach of a wider audience. The DoD also insisted that TCP/IP should be used for network functionality in all computer software sold to the DoD. To improve TCP/IP technology, the DoD also funded the development of a communication network, the ARPANET, which functioned from 1969 to 1990.

Eventually, all computer manufacturers replaced their proprietary network- and transport-layer networking technologies with TCP and IP, enabling TCP/IP to provide a standard platform for computer communication across the globe.

## The early Internet, funded by the National Science Foundation

The National Science Foundation (NSF) is the primary agency of the U.S. government that funds research in nonmedical disciplines. NSF initiated a program in 1985 to fund the development of a nationwide network, NSFNET, to serve the entire academic community in the United States. NSF required U.S. universities requesting NSF funding for an Internet connection to make the connection available to all departments on campus. This initiative liberated the Internet from the confines of Computer Science departments and enabled nontechnical departments to get access to the Internet. NSF chose to use TCP/IP for the NSFNET program, thereby introducing the Department of Defense's TCP/IP to the nontechnical community. In some sense, NSFNET may be considered the earliest version of the Internet.

NSFNET functioned until 1995, by which time the Internet had become wildly popular and commercial service providers had emerged to offer the functionality provided by NSFNET, even to home users. In April 1995, funding for NSFNET was stopped, and universities began to use commercial ISPs for Internet connectivity.[6]

---

[6] Leiner, B. M., V. G. Cerf, D. D. Clark, R. E. Kahn, L. Kleinrock, D. C. Lynch, J. Postel, L. G. Roberts, and S. Wolff, "A Brief History of the Internet." www.isoc.org/internet/history/brief.shtml (accessed April 30, 2010).

## The development of the web browser at the National Center for Supercomputing Applications

TCP and IP were very useful for computer communication. However, early applications that used TCP and IP were not very user friendly. The primary mechanism for interacting with these applications was through the command line interface (CLI). The DOS prompt that you have used in the hands-on exercises of earlier chapters is an example of the command line interface. Most users are very uncomfortable with the command line. Therefore, the Internet did not become useful for the masses until the graphical web browser was developed. This happened at the National Center for Supercomputing Applications (NCSA) at the University of Illinois. Two students at the center, Marc Andreessen and Eric Bina, developed a graphical web browser for UNIX computers. The first version of the browser was released on January 23, 1993, as an application that ran on X-Windows, the UNIX GUI. Soon thereafter, the browser led to the boom in the PC industry, e-commerce, the dot-com era, and related developments. The dot-com boom ended badly for many investors, but the user-friendly web has changed our lives forever.

NCSA and the students who developed the first browser were largely funded by the U.S. National Science Foundation.

## Wireless spectrum

We saw in Chapter 11 how the government has identified some wireless bandwidth for free use by wireless LAN and other technologies. This allocation of bandwidth has enabled the development of many generations of 802.11 WLAN technologies. This, in turn, has enabled free wireless Internet access at many offices and commercial establishments, allowing professionals to become more mobile using laptops. Without the availability of this free ISM bandwidth, cell phones would probably have been used for wireless LANs. This would have raised the costs of wireless Internet access because cell phone service is not free. It would not have been surprising if the costs of wireless Internet access would have been comparable to the costs of using a cell phone.

## AT&T split

We saw in Chapter 12 how the government took an active role in breaking the monopoly of AT&T in the phone business in the United States. In 1982, the U.S. government and AT&T settled on a judicial agreement that generated competition in long-distance phone calls. The government initiates such antitrust proceedings when it believes that a company is using its monopoly position in an industry in an unfair manner. Antitrust proceedings are contentious and often controversial. However, the authority of the government to intervene and prevent the misuse of monopoly power is well-recognized. The AT&T divestitures are a good example of the government's role in preventing abuse of monopoly power. Today, two decades after that judgment, competition and technology development has made long-distance phone service almost free, even to many international destinations.

We also saw how the courts and the legislature were involved in the process of enabling competition in the phone industry, ultimately changing the law that governed how telecommunication companies operated in the United States. In 1996, the Telecommunications Act was passed to open all forms of communication to competition. As a result, today we are beginning to see the web emerge as a viable competitor to cable TV service.

## Net neutrality debate

At the current time, the government is involved in a debate between the telecommunication companies, such as Verizon, and information service providers, such as Google. Google is a search-engine company that is trying to establish a presence in voice telephony, primarily through Google Voice. When a call is made to any number of a Google Voice subscriber, a ring is heard at all the registered phone numbers of the subscriber. The subscriber can pick up any one of these phones to take the call. Cell-phone service providers believe that though Google can find ways to earn revenues from the idea, their own networks are likely to get heavily burdened from the additional call volume. They also believe that Google is not likely to compensate the carriers for carrying this traffic. Cell-phone companies have therefore occasionally blocked Google Voice calls from being forwarded on their networks. Google believes that all traffic on a network should be treated equally; i.e., carriers should be neutral about the source of traffic and should treat all data packets neutrally. Hence the term, "net neutrality."

The telecommunications industry believes that if cell-phone providers are not allowed to decide how to charge for different traffic streams flowing on their networks, and other companies can send traffic through their networks for free, they will have no incentive to invest in upgrading their networks. After all, why should cell-phone companies bear the expenses of upgrading and maintaining their networks if other service providers can push traffic through these networks without compensating the cell-phone companies.

The issue has not yet been settled. It is, however, clear that the government, courts, and the legislature will play key roles in resolving the dispute in a manner that helps new services to be created without discouraging investments to upgrade the telecommunication infrastructure in the country.

In general, government has three roles—executive, regulatory, and legislative. We saw in this section that the involvement of the government in data communications has emerged from all these three roles of the government. In the executive role, the government is one of the largest users of technology and invests in technology development to meet its own needs. In this role, the government funded the development of TCP, IP, and a host of other Internet technologies in widespread use today. When a technology developed by the government is not considered confidential, it is made available for civilian use. If there is demand for any such technology, commercial vendors integrate the technologies into consumer products. The GPS system is another example of such a technology developed by the government for its own needs, but which is now available for civilian use.

The second role of the government is that of a coordinator or a regulator. In this role, the government envisions itself as a protector of consumer interests over corporate greed. As a regulator, the government intervenes, as in the case of AT&T, when it believes that consumer interests are being harmed by a company with monopoly power in the market.

The government, in its regulatory role, also facilitates the allocation of scarce resources. Though most resources in the world are allocated through the price mechanism, the government has historically coordinated the allocation of scarce wireless spectrum to protect the public interest. For example, the government believes that general news should be accessible to everybody, not just those who can pay for expensive cable service. Therefore, wireless bandwidth for broadcast TV has been made available at almost no cost to the broadcast channels. Similarly, the ISM bandwidth has been allocated for free use over very short ranges and has been extremely useful in enabling wireless LANs. Other frequencies made available to agencies for free by the government include frequencies for police, fire, and the Department of Defense.

In the legislative role, the government passed the Telecommunications Act in 1996 to generate competition in all telecommunication services. The industry is continuing to evolve in response to this development in the legal infrastructure of the country.

---

**CASE STUDY** | AS NETWORKS GO FAR, COWORKERS & PHYSICIANS GET CLOSER: TELEWORK, TELEMEDICINE

---

*The cases in the previous chapters have looked at how computer networks have affected various industries. As we come to the end of the book, it is time to see how computer networks are helping the people who work in these industries. Computer networks are enabling new work practices, changing old practices, and lowering business costs across industries. With the help of computer networks, many professionals are able to work from homes and central offices, saving commute time and bringing world-class services to the remotest corners of the world.*

Consultant Jack Nilles is credited with coining the terms "teleworking" and "telecommuting" in 1973. *Teleworking is any substitution of information technologies for work-related travel.* Teleworking moves work to the workers instead of moving the workers to work. Telecommuting is a form of teleworking where workers work away from their primary office space, at least one day per week.

Telecommuters may work at home, client sites, or at a telework center. Telecommuting substitutes information technologies for the commute to work.

Telecommuting is gaining popularity in the United States and around the world. In 1997, approximately 3.6 million people were telecommuting. According to an estimate by Forrester Research, this number exceeded 34 million in 2009. With a U.S. civilian workforce of slightly over 150 million, this implies that slightly over 22% of the U.S. workforce telecommutes. Technology companies such as IBM and AT&T are big adopters of telecommuting.

Telecommuting offers many advantages and some risks. Real-estate cost savings can be considerable. CISCO estimates annual savings of $277 million (compared to annual profits of $6 billion) from telework and telecommuting. During the workday, employees generally find fewer distractions at home than at work and can therefore be very productive. Employees report significant increase in productivity and overall satisfaction as a result of their ability to telework. There are also other social benefits that are not captured by the organization such as reduced traffic congestion and lower fuel consumption.

Telecommuting has risks. Many workers are not able to separate their work and professional lives effectively. Telecommuters can feel left out of happenings in the workplace. The productivity of workers involved in activities that need face-to-face interaction can be dramatically reduced through telecommuting. While technology can facilitate telecommuting, it cannot address these risks. These risks have to be managed through well-developed managerial practices.

The field of medicine has successfully developed variations of telework to reduce medical costs and to bring medical expertise to remote regions of the world. This is called telemedicine. *Telemedicine is the application of computer networks to transfer medical information through the phone or Internet for medical consultation, and even to remotely provide medical examinations and procedures.*

Telemedicine traces its origins to NASA's space program, which developed procedures in the 1960s to serve astronauts in outer space. In the best known examples of telemedicine, medical data like medical images and bio-signals (such as ECGs and EEGs) are transmitted to doctors or medical specialists for assessment. Even in traditional medicine, such assessment is not done face to face and the information required for such assessment can be completely digitized. Therefore, such assessments are excellent candidates for telemedicine.

In another category of telemedicine, medical professionals use networking technologies and applications to remotely monitor patients with chronic diseases or specific conditions, such as heart disease, diabetes, or asthma. Not only does remote monitoring reduce the need for patients to commute to hospitals and clinics, it can be cost-effective and provide health outcomes comparable to traditional medical visits.

In the most advanced category of telemedicine, telemedicine can be interactive and provide live interactions between patients and providers. Psychiatric evaluations and ophthalmology assessments are considered prime candidates for interactive telemedicine.

## Advantages of Telemedicine

Telemedicine offers many advantages. Rural populations that typically do not have the resources to support specialty-care clinics can be served by telemedicine using video consultations. Such technical solutions can significantly reduce costs for patients. Additionally, healthcare workers in isolated or low-income areas can undergo regular continuing-education programs using simple video technologies.

## Barriers to Telemedicine

As with most technology-driven advancements, barriers continue to exist that prevent rapid adoption of telemedicine. Many states require state licenses to provide medical consultations to patients in the state. Physicians have to consider the possibility of malpractice suits if a patient is dissatisfied with the treatment. Many physicians are not comfortable with information technology and have strong preferences for personal interactions with patients. Reimbursement practices of many private insurers and Medicare may discourage telemedicine. Many target sites lack appropriate telecommunications infrastructure because rural areas still generally lack access to high-bandwidth data networks to transmit video and medical images. Regular telephone lines are available everywhere, but provide insufficient bandwidth for telemedicine applications. Unfortunately, therefore, telemedicine may be least available to those who could benefit most from it.

## Telemedicine success

To end the case, chapter, and text on a positive note, let us look at a recent success story in telemedicine. After the earthquake in Haiti on January 12, 2010, the University of Miami established a 240-bed tent hospital near the airport in Port-au-Prince, Haiti. Volunteer surgeons from the United States have performed over 1,000 on-site surgical procedures at the site. For ongoing operations, experts who helped develop telemedicine applications for space shuttles have installed systems to enable on-site doctors to consult with specialists in Miami and other medical centers via satellite. The satellite connection will provide sufficient bandwidth for telemedicine consultations and is unlikely to be affected by terrestrial phenomena. While it is difficult for busy physicians to stay for long at disaster sites, after a visit, they are usually available for telemedicine consultations. If video sessions are necessary, e-mail and secure Internet messaging is used to exchange pictures, X-rays, and pathology reports beforehand to optimally use physician time during the video session.

## REFERENCES

CISCO. *"Cisco Study Finds Telecommuting Significantly Increases Employee Productivity, Work-Life Flexibility and Job Satisfaction."* http://newsroom.cisco.com/dlls/2009/prod_062609.html (accessed 2/12/10).

Freudenheim, M. "In Haiti, Practicing Medicine from Afar." *New York Times,* February 9, 2010, D5.

Healy, M. *"Wounded Soldier's Shattered Pancreas Gets Replaced in a Whole New Way."* Los Angeles Times, December 15, 2009. http://latimesblogs.latimes.com/booster_shots/2009/12/ wounded-soldiers-shattered-pancreas-gets-replaced-in-awhole-new-way.html (accessed February 13, 2010).

Jala International. www.jala.com.

Jennings, J. *"Less Is More: How Great Companies Use Productivity."* New York: Portfolio (Penguin Putnam), 2002.

Mariani, M. "Telecommuters." *Occupational Outlook Quarterly* (Fall 2000).

Nilles, J. M. "Telecommunications and Organizational Decentralization." *IEEE Transactions on Communications 23(10)* (October 1975).

Schadler, T., and M. Brown, *"US Telecommuting Forecast, 2009 to 2016."* www.forrester.com/rb/Research/us_telecommuting_forecast,_2009_to_2016/q/id/46635/t/2, 03/11/2009 (accessed 2/12/10).

U.S. Bureau of Labor Statistics, "Table A-1." http://stats.bls.gov/ news.release/empsit.t01.htm (accessed 2/12/10).

*"Telemedicine."* Wikipedia. http://en.wikipedia.org/wiki/Telemedicine.

## SUMMARY

This chapter introduced the managerial and procedural issues in computer networking. Computer networks are designed following standard systems-analysis and design procedures. Some standard designs have evolved to build networks. These standard designs are used in a modular manner to create larger networks. Once deployed, hardware and software in networks need to be monitored and maintained. Protocols such as SNMP have been developed to automate many of these maintenance functions.

Computer networks have benefitted immensely from the development of standards for communication. As a result, users can use any network application running on any operating system and hardware to communicate with applications running on any other operating system and hardware. Many organizations, including the IEEE, ITU, and IETF, are responsible for the successful development of these standards.

Over the years, the government has played a very significant role in funding the development of many critical components of the Internet. These include the TCP and IP protocols, the early Internet, and the early Internet browser. The regulatory role of the government has also become increasingly important in facilitating the orderly development of business data-communication technologies.

## ABOUT THE COLOPHON

Standards are extremely important elements in ensuring the smooth operation of a community. This book has focused on technical standards that are important for data communications. Standards exist in many other technical domains as well, for example, the voltage levels on a wire.

But standards can have even wider impacts. As the colophon to the chapter indicates, the constitutional convention, which created the Constitution of the United States, started with the goal of creating a standard documenting the highest ideals for a society. The resulting standard is the Constitution of the United States. For years, this standard has served as a guiding light for lawmakers in creating laws, rules, and conventions that govern life in the United States. Standards can help guide activities whenever coordination among multiple entities is required to accomplish a goal.

# REVIEW QUESTIONS

1. What are the goals of network design and implementation?

2. What are some of the important pieces of information you should gather during the requirements-analysis phase of network design?

3. What is a logical network design?

4. Why is it useful to represent the logical network design as a drawing?

5. What are some important pieces of information you should show in a drawing of the logical network design?

6. What is a physical network design?

7. What is a building network? What data-link-layer technology are you most likely to see in a building network?

8. Why is it useful to develop a standardized design for the building network and to use it as a building block to network every building, even buildings that have much lower network demands?

9. What is a campus network?

10. What is the core layer in a campus network? What is the role of the core layer?

11. What is the distribution layer in a campus network? What are the roles of the distribution layer?

12. What is the access layer in a campus network? What service is offered by the access layer?

13. Which layer in the campus network is most suitable to provide Internet connectivity? Why?

14. What is an enterprise network?

15. What is *network maintenance*? What are the important activities in network maintenance?

16. What is *SNMP*? Briefly describe how it is used to maintain network hardware.

17. What is the management information base (MIB)? What are some pieces of information you are likely to find in an MIB?

18. What are the typical concerns in software maintenance on the network?

19. What are *standards*? How are they useful?

20. What is the typical procedure by which a standard is developed?

21. How did the government facilitate the development of the technologies (TCP and IP) on which the Internet is based?

22. How did the government facilitate the creation of the Internet?

23. What is the role of the government in facilitating wireless LANs?

24. What has been the role of the government in the evolution of the phone industry?

25. What are the general ways in which the government influences the development of the data communication industry?

# HANDS-ON EXERCISE

For this exercise, revisit OPNET IT Guru and complete the LANs project (File → Open → LANs). Read all the instructions. Run the switched_ethernet, switched_ethernet_LANs, and Loaded_Fast_Ethernet scenarios with the default parameters.

　　You can use this exercise to quickly see how OPNET simulations are set up. We define the following elements:

a) Applications: We can define the traffic patterns generated by all the applications deployed on the network. These definitions are accessed from APP DEFS → Edit Attributes → Application Definitions. This is shown in Figure 7.

b) User profiles: Different categories of network users have different levels of usage of the different

**FIGURE 7** Application definitions in OPNET

applications. OPNET allows specification of different user profiles, each with its own levels of usage of the different applications. For example, developers may be using more of the FTP application, receptionists may be using more of the e-mail application, and sales people may be using more of the database application. These user profiles are defined in PROFILE DEFS and can be accessed using PROFILE DEFS → Edit Attributes → Profile configuration. This is shown in Figure 8. In the example, there is only one profile defined—Ethernet LAN User.

Once the applications and profiles are defined, we can assign profiles to each computer user. For example, if we had different profiles for developers, receptionists, and salespeople, we could assign the respective profiles to each user. However for convenience, in this example, all users have been assigned the same profile—Ethernet LAN User. As an example, in Figure 9, we see that the profile

name associated with the receptionist workstation in the switched_ethernet scenario is Ethernet LAN User. This is the same profile defined in Figure 8. Figure 10 shows the advanced results for the switched_ethernet_LAN scenario. It shows that the two scenarios (switched_ethernet and switched_ethernet_LAN) are essentially identical, but the network models are more convenient to use when we are only interested in the average response times for all users on a network.

Answer the following questions:

1. What are the traffic characteristics of the e-mail heavy application?

2. What are the applications associated with the Ethernet LAN user profile?

3. What are the TCP protocol specifications for the different applications associated with the Human Resources workstation in the switched_ethernet

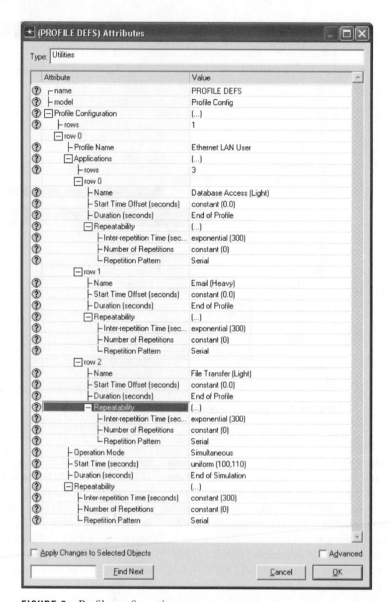

**FIGURE 8** Profile configurations

scenario? These are accessed from the Application: Transport Protocol Specifications node when you edit attributes for the host.

4. Show and briefly describe the results from Results → View Results (Advanced) in the switched_ethernet scenario.

5. (Optional) If you would like to learn how to use OPNET to set up a LAN and simulate it, please visit the companion website and follow the instructions for the OPNET LAN lab. These are included in the readings for this chapter.

**FIGURE 9**  Assigning profiles to hosts

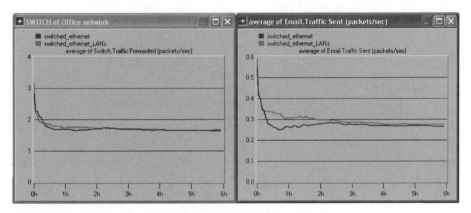

**FIGURE 10**  Results from the switched_ethernet_LAN scenario

## NETWORK DESIGN EXERCISE

Your network is ready to use in most respects. To maintain the network, Coolco has decided to hire a network administrator. Answer the following:

1. Create a job ad that Coolco can use to attract the right individual to the job. In the ad, include all the relevant information to maximize the likelihood that the most suitable individuals will be attracted to the opening.

2. Recommend three media outlets to advertise the opening.

## CASE QUESTIONS

1. What is your desired career path? Look at the characteristics of tasks for which you could telecommute, found on pages 15–16 of the article by Matthew Mariani. (Please see references in the case; the article is available online.) Which of these characteristics does your dream job possess? Based on these characteristics, how suitable is your career path for telecommuting?

2. Use the "Telecommuter self-assessment" in the same article (pages 16–17) to assess your ability to succeed at telecommuting. What is your score on the self-assessment? In what areas do you need to improve to be able to telecommute successfully?

3. What practices would you recommend to a manager who is supervising teleworkers, to optimize their professional performance?

4. The University of Miami is a leading center for telemedicine in the United States. Visit the telemedicine site at the University of Miami (www.med.miami .edu/telemedicine/, accessed February 12, 2010) and briefly describe at least three telemedicine projects/ activities being run by the group.

5. Recall a medical procedure that was performed on someone you know. If telemedicine was used during any stage of the disease, briefly describe how telemedicine was used in the case. If not, briefly describe how telemedicine may have been used in the case (Assign anonymous names, such as A, B, etc. to prevent revealing personal information).

# Networking Careers

*The person who knows "how" will always have a job.*
*The person who knows "why" will always be his boss.*
—DIANE RAVITCH

*I don't think of my life as a career. I do stuff.*
*I respond to stuff. That's not a career—it's a life.*
—STEVE JOBS, *Time*, December 4, 2010

Hopefully the book has gotten you interested in exploring opportunities in the IT sector that relate to networking. To help in your job search in this sector, a short summary of the jobs performed by networking professionals is provided here. There are many ways of classifying networking jobs. The approach used here parallels the chapter structure of the book. In general, each layer creates professional opportunities.

Many entrepreneurs get started with cabling. Schools and small or large business are constantly investing in installing and upgrading networks, which usually requires running Cat5 or Cat6 cabling through the structures. This job mostly involves using elbow grease and may be considered the most easily attainable job opportunity in IT.

Moving up to the data-link layer, small businesses start with buying a switch to set up an Ethernet LAN to share an Internet connection, and hardware such as printers among the computers in the organization. Most such organizations need someone with at least rudimentary expertise to set up equipment, trouble-shoot problems with network connectivity, isolate faults, and generally ensure that the network is operating without problems. A popular certification for professionals who attend to these networks is offered by Cisco, and is called CCNA (Cisco Certified Network Associate).

When organizations are successful, they grow larger and establish presence in multiple locations. Each of these locations typically has a LAN. Routers are used to exchange traffic between these LANs. Layer-3 (network layer) technologies form the core of the network in these organizations. The organization now interfaces with telecom carriers and needs to select suitable network technologies that will provide the most cost-effective solution for its data-transport needs. The organization now needs access to expertise in operating and maintaining routers and designing and managing the network. One of the certifications that professionals seek to obtain to demonstrate expertise in this area is the CCIE (Cisco Certified Internet Expert).

Transport layer details are generally hidden from endusers, but two categories of professionals are interested in transport-layer details: network security administrators and application developers. Network security professionals are very interested in ensuring that there are no unnecessary ports open on computers on the network. Unnecessarily open ports represent applications that may expose software vulnerabilities. Security professionals routinely scan computers on the organization's network to ensure that all non-essential computer ports are closed. Web-application developers are interested in developing session-aware applications to improve the customer experience. Most high-level applications development frameworks such as .NET and JSF support the development of session-aware applications.

The application layer has revolutionized business and has created professional opportunities even in non-technical functional areas of the business. As an example, search-engine optimizers help marketing and are widely quoted as an example of a completely new category of professionals that did not exist a decade ago and would not have existed were it not for the Internet.

A lot of the day-to-day network-operations work involves the support functions. Network professionals who maintain the WAN typically also maintain network services such as DHCP and DNS. These professionals also periodically are involved with carving out new subnets to accommodate organizational growth.

More and more organizations are using wireless LANs instead of wired Ethernet LANs. Network technicians who maintain LANs also typically maintain the wireless LANs. In larger organizations, the creation of a wireless network is typically accompanied by the creation of new subnets and NAT domains to accommodate wireless users.

WANs are almost exclusively operated by the telecom carriers. These organizations (e.g. AT&T, Verizon, and Comcast) specialize in long-distance data transport and employ large cadres of network experts to manage all parts of their networks. These experts are responsible for routing and optimizing the paths taken by packets through their networks. These experts also design networks to accommodate traffic growth created by video and cell phones (recall the statistics from Chapter 1).

Landline phones are now a declining business. But cell phone networks are growing rapidly. Operators of these networks need experts to keep the networks running even as traffic volumes grow rapidly.

Network security is experiencing rapid growth at this time. The Committee on National Security Systems of the Department of Defense has defined various certifications (CNSS 4011–CNSS 4016) for professionals involved in various network- and information-security roles in the organization. These professionals ensure that the organization complies with information-security requirements specified by law. They also deploy solutions such as single sign-on that simplify network security.

Finally, all keen IT professionals have the opportunity to provide their input on network standards through voting memberships in organizations such as IEEE.

## ABOUT THE COLOPHON

This colophon closes the book with an idea that I believe students should always keep in mind as they start their careers. It is important to know how to perform the essential tasks in the job. In our context this would mean being able to troubleshoot network problems and deploying

essential information-security controls for an organization. At the end of the day, the ability to perform pays the bills.

However, knowing *why* allows you to identify the most appropriate solution for a task and to recognize when a specific know-how is obsolete and a new one needs to take its place. Knowing *why* also allows you to recognize the potential of new opportunities and technologies before competitors. This is essential to growth and prosperity. Therefore, those who know *why* enjoy good careers.

To summarize, knowing *how* is essential to getting and keeping a job. Knowing *why* is essential to building a career and successful organizations.

In the other quote, Steve Jobs reminds us that ultimately, a career is only one component of a larger expedition—life.

# INDEX